# THE NEW GULF

## HOW MODERN ARABIA
## IS CHANGING THE
## WORLD FOR GOOD

# THE NEW GULF

## HOW MODERN ARABIA IS CHANGING THE WORLD FOR GOOD

### EDMUND O'SULLIVAN

**MOTIVATE**
PUBLISHING

Published by
**Motivate Publishing**

**Dubai:** PO Box 2331, Dubai, UAE
Tel: (+971 4) 282 4060; fax: (+971 4) 282 0428
e-mail: books@motivate.ae   www.booksarabia.com

Office 508, Building No 8, Dubai Media City, Dubai, UAE
Tel: (+971 4) 390 3550; fax: (+971 4) 390 4845

**Abu Dhabi:** PO Box 43072, Abu Dhabi, UAE
Tel: (+971 2) 677 2005; fax: (+971 2) 677 0124

**London:** Acre House, 11/15 William Road, London NW1 3ER
e-mail: motivateuk@motivate.ae

| | |
|---|---|
| Directors: | Obaid Humaid Al Tayer and Ian Fairservice |

| | |
|---|---|
| Consultant Editor: | David Steele |
| Production Editor: | Albert Harvey Pincis |
| Deputy Editor: | Moushumi Nandy |
| Assistant Editor: | Zelda Pinto |
| Senior Art Director: | Fredrick Dittlau |
| Senior Designer: | Cithadel Francisco |
| Designer: | Charlie Banalo |

General Manager Books: Jonathan Griffiths

© Motivate Publishing and Edmund O'Sullivan 2008

ISBN: 978 1 86063 229 7

British Library Cataloguing-in-Publication Data. A catalogue record for this
book is available from the British Library.

Printed by Rashid Printing Press, Ajman, UAE

# CONTENTS

Preface                                            1

1  Rise of the New Gulf Civilization              17
2  In the Kingdom                                108
3  Kuwait and the Feminine Mystique              162
4  Making a New Eden in Bahrain                  186
5  Getting Rich Quickly in Qatar                 206
6  The Last Arabian Sultanate                    224
7  The UAE and the New Gulf                      250

   Chronology of Arabia                          318
   Index                                         335

*For Justin Gibbons*
*and Charlotte Thompson*

# PREFACE

Imagine it is 2030. . . . The six Arabian states that are the subject of this book – Bahrain, Kuwait, Oman, Qatar, Saudi Arabia and the UAE – have a combined population in excess of 80 million people, more than double the 2008 figure. Most live on, or near, Arabia's east and west coasts. An unbroken chain of development extends from Ra's al-Khaimah along the Gulf littoral to the Iraqi border and down much of Arabia's 1,600 km Red Sea coastline from the Gulf of Aqaba to Jizan. Arabia in 2030 has eight cities with more than five million residents. Riyadh, the largest, has more than 10 million.

Hydrocarbons continue to drive the Gulf economy. But its leaders have long realized that the least productive use of Arabia's oil was sending it in a crude form to be burned in foreign cars and power stations. Most is processed before export in the world's largest refinery network. Gulf gas is converted into plastics or used to fuel heavy industries, electricity plants and water desalinators. The Gulf, nevertheless, remains the world's principal energy supplier. The Gulf Six produce 25 million barrels a day (b/d) of oil, more than 20 percent of the world total, compared with some 16 million b/d in 2007. Gulf gas accounts for one-fifth of world consumption.

Sources of oil outside the Gulf are rapidly depleting. World demand continues to grow. But no one worries about energy shortages. The Gulf has enough to meet every contingency for at least another century. And despite fears of relentless price increases, oil in 2030 is in real terms no costlier than in 2008. In 2030, the Gulf Six have a combined gross domestic product (GDP) of US$2 trillion at 2007 prices, three times the figure recorded 25 years earlier. This makes the region the sixth-largest economy in the world after China, the US, the EU, Japan and India. Oil and gas were behind the boom that has transformed Arabia since oil prices rose to more than US$30 a barrel in 2004. But energy accounts for a fraction of the region's economy. Services are the most important source of income and jobs. Logistics is the biggest employer of Arabians and great highways cross the peninsula from east to west and from north to south. The rail link between Jeddah on the Red Sea and Dammam on the Gulf is one of the busiest on earth.

Income from tourism and travel has overtaken earnings from oil and gas. In 2030, more than 150 million foreigners will travel to the Gulf. Nearly 20 million pilgrims will visit the Muslim Holy Cities of Mecca and Medina which are linked by trains travelling at up to 800 km/h. Gulf airports handle 400 million passengers a year. Gulf towns support enviable lifestyles. Many Gulf professionals have a house or apartment convenient for work, a weekend condominium home by the sea and a boat moored in one of Arabia's coastal marinas.

Gulf scientists are advancing the frontiers of knowledge. Technology developed in Arabia made the production of potable water from the sea possible at a fraction of the cost of extracting groundwater. The decline in the peninsula's groundwater reserves has been reversed. In Gulf towns, all wastewater is being recycled. Solar power is used extensively to generate electricity for air conditioning in Gulf homes.

Gulf corporations are among the world's largest. Saudi Basic Industries Corporation (Sabic) has become one of the biggest manufacturing companies in the world. Gulf banks have merged and compete on an equal footing with Citigroup and HSBC. Gulf airlines span the globe. The integrated Gulf stock market is one of the world's biggest.

The Gulf has recorded balance of payments surpluses since 1998 and has accumulated the world's richest portfolio of international financial assets. The political row in 2006 about DP World's plans to take over the management of six American ports deterred Gulf investment in the US for a decade. But America's loss was a huge gain for others. Gulf money flooded into Asian economies and was seminal in the African economic renaissance.

But it is not all work. Sports are booming and the arts are flourishing. Religion continues to be the cornerstone of Gulf society, but Arabia has become the centre of a tolerant and middle-class Islam. Women are playing important roles in Gulf mosques and Islamic universities as they have for decades in business and government. Islamic banks and insurance firms offering a low-cost alternative to conventional financial institutions are welcomed on every continent.

The Gulf Six have integrated with neighbouring economies and are the engine of a dynamic Middle East peace economy. The Gulf, once the zone of conflict, has become a waterway of peace. The world looks to a region transformed by the Gulf's prosperity for the solution of apparently intractable conflict. . . .

This vision of the future is a work of fiction. Many would consider it to be fantasy, not a forecast. You can understand why. Since the mid-1970s, the Gulf has seen a revolution and three all-out wars. The region's bad reputation can be traced back even further. In the 19th century, the German chancellor, Otto von Bismarck, described the Gulf as a "hornets' nest". Recent headlines seem to confirm this.

This is being written soon after the fourth anniversary of the US-led campaign to bring freedom, peace and prosperity to the people of Iraq. Today, few Iraqis live free of fear, there is little peace and living standards are little better than before the deposition of the Iraqi Baath regime in 2003. The British medical journal, *The Lancet*, estimates there have been more than 600,000 Iraqi civilian casualties since then.

Terror's shadow has fallen across the Gulf. In 2003, 2004 and 2005, killings of civilians in Kuwait, Qatar and Saudi Arabia shook international confidence in the region's stability. A new US war, this time to bring about regime change in Iran, is possible. The troubles that have tortured the Gulf for three decades seem endless.

But a New Gulf is rising, one that will be radically different to the old. This book is about the economic, social and political transformation sweeping the Gulf Six that in 1981 formed the GCC, an association loosely modelled on the EU. In 2007 they were the fastest growing part of the world economy. The vision of the Gulf in 2030 is based on their ascent and the new civilization emerging in the heart of the Middle East that will transform the region and the world for good.

Oil and gas underpin the Gulf 2030 vision. The countries of the GCC have more than 40 per cent of proven world oil reserves and a fifth of world gas. This figure is likely to rise, not fall, in the years to come. Across Arabia, there is more exploration than at any point in oil-industry history. At the end of 2005, drilling started as part of Saudi Arabia's quest for gas in the Rub al-Khali desert, also known as the Empty Quarter. The kingdom is implementing the world's largest oil-development programme. It will increase Saudi Arabia's reserves and could raise its capacity to pump crude to 15 million b/d by 2020. In March 2006, Kuwait announced a gas discovery that more than doubled its proven reserves. Qatar is confident it will make major new oil discoveries and that increases will be announced in its gas reserves, the world's second largest. Oman is implementing the most ambitious advanced oil-recovery programme in oil-industry history. Bahrain has resumed extensive oil exploration.

New technology is squeezing more out of existing reservoirs. Qatar's Al Shaheen offshore field's production will be doubled to 500,000 b/d by 2009, purely as the result of using new techniques. Similar initiatives are taking place across the region. These and other developments substantiate the Gulf's assertion that the world should stop worrying about depleting oil and gas. The region has plenty and is discovering more.

In contrast, the rest of the world's oil resources are declining. The US Department of Energy's long-term energy forecast shows US oil imports rising by more than 70 per cent to 18 million b/d in 2030. The consensus is that the US and the world as a whole will rely increasingly on Gulf oil and gas.

The other part of the oil market balance is demand. Here, the news for the Gulf is also good. Despite record prices in 2008 and energy-saving technology that has slashed the intensity of energy use in Western economies, world oil demand is continuing to rise. Car ownership in China and India is soaring as living standards and expectations rise. There is no prospect of gasoline consumption slumping. Demand for gas is being driven higher by a global shift towards fuels with lower carbon emissions in power generation.

But will wind power, solar energy, nuclear fuel or even cold fusion make hydrocarbons redundant? The answer is not yet and, probably, not soon. The International Energy Agency forecasts that 80 per cent of world energy needs will be met by oil, gas and coal for 30 more years at least. Interest in nuclear power has been stimulated by forecasts of a world energy shortage. But it will take many decades before it will account for more than a minority of world electricity production.

An obstacle to the irresistible rise in Gulf oil and gas is environmental. Higher global temperatures, melting ice caps and rising sea levels have once again raised questions about carbon emissions caused by the burning of hydrocarbons. Governments in the principal consuming nations are beginning to tackle the issue seriously, but there is no prospect they'll be able to do more than restrain the growth of hydrocarbons consumption. The UN's Kyoto Climate Change Protocol is set to expire in 2012 and tighter carbon limits are certain in the agreement that will replace it. But the principal new polluters are developing nations such as China and India that are reluctant to slow growth when most carbon emissions are coming from rich countries. The main hope lies in new inventions that capture or reduce emissions. And it is in the Gulf's interest that this should happen since it will sustain demand for the region's principal hard-currency earner.

With oil and gas demand set at least to match supply for the indefinite future, energy prices will remain buoyant. The US Department of Energy has revised its long-term forecast and says that oil prices are likely to stay high until at least 2030. The higher oil prices seen since the end of 2003 will encourage energy saving and the development of high-cost alternatives such as shale oil. But they will also spur investment in oil exploration and development in the region where energy is cheapest: the Gulf. The economic implications for the Gulf Six will be profound and far-reaching. Oil and gas sells in world markets for at least 10 times the cost of production. That's why Gulf national oil companies are today the most profitable corporations on earth. In 2007, GCC oil companies recorded export sales worth about US$350 billion. At least 80 per cent was profit. With these surpluses likely to continue indefinitely, Gulf oil corporations will have more than enough money to finance further capacity increases, extend their distribution networks through international acquisitions and finance high levels of expenditure by the governments that own them.

A huge hydrocarbons endowment is only part of the reason why the Gulf's growth will remain high. Since energy accounts for more than one-third of the cost of producing plastics, steel, aluminium, fertilizers and other basic industrial commodities, Gulf manufacturers of these products with access to low-cost gas can undercut producers in other parts of the world. Practically all plastic production in North America and Europe will close in the next 20 years. Most new capacity will be built in the Gulf where access to low-cost gas has been guaranteed. To a lesser extent, this is also true for steel, aluminium and fertilizers. The new heavy industries will feed new factories that use their output to make finished products from plastic bags to aluminium door frames.

The economies of the Gulf Six are also being driven by a service industry boom. After half a century of oil-financed development, per capita national income in the Gulf states is high by developing world standards. In 2008, the GCC average was about US$20,000, below Europe but several times higher than elsewhere in the region. High income leads to spending on services and the sector is flourishing across the region.

Gulf banks, the largest in the Middle East, are the world's most consistently profitable financial institutions. The enormous increase in cash in the hands of governments, companies and households is fuelling a startling growth in demand for financial services. In 2005, most Gulf stock exchanges appreciated by up to 100 per cent. The Saudi Arabian share market became the largest by turnover in emerging economies.

The Gulf share crash at the start of 2006 has extinguished the euphoria about equities, but the tide of money flowing into the Gulf finance system is unstoppable. The Gulf banking industry will probably double within five years. Mergers among the region's banks are beginning. At least one will have emerged by 2030 big enough to join world banking's top tier.

Tourism is growing faster in the Gulf than anywhere in the world. Gulf states are promoting holidaymaking, particularly from Europe, during November to April when Arabia's weather is most pleasing. The biggest initiative is Dubailand, a swathe of desert in Dubai that is to be converted within 20 years into the world's largest integrated leisure resort, to attract up to 100 million visitors each year. But every country in the region is searching for the tourist dollar. Old Arabia is being opened up to new visitors to an extent that was inconceivable 20 years ago.

Saudi Arabia's additional advantage is that it's the site of the Muslim Holy Cities of Mecca and Medina. Since there are about 1.5 billion Muslims, all of whom are obliged if possible to complete a pilgrimage to Mecca, the potential is obvious. Saudi Arabia plans to quintuple the annual number of pilgrims by 2020.

To facilitate the tourism boom, Gulf airports are being expanded. Three new ones are being built: one in Dubai big enough to handle 120 million passengers a year, another in Doha with capacity of up to

60 million and a third in Abu Dhabi with twice the capacity of its existing facility. Saudi Arabia, which already has 26 airports, plans to build at least three more. Gulf airports are being filled principally by national airlines that are growing at a startling rate.

Emirates, the international airline based in Dubai, is reporting passenger growth of more than 20 per cent a year and forecasts it will have more than 170 million customers in 2025, compared with almost 20 million in 2006. Etihad Airways, the international airline of Abu Dhabi launched in 2003, aims to have six million by 2009 and Qatar Airways has even larger ambitions. To attract tourists, more than 200 first-class hotels will be built in the GCC by 2010 and the biggest expansion in retail history is taking place in the region.

With every economic sector booming, the GCC is being transformed by the world's greatest construction bonanza. By the start of 2008, US$2 trillion worth of new projects were under way in the Gulf, most of it in the Gulf Six. Millions more construction workers will be needed. They in turn will add to the soaring demand for goods and services in the GCC.

The principal constraint on Gulf growth is the limited supply of skilled local labour. But there's change here too. The Gulf Six have a natural population growth rate of more than two per cent on average. The challenge is equipping future generations with the skills needed by Arabia's high-tech service economies. The governments of the region are responding with far-reaching education and vocational training initiatives. Projects such as Doha's Education City and DuBiotech in Dubai are also laying the foundations for a technological revolution. Their focus will be on scientific challenges relevant to the Gulf. Diabetes is the new Gulf plague, the result of the coming of a high-calorie diet. This and other endemic health problems are under scrutiny in Gulf research institutes. Remarkably, stem-cell research using embryos will probably be permitted in Dubai. Arab Nobel prizes for science may be a distant prospect, but they will be attainable in the New Gulf.

The region is also willing to import the skills it needs. Most new arrivals to the UAE are professional middle-class people seeking employment in the service sector. A similar pattern is developing elsewhere in the region. Nowhere welcomes skilled white-collar workers more readily than the New Gulf. New financial centres in Dubai, Doha, Manama and Riyadh are being developed to attract the world's leading financial institutions. They've got everything top financiers require, from marbled conference halls to designer coffee shops with the added bonus that there's no personal income tax. Accountants, lawyers, management consultants and other professional service workers are flocking to the region.

A key factor behind the growing attraction of the Gulf to skilled workers is property. Until the start of this decade, non-GCC nationals could not own homes in Gulf states. Then Dubai broke the mould by offering apartments and houses in selected developments. Today, foreigners can buy homes in the GCC.

Foreign ownership is the basis of some of the region's biggest developments. Dubai's enormous Palm Island projects are principally aimed at resident and non-resident foreigners. Across the region, a home-building boom is transforming the face of Gulf cities. And unlike in Europe, North America, Japan, Singapore and Hong Kong, there's no shortage of land. Arabia has a total area more than five times larger than California. Most of its coastline is undeveloped. In 2006, the Saudi government handed over 100 kilometres of Red Sea coast to the developers of King Abdullah Economic City, a new town being built north of Jeddah. More giant urban initiatives are coming.

In 2007, the combined population of the Gulf Six was about 35 million people, roughly the same number as California. The high birth rate and immigration will rapidly lift this figure. Abu Dhabi could have a population of four million by 2020. Qatar's population is growing at a similar rate. Kuwait, where nationals account for less than half the total population, will have more than four million people in 2020. Bahrain and Oman, which have youth unemployment problems, will probably continue to restrict immigration. But Saudi Arabia's long-term economic plans are so vast that immigration of skilled workers is essential. These trends suggest a combined population of more than 80 million people is conceivable.

The growth of Gulf cities is expressing itself mainly in high-quality suburbs designed to please professionals. The New Gulf will look like southern California, not a slum. For young Arab professionals, Gulf cities offer the opportunity to satisfy the desire for travel where they can enjoy more personal freedom and practice their profession in an international environment that's a comparatively short flight from home. It is for this reason, as much as the skyline, that Dubai is sometimes described as the New York of the Middle East.

The final cause of the long Gulf boom is globalization. Arabia is becoming the cross-roads for world commerce for the first time since the fall of the Roman and Persian empires. The peninsula lies half-way between the EU, the world's largest economy, and China and the Far East. As trade flows increase between these two great engines of global trade, more of it will pass through the ports, airports and cities of the Gulf.

So the new Gulf economy is being created by five abiding factors: the world's dependence on hydrocarbons, the shift of heavy industry to the region, a service boom, a population explosion and globalization. They are combining to fuel at least a generation of high rates of real economic growth. And the Gulf boom is being accompanied by huge financial surpluses that are likely to be worth at least US$500 billion in the next five years. These surpluses are now looking for a safe haven and major Western businesses are potential takeover targets. The Abu Dhabi Investment Authority (ADIA), with assets of more than US$500 billion, the Kuwait Investment Authority (KIA) and the Saudi Arabian Monetary Agency (SAMA), each with more than US$200 billion, are established players in world capital markets. They will be joined by Qatar, on a per capita basis the richest Gulf state, which is accumulating reserves at the rate of more than US$5 billion a year. The total pool of private Gulf wealth is even larger. The DP World takeover of Peninsula & Oriental (P&O) is just the first part of a new wave of international Gulf investment that will have growing implications for every economy on earth.

The Gulf's social character is evolving with its rapid economic development. The biggest change is in the role of women. More graduate from Gulf universities than men. They are joining the labour force in growing numbers and making life choices with growing confidence. The change is being reflected at the highest levels of government. In Oman in March 2004, Rawya bint Saud Al Bousaidi was appointed minister for higher education and became the first woman in a GCC cabinet. Nada Haffadh, a doctor and a member of Bahrain's upper house of parliament, was made health minister the following month. In November 2004, the UAE appointed Sheikha Lubna bint Khaled Al Qassimi as economy and planning minister and the first woman member of the federal council of ministers. Kuwait followed the pattern in 2005 by appointing Dr Massouma Al Mubarak as planning minister and the UAE appointed a second woman, Dr Mariam Al Roumi, to the council of ministers formed in January 2006 following the death of federal prime minister and Dubai ruler, Sheikh Maktoum bin Rashid Al Maktoum. Two more women joined the cabinet in 2008.

One of the most telling images of 2006 was Qatar's Sheikh Hamad bin Khalifa Al Thani and his wife, Sheikha Mozah, photographed together with UK Prime Minister Tony Blair and his wife, Cherie, outside Number 10 Downing Street. In March, the couple posed with President Chirac and his wife outside the presidential palace in Paris. Never before had a Gulf leader been seen sharing the limelight equally with his spouse. It is a sign of the new times and the rise of the New Gulf.

The Gulf cultural landscape is being transformed by migration to the region and growing exposure to the outside world. Most middle-class Arabians watch satellite television and travel internationally. With the exception of Saudi Arabia, the door is open to most forms of performance art. The cosmopolitan mix of nationalities is inspiring new creative activity. The Gulf media industry is booming thanks to soaring advertising spending.

The greatest enigma of the New Gulf is how modernization, the influx of foreigners and the coming of alien cultures, can be reconciled with Islam and societies that are among the most conservative on earth. As this book shows, history may be a guide.

The Gulf has been engaged with the world outside for millennia. For most of the past 1,500 years, Arabia has been controlled by foreign powers. Less than 50 years after the coming of Islam, power shifted to Damascus and from there to Baghdad and then to Istanbul. Starting in the early 16th century, Europe started to dominate the Gulf region. Britain's control of the coasts of the Gulf and the Red Sea began in the early 19th century. For thousands of years, the people of coastal Arabia have travelled to and traded with distant regions. Involvement with the outside world is nothing new. This time it is happening on terms defined by the Gulf, not imposed upon it.

This book shows that the New Gulf has been emerging for decades. Britain's retreat from the Middle East after 1945, the rise of OPEC and the 1973/74 oil price increases that presaged the nationalization of Gulf oil were behind its first flourish. But the capacity to manage the implications was limited and mistakes were made.

The rise of the New Gulf was interrupted by the regional setbacks that culminated in the 1979 Iranian Revolution, the 1980–88 Iran-Iraq War and the 1986 oil price crash. Revolutionary Islam captured the imagination of many in the Middle East. It remains a potent challenge to the Middle East status quo.

For decades, Gulf governments promoted modernization while appeasing Islamic conservatives. The 9/11 atrocity and the US response to it convinced the region's leaders that there could only be one choice. Arabia has since decisively opted for accelerated modernization, including political and economic liberalization. Votes for women in Kuwait, nationwide local government elections in Saudi Arabia and the 2006 national ballot in the UAE would have happened without 9/11 and the invasion of Iraq. But they would not have happened so quickly.

Gulf modernization has been facilitated by generational leadership change in the past decade. Qatar's ruler, Sheikh Hamad, replaced his father in 1995 and set his country on the modernization track. Sheikh Isa Al Khalifa's death in 1999 cleared the way for Bahraini political reform. UAE president and Abu Dhabi ruler, Sheikh Zayed bin Sultan Al Nahyan, passed away in November 2004 and was succeeded by his son, Sheikh Khalifa, who is pursuing the modernization agenda. King Fahd's death in August 2005 has had a similar impact in Saudi Arabia.

But are the people of the GCC ready for rapid change? The majority of GCC nationals are members of tribes that have dominated Arabia for thousands of years and still provide the Gulf ruling class. Gulf government policy for decades has been to build state institutions and to promote economic development evenly across the peninsula. Tribal loyalties, as a result, have begun to fade, but still count. Arabia is several generations away from having a coherent national identity, but it is coming. Urbanization, the growth of a Gulf middle class and the influx of expatriate professionals are contributing towards this goal. Even participation in major world sport events, such as the FIFA World Cup finals in Germany in the summer of 2006, where Saudi Arabia was represented, is having an impact. But it would be premature to dismiss the appeal of sectionalism.

Most Gulf nationals are Muslims, but there is greater diversity within Islam than many suppose. About 15 per cent of Saudi Arabians are Shiite Muslims, the largest minority sect within Islam, the official religion of Iran and the majority religion of Iraq. But there are other groups: Ibadhis in Oman and south-east Arabia, Zaydis in Yemen, Ismailis in the Arabian south-west and a multitude of sects introduced by the presence of millions of foreign-born Muslims. Arabia is the Islamic melting-pot of the 21st century.

Gulf governments have invariably attempted to promote moderate Islam, but they have been constrained by powerful forces, particularly in Saudi Arabia, where economic and social reforms were blocked. But time is not on their side in the New Gulf. Conservative Gulf Muslim leaders are fighting a rearguard action against an irresistible and popular wave of modernization that, if applied properly, is profoundly appealing to the young Arabians who account for the overwhelming majority of the population of the Gulf Six. In the next 25 years, a new generation of Muslim leaders will be in place across the region. Their challenge will be synthesizing the new ideas with the old, not blocking them.

The greatest moderating influence on religious attitudes will be the New Gulf's growing affluence. Islam is comfortable with personal wealth provided it's used appropriately. Early objections to modern technology have been replaced with an amazing appetite for the new. In every area of life, attitudes and behaviour are changing as the New Gulf's prosperity increases the size and confidence of Arabia's middle class.

Sharia-compliant banking is the most distinctive emblem of the New Gulf. Until modern times, banking was deemed to be un-Islamic. Dubai Islamic Bank, the world's oldest Islamic deposit bank, was set up in 1975. For the next 20 years, the Sharia-compliant banking movement battled objections from regulators at home and abroad, the doubts of local business communities and the scepticism of the banking establishment. And yet, Muslims found the idea irresistible.

Islamic banking is now the fastest-growing service industry in the Islamic World, a unique example of grassroots pressure overcoming establishment opinion. Today, Islamic banking has effectively conquered the retail-banking market of Saudi Arabia and is set to dominate others in the Middle East and beyond. The new target is the corporate and investment-banking markets of the Muslim World. The cornerstone of its success is the growing affluence of the people of Arabia.

The Islamic-banking movement is Muslim moderation in action. Champions of Islamic banking say it's a system for all humanity. You do not have to be a Muslim to use, or work for, a Sharia-compliant bank or insurance firm. Since it is also based on risk and profit-sharing and abjures interest, it echoes original Christian teaching about usury and may offer Western borrowers a lower-cost source of finance than conventional banks. The fact that Sharia-compliant banks refuse to invest in companies producing alcohol and tobacco enhances its potential appeal to conservatives of all religions.

A central objective of New Gulf government policy is producing educated people with a tolerant outlook. Whether this succeeds depends on several factors, but two stand out. The first is raising living standards and creating jobs for the hundreds of thousands of young Gulf people entering the labour market annually. The chances of achieving this objective have been greatly improved by quickening Arabian economic development. The second is demonstrating Gulf leaders have a long-term vision relevant and applicable to the wider Middle East.

Here too, there's substance in the 2030 vision. New leaders and new economic opportunities are combining in the New Gulf to produce farsighted thinking. Co-operation is accelerating among GCC states. There are plans for a rail link along the east Arabian coast, power and water connections among the Gulf Six and currency union. Economic policies are converging towards the liberal consensus. It is being made easier to travel across borders to trade, invest or just have fun. Arabians speak a common language. Most are of the same religion. Their economies are similar. And their leaders are Muslim moderates open to the West. Europe has integrated despite differences in language, religion and economic systems. The GCC, with fewer obstacles, should be able to do the same.

Some GCC states have more in common than others. As chapter seven on the UAE shows, the original plan for the UAE was for a federation of nine states: the seven that joined plus Bahrain and Qatar. This vision was shattered by the Iranian threat to Bahrain's independence and territorial rivalry between Doha and Manama. Today, these issues have evaporated. Qatar and the UAE are on a convergence fasttrack which could encompass Bahrain. Increasing trade and investment among GCC states is drawing them closer together in all areas.

A dynamic association of Gulf Arab states is emerging that will have a broader impact. The Middle East's greatest failure since 1945 has been the limited flow of goods, capital and labour across Arab borders. Of the millions of foreign workers in the GCC, less than a quarter come from other Arab countries. This is a consequence of the division between the republican regimes of the Middle East and the traditional governments of Arabia that originated in the deposition of the Egyptian monarchy in 1952 and the coming of the Cold War to the region.

This division is now redundant. Since the start of the century, there's been a steady growth in investment from the GCC into other parts of the Arab World. The rise of the New Gulf is transforming economic relations. This in turn should create the conditions for the settlement of political rivalries that mean little to young people of the Middle East yearning for a better life. The New Gulf in the years to come is well placed to play its proper role as the locomotive of the Arab economic train. As that happens, wider Arab integration, a dream of many Arab generations, will become possible.

A further incentive for regional integration is the challenge presented by the Islamic Republic of Iran, a country with more than 70 million people and the second-largest Middle East economy. The June 2005 Iranian presidential election was won by Mahmoud Ahmadinejad, the embodiment of radical Islamic conservatism. The Middle East faces two compelling and contrasting models: Iran, where government is dominated by anti-Western Shiite clerics, and moderate and modernizing Gulf states such as Qatar and the UAE. There's no third way left. And unless there are more Dubais, Dohas and Abu Dhabis, there will be more Irans. A successful New Gulf could tip the regional balance decisively in favour of moderation.

And what role will the outside world play in the New Gulf?

As this book shows, the US has been directly involved in policing, defending and intervening in the Gulf since it reflagged Kuwaiti oil tankers to protect them against Iranian attack in 1987. But the 2003 war for Iraq has proved that even the world's sole superpower is no longer up to the task. According to Nobel Prize-winning economist, Jo Stiglitz, in a report published in 2006, the full economic cost of the Iraq War alone is already more than US$1 trillion. The total for the US's 20-year Gulf adventure is several times that figure.

American voters are concluding that the results are failing to justify the price paid in money and lives lost and they're losing their appetite for costly and ineffective Middle East adventures. A group of US thinkers – sometimes called neo-conservatives – is continuing, nevertheless, to influence Washington's Gulf agenda with calls for military intervention in Iran to extinguish its nuclear programme and, ultimately, to change the Iranian regime.

Gulf leaders regard nuclear Iran as a threat but fear a unilateral US attack will cause even more serious long-term problems. The Shiite majority in Bahrain, a large Shiite minority in Saudi Arabia and significant Shiite populations in all four other GCC states, are further reasons for anxiety about American intentions towards Shiite Iran.

These concerns underpin the desire among the Gulf Six for dialogue with Iran. The Gulf view is that there's no hope of regional stability without compromise with Tehran. The challenge is to find an approach that addresses America's legitimate concerns about Islamic radicalism and energy security. This requires an historic understanding with Iran about issues including Iraq's future, weapons of mass destruction and the role of foreign forces in the Gulf.

Economics could be the key to unlock the door to lasting cross-Gulf détente. The benefits that would accrue to the people, businesses and government of Iran from sharing in the New Gulf's prosperity are a compelling incentive for moderation in Tehran. As Europe's experience since 1945 has shown, mutually beneficial trade can erase even the bitterest of divisions. Peace in the Gulf requires economic co-operation across the waterway, not a new Iron Curtain that an international trade embargo on Iran could bring. And if there is peace and prosperity in the Gulf, why would the US want to have hundreds of thousands of troops in the region? More to the point, why should they be allowed to?

The greatest challenge now facing the leaders of the New Gulf is persuading Iran to collaborate with them in creating a Gulf peace economy and convincing the US that it is in its interests that this should happen. These points would have been raised in May 2007 with US vice-president Dick Cheney who visited Abu Dhabi less than two days before Iran's Ahmadinejad arrived in the UAE capital for his first official visit to the federation.

So, the outline of a final solution to the agonies that have tormented the Gulf for decades can be discerned amid the storm about Iran. Cross-Gulf détente will help deliver prosperity, peace and growing global influence. For America and the West, it would create the opportunity to collaborate constructively with the region controlling world energy and at the head of the most dynamic religious movement of our age. It could lead to an historic compact between the West and the wider Islamic World as well. This is a prize worth arguing for and, perhaps, worth fighting for.

There's a further goal that a prosperous, united New Gulf could help deliver. Attempts by force to rectify the wrongs inflicted upon the region since the Balfour Declaration of 1917 have failed to end the suffering of the principal victims: the Palestinian people. Decades of confrontation with Israel have not delivered the original goal of a unified, multi-confessional state in the lands of the Palestinian mandate approved by the League of Nations in 1922. The limited objectives of an independent Palestinian state in the West Bank and the Gaza Strip, the withdrawal of Israel from land seized in the 1967 war and justice for millions of Palestinian refugees and their descendants remain frustratingly elusive.

The New Gulf could break this tragic deadlock. A prosperous and stable association of moderate Arab states working constructively with its neighbours and in dialogue with the US would be in an excellent position to negotiate from a position of strength about an issue that should have been settled decades ago. The New Gulf properly led is, perhaps, the only agent capable of bringing peace to the Holy Lands of the Jews, Christians and Muslims, and a tranquility to the wider Middle East not seen for almost a century. Because, even in matters of faith and principle, money counts.

This book is based on my experiences in the Gulf since joining *MEED* in August 1979. In this time, I have witnessed remarkable events and tragedies. The region was rocked by the Iranian Revolution, the Iran-Iraq War, the 1982 Lebanon invasion, the Libyan bombing in 1986, the oil-price crash of the same year, Iraq's invasion of Kuwait, the in-humane sanctions against the country that followed and the 2003 war that led to the deposition of Saddam Hussein. There have been very bad times, none worse than the slaughter of Palestinian civilians in the refugee camps of Sabra and Chatila in 1982 and the poison-gas attacks on the Kurdish people of Halabjeh in 1988. I've often retired to bed in a sad and angry mood. That's why I can recognize a good time when I see it. And this is a very good time for the Gulf and, potentially, for the wider Middle East and its people.

The Iraq War of 2003 was another depressing experience involving many of the worst themes of the past quarter century: a festering humanitarian crisis, a leader out of touch with reality, an American president dancing to a domestic political constituency ignorant of the needs of the region and, finally, more destruction and death in a Middle East country that should have been rich and free. The war's end did not bring peace to Iraq. But it marked the start of what in hindsight can be seen as the ascent of the New Gulf. Since I moved permanently to Dubai in September 2003, Gulf modernization has quickened to an extent none forecast. My arrival came just before the annual IMF/World Bank meetings held in the Gulf for the first time at the new Dubai International Convention Centre. Some forecast it would be a mess and others believed it would be cancelled because of post-war security worries. It proceeded more smoothly than anyone could have hoped. International financiers came, saw what was happening in the New Gulf and declared it to be good.

*The New Gulf* has been written to provide a concise and complete description of Arabian countries that are benefiting most from the affluence sweeping the Middle East in the 21st century's first decade. It is also designed to be an accessible reference that answers questions that might be asked by seasoned residents as well as by first-time visitors. I have drawn principally upon three sources: the first is the numerous books, reports and manuscripts about the region. The second is the extraordinary detail published weekly since March 1957 in *MEED*, where I've worked for more than a quarter of a century. The third source is my own memories and experiences that have included living full-time in the UAE and hundreds of visits in this time to all the other countries of the region.

*The New Gulf* has several themes. It places developments in each Gulf state within their proper regional historical context. It details the origins, achievements and evolution of Islam, Arabia's greatest gift to the world. Its focus is on the people who've shaped its past and are leading it into the future; I leave the task of writing a definitive academic book to others. Finally, *The New Gulf* is written in an optimistic spirit. Something remarkable is happening in the Gulf. Much is encouraging.

I must now thank all those who have helped me write this book. Special thanks are due to Angus Hindley, a *MEED* writer since 1989 and I would also like to offer my thanks to all past and present members of the award-winning *MEED* team.

Working at *MEED* has given me the opportunity to meet some of those who are building the New Gulf. I would like to thank them for sharing their experiences and wisdom. Motivate Publishing, the Gulf's first English-language publisher, took the bold decision to publish this book. I'm deeply grateful to Motivate managing partner and group editor, Ian Fairservice, Motivate general manager business development, Simon O'Herlihy and the company's consultant editor, David Steele.

This book would also have been impossible without the co-operation of the governments of Dubai and of the United Arab Emirates. Dubai Media City, under the leadership of Dr Amina Al Rostamani, provides one of the finest venues on earth to be a current affairs reporter. Thanks are due to Ibrahim Al Abed, director general of the UAE's National Media Council, and also to Peter Hellyer, adviser to the council, for his advice, particularly about the history and archaeology of the UAE.

A large number of books and other sources have been very helpful in writing this book. In chapter one, they include *The Arab Awakening* by George Antonius, *A Peace to End All Peace* by Daniel Fromkin, *The Encyclopaedia of Islam* and *The Prize: The Epic Quest for Oil, Money and Power*, Daniel Yergin's definitive history of the oil industry. The author would also like to acknowledge *From Trucial States to United Arab Emirates* by Frauke Bey-Heard, the best book yet written about the modern history of the federation.

Home is where the heart is. And so my final words of thanks are for my family. I would like to express my love and loyalty to my father Edmund, my mother Patricia and to my five brothers and sisters: Marian, Bernard, Catherine, Stephen, Richard and their families.

Thanks are also due to Teresa and Frank Rodger, Monica Kasinathan and Eddie Brigdale and to their families. For thousands of reasons, I would like to thank Heather Rabbatts, her sister Emerald and their much-missed parents Hyacinth and Tom. There has been joy in the time this book was written, but also much sadness. I dedicate it to the memory of Justin Gibbons, son of my sister's partner Roger, and to Charlotte Thompson, daughter of my cousin Hilary and her husband Reg, who both died prematurely in 2005. I hope *The New Gulf* will interest my son Euan. Above all, I want to say an endless thank you to my wife, Maria, who encouraged me to start this project and to persist when the spirits flagged, and who then proofread the transcript with an unerring eye for detail. I could not have done it without you.

CHAPTER 1

# RISE OF THE NEW GULF CIVILIZATION

This story starts with an ending.

It was the afternoon of Wednesday November 3, 2004. Leaders of the Islamic World had gathered to honour Sheikh Zayed bin Sultan Al Nahyan, ruler of Abu Dhabi and president of the United Arab Emirates (UAE) since it was founded; Sheikh Zayed's death had been announced the day before. With the shadows lengthening, they assembled in Abu Dhabi's main mosque before a wooden coffin. It contained Sheikh Zayed's body, wrapped in the flag of the federation he created. The mourners were greeted by Sheikh Mohammed bin Zayed Al Nahyan, pilot son of the late ruler, who'd been named Abu Dhabi's new crown prince.

General Musharraf, president of Pakistan, was among the first to arrive, followed by President Karzai. (The next day, Karzai was elected president of Afghanistan after the first democratic polls in its history.) Abdelaziz Bouteflika, president of Algeria, pressed into the front row on Karzai's right. Yemen's President Saleh, another former general and a 1960s republican rebel, was followed by King Abdullah of Jordan, the half-British son of the late King Hussein. Sultan Qaboos, Ruler of Oman since 1970, joined the throng. Hurrying in last was Bashar Al Asad, an opthalmologist who succeeded his father Hafiz as Syrian president in 2000.

Sheikh Sayed Ali Al Hashemi, Sheikh Zayed's religious affairs adviser, led the prayers. Standing with him before the coffin was the ruler of Ra's al-Khaimah, Sheikh Saqr bin Mohammed Al Qassimi, the oldest of the seven rulers of the UAE. Sheikh Saqr's dark, full beard belied the fact that he was then 87 and had been ruler since 1948. He was now the final survivor of the UAE's founders. Facing the coffin was Sheikh Mohammed bin Rashid Al Maktoum, the mastermind behind Dubai's drive to become a global city, who was to succeed his brother, Sheikh Maktoum bin Rashid Al Maktoum, as vice-President and prime minister of the UAE and the emirate's ruler 14 months later.

Qatar's crown prince, Sheikh Tameem bin Hamad Al Thani, representing what will soon be the richest country on earth, stood close by. Saudi Arabia's Prince Abdullah bin Abdelaziz Al Saud, crown prince

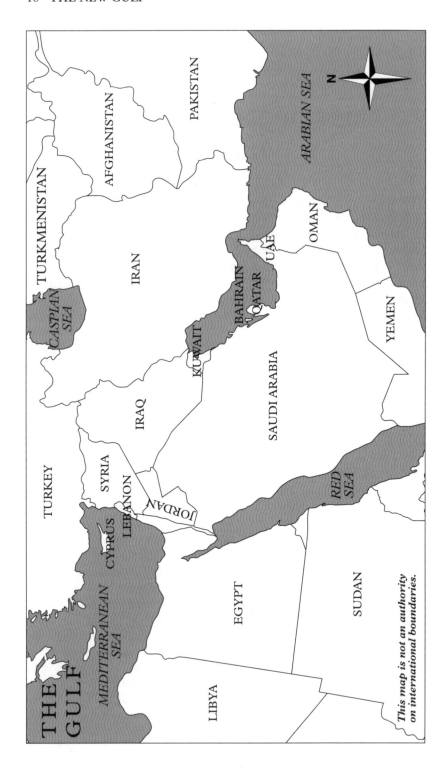

since 1982, was at the centre of the front row. (The following August, he became the Saudi king and ruler of the world's biggest oil exporter and guardian of Islam's holiest sites.) To Prince Abdullah's left was Bahrain's King Hamad bin Isa Al Khalifa, who succeeded his father in 1999 and reintroduced parliament and elections. On Abdullah's right was the principal mourner, Sheikh Khalifa bin Zayed Al Nahyan, who had succeeded his venerated father as ruler of Abu Dhabi. That evening, he was to be elected president of the UAE by the six other UAE rulers. His inheritance is the world's fifth greatest petroleum reserve and more than US$500 billion worth of financial assets.

Next to King Hamad, Kuwaiti Prime Minister Sheikh Sabah Al Sabah represented the ailing emir Sheikh Jaber Al Sabah, who was too ill to attend and was to die in January 2006. Sheikh Sabah succeeded. Beside the future emir was Ghazi Al Yawar, then interim president of Iraq. Before Al Yawar, the presidency had been held for almost 24 years by Saddam Hussein who that day sat in a Baghdad prison.

Al Hashemi began the Islamic prayers for the dead. *Allahu Akbar*, he intoned four times. *Assalaamu alaikum*. The mourners repeated the words. The funeral service was over. Sheikh Zayed's family carried the coffin to a waiting vehicle. The funeral cortege slipped through silent streets to the Sheikh Zayed Mosque. On its east side, a grave had been prepared and Sheikh Zayed's body was tenderly laid in its final resting place. Sheikh Mohammed bin Zayed threw off his headdress and stepped into the grave to arrange his father's body as Islam required. Sudan's President Omar Al Bashir and Iyad Allawi, then interim prime minister of Iraq, joined the group around the grave. The tie-less Shiite Iranian vice-president, Dr Mohammed Reza Aref, and Lebanon's Christian President, Emile Lahoud, circulated discreetly.

Every government in the Islamic World was represented. That night, emissaries from everywhere else arrived to salute Sheikh Khalifa. But the funeral was principally an Arabian occasion.

When Sheikh Zayed was born, the peninsula was unrecognizably different. It had no oil, the people were poor and Britain controlled most of the Middle East. Arabia's map had radically changed during Sheikh Zayed's long life. But Arabians of all ages knew the austere funeral rites of an honoured leader. So, with the sun setting swiftly, an era ended.

It was witnessed by men controlling the destiny of almost 400 million people, a region stretching from the Atlantic Ocean to the Arabian Sea, the future of Islam and most of the world's oil reserves. At that moment, more than 6,000 miles to the east, America was waking to the news that President George W Bush, conqueror of the Taliban and Saddam Hussein, had defeated Senator John Kerry in the race for the White House. Where would Arabia go now?

## The people of Arabia

Gulf nationals are diverse. Some are descended from the peninsula's original inhabitants who were among the first humans. These people were supplemented by those whose ancestors were immigrants, invaders, pilgrims, traders, exiles, prisoners and slaves. They come in every size and colour. Most speak Arabic, a great language, but not an old one. It emerged around the 4th century of the Christian era as the result of a fusion between older Semitic tongues and Aramaic, the language Jesus spoke.

In Arabian tradition, the peninsula's original people are descended from Adam and Eve, the first humans God created, according to Islam, Christianity and Judaism, to live in the Garden of Eden. Anthropologists say there's a difference between the people who came from north Arabia and those from the south. In the north, where desert prevailed, society was shaped by migrating tribes and sedentary oasis dwellers. In the south, regular rain allowed the development of villages and towns that produced a different social structure. It has even bequeathed physical differences.

The people of the desert are called Bedouin, a French word derived from *Bedu* which is Arabic for 'without'. In Arabia, Bedouin tribes remain a vital part of modern society. Arabian tribes began as groups bound by kinship. The tribes expanded through marriage and alliance into confederations that sometimes numbered thousands of individuals. No borders divided one from another. But each Arabian waterhole and wadi was controlled by a tribal group and in old Arabia feuding over water and grazing was endemic.

Tribes are patriarchal, though political power ran through the women's side in pre-Islamic Arabia. A tribal leader, or sheikh, normally inherits his status from his father. But tribes are egalitarian. The leader must protect its members and be open to their views. A sheikh who betrays can be deposed. Leaders know their position depends on ensuring wealth is distributed fairly, though absolute equality is considered impractical and subversive to God's order. Women's influence can be decisive. Through Arabian history, marriage has been a means of forming alliances.

The great tribes have supplied most modern Arabian leaders. Descendants of the Shammar confederation of central and northern Arabia include Saudi Arabia's King Abdullah on his mother's side. Their old rivals, whose lands extended from north-central Arabia to Kuwait, are the Anaizah confederation. The Al Saud and the ruling families of Bahrain, Kuwait and Qatar are all descended from the Anaizah. The greatest confederation of the Arabian south-east is the Bani Yas (the children of Yas). It provides the leading families of Abu Dhabi, including the Al Nahyan, and the Al Maktoum of Dubai. The Al

Qawasim (Al Qassimi in the singular) produced the ruling families of Ra's al-Khaimah and Sharjah in the UAE. The principal exception is the governing Al Bu Said family of Oman, which is not of Bedouin descent. It traces its origins to south Arabia's first Muslim converts.

Most celebrated Arabian tribes are subsets of the great confederations. The Murrah, famous for their desert tracking ability, are considered the purest of Arabian Bedouin. The Saar, who once ranged along the southern edges of the Empty Quarter, are also renowned trackers. The Saar's great rivals were the Al Rashid (Al Rawashid) who dominated the southern fringes of the Empty Quarter. The Duru dominated the area between the east of the Empty Quarter and the Hajar Mountains of south-east Arabia. The Al Manasir (Al Mansouri), one of the great tribes of Abu Dhabi, are found between the base of the Qatar Peninsula and the lands of Abu Dhabi.

South of this and stretching deep into the Empty Quarter are the traditional lands of the Awamir (Al Amiri), historic rivals of the Al Rashid. The north-east of the Empty Quarter is the land of the Al Dawasir (Al Dossary), a people who settled in the wadi that bears their name, but who have since spread widely across eastern Arabia. The Al Ghamdi, one of the largest of Saudi Arabia's tribal groups, originate in the kingdom's south. The Ajman, rivals of the Al Saud, are found in the kingdom's Eastern Province as are the Bani Khalid, once the masters of north-eastern Arabia, the Al Jabri, the Bani Hajir and the Awazim. The Al Mutair (Al Mutairi) live mainly in north-east Arabia.

Arabian tradition says that the people of the north are descended from Nizar bin Majid bin Adnan, one of Ismail's sons and Abraham's grandson. Those of the south are said to descend from Qahtan, one of Noah's sons. Adnani tribes are also known as Nizari. The Qahtani are alternatively called Yamani. In the area now comprising the UAE and northern Oman, a civil war in the 18th century led to the emergence of two opposing confederations roughly corresponding to the northern Adnani/Nizari Arabs and southern Qahtani/Yamani Arabs. In the war, Nizari Arabs took the name of the Bani Ghafir, the tribe of the leader of that confederation. Qahtanis were called the Hinawi after the Bani Hina, the leading tribe of that section.

Ghafiri tribes include the Al Qassimi, the Al Nuaimi (the ruling family of Ajman in the UAE) and some of the tribes of the Buraimi Oasis, the Musandam Peninsula, Dibba and Umm al-Qaiwain. Hinawi tribes include the Bani Yas, the Awair, the Afar, the Manasir, the Al Dhaheri of Al Ain and the Sharqiyin (Al Sharqi) ruling family of Fujairah. In periods of tension, the Ghafiri and Hinawi divide has been significant. It is dormant at present. Oman's Musandam Peninsula is home to the Shihu, recognizable by the small, tomahawk-like hatchet its men carry or have tucked in their belts.

The tribal arrangements are complex in Arabia's rugged south-west. The Al Kathir are prominent in Oman's Dhofar province and Wadi Hadhramaut in Yemen. Some speak the *Jabali* (mountain) language, which comprises four pre-Arabic tongues believed to be similar to the language of the ancient kingdom that dominated Yemen almost 2,000 years ago. The Al Kathiris had an independent sultanate in what was South Yemen before British withdrawal in 1967. The Al Qara, which comprises more than 10 clans, is the largest tribe in Oman's Jebel Dhofar region. Many speak *Jabali*. The Al Shahra, who do not have a tribal structure, are scattered among the Al Qara lands and are found on the Kuria Muria (Al Hallaniyat) Islands off the Omani coast. The Al Mahra live on both sides of the Oman-Yemen border.

The highlands of north and central Yemen are dominated by two confederations: the Hashid and the Bakil. Both trace their origins to pre-Islamic times and both are predominantly Zaydi, a Shiite sect found mainly in south-west Arabia. The Hashid have fewer constituent tribes and have played a more significant role in recent Yemeni history. Ali Abdullah Saleh, president of Yemen since 1990 and of North Yemen for 12 years before that, is a member of the Al Ahmar family that's connected to the clan that has provided the paramount sheikhs of the hashid for generations. The Bakil, with more divisions that have fought over the title of paramount sheikh, believe Yemen's government is dominated by the Hashid. Bakil tribes may have dallied with Al Qaeda and some believe its members were involved in the October 2000 attack on the USS *Cole* in Aden harbour.

In south-west Saudi Arabia, the Al Qathani are the most notable tribal grouping. The Al Yam, some of whom are Ismailis or Zaydis, are numerous around Najran. In the west of Arabia, the great tribes are the Al Utaiba; the Bani Harb; the Juhaina, traditionally a clan of watchmen and guides; the Billi, who are numerous in the north-west; the Muttar and the Bani Atiya. Settled tribes include the Solaib, who in the past were tinkers, hunters and medicine-men; the Agail, a brotherhood of camel-dealers and guides; the Bani Saad, who were farmers; and the Bani Salem, who traditionally lived north of Rabigh and around Yanbu. The Bani Thaqit come from Taif, south of Jeddah.

In the far north-west, the Huweitat and Ruwallah once roamed from Syria to northern Saudi Arabia.

Distinguished families of tribal descent settled in Arabian towns. The Al Zamil were the feudal lords of Unaizah in the central Saudi Arabian province of Qassim. The Olayan family, which is descended from the Shammar confederation, held a similar position in Buraidah, also in Qassim. The prominent Al Turki business family is descended from the Bani Khaled, the dominant tribe of eastern Arabia until the rise of the Al Saud.

Some prominent families trace their origins to the Prophet Moham-med (PBUH) and his companions. The Barooms of Jeddah are a fami-ly of Sayyids, or descendants of the Prophet (PBUH). There's a tradition that the Attar family, also of Jeddah, descends from the Caliph Abu Bakr, the first Islamic leader after the Prophet (PBUH). The Juffali family of Jeddah are said to descend from Khalid bin Al Waleed, the Prophet's (PBUH) greatest general.

Around the coast of Arabia are Arab Sunni Muslims, who originated from southern and western Iran and are known as Huwala (those who have changed) Arabs. Hundreds of thousands were expelled from Per-sia at the end of the 19th century. Many left for Dubai, where they still trade with Iran. The Al Fahim family of Abu Dhabi traces its origins to Sirri Island, now part of Iran, where they lived until the end of the 19th century. The family of Easa Al Gurg, the UAE ambassador to London, originated from Lingah in Iran. Others made similar journeys. They in-clude the Kanoos, who can trace their origins from a section of the Al Dawasir that migrated into Mesopotamia and then to the coast of Iran before moving to Bahrain in the early 19th century. The name, which is derived from the Arabic word 'lawful', was a nickname that stuck.

Other Bahraini Huwalas include the Mannais, who are also found in Qatar, and the Koohejis. The Alireza family, which has branches on the east and west coast of Saudi Arabia, was forced out of what is now Iran in the early 16th century. Zainal (also referred to as Xenel) moved to Jeddah in about 1845 and founded the Hajji Abdullah Alireza Com-pany. His descendant, Abdullah Alireza, a prominent businessman, has been a member of the Saudi cabinet since 2003. Teymour Alireza of the Al Khobar-based Rezayat Group has been a non-executive director of the Shell Group since 1997.

The Linjawis (a derivative from Lingah, or Lingeh, the name of the principal port of the former Persian Arab lands) settled in different parts of what is now Saudi Arabia. And then there are Arabian clans with individual tales. The Al Fitaih originated in Mecca al-Mukarra-mah (Mecca the Honoured) where they made a living as silversmiths. They serviced pilgrims and subsisted by selling jewellery. Legacies of Ottoman rule in Arabia include the Khashoggi and Khazindar families, whose names derive from the Turkish for 'guardian of the treasury'.

Arabia has been enriched by the enterprise of the people of the Wadi Hadhramaut that runs from the Yemen to the coastal plain near the Oman border. It had once been rich, but its agricultural system was wrecked in internecine war in the 18th century. From the 1830s, and after the opening of the Suez Canal in 1869 in particular, emigration began. Hadhramis settled across Arabia, East Africa, India and the Far East. During the 1991 Somali Crisis, there was a flow of Hadhramis attempting to return to Yemen. Because of their comparative wealth, returning migrants gained political influence in the Hadhramaut in the 19th and first half of the 20th centuries. Some who'd risen in the service of the Nizam of Hyderabad in India established the Kathiri and Quaiti sultanates, which were autonomous members of the short-lived South Arabian Federation set up by Britain in 1959. The Bin Ladens, the Bahamdans, the Bin Mahfouz, the Kaakis, the Bugshans and the Binzagrs all trace their origins to the southern wadi.

Around Arabia's Gulf coast, there are pockets of Baharanis, Shiites who trace their origins to the Bahrain archipelago. In Oman, Persians, Pakistanis and Indians have settled for centuries. Many families with Gulf passports arrived in the past half century as exiles or refugees from other Arab countries. Iraqis, Syrians and others were granted asylum after revolutions and coups in their homeland and sometimes served in local armed forces. Palestinian refugees settled in the Gulf. Some were granted nationality or intermarried locally.

Finally, there are names that on their own provide clues to family origins. Hajji was adopted by men who'd completed the pilgrimage. Throughout the Arab World, families adopted or would be given names based on their origins: Al Bokhari from Bokhara, Al Fezzani from Fez, Al Baghdadi from Baghdad and so on. And then there are the names that make sense only to their owners. Fadil Jerman, assistant to the managing director of Kuwait's national oil company, inherited his family name from an ancestor who had greenish-blue eyes and was nicknamed 'The German', or Al Jerman.

Arabic family names beginning with the definitive article have for decades been transcribed into English from Arabic script as beginning with Al-, as in Al-Saud and Al-Nahyan. It appears that this way of naming people is being destroyed by the fact that new digital machines installed to read passports cannot cope with hyphens. Because the hyphen is out, it is now Al Saud or AlNahyan. A further twist is that the Saudi interior ministry has insisted all Saudi Arabians should adopt their tribal names, if they have one, even if they have not used them for years or ever. One prominent Saudi business executive has thus lost, in his passport at least, his preferred name and suddenly become, in the sixth decade of his life, Mr Aldossary.

Arabians love talking about their families' history and origins. The stories are invariably fascinating and provide a connection with an unrecorded past.

## Persian Gulf versus Arabian Gulf

You might be confused about the difference between the Persian Gulf and the Arabian Gulf. Don't be. They are the same thing. The term Persian is derived from the Ancient Greek word *persikos*, which appears to have originated from Parsa, the name of an Indo-European people who migrated into what is now south Iran in about 1000 BC. The Greeks used the term for all the inhabitants of the Iranian Plateau. But the ancient Persians preferred to use the word *Aryan*, which means noble, to describe their descent and language. This is the source of Iran, which can be translated to mean the land of the Aryans. It was adopted by the Iranian government in 1935.

Ancient texts and maps refer to the Gulf as Sinus Persicus, a Latin term translatable into Persian Gulf that the ancient Persians themselves would not have accepted. Erythraean Sea was used by the ancient Greeks for what is now the Red Sea, the Indian Ocean and the Gulf. Erythraean is derived from the Greek word *erythros*, which means red. For this reason, the Gulf has in the past also been called the Erythraean Sea. This in turn was translated into Latin as *Mare Rubrum* or Red Sea. To increase the confusion, the ancients also sometimes referred to the Red Sea as *Sinus Arabicus* or Arabian Gulf. The use of the term Persian Gulf is a recent development. It reflected growing Persian national consciousness that followed the accession of the Safavid dynasty at the start of the 16th century. As the Safavid domain was pushed west it came into contact with the expanding realms of the firmly Sunni Muslim Ottomans. Almost three centuries of intermittent Ottoman-Persian conflict followed.

At the end of the 18th century, the British started to compile detailed charts. They used Persian Gulf in their maps. The emergence of independent Arab states following the dismemberment of the Ottoman Empire during and after the First World War from 1914–1918 gave the issue a new twist. Egypt's President Nasser, the first modern Arab champion, called the waterway the Arabian Gulf. The term is generally used by Arab governments to the irritation of the Iranian government. Publishers using it will get a letter from the Iranian authorities, complete with copies of maps and statements, demonstrating that the proper name is, in fact, the Persian Gulf.

So who is right? Persian Gulf is indeed correct. But there is no consensus that this is the sole accurate name or that Arabian Gulf is wrong. The US government, in a rare agreement between countries that have been adversaries for more than 25 years, continues to call the waterway the Persian Gulf.

**The morphology of the Gulf**
The body of water with two names is both narrow and shallow. It stretches in a crescent 1,000 km from the Shatt al-Arab in the north to the Strait of Hormuz in the south-east. Torrents crash into it on the Iranian coast but no river enters from the Arabian side. It can take up to 200 years for its water to be replaced by inflows and outflows through the Strait of Hormuz, a channel some 50 km wide at its nar-

rowest. Coastal water temperatures range between 10°C in winter and 35° in the summer. Salinity can reach 70 parts per thousand, more than 50 per cent higher than other seas and oceans.

The Gulf embodies the borders of eight states: Iran, Iraq, Kuwait, Saudi Arabia, Bahrain, Qatar, the UAE and Oman. It is also the frontier between the Arab-speaking world and Farsi-speaking world, a divide that stretches back to the time of the Prophet (PBUH) and before.

In the far north, nine alluvial Kuwaiti islands, including Boubiyan, Failaka and Warba, are the result of thousands of years of silt flowing down the Tigris and Euphrates. Significant islands, including Tarut, lie off the coast of Saudi Arabia. Bahrain is an archipelago comprising 33 islands. The shallow water between it and Qatar includes Bahrain's low-lying Hawar Islands and other smaller isles and reefs. Great islands lie along the coast of Abu Dhabi, including Abu Dhabi Island itself. Umm al-Nar, Marawah and Sir Bani Yas are the sites of some of the most important Arabian archaeological finds. Das Island accommodates an oil-and-gas complex. Saadiyat and Reem, both east of Abu Dhabi, are being turned into tourism, residential and commercial centres.

As the Gulf narrows towards the Strait of Hormuz, rocky islands feature in the region's recent history. They include Abu Musa and the Greater and Lesser Tunbs (derived from the Farsi for 'hilly place') that figure in present disagreements between Iran and the UAE.

In the Red Sea and off the southern coast of Arabia, the islands are more dramatic. Yemen's Socotra Archipelago in the Gulf of Aden comprises four islands. Socotra, the largest of the four, is about 120 km by 48 km and rises to more than 1,500 m. Despite their remote location, the Socotra Islands support a population estimated at 40,000 people. But only Socotra itself has a significant number of inhabitants. The island was settled by the Persians and Romans and seized by the Portuguese in 1507. The Omanis tried to capture it in 1669 and the British used it as a coaling station before opting for Aden.

Saudi Arabia's Farasan Islands are limestone outcrops off Jizan in the far south-west of the kingdom. They comprise 20 large isles and are part of more than 800 km of coral shoals called the Farasan Banks that extend parallel to Saudi Arabia's Red Sea coast. In 1963, the French underwater explorer, Jacques Cousteau, wrote *The Living Sea* about the abundance of life he found there.

Large islands lie off the coast of Oman. Masirah was used by the Royal Air Force (RAF) as an emergency landing ground from 1932 until March 1977 and accommodates an American military staging post. The Al Hallaniyat Islands were ceded by Muscat to Britain in 1854 but were returned on November 30, 1967 as part of British disengagement from Aden and south Arabia. They are inhabited by a few families and yield guano.

**The Gulf Cooperation Council (GCC)**
The political shape of the Gulf is being remade by the Gulf Cooperation Council (GCC), an association created in 1981 of Bahrain, Kuwait, Oman, Qatar, Saudi Arabia and the UAE, loosely modelled on the
EU. The GCC six have common characteristics. Their nationals are
mostly Arab and the majority are Sunni Muslims, though there are indigenous communities of minority Muslim groups that perhaps account
for about 10 per cent of the Arabian total. The GCC had a combined
population at the start of 2007 of about 35 million people. About 20
per cent are non-nationals, some born in the GCC. GCC birth rates are
among the world's highest and the majority of nationals are under 21.
The governments of the Gulf Six are dominated by traditional ruling
families. None can be called liberal democracies. All accept with vary-
ing degrees of diligence that the Sharia, or Islamic law, is supreme.

There are also substantial differences. Saudi Arabia has 24 million
people and is roughly the size of the US west of the Rockies. Bahrain
and Qatar each have fewer than one million. Bahrain is smaller than
Greater London. Saudi Arabia has one quarter of the world's proven
oil reserves. Qatar owns the largest non-associated gas field on earth.
Bahrain has almost run out of oil. Qatar's average per capita national
income is more than three times that in Oman and Saudi Arabia. But
all six are comparatively wealthy. Per capita income on average is about
US$20,000. In places, average per capita income for nationals is among
the world's highest. Qatar's is US$50,000 and rising by more than 10
per cent annually.

The Gulf Six are wealthy because of oil and gas. They account for
almost 20 per cent of world oil production and one third of the oil sold
internationally, and own 40 per cent of proven reserves. Demand for
GCC oil is rising by more than five per cent a year and the price at
which it is sold rose by 30 per cent in 2004 and in 2005, and reached a
record high of more than US$120 a barrel in May 2008. GCC econo-
mies are supplemented by gas exports, earnings from plastics and other
products made from hydrocarbons, as well as by income from more
than US$1 trillion in savings. Service industries of all kinds are rising.
GCC growth will be high for at least five more years and US$500 bil-
lion of balance of payments surpluses will be banked by 2011.

**The climate of Arabia**
There are major differences in climate between the north, which borders Iraq, and the south, where it meets the Indian Ocean, between the
coast and the interior and between the lowlands and the highlands that
can rise above 3,000 m.

In August, the Empty Quarter is one of the hottest places on earth.
In the same month, a localized monsoon in south-west Oman brings

rain, low clouds and temperatures barely above 20 degrees. Temperatures in summer can linger above 40 degrees. But as the sun sets, the temperature tumbles. Throughout summer, in most of Arabia, it is possible to sit outside comfortably at night, unless you're in one of the humid coastal areas. In summer, desert nights are usually fresh and sometimes chilly. In winter, the desert can be damp during the day and icy at night. Snow fell in the Hajar Mountains in the UAE in the winter of 2004. And it rains. . . .

On the year's hottest day in July 2004, a violent thunderstorm swept Al Ain in the UAE. In November, a hail storm battered Dubai. Most of the Gulf was swept by storms in early January 2005 and the winter of 2006 was particularly wet. In June 2007, the strongest storm in the Gulf region since 1945, Cyclone Gonu, hit large parts of Oman and the east coast of the UAE, leaving 49 people dead and 27 people missing in Oman alone. Dry wadis can be inundated in minutes by torrential downpours. In the south of Arabia, people are sometimes swept with their vehicles down wadis and clear out to sea.

As the seasons turn, desert air sweeps in from central Arabia bringing clouds of dust. In the winter, cold winds blow from the western mountains and, in the early summer, from the north (*shamal* in Arabic). Temperatures can then fall uncomfortably low, particularly in highland regions. Arabia is a place where it can average less than 15 degrees on a winter's day to 50 degrees in summer. The difference between day and night can be more than 30 degrees.

### The making of Arabian oil

Arabia slopes from the west, where a line of mountains runs the entire coast to rise to about 3,650 m in Yemen. In the east, some land lies below sea level. It is big enough to accommodate all the countries of Western Europe and throws up many questions. Why is it so hot? Why so arid? Why so much sand? And why does it have more oil than any other place on earth?

The answer starts with the origins of the world. The earth is 4.5 billion years old. It took almost two billion years for oxygen and hydrogen to combine to create seas and cloud, and another one billion years for life to emerge in oceans and lakes. About 1.5 billion years ago, lava broke through the earth's crust and drove volcanoes through a giant ocean north-east of Africa. These eruptions were caused by the collision of two tectonic plates, slabs of crust that float on a viscous layer of molten rock. The volcanoes are called the Asir Island Arc after the south-western region of the peninsula that owes its existence to their violence. They are the original parts of Arabia.

A collision further north about 100 million years later threw up the Hejaz arc of volcanoes, the origins of Arabia's north-west mountains.

Millions of years later, the Asir and Hejaz arcs collided. Further collisions and eruptions during a period of almost 500 million years created
the jumble of igneous (formed from volcanic eruptions) and metapho-
ric (changed by heat and pressure) rock that is called the Arabian
Shield. This ancient structure accounts for almost half of visible Arabia
including the mountains and plateaus of the Hejaz and the Asir.
Produced by great heat and pressure, the Arabian Shield contains
abundant minerals.

The tectonic plate upon which Arabia was built, moving fractions of
a centimetre a year, then made a vast journey. Some 300 million years
ago, the peninsula was further south than New Zealand and was probably covered with glaciers. Since then, Arabia has moved north-east.
Some 200 million years ago, it crossed the equator and was then probably covered with tropical rain forest. Today, half of it straddles the
Tropic of Cancer. In 500 million years, it could be near where Siberia
is now and once more covered in snow and ice.

Between 600 and 200 million years ago, Arabia was part of a land
mass known as Gondwanaland that also comprised what are now
Antarctica, Australia, India, Africa and South America. For the final
100 million years of this period, Gondwanaland was linked to Eurasia
and North America in a single land mass called Pangea.

Pangea disintegrated. As tectonic plates separated and collided, deep
trenches were created, allowing molten rock to escape from the earth's
inner crust. These collisions threw up new mountain ranges. Trenches
caused by continental drift run under the Red Sea and between the peninsula's south coast and the Horn of Africa. Here, the sea floor plung-
es thousands of metres. In the north, plate collision created the Zagros
Mountains that run from south-east Iran to the Black Sea.

As the Arabian plate drove north beneath the Eurasian mass, it pushed up the peninsula in the west and south-west. In the east, Arabia was
pushed below sea level and flooded. It was this that has given the Arabian Peninsula its west-to-east tilt, crucial in the development of oil
and gas. In the south-east, a plate beneath the sea rammed into Arabia
and rose up to form the Hajar Mountains. Africa moved south-west
while Arabia inched to the north-east. This created another trench that
runs under the Gulf of Aqaba, through the west of the Sinai Peninsula
and into the eastern Mediterranean.

Friction between plates is the source of shattering earthquakes like
the one that destroyed the Iranian city of Bam on New Year's Eve
2003. The Arabian side of the Gulf has no great geological faults. And
yet, it sits less than 150 km south from a zone where earthquakes are
common. In June 2004 two distinct subterranean shocks, that might
have presaged a further serious earthquake in southern Iran two days
later, were felt in Dubai. A year before, an earthquake registering five

on the Richter scale was recorded in the mountains east of Dubai.

Tectonic plate movement and volcanic eruptions formed Arabia, but the sea shaped it. About 550 million years ago, sea levels began rising with the earth's temperature. At its peak, water covered everything with the exception of the extreme north-west and part of what is now Yemen. In the ages that followed, the ocean ebbed and then returned, inundating Arabia more than a dozen times, for millions of years on each occasion. Silt washed by erosion poured into the ocean that would eventually shrink to become the Gulf. It settled on the seafloor and took with it the remains of trillions of tiny sea creatures called graptolites. These animals formed the material from which some of the greatest oil and gas discoveries were made. Eastern Arabia's sedimentary layers are principally carbonates, mainly comprising limestone but also chalk. It is unique for a richness resulting from long periods of relative calm that allowed life to develop, die and become entombed.

As the ocean fell, these sedimentary layers were exposed to wind, rain, snow and ice and, over millions of years, gradually eroded. When it rose, sedimentary deposition resumed to be followed by more ocean retreat and erosion. The sea level is now well below the highest levels recorded in the distant past. Most of Arabia is exposed and about two-thirds is covered in rocks deposited by the sea. In many places, fossils are easily spotted. Where ancient rivers flowed and ocean waves once crashed, deep valleys and soaring cliffs have been left, a reminder in a land now dry as a bone of a previous presence of water in motion.

As Arabia smashed into Eurasia, the surface crust buckled and curved. Heat and pressure cooked the remains of the sea organisms to produce oil and gas, which migrated along sedimentary bands to settle under domes created by plate collision. This took at least 100 million years. The final phase of Arabia's creation involved volcanic eruptions in the Hejaz Mountains that spread black basalt over more than 300,000 km². These eruptions continued into recent times. Twice in recorded history, Medina (Madinah) was threatened by violent eruptions. Hundreds of dormant Hejaz volcanoes have been counted.

So Arabia was formed by volcanoes, tectonic-plate shift, the rise and fall of the sea, fresh eruptions and the work of the elements during hundreds of millions of years. Because it's stripped of vegetation and topsoil, its origins are exposed. It's impossible to avoid the evidence of the agonies of the earth's crust, the power at work beneath our feet and the unbelievable reality that most of this desert land, even Oman's Jebel Akhdar which soars to 2,000 m, once lay beneath the sea.

**Arabia's deserts**
A million years ago, when rain fell regularly, rivers crossed Arabia. One flowed from the northern Hejaz and then north-east to connect with

what is now the Shatt al-Arab, the sluggish confluence that marks the southern border between Iran and Iraq. Another waterway originating in Arabia's central plateau entered the Gulf below the Qatar Peninsula. The longest river flowed from the mountains of central Hejaz through south-eastern Arabia to supply what may have been a lake occupying a large part of today's Empty Quarter before flowing north to the Gulf west of Abu Dhabi. The fourth lost river carved a valley through the mountains to the Arabian Sea.

The Arabian drought began about one million years ago. As rain dwindled, forest gave way to grasslands. About 50,000 years ago, aridity set in. For a period of no more than 12,000 years, rainfall again became frequent. The Gulf, when the last Ice Age peaked, was a broad, shallow valley cut by a river and connected marshes that meandered from the Shatt al-Arab to the Strait of Hormuz. It slowly flooded as sea levels rose with the melting ice. Higher temperatures as the Ice Age ended 18,000 years ago again brought a dry climate. Wet weather began about 10,000–12,000 years ago and grasses covered the sand dunes while water settled in dry river beds. It lasted until about 4000 BC when rain stopped for most of the time across most of Arabia. The rivers gradually died. The four giants nevertheless left a lasting imprint. The northern river is now Wadi al-Rimah, which connects with Wadi al-Batin in the north-east. The river delta is today the Dibdibah gravel plain that stretches from southern Kuwait into the Divided Zone with Saudi Arabia. The central river is now the Wadi Hanifa that runs through Riyadh and Kharj. Wadi al-Dawasir runs through south-central Arabia and peters out in the Empty Quarter where a lake was once present. Wadi Hadhramaut is the legacy of the southern river. The wadis, and the oases, springs and wells they contain, became the highways and havens of Arabia's desert nomads.

Eight Arabian subterranean rock systems contain water more than 20,000-years old. In the Gulf, it drives up from the seabed in many places. Until the middle of the last century, potable water was harvested from the sea around Arabia's east coast.

The line that marked the division between land and ocean when the sea level was higher remains throughout eastern Arabia. It takes the form of the Summan Escarpment, which extends from north-east Saudi Arabia more than 800 km to the north of the Empty Quarter. It is a sea cliff that's been marooned by the retreat of the Gulf. Made of soft carbonate rocks, the Summan has been eroded and broken to form *jebels* (mountains). To its east lie all the great concentrations of oil and gas including the Ghawar Field, the world's largest single oil reservoir.

More than one-third of Arabia is mountain, created by tectonic plate movement and volcanoes. Most of the rest is desert, but not all of it is sand. Vegetation was killed by the absence of rain and the topsoil was exposed. Wind turned earth into dust and the residue left by the dried rivers became fine sand. Together, they have engulfed more than 1,165,000 km² to create five significant sand deserts. These deserts are the Empty Quarter, the world's largest sand desert; the Nafud, which separates central Arabia from Syria and Jordan; the Dahna, east of Riyadh; a narrower band of desert west of the Saudi capital; and the Jafurah, which separates the Al Hasa Oasis from Qatif and the Gulf.

The dunes of the Dahna, which is more than 1,100 km long and up to 80 km wide, follow the direction of the prevailing north-south winds, forming structures known as uruq. In the Empty Quarter, crescent-shaped barchan dunes have been created with their tips pointing downwind. The light-coloured sands of the Jafurah are dominated by fast-moving, low dunes.

Animals and plants adapted to the desert climate as vegetation died across Arabia from about 15,000 BC. There are 400 Arabian species including baboon and leopard in mountain areas, giant spiny-tailed lizard, gazelle and oryx, desert wolf, the long-eared Arabian hare, sand rats, the desert hedgehog, jerboa and birdlife which encompasses flamingos, eagles and cormorants. The greatest symbol of life flourishing in the desert is the camel, which, in its single-humped form, is probably native to Arabia.

In depressions in the wadis, water percolating to the surface from the aquifers was sometimes sufficient to support bushes and trees. The oases of Al Hasa and Qatif in eastern Saudi Arabia became giant palm plantations that have been cultivated from such sources for at least 2,000 years. Even 2,000 years ago, it may have been possible for water flowing from artesian wells in Al Hasa to flow on the surface, possibly draining into Half Moon Bay south of Dhahran.

The memory of a time when Arabia was wetter and cooler is preserved in the trees in Arabia's mountains. South of Jeddah, the Asir Escarpment rises almost 1,500 m. The road to Taif passes through stands of mimosa and, at the higher altitudes, junipers. These trees, which are found in no other part of the peninsula with the exception of the highlands of Oman and the Musandam Peninsula, rarely survive in Arabia at less than 1,800 m and more than five kilometres from the coast. They are the residue of the last Ice Age when a Mediterranean climate prevailed across the Red Sea region. They've survived in Arabia because of moisture-laden winds from the Red Sea and, in the case of Oman, from the Indian Ocean. In the Asir region, the warm, wet air collides with cold air in the higher altitudes to form thunderclouds that produce violent storms in April and May. During August–September, a monsoon effect brings thick clouds and gentle rain. In August around Salalah in the Dhofar region of Oman, the effect creates the annual *khareef* that brings temperatures down to 20 degrees. Visitors from across Arabia come to enjoy the marvel of rain, rivers and abundant greenery at a time when the rest of the peninsula is scorching. Arabia has mountains as well as deserts. There are, in places, lakes and rivers as well as dunes and dry wadis. But rain is rare. Why did people come to this place? And how did they survive?

## The first Arabians

Near Sakakah in the north of Saudi Arabia, flint tools about one million years old that were left by a family of pre-human creatures known as *Homo erectus* have been found. Only in East Africa, where *Homo erectus* originated, have older remains been found. It's believed that they walked out of Africa into Arabia across the Sinai Peninsula. Human remains, including flint quarries, become more plentiful from 500,000 BC. *Homo erectus* was replaced about 100,000 years ago by the Neanderthals, who left many remains in Arabia. They in turn were gradually displaced and then eliminated by *Homo sapiens*, modern man, some 35,000 years ago.

The wetter weather that began 10,000–12,000 years ago was conducive to human settlement. Stone Age people carefully engraved sandstone rocks with drawings of hunting, wild camels and cattle. In Saudi Arabia, 2,000 rock-art sites have been found. The greatest concentrations are west of Hail near the Nafud Desert and in Shuwayhitiyah in the north, where there are carvings of lion, cheetah, hyena, oryx, camel, cattle and ostrich. Human figures and footprints have been engraved into the rock and writing in Thamudic, the oldest known Arabian script, has also been recorded. Carvings of a similar type and age are being identified elsewhere. In the Hajar Mountains of the UAE, there are carvings that may have acted as signposts for ancient Arabians. Tribal stone markings called *wasum* are used to this day by Bedouin to delineate territory.

Around 7,000 years ago, not long before the emergence of the river-based civilizations of the Indus, the Tigris and Euphrates, and the Nile, Gulf waters were almost three metres higher than today. Much of eastern Arabia was submerged. The coastline was fringed by mangroves with enough fish, birds and mammals to support human settlement. According to archaeologists, the first human civilization was created by the Ubaid people, who are believed to have migrated from southern Mesopotamia. They spread into what is now Syria, Arabia and the southern shores of the Gulf, and laid the foundations for humanity's shift from being nomadic hunter-gatherers to a settled life.

Arabians probably came into contact with the Ubaid people and Ubaid pottery has been found along the Gulf including at Ayn Qanas north of Al Hasa, near Jubail on the Gulf coast, and on the UAE coastline and islands from Dalma to Ra's al-Khaimah. People by this time were using boats made from palm fronds and reeds to make coastal trips. There is evidence that Gulf settlements began before the Ubaid era. In March 2004, the Abu Dhabi Islands Archaeological Survey (ADIAS) found a skeleton at least 7,500 years old in an ancient stone building buried on Marawah Island.

About 5,000 years ago, Arabians started smelting copper and gold. Using charcoal produced from forests that no longer exist, 50,000 kg of gold is estimated to have been produced in Mahd al-Dhahab in the Hejaz. Copper mixed with tin makes bronze, a hard alloy used in weapons and tools. Bronze, coupled with cereal cultivation, made possible the civilizations of the Tigris, Euphrates and Nile, and the rise of the pharaohs, Babylon, Persia and Greece. Arabia became one of the ancients' most reliable copper suppliers.

The Ubaid Civilization was replaced by that of Sumer which was created by people who appeared in the south of what is now Iraq by 3500 BC. The Sumerians founded small cities. Ur, Uruk, Lagash and Nippur were built on the banks of rivers that have since meandered far away, leaving these places in desert plains. Around the time the Sumerians were founding the first towns, villages were emerging along the Gulf coast. Evidence suggests there were links between Arabia and the lands of Sumer.

The most significant Gulf discoveries dating from the early Sumerian period have been made on Tarut Island, three kilometres off the coast town of Qatif; in Al Hasa; in northern parts of what is now Bahrain; on Umm al-Nar Island near the present city of Abu Dhabi and in an area known by the Sumerians as Magan, a term that was applied to the whole of southeastern Arabia. By 2100 BC, Magan was supplying copper to southern Mesopotamia. The settlements at Umm al-Nar and Tell Abraq, in what is now the Emirate of Abu Dhabi, may have been shipping terminals for copper destined for the north.

With practically no written records, imagination has taken the place of fact in attempts to understand this period. The most compelling theory is that Bahrain was the site of a place referred to in Mesopotamian writings as Dilmun, a land of plenty. It has one of the world's most extensive ancient burial grounds. Almost 200,000 Bahraini gravetombs dating from the Sumerian period have been counted.

The original explanation was that the Egyptians, starting 5,000 years ago, placed their dead on ships that sailed down the Red Sea, along the Omani coast and then through the Strait of Hormuz to their final resting place on the archipelago. The consensus now is that the graves were for local people, evidence that Bahrain and the surrounding islands were watered sufficiently to support a significant population for many centuries, perhaps as many as 10,000 people at one time.

Some 50,000 tumuli, now mainly destroyed, were counted around the Dammam Dome in eastern Saudi Arabia in the 1940s. Others were located near Abqaiq, 30 km from the Arabian coast. Gulf towns in the Sumerian era depended upon long-distance sailing based on coastal hops using reed boats. To demonstrate they could travel huge distances, Thor Heyerdahl in the 1977 built one, which he called the *Tigris*, and sailed it down the Gulf, around Arabia and into the Red Sea. The trip is detailed in Heyerdahl's book *The Tigris Expedition*, published in 1979. Unlike his claim that the people of Easter Island came from Latin America, this theory has stood the test of time.

The city states of Sumer could not fend off new regional forces. Around 2400 BC, the Akkadians, who originated in the city of Akkad in northern Sumer, created the first empire where a Semitic language was dominant. The Nile Civilization of ancient Egypt, which emerged before 3000 BC, grew into a magnificent additional challenge to the regional order. After the last Sumerian dynasty fell around 2000 BC, Mesopotamia collapsed into chaos.

A century later, a new system emerged under another group of Semitic-language speakers called the Amorites. Like the Akkadians, the Amorites had a centralized system of government and founded Babylon on the site of Akkad. Their rule did not last. In 1400 BC, northern Mesopotamia fell to the Iron Age Hittite Civilization, the centre was taken over by the Hurrian people of the Mitanni kingdom and the Kassites seized the south-east.

The Assyrians in turn rose to replace the Hittites and dominate northern Mesopotamia. In the 9th century BC, they established their capital at Nineveh, near present-day Mosul on the upper Tigris River. Equipped with iron weapons and famous for their military prowess, the Assyrians extended their domain to encompass what is now Iran, Iraq, Jordan, Syria, Palestine and Israel and most of present-day Egypt. They created roads, a postal system and a silver currency. Royal libraries comprising clay tablets were established. But military over-reach led to their fall.

In 612 BC, the ruler of Babylon united with the Medes, an Indo-European people from the east, to destroy the Assyrian state. A new empire based on Babylon emerged to outshine all predecessors. The city's Hanging Gardens, planted to adorn a giant ziggurat – or rectangular stepped tower – were one of the Seven Wonders of the Ancient World. The New Babylonians deported the Hebrew people to captivity in their capital.

In 539 BC the New Babylonians were conquered by Cyrus the Great of Persia, who gained sovereignty over the Medes 10 years later. His new state, known as the Achamaenian Empire, swallowed the lands of Babylon and extended its influence along the coast of Arabia into what is Oman. The Persians were ambitious and powerful. But they were tolerant and competent. Cyrus freed the Jews. His name is celebrated in the Torah and the Bible.

### The rise of Arabia's Oasis Civilization

Arabia throughout these dramas was arid. Arabians nevertheless managed to inhabit the interior of the peninsula by moving in search of grazing and water from oasis to oasis. Their civilization was made possible by two breakthroughs: the artificial cultivation of the date palm (*Phoenix dactylifera*), which originated in North Africa, and the domestication of the camel.

Surviving on moisture drawn from the subsoil, palm trees provided food and shelter for humans and livestock and shade for cereals, fruit and vegetables. The impact of the date palm is reflected in Al Hasa in Saudi Arabia, which was known as Hajar in ancient times. It has more than 100 natural springs and artesian wells, some of which flow with hot water. Its alkaline and sandy soils, combined with the heat of the desert, make the area ideal for date cultivation. Almost a quarter of the world's date palms are found in the kingdom and about three million of them are in Al Hasa. The other major date-growing areas of Saudi Arabia include Qassim, in the centre of the kingdom; Qatif, north of Dammam; Bisha, which lies in the mountains south of Jeddah; and Medina. Date palms grow quickly and produce fruit within a couple of years of being cultivated from offshoots cut from the base of a mature tree. The trees normally produce good harvests for about 75 years.

Dates grow in bunches like grapes. They can be harvested at any time of the year and at several stages of ripeness from green and unripe to very dry when all the syrup in the fruit has gone. Dates have multiple uses including as a meal, as a sweetener in drinks and as a colouring agent in rice or couscous. There are almost 400 date types and intense debate about which is the best, though there is consensus that the *khalasah* (quintessence) variety is in the premier league. For Arabs, dates are more than simply food. They are part of a culture stretching back to the time of the Prophet (PBUH) and before.

The camel made long-distance oasis travel and the culture of the Bedouin possible. Capable of drinking half its weight in water, camels have a blood system that regulates their temperatures. Domesticated about 3,200 years ago, camels are now never seen in the wild in Arabia. They continue to serve as a source of milk and meat, their use as a beast of burden long superseded by the motor vehicle and the aeroplane. Camel-racing, still popular throughout Arabia, is a living memorial to the time when he who rode the camel commanded the desert. And the masters of the desert ruled Arabia for thousands of years.

By about 1000 BC, trading settlements had developed on camel routes running from Yemen to the north. They gained favour because

they avoided the hazards of sea travel and political instability in Mesopotamia. The first major trading centres in inland northern Arabia
were established some 300 years later. Arabia had by then acquired a
new reputation. The first reports of camel-riding Arab warriors start to
emerge from about the 9th century BC.

The boom period of the camel and oasis was in the early Roman era.
The empire's demand for luxury goods was satisfied by deliveries of
spices and aromatics from southern Arabia, East Africa, India and
China. The gateways to the Roman Empire by land were Sayhut, Bir
Ali, Aden and Mukha in what is now Yemen. Caravan routes ran from
these ports to Najran, which was a key way-station on the route north.
From there, two parallel highways east and west of the Hejaz headed
north and then joined to pass through Taif, Mecca (Makkah) and
Yathrib, as Medina was then known, to Dumat al-Jandal, or Tayma as
it is now known, and finally to Tabuk in north-west Arabia. From there,
the route entered Roman domains to connect with the Mediterranean.

A later route was opened across Arabia from Najran to Qaryat al-
Faw in Wadi al-Dawasir in central Arabia and from there to Layla and
Kharj and finally to Gerrha, the principal trading centre of eastern
Arabia in the early Roman period. Gerrha is now lost. It probably lay
on or near the coast of present-day Saudi Arabia, possibly where Jubail
Industrial City is now situated. A subsidiary route cut through the
Najd along Wadi Fatima to Buraidah and Unaizah in Qassim and from
there to Hail before crossing the Nafud to Tayma.

**Frankincense and myrrh**
Death in ancient times was more real than life, which was short and
full of grief. Across arid Arabia and the Middle East, ancient people
sought comfort in the sparkle of stars in the night sky. The ancient
Egyptians believed their kings, as Gods, found an eternal home in the
heavens. They built their greatest pyramids to emulate the constella-
tions they could see to honour ancestors and provide a link between
earth and eternity. The vision of an afterlife that could only be reached
after a long journey demanded that the dead had to be carefully prepared. They needed food and drink, clothes and trinkets, utensils, car-
riages and, sometimes, companions. The body had to be preserved and
the smell of death eliminated. And this is why frankincense and other
heady aromatics found in Arabia became the most valuable commodities on earth.

The frankincense tree is found only in Dhofar and the Horn of
Africa. Its sap oozes like milk from its bark and branches when cut.
Once in contact with air, it hardens into a crumbly, semi-transparent
golden crystal. The crystals burn giving off clouds of aromatic smoke.
They can be dissolved into water and oil to produce scents and per-

fumes. The ancients prescribed frankincense to cure many illnesses.

No one can say when incense trade began but the civilizations of Mesopotamia, the Nile, Greece and Rome incorporated frankincense into their religious rituals. Incense harvesting flourished as demand boomed in Egypt and Mesopotamia. History is in awe of the scarcity of frankincense and records how Rome was shocked when the Emperor Nero ordered the burning of the entire annual Arabian frankincense supply to mark the funeral of his wife Poppaea. In the New Testament Gospel according to Matthew, the three wise men that travelled from the east to honour Jesus brought gifts in the form of gold, frankincense and myrrh, another aromatic sap originating from south Arabia. These were the most valuable things they could buy.

### The Civilization of Saba

The kingdom of Saba or Sheba, south Arabia's first civilization, lasted from the 12th century BC to the 1st century AD. It occupied what is now western Yemen, but some say it held at least part of what is now Ethiopia. For centuries the Sabaeans controlled the straits leading into the Red Sea and their queen, according to the Bible and the Koran (Qur'an), visited the Hebrew King Solomon who lived in Jerusalem around 900 BC. The Sabaean capital for most of this time was Marib, east of the Yemeni mountains at the start of the Arabian Desert. Other civilizations developed in the region: in Main north of Saba, in Qataban and along Wadi Hadhramaut.

The wealth of Saba resulted from agriculture made possible by a sophisticated system of irrigation. Its crowning glory was the Marib Dam. Some 600 m across, the dam spanned Wadi Adhanah near the Sabaean capital. According to inscriptions, it was built in the 7th century BC. Saba's economy was supplemented by trans-shipping Chinese silk, commodities from East Africa and cinnamon, pepper, gold and precious stones from India. The cream came from trade in frankincense and other aromatics.

Around 25 AD, Saba was conquered by Himyarite kings. The new rulers consolidated the fragmented states of south-west Arabia and dominated Yemen until the 6th century. The Himyarites continued to control the frankincense and myrrh trees. But the spread of Christianity, which initially discouraged incense burning as a pagan practice, reduced the demand for aromatic tree sap.

The region was occupied by Christian Abyssinia in 335. Christianity was introduced in southern Arabia with centres in Najran, Aden, Sanaa and the Hadhramaut and on Tarut Island off the Arabian east coast. Christian and indigenous Jewish peoples clashed. A king who'd converted to Judaism attacked Najran in the 6th century. Abyssinian forces crossed from the Horn of Africa in 525, established a new protectorate over south Arabia, and eventually ended Himyarite rule. The Abyssinians in turn were displaced by the Sasanians of Persia who absorbed southern Arabia at the end of the 6th century. Under the Himyarites, the Sabaean knowledge of hydraulic engineering was lost. The maintenance of the Marib Dam became increasingly difficult. It broke and was repaired in 450 and gave way again in 542.

But catastrophe came, according to Muslim historians, in 575 when the dam collapsed for the third and last time. Water stopped flowing through the irrigation channels. Crops died. Marib farmers migrated. Whole tribes moved to Syria. The Koran has a simple explanation. It was punishment for their ungratefulness to God. And it paved the way for Islam.

### The Gulf goes Greek

In 334 BC, Alexander the Great launched a campaign to unify the world under his leadership. Egypt was captured and the Achamaenian Persian Empire smashed. Alexander reached the Indus Valley. At this point, he decided to return to Babylon, his eastern base. Alexander split his forces into two. One returned by land along the south coast of what is now Pakistan and Iran. The other journeyed home by sea through the Gulf.

Back in Babylon, Alexander ordered the exploration of eastern Arabia in the hope of establishing a Greek trade route from India to the eastern Mediterranean. It is likely that one of three expeditions he dispatched located and explored Bahrain. Alexander's general Nearchus landed on Failaka Island in Kuwait Bay and a permanent settlement, which lasted from 230 BC to 110 BC, was established there. For a while, Arabia was defined in Greek. Failaka was named Ikaros and Bahrain Tylos. Greeks traded with Thaj, Al Hinnah and Gerrha, all in what is now eastern Saudi Arabia.

Alexander was planning to invade Arabia when he died in June 323 BC. His empire was divided. A dynasty founded by his general, Seleucus, governed the eastern section, comprising parts of the Gulf coast, Iran, Iraq, Syria, and Lebanon as well as what are now areas in Turkey, Armenia, Turkmenistan, Uzbekistan and Tajikistan. During the Seleucid period, Gerrha was the most important Gulf trading centre. The Romans replaced the Greeks as masters of the Mediterranean, Syria and Egypt following the defeat and suicide of Cleopatra in 30 BC. Nomadic Parthians seized the east. Between them, they destroyed the Seleucid Empire.

All these conquests established the frontier between the Greek-speaking East Mediterranean world and the Parthian and subsequent Persian empires in the East. It divided Arabia. For the Romans, and the Greeks before them, the Red Sea was the sea route to the frankincense lands and further east. The northern Gulf was controlled by the Parthians who established garrisons as far south as Oman.

In 225 AD, the Parthians were replaced by the Sasanians, who made Ctesiphon in what is now Iraq their capital. They aimed to control the Gulf and undermine the Red Sea's significance. The Sasanian King Ardashir invaded eastern Arabia to depose one of the last remaining Parthian governors. He founded a new town that was called Batn Arda-shir. Its site has been lost, but it is believed to be in the Qatif Oasis.

In 325 AD, the Sasanian King Shapur II responded to attacks on the Persian coast by Arab raiders with campaigns that eventually took his army across the peninsula to Yathrib (Medina). There, he turned north and probed Roman territories. Shapur was brutal. His prisoners had their shoulders pierced so that they could be roped together. For this, he was named Dhu al-Aktaf, or Lord of the Shoulders.

### The Nabataeans build Petra, Rome's gateway to Arabia

The Nabataeans dominated north-western Arabia for more than 500 years, starting from around the start of the Christian era. Their greatest legacies are the abandoned city of Petra in southern Jordan, and Madain Saleh in north-west Saudi Arabia. The Nabataeans were prob-ably Arabs who migrated into the Negev Desert and Sinai over the centuries. They applied their skills in water collection to create stations for the caravan trade from southern Arabia to Egypt and Mesopotamia. At its peak, the Nabataean domain may have stretched from Yemen to Damascus and from the west of Iraq into the Sinai. Their knowledge of sea and land routes created a link between the sources of the luxu-ries of the south and east and the markets of the north and west.

Following their conquest of Egypt, the Romans became neighbours. In 24 BC, the Romans tried to bring Arabia within their realm. Egypt's pro-consul, Aelius Gallus, under the directions of Augustus Caesar, led an army 1,450 km from Petra into the peninsula. Gallus returned empty-handed. Some believe he may have got as far as Abha in the Asir. Around this time, human ingenuity dealt Arabia a blow from which it never recovered until the discovery of oil. Arab navigators of the Gulf had discovered how to sail to India and back and were trading in the region's pearls that were also exported to imperial Rome. This skill was exclusively theirs until, about 2,000 years ago, Greek sailors learned how to use south-westerly monsoon winds to sail from Egypt to India and return safely. This allowed the development of Red Sea shipping routes that could bypass the Arabian caravan highways and avoid Yemen altogether.

The rise of Red Sea routes led to economic decline in the Arabian interior. Nabataea was absorbed by Rome in 106 AD. After the annex-ation, the Romans preferred to peer into the south from their garrisons, fantasising about Happy Arabia, Arabia Felix, one of the earliest El Dorado myths. Rome's decline and conflict with Persia were further blows. Petra was destroyed, either by earthquake or war, in the middle of the 6th century AD. It was abandoned and never reinhabited.

In the Gulf, the town of Mleiha south of Dhaid in the UAE flourished in the final three centuries BC. The Roman writer Pliny the Younger, who lived in the first century AD, said south-east Arabia was full of towns. Omana, which is believed to have been on the UAE's Gulf coast, was a trans-shipment centre for goods going to India from Syria and southern Iraq. The other main settlement in the area was Al Door in what is now Umm al-Qaiwain. Some archaeologists believe Omana and Al Door are different names for the same place. The Persian Sasanian Dynasty introduced Zoroastrianism, the Persian Empire's official religion, and Nestorian Christianity, which it tolerated.

By the start of the 6th century, the Roman Empire had been divided for 200 years. Rome and Western Europe had fallen to barbarian invaders. But the eastern empire with its capital in Constantinople remained largely intact. Greek-speaking Byzantium, as we now know it, ruled a vast area including Syria and the Arabian frontier. Byzantium's rival was the Sasanian Empire. The Sasanian domain in 500 extended east from Byzantium to the Indus Valley. Its northern borders were defined by the Caucasus, the Caspian Sea, the central Asian Desert and the Karakoram Mountains. The southern frontier comprised the Gulf and the Euphrates Valley, which marked where the settled lands of Mesopotamia met the deserts of Arabia.

The Byzantines and the Sasanians from the third to the sixth centuries encouraged Arab buffer states between their lands and the territories of the Bedouin. The Ghassan, a Christian people of Yemeni stock, were clients and allies of Constantinople. The Lakhmids, who were based on the city of Hira in north-east Arabia, dominated southern Mesopotamia and eastern Arabia. They served the equivalent purpose for the Sasanians. The land of the Lakhmids bordered Kinda, a Bedouin state supported by the Himyarites of Yemen, which controlled most of central Arabia including the Najd. In about 500, the rule of the Lakhmids was broken by the Kinda. For about three decades, the Kinda governed eastern Arabia before they were in turn defeated and the Lakhmids restored. Some historians believe Kinda was the first independent Arab state.

The Byzantines and Sasanian Persia provided uneasy stability in the central Middle East for three centuries but the system was under pressure. Incompetent rulers in Constantinople and Ctesiphon, together with the waste of resources in wars between the two empires, weakened the economy. Byzantine religious intolerance had alienated many of its people. The buffer states of the Ghassan and the Lakhmids were weak.

This made the status quo much more fragile than the magnificence of the two imperial capitals suggested. It was vulnerable, to an extent no one imagined, to the shock that was about to be delivered from the south by the Arab armies of the Prophet Mohammed (PBUH).

## The Prophet Mohammed (PBUH) and the Islamic revelation

The movement that was to change the face of Arabia and the world was inspired by the same story of creation by one, omnipotent, God who made the world in seven days that is accepted by Christians and Jews. God created Adam and Eve and expelled them for their disobedience from the Garden of Eden. Muslims, Christians and Jews agree that Noah built an ark, or boat, to save his family and all God's creatures during a great flood.

The disagreements start with Abraham (Ibrahim in Arabic). He was a shepherd descended from Adam and Noah who left the Sumerian city of Ur on the Euphrates on a journey west at the direction of God.

According to the Bible, Abraham's wife Sarah was unable to have children. She called on the patriarch to father a child through her servant Hagar. The fruit of this union was Ishmael or Ismail. Fourteen years later, when Abraham was 100, Sarah gave birth to Isaac. Jealous of Ismail, Sarah pressed Abraham to eject Hagar and her son. This he did but God saved the mother and child, declaring to Hagar: "Arise, take up the boy, and hold him by the hand; for I will make him a great nation." (Book of Genesis, chapter 21, verse 18) The great nation would be the Arabs.

The Muslim version of this story is that Sarah told Abraham to marry Hagar and, consequently, Ismail is the great man's legitimate, eldest son. According to Muslims, Abraham, who'd settled in the Mecca Valley in western Arabia, did not expel Hagar and Ismail willfully but as a result of a divine order. Alone in the desert, Hagar and Ismail were saved when God made a freshwater spring burst forth at Ismail's feet. Hagar enclosed the spring, called Zamzam, which later became a well.

The second great divergence comes years later. Again in obedience to God's instructions, Abraham, according to Jewish and Christian versions, took his son Isaac to a mountaintop and prepared to slaughter him as a sacrifice. At the last moment, an angel sent by God restrained him. For Jews, this marks the moment when Abraham and his descendants became God's chosen people. For Christians, the covenant between God and Abraham establishes the bloodline from which their redeemer Jesus was born. According to Muslims, God commanded Abraham to sacrifice his first born, who was Ismail not Isaac. In Islam, all the other details remain the same with the exception that they involve the son of Hagar not the son of Sarah. The slaughtering of a ram instead of a boy is commemorated by Muslims in the Eid al-

Adha (Feast of the Sacrifice) which follows the annual Hajj. Muslims believe Ismail had 12 sons, among them Kedar. The Prophet (PBUH) is a descendant of Kedar, which places the Prophet of Islam directly in line from Abraham, father of the three great monotheistic faiths.

Jews and Christians focus on Isaac and his son Jacob, the father of Joseph with the multicoloured cloak. Isaac, whom God named Israel (You Have Struggled With God), had 12 sons who are the founders of the tribes of Israel. The line of Isaac and Jacob was to lead to another Joseph, the husband of Mary who was the mother of Jesus. In the Muslim version, Ismail and Isaac are equals. But Ismail is the greater of the two and he helped his father Abraham build the Ka'bah in Mecca. These contradictory accounts lead to the conflicting claims of legitimacy at the heart of the religious divide between three great faiths. The differences are irreconcilable. But the three have a common source, the patriarch Abraham.

The biblical story of the Jews continues through Babylon and Egypt. Moses led his people out of bondage into the Promised Land. We shall advance to the birth of Jesus in Bethlehem in Judea in Palestine. Joseph and his betrothed Mary, who was pregnant but (according to most Christians) still a virgin, lived in Nazareth in Galilee. They travelled to Bethlehem to participate in a census ordered by the Roman Emperor Augustus. The Bible says Joseph was descended from the Judean King David, who founded Jerusalem as the religious centre of Judaism. David had been born in Bethlehem. Jews were required to gather in their tribal centres for the census. That's why Mary and Joseph went to the city and why Jesus was born there.

In the Christian version, it fulfilled prophecies that the Messiah, or the saviour of the Jews, would be born of the House of David. The three-year mission of Jesus in Galilee, Judea and Samaria that concluded in his crucifixion, death and resurrection is at the centre of Christian belief. In his final acts on earth, Jesus demonstrated he was both God and man and the saviour of the world promised by the prophets. Because Jerusalem is the site of the crucifixion as well as some of the miracles of Jesus, the city has special status for Christians.

For Jews, Jerusalem matters as the centre of their faith and because of the orthodox belief that God will choose a *Mosiach* (Messiah), a man who will put an end to all evil, rebuild the Temple in Jerusalem, bring all Jewish exiles back to Israel and usher in the world to come. Jews regard Jesus as a false Messiah, of which there have been several.

For Muslims, Jesus, or Isa in Arabic, is the penultimate prophet who presaged Mohammed. Of all the prophets, Jesus is probably the most written about in the Koran. It states that Jesus was chosen by God to teach his people. But he is not associated with nor part of God himself. Muslims believe he performed miracles by the grace and power of God alone. They reject the notion of the Trinity, which is central to the teaching of most Christians, in which God is made up of three parts: the father, the son Jesus, and the Holy Spirit. Islam also teaches that God is merciful and forgives all sins. There was no need for a saviour or a blood sacrifice such as the crucifixion. Muslims believe the message of Jesus was the same as the message of all the prophets: worship God, and him alone.

More than five centuries after the crucifixion, Mecca was a settlement off the principal Arabian caravan route. Its inhabitants included Jews, Christians, Zoroastrians and people with older faiths who saw spirits in rocks, the sea and even in the wind. For centuries, a black meteorite in Mecca had attracted attention. Its compelling shape and texture made it a magnet for those seeking an explanation for the mysteries of human existence. A wall surrounded the stone to create a sanctuary where pilgrims left idols and tribal tokens. The pilgrimage climaxed at an annual Mecca fair.

Sometime before recorded history, a square building was erected with the black stone protruding from its eastern corner. Some versions say that the original building was constructed by Adam, the first man. Muslims believe that a new structure, called the Ka'bah (cube), was built under Ismail's guidance by the Prophet Abraham, who was handed the black stone by the Archangel Gabriel and erected the *Ka'bah* on the remains of the original temple. The descendants of Abraham through Kedar are also believed to have acted as guardians of the Ka'bah until the time of the Prophet (PBUH). The valley in which Mecca is set is called the Valley of Abraham (Wadi al-Ibrahim).

The Ka'bah is mentioned by ancient historians. In the 1st century BC, the Roman Diodorus Siculus described what seems to be the Ka'bah. Ptolemy, the Greek geographer and author of what is considered to be the first atlas, also mentions a town that could be Mecca. The Koran describes it as the first place of worship selected by God and calls it Umm al-Qura (The Mother of Settlements).

The Ka'bah has been demolished and rebuilt several times. Today it is oblong in shape – 12 m long, 10 m wide and 16 m high – and made of grey stone from the Mecca region. The building is hollow and was used to accommodate pagan statues until the coming of Islam. It is opened twice a year for ritual cleaning and draped in a gold-embroidered black silk cover called the *kiswah*. A new one is made each year and ceremonially delivered to Mecca. Around the Ka'bah are places of special importance in Islam, including the graves of Ismail and Hagar and the stone on which Abraham stood when the Ka'bah was being built and upon which has been miraculously engraved the patriarch's footprints. The Zamzam Well is hidden from view near the Ka'bah's north-east corner. The Great Mosque of Mecca now encompasses the hills of Al Safa and Al Marwa between which Hagar ran in search for water for her son before God's miraculous intervention.

During the 5th century, Mecca was controlled by the Quraysh family. They had grown rich on trade and the annual fair. The Prophet (PBUH) was born in Mecca around 570. His clan was the Bani Hashem, children of Hashem, a unit of the Quraysh family who were guardians of the Zamzam Well. Mohammed's (PBUH) father, Abdullah bin Abd Al Muttalib, died before He was born and His mother, Aminah, died when He was six. He was subsequently raised in the home of His grandfather Abd Al Muttalib, who died when Mohammed (PBUH) was eight. Mohammed (PBUH) was then protected by His uncle, Abu Talib, whose son Ali later became the fourth caliph. When he was old enough, Mohammed (PBUH) worked as a caravaner on long journeys from Mecca into the north of Arabia, Byzantium and, possibly, into Persia. Mohammed (PBUH) is believed to have remained illiterate all His life.

Aged 25, Mohammed (PBUH) married Khadija bint Khuwaylid whose wealth in camels was managed by her devoted husband. They had two sons, who both died in infancy, and four daughters. It was from these bonds of kinship that the Islamic revolution was born. Mohammed (PBUH) would frequently retreat to the mountains around Mecca to meditate and pray. He was originally from a polytheist family but may have received religious guidance from a monotheist living in Mecca. Some time in 610, Mohammed (PBUH) received without warning His first revelation. It was dictated by the Archangel Gabriel who revealed himself while the Prophet (PBUH) was in retreat in a cave on Mount Hira near Mecca. Gabriel (Jibreel) is one of four archangels believed to be able to act as God's emissaries to humanity.

Standing before the wondering Mohammed (PBUH), the archangel declared: "Recite: In the name of thy Lord who has created man from a clot."

"I cannot recite," Mohammed (PBUH) replied.

Gabriel then grasped Him and squeezed Him until He was exhausted. The angel repeated the command twice more. Twice more Mohammed (PBUH) gave the same response and on each occasion He was squeezed in the same manner. Finally, after the third time, Mohammed (PBUH) received His first revelation and recited the words of what are now the first five verses of the 96th sura, or chapter, of the Koran. This proclaims that God is the creator of man and the source of all knowledge.

The revelations continued during most of Mohammed's (PBUH) life. For three years, He shared them only with close family and friends, His kinsman Abu Bakr, the Mecca merchant, Uthman bin Affan, and His cousin Ali, son of His guardian and uncle Abu Talib who was later to marry Mohammed's (PBUH) daughter Fatima. Mohammed (PBUH) would recite what He'd been told. This select group became the first converts to Islam. The revelations completed the work of earlier prophets. There was one God, whose wishes would be revealed in prophecy, and religious rules to be rigidly applied. The world would end in disaster and glory. There would then be a final judgement by God and bodily resurrection and eternal life for the righteous. The power of the message and the beauty of the poetic form in which it was delivered are compelling. It is universally said that it is barely translatable from Arabic without loss of meaning and lyricism.

In 613, Mohammed (PBUH) received a revelation that begins 'Rise and Warn', a command to take God's message to a larger audience. He began to preach in public, calling for repentance and submission (Islam). The message found a following among the poor and rootless who were galvanized by the idea of a society where all were equal before God and that heaven was open to the righteous regardless of social status or race. To the Medinan establishment, Mohammed (PBUH) was a troublemaker, propounding a new religion that would, by taking precedence over all other faiths, destroy their city's prosperity. The revelations continued, including in the Lailat al-Miraj (The Night Ascent) when the Prophet (PBUH) was visited in 620 by two archangels while he was asleep. The angels purified his heart and filled him with knowledge and faith. The Prophet (PBUH) is said to have travelled from Mecca to Jerusalem in a single night on a winged creature called Buraq. From Jerusalem, He ascended into heaven, where He met the earlier prophets and God. During his time in heaven, Mohammed (PBUH) was told of the duty of Muslims to recite salat (ritual prayer) five times a day.

After more than a decade of preaching, Mohammed (PBUH) had perhaps no more than 100 followers. He made contact with leaders of Yathrib who promised Him a haven. On the day corresponding to July 16, 622, Mohammed (PBUH) led the Muslim community on the 336 km journey north to the city which was subsequently renamed Al Medina Al Munawarra (The City of Light). The departure, or flight, from Mecca is memorialized as the Hegira, which literally translates as the migration. The Muslim calendar, based on a year comprising 12 lunar months, begins at this moment. Medina provided a base from which Mohammed (PBUH) and His followers launched campaigns of conversion and conquest. The confrontation with Mecca continued.

In Islam's first battle in March 624, a Muslim army of 300 men led by Mohammed (PBUH) defeated a superior force from Mecca at Badr, a town south-west of Medina. The following year, the Medinans sent an army of 3,000 men to attack Medina and met a Muslim force one quarter its size at Uhud, a ridge outside Medina. Despite the odds, the Muslims were close to victory when the Medinan cavalry launched

a flank attack that forced them to retreat. Mohammed (PBUH) was
seen to fall and the Muslims withdrew. The Prophet (PBUH), however, was only wounded and the battle ended in a draw with the Medinans failing to destroy the Muslim army. A third attack on Medina was
launched in 627. The Muslims dug a trench across the northern side of
the Medina Oasis. The invasion turned into a siege. When the weather
worsened, the Medinans lost heart and withdrew. It was not a complete Muslim victory, but it was decisive. Mohammed (PBUH) then
built alliances with Bedouin tribes of the Hejaz and the Red Sea coast.
He won over leading figures from Mecca including Amr ibn Al As and
Khalid bin Al Waleed, leader of the Medinan cavalry that had inflicted
so much damage on the Muslims at the Battle of Uhud.

With an army of 10,000, Mohammed (PBUH) and the Muslims
went on the offensive. His opponents collapsed and, on January 11,
630, Mohammed (PBUH) re-entered Mecca virtually unopposed. The
pagan idols in the Ka'bah were destroyed, though a statue depicting
Jesus was preserved on Mohammed's (PBUH) direct orders. The sanctuary was declared to be the holiest shrine in Islam, replacing Jerusalem
towards which Muslims had prayed since moving to Medina.

Mohammed (PBUH) addressed the enemy he had just vanquished.
"Men of Quraysh, what do you think I am about to do with you?"

"Everything good, for you are a noble and generous brother, son of
a noble and generous brother," they replied.

The Prophet (PBUH) then said: "Rise and go, for you are free."
This exchange set the merciful standard, though it was not always met,
for every future Muslim leader when dealing with a defeated foe.

Immediately after Mecca was recovered, a new threat emerged when
hostile Bedouin tribes gathered at Hunayn near Taif, south of Mecca.
This time the people of Mecca formed an army and marched out to
defeat them. The victory made the Prophet (PBUH) the undisputed
leader of the Hejaz. The settlements of east Arabia were among the
first outside the birthplace of the Islamic movement to hear the message of the Prophet (PBUH). Control of the Al Hasa Oasis was divided
between a Sasanian governor and a Christian Arab named Mundhir
ibn Sawa. Mundhir adopted the new faith and sent a delegation to
Medina to sign a treaty. In Hofuf, capital of Al Hasa, the first mosque
in eastern Arabia was built in about 635. The conversion of Bahrain is
believed to have taken place between 627 and 629 and the island was
incorporated into the Muslim Empire in 633.

The Muslims had by then conquered the south. In 630, Amr ibn Al
As, who was later to capture Palestine and Egypt, carried a letter from
the Prophet (PBUH) to the rulers of the Azd people of inland Oman,
then under the rule of the Persians, calling for them to adopt the faith.
Tribal leaders travelled to Medina to find out more. The Azd, to whom

the ruling family of Oman traces its descent, were convinced. The Azd converts sent a letter to the Sasanid governor of Rustaq, in what is now Oman, inviting him to follow their lead. When he refused, they defeated him in battle and besieged the Persian garrison at Sohar. It surrendered, the Persians left and Sohar became Islam's gateway to the Indian Ocean and the Far East. The Azd, led by their general, Al Muhallab ibn Abi Safra, then carved their name into Muslim history by taking part in the conquest of Khorasan, the giant north-east province of the Persian Empire. Many Azd people initially settled in Basra, which was founded by the second Muslim caliph, Omar. The Prophet (PBUH) sent his son-in-law Ali to the Yemen, also then a part of the Sasanian Empire, where the people were mainly Jews or Christians. The conversion was spontaneous and almost complete. All 14,000 members of the powerful Hamdan tribe are said to have adopted Islam on a single day.

The campaign then shifted to the north. In October 630, Mohammed (PBUH) led an army of 30,000 men and 10,000 horses on his greatest campaign, this time against the town of Tabuk in north-west Arabia. Without a single military engagement, the Prophet (PBUH) secured the capitulation of the region. One of the features of the largely bloodless campaign in the north-east was the practice of establishing treaties of co-existence with Jewish and Christian populations. They established the *dhimmi* (in the care of) system, an arrangement that provided for their protection, secured all their rights in property and allowed them to profess their religion provided an annual tax was paid.

Mohammed (PBUH) died in 632 and was buried in Medina. Around his tomb, a mosque has been built which is now the second holiest place in Islam. Abu Bakr, the father of Mohammed's (PBUH) influential wife, Aisha, was named by the Muslim community as his heir, or caliph, which is derived from the Arabic word *khalif*, which means 'successor'.

The following year, the forces of Islam reasserted control over south-eastern Arabia, which had fallen into rebellion and disbelief, smashing the rebel army of Dhul Taj Lakit bin Malik in a battle near Dibba on what is now the border between Oman and the UAE. It's said that nearly 10,000 people died in what is known in Muslim history as the 'Day of Dibba' and the headstones marking their graves can still be seen. The first confrontation between Muslims and the Byzantines took place at Mutah, in what is now Jordan, in 632. The battle was a Muslim disaster. Zayed ibn Harithan, one of Mohammed's (PBUH) closest companions, was killed and two other leaders died. Khalid bin Al Waleed led the defeated army home. Abu Bakr then launched simultaneous campaigns against the Byzantines and the Persians. Khalid bin Al Waleed, known in Islamic history as 'The Unsheathed Sword of God', led a column against the Persian city of Hirah which submitted.

Two other columns under Amr ibn Al As drove into what is now Jordan and southern Palestine.

Abu Bakr died in 634 and was succeeded by Caliph Omar who was to witness many Muslim triumphs. In July 634, the Byzantines were defeated at the Battle of Ajnadayn. Damascus fell in September 635. The Christian cathedral at its heart, built round a pagan Roman temple, was converted into the first great mosque of Islam. The Byzantine Emperor Heraclius sent a relieving army but this was defeated in a dust storm at the Battle of Yarmuk in 636. Jerusalem sued for peace. Caliph Omar amazed the people of the city by entering wearing a coarse mantle. He cleansed himself and then prayed in the southeastern section of the city, the site of the temple destroyed by the Romans in 70 that was still a rubbish-strewn heap of rubble. Omar commissioned the building on this site of a modest mosque. The first Jerusalem mosque was replaced in 684 by the Qubbat al-Sakhrah (Dome of the Rock) which encloses the place from which Mohammed (PBUH) is said to have made His nocturnal ascent to heaven 64 years earlier.

Syria was now in Muslim hands. By the end of 643, Egypt was part of the Muslim Empire. Tripoli in modern-day Libya fell the same year, but it took another 75 years to complete the conquest of North Africa. Campaigns northwards in 673 and 717, when the Muslim army besieged but failed to capture Constantinople, were unsuccessful. Muslim armies entered France from Spain in 768. They were held at Poitiers by a Christian Frankish army. This defined the high watermark of Muslim conquest in Europe until the Ottoman advance to Vienna at the end of the 17th century.

The success in the east was equally dramatic. Initially defeated at the Battle of the Bridge in 634, the Muslim army beat the Persians at Buwayb the following year. At Qadisiya in 636, south of what is now Baghdad, the Persian army, complete with elephants, was comprehensively defeated. The Sasanian capital Ctesiphon was captured. The Muslim army pursued the Persians across the Iranian Plateau and in 642 won a battle at Nihavand known in Muslim history as 'The Victory of Victories'. Muslim control now extended to the gates of central Asia. The Abd Al Qais of Al Hasa mounted sea expeditions against the Persian coast and played a role in the conquest of the Pars province during 649–50. The Sasanian Dynasty was finally extinguished in 651 when its last emperor, Shah Yazdegerd, was assassinated in Merv in what is now the Republic of Turkmenistan. The expansion to the east stopped at this point though it was to resume 60 years later in a drive across the Oxus into the heart of central Asia.

Eastern Christians adapted themselves to the new rulers. Muslims initially suppressed Jewish influence in Arabia. But, with the capture of Babylon and Syria, and their large Jewish populations, a different attitude emerged. Mohammed (PBUH) taught that Jews, like Christians, were people of the book (Ahl Al Kitab), mistaken in their unwillingness to accept Mohammed's (PBUH) message, but still open to conversion. Their treatment in most Muslim territories contrasted with the bans, discrimination and persecution that were a feature of Jewish life in the Christian World.

Omar, the second caliph, died in 644, having moved the capital of the Islamic state to Damascus from Mecca. He was replaced by Uthman ibn Affan, who has an honoured place in Muslim history for ordering the writing of a definitive version of the Koran in about 651. He was assassinated by Muslim opponents in 656. Ali, the Prophet's (PBUH) cousin and son-in-law, was made caliph. Ali was a kind-hearted person who did not contest the choice of Abu Bakr as first caliph and assented when the Muslim elite selected Omar and then Uthman as their leader.

Ali's moderation was tested when the Caliph Uthman's cousin, Muawiya bin Abu Sufyan, rebelled in the first Islamic civil war which was to last until Ali's death. The two sides met at the Battle of Siffin on the upper Euphrates in 657. The army of Muawiya was being defeated when some of his soldiers raised scrolls from the Koran on their lances in an appeal for the conflict to be resolved through arbitration (*takhim*). Ali ordered a halt to the fighting and agreed to negotiate with Muawiya. Some of Ali's supporters were outraged by his moderation and left the battlefield. They were given the name Kharijite – 'those that departed'.

Ali argued that authority within the Muslim community should rest on the pious and those with a close connection to the Prophet (PBUH). He was assassinated by a Kharijite as he left a mosque in Kufa in what is now Iraq in 661 and is buried in Najaf. A huge mosque has been built around his tomb. The Muslim majority accepted Muawiya as caliph, the first in the Umayyad Dynasty that was to last until 750, while the followers of Ali rejected his right to govern. These differences were managed until Muawiya's death in 680 when the civil war between the Umayyads and the followers of Ali resumed and continued until the Umayyad caliphate was ended. Muslims still yearn for the era of Islamic unity that occurred during the time of the Prophet (PBUH) and the 39 years of the Islamic revelation under the first four caliphs, known as the *Rashiduun*, or rightly guided caliphs: Abu Bakr, Omar, the first part of the rule of Uthman and Ali before the arbitration with Muawiya.

**What Muslims believe**
The Muslim creed comprises the following. The religion of God is Islam. The only way to know Islam is through the Koran, the Sunna (actions of the Prophet [PBUH] meant to teach the faithful how to conduct themselves in a way that earns a reward from God) and the

approved Hadith (what Mohammed [PBUH] said). God is one and transcendent. Mohammed (PBUH) is his last prophet. All humans will be resurrected at the last judgement and tested about their beliefs and actions during life. God will then decide which of them will be elevated to God's eternal kingdom and those consigned to hell. Anyone that does not believe in the oneness of God, that Mohammed (PBUH) was his final prophet and in the bodily resurrection and the final judgement cannot be a Muslim.

Believers are given the freedom to decide what the proper fulfilment of God's will entails, but up to a point. Conventional Muslim thought places humans in the hands of an all-powerful and all-knowing God. The fatalism some Muslims express in the frequently repeated phrase *Insha'allah* (God willing) is attributed to this characteristic of the faith. Human predestination, or the idea that God already knows who will be redeemed and who will be damned, is a concept widely held in the Islamic World.

The word Islam means 'surrender' or 'submission' (to the will of God). This is expressed in Islamic law that regulates relations between humanity and God and among human beings. The Koran, which comprises 114 chapters, is the first source of Islamic law. No orthodox Muslim disputes that it is the literal word of God revealed in phases over several years to his final prophet. The Koran is supplemented by the Sunna and the Hadith. Muslims recognize two other sources: comparative analogical reasoning (*Qiyas*) and consensus (*Ijma*). *Qiyas* is used when there is no clear guidance in the Koran or Sunna. *Ijma* requires agreement among religious scholars, and not the Muslim community as a whole.

Muslim scholars diverge about the emphasis to be placed on various Sunna and Hadith. There is, therefore, a higher degree of pluralism within Muslim belief than most non-Muslims imagine. And yet, with the Koran's 6,226 verses (sura) at its centre, supplemented by the guidance provided by the Prophet's (PBUH) actions and words, Muslim faith and practice has been comprehensively codified into the Sharia (the way or road). The faithful believe it is the complete answer to every question that humanity has about life and its purpose.

The key elements of Muslim religious practice can be simplified into the five pillars of belief. The first is the profession of faith (*Shehadeh*) which simply entails a believer stating with absolute conviction "*Laa il-aaha illallaah. Mohammedun Rasul Allah!*" This can be translated as: "The only God is God. Mohammed (PBUH) is the Prophet of God!" The words are inscribed in silver in the green national flag of the Kingdom of Saudi Arabia.

The second pillar is prayer (salat) at the prescribed moments of the day. Each time, Muslims are summoned by the chanted call of the muezzin or prayer leader. The first prayer of the day is at dawn (*Fajr*) when the faithful are wakened by the muezzin with the cry that "Prayer is better than sleep!" *Fajr* prayers can be performed up to two hours after daybreak. The noon prayer (*Zuhr*) may be offered anytime after the sun begins to decline from its zenith until it is about midway on its course to setting. The third prayer (*Asr*), or mid-afternoon prayer, begins immediately after the end of the time for noon prayer. Sunset prayer time (*Maghreb*) begins after sunset and extends until the red glow in the western horizon disappears. This normally lasts for 80–90 minutes. Evening prayer time (*Isha*) begins after the red glow in the western horizon disappears and lasts until dawn. When travelling, Muslims are allowed to combine *Fajr* and *Zuhr* prayers and *Asr* and *Maghreb* prayers.

Before praying, faces, heads, hands and arms to the elbow and feet have to be washed. All Muslims begin with the *Qiyam*, the standing posture. The hands are then raised to the ears and *Allahu Akbar* is said. Orthodox Sunni Muslims will then fold their right hand over their left across the chest. Shiite and other Muslims, in contrast, keep their arms by their sides. The first chapter of the Koran (*Al Fatiha*) is then recited. The hands are raised again and *Allahu Akbar* is said once more. The worshipper then bows (the *Ruku*) and recites three times: *Subhana Rabbiyal Adheem* (Glory be to my Lord Almighty). While standing and reciting: *Sami Allahu liman hamidah, Rabbana wa lakal hamd* (God hears those who call upon Him; Our Lord, praise be to You), the worshipper raises his or her hands. After saying *Allahu Akbar*, the prostration (the *Sajdah*) is then performed which involves kneeling and touching the forehead on the ground whilst reciting *Subhana Rabbiyal Aala* three times. The worshipper rises to a sitting position while saying *Allahu Akbar* and then prostrates himself or herself again. This concludes one *Raka* or cycle of prayer.

*Fajr*, *Eid* and Friday (*Jumah*) prayers require two *Rakas*, *Maghreb* prayers require three and *Zuhr*, *Asr* and *Isha* four. After the final *Raka*, the worshipper remains seated and recites the first part of the *Tashahhud* prayer. The greeting *Assalamu alaikum wa rahmatullah* (Peace be upon you and God's blessings), is then said to the right and then to the left. This is known as the *Taslim*. The conventional explanation is that the worshipper is greeting fellow Muslims. Some believe a greeting is being voiced to two invisible angels that sit on each of a Muslim's shoulders and judge behaviour.

This is the simplest form of prayer. It can be extended by reciting passages from the Koran. On Fridays, the congregational prayer replaces the midday prayer. Worshippers gathering for *Jumah* also listen to a sermon. In addition to the five daily prayers, there are the *Tahajjud* prayers, a late-night ritual practised but not commanded by the Prophet (PBUH). The *Tarawih* prayers are held after *Isha* during Ramadan. Birth, marriage, death and other events in life are marked with special prayers. And there are prayers that can be said at any time. Muslims believe it's better to pray in a group and that the bigger the gathering the more powerful each prayer becomes. There's gender separation, but all line up regardless of status and perform prayers simultaneously and identically. For Muslims, salat is a public occasion. There is no embarrassment in the act of worship.

Ideally, prayer should take place in a mosque where worshippers can also hear sermons from their religious leaders. Muslims believe there should be a mosque within walking distance. Saudi Arabia has no fewer than 70,000 mosques, one for every 300 people. The mosque is the greatest physical manifestation of Islamic faith and it has produced some of the world's most beautiful buildings. The Blue Mosque in Constantinople and the Kalyan Mosque in Buhkara are among the finest examples. A new generation of mosques is appearing. In Casablanca, the King Hassan II Mosque dominates the city's coastline. The white marble-clad Sheikh Zayed Mosque in Abu Dhabi is among the biggest new projects in Arabia.

The third pillar is the giving of alms, known as zakat (growth or goodness). This is the amount of money every adult who is mentally stable, free, and financially-competent is obliged to give to specific categories of people. The amount paid is related to net wealth and not income. The majority view is that Muslims, once they have more than the required minimum, are obliged to give the equivalent of 2.5 per cent of this figure. Giving is one of the cornerstones of Arabian society.

The fourth pillar is fasting during Ramadan, the eighth month of the Islamic year, which is based on a lunar calendar and has about 355 days. Each month is 29 or 30 days long. During Ramadan, Muslims are obliged to abstain from food and drink and any stimulant between dawn and sunset prayers. Ramadan is a period for self-examination and prayer. In addition to the five normal prayer times, there is one starting as late as 2 am in the morning called *Qiyam Al Ail*. This was recommended by the Prophet (PBUH) and can be offered either late at night or in the early hours of the morning. Ramadan's final 10 days are special. The Koran's first verse was revealed in this period. The Night of the Revelation, known as the Blessed Night or Night of Power (*Lailat al-Qadr*), is a crucial moment. Mohammed (PBUH) said the sins of anyone who stays up during *Lailat al-Qadr* out of faith will be forgiven. There's no agreement exactly which of the 10 nights is the right one, but by tradition the evening of the 27 Ramadan has been chosen.

Ramadan combines each day an intense form of Christian Lent, a 40-day period of self-denial, with the joyful feasting of Christmas which gets under way with the Iftar ('break fast') meal at sundown. This is accompanied by socializing that can go on late into the night. Meals served during this time are called *Surour* and can include grilled meats, cheese-filled pancakes and honey cakes. People gather in Ramadan tents to contemplate the changing phases of the moon, chat and smoke a *nagile* (water pipe). The further purpose of Ramadan is to remind the faithful of the needs of the poor and the importance of family. Ramadan ends at sunset on its final day. After breaking their fast and enjoying the company of friends and family, the faithful retire that evening with the pleasure of contemplating Eid al-Fitr (Feast of the Holy Day), a public holiday lasting at least two days.

Muslims are required once in their lifetimes to make the journey to Mecca at the point in the Islamic calendar that marks the anniversary of the Prophet's (PBUH) last sermon to the faithful. Those seeking to complete the Hajj, the fifth pillar, are required to meticulously complete a complex sequence of activities for the blessings of the pilgrimage to be fully enjoyed. The elements of the Hajj were defined by the Prophet (PBUH). It always takes place on the same six days of the lunar calendar and begins on 8 Dhu al-Hijjah, the final month of the Islamic year. Rituals take place in five locations in and near Mecca.

The first ritual, called *Ihram* or purification, can begin up to 14 days before the Hajj. Before entering Mecca, pilgrims are obliged to cleanse themselves spiritually and physically at designated times and places around the border of the holy precinct surrounding the city. Their intention to perform Hajj is declared through an invocation called the *Talbiyah*. Men must replace their clothing with two pieces of seamless white cloth that are worn for the duration of the Hajj. Women can wear modest clothing of any colour but their heads must be covered.

At some time between their arrival in Mecca and 8 Dhu al-Hijjah, pilgrims are required to walk seven times counterclockwise around the Ka'bah within the Holy Haram and the Great Mosque. The purpose of this exercise, which is called the *Tawaf*, is to express God's central place in life. Pilgrims then run or walk seven times between the hills of Safa and Marwah to commemorate the search for water by Abraham's wife Hagar. This ritual, called *Say*, now takes place in a 400-metre covered arcade. The Zamzam Well is located in the same area. Later, the pilgrims assemble in the Valley of Mina that lies about five kilometres east of Mecca. Most spend the night in tents.

The Hajj climaxes the following day on 9 Dhu al-Hijjah when the pilgrims walk east to the Plain of Arafat. From noon prayers until sundown, they stand or sit and offer prayers for mercy and renewal. The Valley of Mina also contains the Jebel Rahmah, or Mount of Mercy, where the Prophet (PBUH) delivered his farewell sermon. After sundown, the pilgrims walk back to Mecca and stop for the night at Muzdallifah where they can gather up to 49 stones that they will throw at the three pillars of Jamarat during the next three days.

On the morning of 10 Dhu al-Hijjah, the pilgrims move to Jamarat where they throw seven pebbles at the first of three pillars that have come to represent Satan. This ritual symbolically repudiates evil and memorializes Abraham's three rejections of the devil when God asked him to sacrifice Ismail. Pilgrims then celebrate by sacrificing a sheep, although this is now done in a slaughterhouse rather than individually, as God ordered Abraham to do. After throwing more stones at the first pillar, men have their heads shaved. Women cut off a lock of their hair.

The three-day Eid al-Adha, or Feast of the Sacrifice, starts on 10 Dhu al-Hijjah and pilgrims can return to the Great Mosque at any time during this period to circle the Ka'bah seven more times. Many pilgrims return to Mina and pass again through Jamarat on the fourth and fifth days of Eid to stone each of the three pillars with seven pebbles. On 13 Dhu al-Hijjah, the pilgrims return to the Great Mosque to make a final circumambulation called *Tawaf al-Ifadhah*. This deconsecrates the pilgrim and the state of *Ihram* comes to an end.

Hajj and Umrah, the lesser pilgrimage that can be done at any time of the year, are also political occasions. The Iranian Hajj mission seeks to visit the graves of the family of the Prophet (PBUH), something that conservative Sunni Muslims find troubling. The tensions expressed themselves horribly in 1987 when about 400 people were killed in clashes with Saudi security forces. No serious confrontations between Iranian Hajjis and the Saudi police have since been reported. There have been further tragedies. In 1997, 340 pilgrims died in a fire that swept the Mina tent camp. In 1998, 180 people died in a stampede. The crush caused by the need to complete the stoning of the pillars in five-and-a-half hours caused hundreds of deaths in the 2004 Hajj and led to more loss of life in January 2006 when at least 363 people died. The authorities are rebuilding the Jamarat area to make it safer and there are suggestions that more time should be provided for the stoning ceremonies to be completed.

**Differences in Muslim belief**
There could be as many as 700 subdivisions of Islam. Sunnis (derived from the word Sunna) account for about 70 per cent of all Muslims though they too are divided in terms of belief, practice and leadership. The followers of the fourth caliph, Ali, called themselves Shiat Ali, or the partisans of Ali, a term that has been abbreviated to Shiites. Initially, the movement was political but it has developed a body of religious thought that varies in important ways from that of Sunni Muslims. The most obvious distinction is that Shiites believe the leader of the Muslim community must be appointed by God. That appointment may have been made public by the declaration of the Prophet

(PBUH) or by succeeding supreme religious leaders who Shiites call imams. Shiites believe that the religious leader must be sinless and possess, above all, the qualities of knowledge, bravery, justice, wisdom, piety and love of God. Shiites argue that Ali had all these qualities, that he was appointed by God to be Mohammed's (PBUH) successor and that this was stated by the Prophet (PBUH) on several occasions. The largest Shiite division, which is dominant in Iran and south Lebanon, believes there was a continuous anointed line of succession from the Prophet (PBUH) until the 12th imam, who was invisible and named Mohammed Al Mahdi (Arabic for 'Messiah' or 'Chosen One'), disappeared into "occultation" in 941. Invisibly, the imam continues to direct the world through selected men in every generation until the time of his return.

Sunnis dismiss any report of the Prophet's (PBUH) life that claims that he anointed Ali. They assert that leadership of the Islamic community rightly runs from Ali to Muawiya and his successors, who Sunnis call caliphs. The caliphate was regularly contested though it was eventually authoritatively secured in the eyes of most Sunnis by the Ottoman sultans of Constantinople in the early 16th century. It was held by the successive sultans until the Ottoman system was dissolved in 1922 and the caliphate was finally abolished in 1924 by the government of Kemal Ataturk, the Turkish Republic's first president. No serious attempt has since been made to restore it. The result is that most Shiites and most Sunnis believe the position of supreme religious leader is, in effect, vacant. Sunnis believe that a ruler of Muslims can be elected, nominated by the previous leader, selected by a committee or gain power by force. Neither sinlessness nor competence nor other qualities are a condition for leadership and a leader cannot be deposed simply because of the lack of these qualities. All that is required is that the leader ensures that the Sharia is impeccably applied. Sunni imams, or prayer leaders, are appointed with the consent of the faithful. They have no permanent status in the Sunni Muslim community.

Most Sunnis argue that only what God has commanded is good. Everything that God has forbidden is evil. This limits the scope for individual freedom of choice and strict Sunnis believe God's path simply involves following God's orders. Nothing is good or bad in itself. The intellect has practically no role. For Shiites, the necessity of religion is proved first by reason. Humans have been endowed with free will, something that conventional Sunnis may deny. Shiites argue that certain courses of action are inherently bad and that God forbids them for that reason. Shiites also accept the existence of God's grace, which Sunnis do not. These are His actions that make men and women more devoted and obedient. God's grace also grants believers the ability to correct their actions. This leads to the Shiite idea that prophets and their successors are necessary since they are the agents of God's grace.

To guide the faithful, four Sunni schools of thought emerged in the early Muslim era. Abdallah Malik ibn Anas, who lived from about 715–795, wrote the earliest-surviving Muslim legal text and is the father of the orthodox Maliki school of Islam. An Numan ibn Thabit (Abu Hanifa – about 700–765), founded the moderate Hanafi school. Mohammed ibn Idris Al Shafi (767–820), who studied under Malik ibn Anas, argued that the Hadith should always be supreme, but subject to the approval of qualified lawyers. The Shafi school he inspired is considered to be conservative. The followers of Ahmed ibn Mohammed ibn Hanbal (780–855) argued there should be no interpretation of the Prophet's (PBUH) sayings which should be accepted literally. The only permissible debate is about the authenticity of the Hadith used to guide the faithful. Hanbalis have been prepared to use force to support their views against alcohol and other abuses. They are also hostile to diversity, particularly Shiism. Hanbalis are, nevertheless, advocates of the idea that a ruler can be deposed for failing to adhere to the divine law. A distinct variety of Islamic thought is known as Sufiism after the Arabic for wool (*suf*). This refers to the coarse woolen garments worn by the first Sufis. They interpreted the Koran freely and pushed out the boundaries of religious ritual.

### The history of Shiism

After Ali's murder in 661, the rivalries between his followers and the establishment were political as well as spiritual. The election of Muawiya disgusted Ali's family and followers, and yet he was a great caliph. Muawiya negotiated with the Byzantines and established the first elements of a centralized Islamic state. His opponents were conciliated if possible. But the conflict with the followers of Ali resumed when Muawiya died in 680.

The second Shiite imam, Hassan, eldest son of Ali and Fatima, had died in 669. In 680, Hussein, Ali's second son by Fatima, journeyed from his home in Medina to link up with anti-government rebels based in Kufa in what is now Iraq. His outnumbered group was surrounded by enemy forces at Karbala, south of the Euphrates. Dying of thirst, Hussein and his band refused to surrender and were slaughtered to a man. This was a shattering blow. Hussein was of the line of succession Shiites recognized. His heroic death was seen as martyrdom accepted in the cause of righteousness and the Prophet's (PBUH) path. On the anniversary of Karbala in the Shiite feast of *Ashura* (the tenth), held annually on the 10th day of the Muslim month of Muharram, Shiites weep openly in memory of the young, slain hero and curse the names of the early caliphs, with the exception of Ali, and their successors. Men pound their chests in despair, whip their backs with chains and even slash their heads with swords. The intensity of the celebration, however, varies from community to community.

Hussein was buried in Karbala. His mosque in the city is second only to Ali's tomb in Najaf as a place of pilgrimage for Shiites. Other major Shiite pilgrimage centres have also developed at Qom and Khorasan in Iran. But Karbala excites the strongest emotions. Hussein is a popular name among Shiite men, though it is not exclusively Shiite. Hassan, the name of Hussein's elder brother and, in Shiite eyes, the second valid Muslim leader after Ali, is also favoured. Among Shiite women, Fatima, the name of Ali's wife and daughter of the Prophet (PBUH), is popular.

Traditionally, Shiites have venerated Mary, the mother of Jesus. Meryem (Mary) is a common Shiite name. Shiites have hymns and poems dedicated to Ali and Hussein. Shiite homes and places of work have images of the martyred father and son. Shiites erect sometimes elaborate structures on and around the graves of their dead and will visit them to leave food, drink and flowers and to pray and sing. This is in sharp contrast with mainstream Sunni practice, where the dead are buried in graves that are unmarked with the exception of a headstone without an engraving. The gap between the two communities continues. In Iraq, the rise for the first time in modern history of an Arab Shiite government is viewed with misgivings by Sunni-dominated Arab regimes that cannot escape the emotions stirred by centuries of competition, conflict and division.

The Shiites themselves split during the caliphate of Ali. Hard-line Kharijites separated themselves from the Shiite majority and intermittently fought their original partners and Sunni forces. They degenerated into armed groups characterized by fanatical intolerance for their opponents. One of their most significant leaders was Najdah ibn Amr Al Hanafi who originated from central Arabia. He and his followers seized Al Hasa and were the dominant powers in much of Arabia until they were suppressed by the Sunni Muslim government based in Damascus. Kharijite leaders eventually moderated and discouraged the fanatics who were dedicated to fighting the caliph and the Sunni establishment. They began to emphasize living in small and exclusive communities with high moral and social standards. The present inheritors of the Kharijite mantle, though they themselves reject this designation, are the Ibadhi Muslims who are mainly found in Oman.

Further divisions soon emerged. Most Shiites believe the line of succession started with Imam Ali and continued until the 12th imam, Mohammed Al Mahdi, who will return at the end of time. They are known as Ithna-'Ashariyya or 'Twelvers'. An influential Shiite group argued that the succession passed through Jafar Al Sadiq, the 6th imam. Jafar Al Sadiq's son Ismail was nominated as his successor, but he predeceased his father. Shiites who follow the line of Ismail, who they call the 7th Shiite imam, are known as Ismaili Muslims or Sevener Shiites. They spread across Arabia, North Africa, Mesopotamia and Iran and preached equality, justice and the imminent arrival of Al Mahdi, the divinely-appointed man who would purify Islam. They follow a continuous visible line to Karim Al Husayni Agha Khan IV who is the 49th hereditary leader of Ismaili Muslims.

Among their beliefs is that there have been six great prophets: Adam, Noah, Abraham, Moses, Jesus and Mohammed (PBUH). Each one had a companion who explained the secret message of the prophets. For Mohammed (PBUH), this was Imam Ali. The seventh and final prophet will be Al Mahdi, the Mahdi. The Ismailis had a huge impact on Islam's middle years. A branch called the Fatimids founded a dynasty in 909 that claimed to hold the caliphate on the basis of descent from Fatima, the daughter of Mohammed (PBUH), Ali's wife and mother of the Shiite imams Hassan and Hussein. Its founder was Said ibn Hussein who lived in Syria.

Fatimid missionaries inspired North African Berbers to rebel against their Sunni rulers. Said ibn Hussein was hailed as the Mahdi and took the name Obaidullah. Under Fatimid leadership, the Berbers conquered Malta, Sardinia, Corsica, the Balearics, and, for a time, Genoa. Fatimid fortunes reached their zenith with the capture of Egypt in 969 and then Palestine, parts of Spain and western Arabia. The Fatimids founded Cairo and made it their capital in 973. Egypt's Fatimids were rulers yet revolutionaries. Their subjects were mainly Sunni Muslims or Christians. But their regime flourished and bequeathed a lovely architectural form best expressed in mosques in old Cairo, including Al Azhar Mosque, which supported the world's first university.

Internally divided, the Fatimids lost Sicily to the Normans and Palestine to Christian Crusaders. In 1131, assassins killed Amir, the last Fatimid caliph of any ability. The final Fatimid ruler died in 1171 and power was seized by the Kurdish leader, Salah Al Din Al Ayyubi (Saladin). He defeated the Crusaders, seized Cairo and founded a dynasty, known as the Ayyubids, that ruled much of the central Arab World until 1250 when they were deposed by the Mamluks, slave soldiers. The Mamluks were the first power to defeat the Mongols in open combat, which they did at the Battle of Ayn Jalut near Nazareth in 1260. They ruled Egypt until the Ottoman conquest in 1517.

A further Shiite splinter group was founded by Hamdan bin Qarmat, an Ismaili cattle breeder who lived in the second half of the 9th century. He argued the Sharia should be replaced and that the revelations of the prophets, including Moses, Jesus and Mohammed (PBUH), were invalid. Believing in reincarnation, the Qarmatians refused to recognize the Fatimid caliphs as their imams. They maintained that the Mahdi would imminently appear. Their rule was established beginning 886 over what is now southern Iraq, eastern Saudi Arabia and Bahrain.

In 899, they captured Qatif. Al Hasa became the capital of the Qarmatian state. In 930, they attacked Mecca during the pilgrimage season and removed the black stone to Al Hasa, apparently to signal the approaching end of the world. In 932, a Persian prisoner was proclaimed as the Mahdi. Chaos ensued and the Persian was eventually executed. From 935, the Qarmatians tempered their policies and started to co-operate with the Sunni Muslim government. The black stone was eventually returned in 954. The Qarmatians declined, in part because of the rise of Egypt and trade through the Red Sea to the Indian Ocean at the expense of the Gulf sea route. In 1078, the Qarmatian state of Bahrain was extinguished. Other Qarmatian communities were absorbed by Twelver Shiism. By the 14th century, the movement was effectively extinct.

In 1021, the Fatimid imam, Al Hakim, died. A splinter group in Lebanon called the Druze concluded that Al Hakim was divine and did not die. Most Druzes, who include Lebanese political leader Walid Jumblatt, are now found in Lebanon, Syria and Palestine. Other Ismaili sects include the Bohras (who were initially known as Mustalians) who followed the descendants of the Shiite imam, Mustali. Bohras now live mainly in East Africa, India and Yemen. Other minority offshoots are the Nizaris, Khoja Ismailis and Agakhannis.

## The Ibadhis of Oman

A native of Oman, named Jaber bin Zaid, established in Basra a school of thought derived in part from Kharijite philosophy. One of his students, Abdallah ibn Ibadh Al Tamimi, founded a movement named in his memory that eventually produced the Al Bu Said family, now the rulers of modern Oman. The followers of Ibn Ibadh, or the Ibadhis, established an autonomous state ruled by an imam in Arabia's Hajar Mountains. Ibadhis, who say they are neither Sunni nor Shiite, are found mainly in Oman, East Africa, the Mzab Valley of Algeria, the Nafus Mountains of Libya, and Jerba in Tunisia. They aim to create a righteous Muslim society and take the view that true Muslims are only to be found in their own sect. Ibadhis refer to themselves as 'the People of Straightness' or simply as 'the Muslims', Al Muslimeen. The sect views non-Ibadhis with tolerance but aims to dissociate themselves from them. Militant action is only justly directed at an unjust ruler who refuses to relinquish power or mend his ways. As is the case with Shiites and Maliki Sunni Muslims, Ibadhis pray with their arms down at their sides rather than folded in the conventional manner. They do not say 'amen' after the *Fatiha* sura that's conventionally recited during daily prayers, and they do not make the *Qunut* invocation in the

Fajr (dawn) prayer. Ibadhis argue that Friday prayer should only be held where just rule prevails. Their imam should be elected by community elders based on the candidate's knowledge and piety and without reference to descent. The position can also be left vacant. The last imam to unite all Ibadhis was Ahmed ibn Said, who ruled in 1754–83 and was the founder of Oman's Al Bu Said ruling family. His descendants took the title of Sayyid, an honorific form of address that can be held by any member of the ruling family, rather than imam. The title of sultan, a concept entailing purely secular powers, was assumed by the Al Bu Said dynasty much later.

The Ibadhi imamate (a system of government based on the rule of an imam) has been disputed on several occasions and its last claimant was driven into exile in the 1950s. The question of how the imamate can be reconciled with the reality of the present Omani system of government is largely thought to be irrelevant. The present Grand Mufti of Oman, Sheikh Ahmed ibn Hamad Al Khalili, is an outstanding moderate who has said that the differences between Sunni and Ibadhi Muslims are subsidiary issues of little eternal consequence. They in no way impede Muslim unity.

### The Zaydis and the history of Yemen

In 740, in one of the many Shiite risings against the caliphate, Zayd bin Ali, a descendant of the first Shiite imam, Ali, died in battle. His followers called themselves Zaydis and established two states: one in Tabaristan south of the Caspian Sea and one in Yemen. Zaydis, also known as Fiver Imam Shiites since they acknowledge only the first five Shiite imams, are the Shiite sect closest to Sunni tradition. Zaydis believe that the imamate can be inherited by anyone of the House of Ali. But they reject the concept of the hidden imam and of the possibility of the return of the Mahdi, a belief held by Ismailis. Their imam is regarded as neither infallible nor able to perform miracles. He is appointed by community elders on the basis of merit.

The Zaydi imamate of Yemen was founded in 780 by Imam Yahya ibn Al Hussein. With brief interruptions until 1962, it controlled most of what are now the northern parts of the Republic of Yemen. The Zaydi people are mainly concentrated in the highlands north of Sanaa and on the Red Sea coastal plain called Tihama. They are also in the majority east of the mountains in the Najran area of Saudi Arabia. South of the lands of the imamate, the majority of the people are Sunni Muslims of the minority and conservative Shafi school. The Shafis of Yemen were ruled by the Fatimids of Egypt during the 10–13th century. Sunni Ottomans controlled the region between 1538–1628 and 1849–1918, providing further reinforcement to the divide within Yemen between Zaydis and Sunnis.

The Zaydi imam launched a rebellion against Ottoman rule in 1897. After more than three decades of guerilla war, Imam Yahya, who'd become leader of the Yemeni Zaydis in 1904, agreed a truce in 1911. He was recognized as the ruler of the Zaydi highlands in exchange for accepting Ottoman rule in Shafi Muslim areas. A border was fixed between Ottoman territory and the port city of Aden and surrounding areas controlled by Britain. Nevertheless, Zaydi imams considered the Aden region as part of their domain.

Following the defeat of the Ottomans in the First World War, the imamate was internationally recognized as an independent nation with Imam Yahya as head of state. He challenged the Saudis for control of the Asir and was finally defeated in the spring of 1933. He invited the Saudi King Abdelaziz to define a new frontier. The Taif Treaty of May 13, 1934 handed back almost half the territories the Saudis had seized.

Imam Yahya did not attempt to convert the Shafis, but Zaydi Muslims dominated the imamate. Resentment among the Shafi merchant class was reinforced by dissident Zaydis who opposed Imam Yahya's conservative and isolationist policies. He irritated Britain by sponsoring raids into the sheikhdoms of south Arabia that were then connected by treaty to British Aden. These tensions combined with growing Arab nationalism after 1945 to precipitate crisis and then revolution. Imam Yahya was assassinated in 1948. He was succeeded by his son Imam Ahmed, who was hostile to Britain and believed his father's death had been plotted in Aden. Border incidents became so frequent that Britain convened a conference in London in 1951 to reaffirm the status quo. Following the overthrow of the Egyptian monarchy in 1952, violent incidents within Aden and British south Arabian territories increased.

Imam Ahmed had domestic enemies, some living in exile in Aden. In 1955, a failed coup produced a bloody government response, including public beheadings of some of the plotters. Nevertheless, the Zaydi imamate for a period won the support of socialist Egypt and of conservative Saudi Arabia. In 1956, it started to receive weapons from the Soviet Union and, subsequently, from Communist China. In 1957, Imam Ahmed announced Yemen would join the short-lived United Arab Republic created by Egypt and Syria. He turned against Egypt in 1961.

Imam Ahmed died in September 1962. His son, Mohammed Al Badr, succeeded as the 69th Zaydi imam. The following week, on September 26, he was deposed in a nationalist army coup supported by the Al Ahmar tribe, who had been alienated by the execution of their leader Sheikh Husayn Al Ahmar and his son for rebelling. The Zaydi imamate has since remained vacant.

The civil war that followed the 1962 revolution was additionally driven by the rivalry between Egypt and Saudi Arabia who supported opposite sides in the fighting. After tens of thousands of deaths, the conflict was ended in March 1970 in a national reconciliation treaty. The army seized control of the government in a coup in 1974. General Ali Abdallah Saleh, a participant in the 1962 coup, became president of North Yemen in July 1978 and has been president of unified Yemen since May 1990.

The state of South Yemen, which came into existence in 1967, was a legacy of the British Empire. The most powerful ruler of the extreme south-western tip of Arabia in the third decade of the 19th century was the Sultan of Lahej. A ship owned by a subject of British India was plundered by the sultan in January 1837. Two years later, British troops captured Aden. The port under British Indian rule served as a refuelling and re-victualling point on the route to India.

Following the opening of the Suez Canal, Aden's importance soared. From the 1930s, Britain started to play a role in the areas east of Aden, principally in the Hadhramaut. In 1935, areas in south Arabia subject to British protection were divided into the Aden Colony and the Aden Protectorate. Aden was made a Crown Colony in 1937. The protectorate was subsequently divided into eastern and western parts.

Following the nationalization of the Abadan Refinery by the Iranian government in 1951, a new refinery was built in Aden and the city's population was expanded enormously. By the end of the 1950s, the trade-union movement was leading opposition to British rule and in 1962 formed the Yemen Socialist Party (YSP) to secure independence by peaceful means.

The Yemeni revolution inspired the southern independence movement. To counter it, Britain incorporated Aden into the conservative South Arabian Federation in January 1963. Fighting between government forces and guerillas of the Sanaa-based National Front for the Liberation of South Yemen, backed by Egypt, started in December 1963. In 1966, the Front for the Liberation of South Yemen (FLOSY) was created to unify the principal parties opposing continued British rule. On February 22, 1966, the British government announced its intention to withdraw from South Arabia. British troops retreated from the protectorates into Aden in June 1967. By the end of August, the National Front controlled most of the interior of South Yemen. The Front and FLOSY split and waged civil war in Aden from September–October 1967. When British forces were withdrawn from Aden on November 30, the Front took control of the city and formed the first government of the newly independent People's Republic of South Yemen. The People's Democratic Republic of Yemen (PDRY), the Arab World's first and only Marxist-Leninist state, was declared on December 1, 1970. The National Front and FLOSY merged into the Yemeni Socialist Party (YSP) which led a coalition government that also included members of the Communist Party and the Baath Party.

South Yemeni dissidents backed by other Arab states launched an attack across the border in September 1972. Aden struck back at insurgent bases in North Yemen. A general war was averted by negotiations mediated by the Arab League. Two agreements signed in October 1972 called for an end to hostile acts and unity between the two states within a year on the basis of a democratic, national and republican form of government with free elections. Unity was blessed in a summit between the heads of state of the two Yemens in Tripoli in November 1972. The deal was never implemented.

King Faisal's assassination in March 1975 ushered in new Saudi policies designed to promote order in North Yemen and moderation in South Yemen. A turning point was the defeat at the end of that year of Oman's Dhofar insurgency, which had been supported by South Yemen and its Chinese, Soviet and East German sponsors. Aden stopped exporting revolution. Relations with Saudi Arabia improved and diplomatic ties were established in 1976. Saudi support for South Yemeni exiles stopped. But south-west Arabia continued to fester. In February 1979, the forces of North and South Yemen clashed on both sides of the border. Once more, all-out war was avoided and once more the two governments announced unity by the end of the summer of that year. Once more, the plans came to nothing.

Tensions within the YSP degenerated into gangsterism in January 1986 when President Ali Nasir Mohammed organized the shooting of most of his party enemies at a specially convened politburo meeting. This was followed by a week of warfare on Aden's streets and President Ali Nasir's departure, first to Ethiopia and then to Sanaa. More than 4,000 people died in the fighting and tens of thousands of South Yemenis fled to North Yemen. But a turning point had been reached. Chaos in Aden, coupled with oil discoveries in North Yemen in 1984 and in South Yemen in 1987, convinced both states a fresh start was needed. South Yemen dropped Marxism-Leninism.

In May 1988, the two Yemens signed a final unification agreement to form the Republic of Yemen. It was confirmed at a summit in Aden in November 1989, ratified in Sanaa on April 22, 1990, and became effective one month later. The new nation run by a republican government comprising former Communists was not welcomed in Riyadh. There were unsettled border issues. Saudi Arabia had opposed North Yemen's membership of the Arab Cooperation Council (ACC) formed with Egypt, Iraq and Jordan in April 1989. Most Arab governments supported the US-led coalition created to force Iraq out of Kuwait. Unified Yemen backed Baghdad. Saudi Arabia retaliated by expelling about 700,000 Yemenis who'd been living in the kingdom.

The northern General People's Congress (GPC) led by President Saleh won Yemen's first free elections in 1993. Fighting between militants of the GPC and the YSP erupted into civil war in April 1994. The following month, Yemeni vice-president and leader of the YSP, Salim Al Baidh, announced the south's secession. Southern forces won the support of the GCC but were crushed in nine weeks. A centre-right government coalition was formed and President Saleh was re-elected in October 1994. The GPC won in a landslide in the 1997 elections. President Saleh then opened a new chapter in Yemen's history. After Al Qaeda supporters attacked a US naval ship at anchor in Yemeni waters in 2000, his government cracked down on Islamist militants. Political reform moved up the agenda. A constitutional amendment ratified on February 20, 2001 created an appointed Shoura Council and an elected 301-member House of Representatives. In elections in April 2003, the ruling GPC won 238 house seats.

Talks about a final demarcation of the Saudi-Yemeni border began in 1995 and a final agreement was signed in June 2000. The border corresponds closely to the frontier defined in the 1934 Taif Treaty between the imamate and Saudi Arabia. Growth in the past decade has been buoyant. Yemen produces 420,000 barrels a day (b/d) of crude oil and exports more than 300,000 b/d. But it remains one of the poorest countries in the world. With a population of about 22 million people at the end of 2006, it has the largest national population of the seven countries of Arabia. Its hopes for the future include admission to the wealthy GCC. President Saleh, re-elected president in 2006, stood by Saudi Arabia's King Abdullah during the funeral for the late King Fahd on August 2, 2005. It was a sign that Saudi Arabia and Yemen plan to be friends.

### From the Abbasids to the sultans

As the previous pages show, rebellious Kharijites, Ibadhis, Qarmatians, Fatimids and Zaydis found havens in Arabia. But most Shiites assented, with occasional periods of open rebellion, to Sunni dominance and waited for the opportunity to strike back. This came in 750 when a faction descended from Abbas, one of the Prophet's (PBUH) uncles, defeated the forces of the 14th caliph, Marwan.

The Abbasids, as they are known, claimed Abu Hashem, a great-grandson of martyred Ali, had bequeathed leadership of his family to them. This connection appealed to the Shiites, who were manipulated into supporting the Abbasid coup. Once in power, the Abbasids rejected the Shiite claimant and made Abu Al Abbas caliph. The descendants of the third caliph, Omar, were completely defeated. Only one of significance – Abdulrahman ibn Muawiya Al Dakhil – escaped the disaster. With a single servant, he fled to Islamic Spain in 756 and set up a new Umayyad Dynasty. It was to become one of the great civilizations of Europe's Middle Ages.

The Abbasids could not bear to live in Damascus, the base of the previous regime. They established a new settlement near their principal supporters in Mesopotamia in the Persian village of Baghdad. By the start of the 13th century, Baghdad had a population of 200,000 people, making it the largest conurbation on earth outside China. The stories of the *1,001 Arabian Nights* and the myth of Sinbad were penned by authors living in the city. In the House of Wisdom (Bayt al-Hikmah), Baghdad scholars translated into Arabic ancient scientific manuscripts stored in Alexandria and parts of the Byzantine Empire within and beyond Muslim control. Algebra was defined in *Kitab al-Jabr Wal Muqabalah*, a book written by Mohammed ibn Musa Al Khwarazmi, a mathematician who lived in Baghdad. Baghdad thinkers made contributions to geometry and astronomy. Abu Bakr Mohammed ibn Zakariya Al Razi wrote 184 books and other works on medicine. Ibn Al Haytham, who was educated in Baghdad, wrote a detailed treatise about the workings of the eye and proposed a dam to regulate the Nile. Abu Nasr Al Farabi explored philosophical and political issues. New crops were developed and long-distance trade connected Morocco, Spain, Tunisia, Egypt and the imperial capital. Abbasid merchants traded with India and China.

But the system was weak. At the start of the 9th century, the Abbasids lost control of what is now northern India, most of modern Iran and then Egypt. By 969, the Fatimids had seized North Africa. In 1025, a Turkish nomadic group named after its patriarch Seljuk crossed the Oxus River from Central Asia. They conquered Persia and in 1055 captured Baghdad where they accepted the nominal authority of the Abbasid caliphates. The Seljuks penetrated Anatolia and defeated Byzantium at Manzikert in 1071. This was to be the catalyst for the Crusades. A Christian army captured Jerusalem in July 1099, crowning the moment by slaughtering every non-Christian and many Arab Christians in the Holy City. The Christian states in Palestine, Syria and parts of Anatolia survived in various forms until the 13th century. The Crusader movement petered out in the 15th century.

One Crusader adventurer created his own Arabian legend of shame. In 1171, Reynauld de Chatillon, a Christian prince who'd made a living by raiding caravans, sailed with an army from the Levant into western Arabia, capturing and looting Medina. De Chatillon escaped, but most of his army died. He was captured in Saladin's victory over the Crusaders on the Horns of Hattin in 1187. He was brought before the Muslim prince. His last words were a defamation of the Prophet (PBUH). Saladin cut off his arm and one of his soldiers took off his head.

The Seljuk Empire began to disintegrate after 1092. By the middle of the 13th century, the Abbasid domain was split with one half governed in Cairo and the rest divided between Christian, Turkish and rebel Muslim rulers. The Abbasid caliphs still ruled Baghdad but their writ was limited to the confines of the city walls. The Mesopotamian irrigation system had collapsed, allowing the encroachment of desert from the west and marshlands from the south, where the Tigris and Euphrates converged. Baghdad's population shrank. The coup de grâce came in 1258. Mongol armies led by Hulagu besieged the city. They stormed the walls and slaughtered, according to some accounts, every Muslim in Baghdad. The caliphate was then claimed by the rulers of Cairo, where a military elite named the Mamluks had seized power.

In 1517, Cairo fell to the Ottoman Turks under the Sultan Selim. The caliphate was transferred to Constantinople where it remained for 407 years. Ottoman rule was extended to Mesopotamia in a campaign that culminated in 1534 with the capture of Baghdad by Sultan Sulayman the Magnificent from the Persians who'd captured the city in 1508. In 1551, Al Hasa submitted but Ottoman control in eastern Arabia was precarious and it was broken by local tribes in 1670. By capturing the caliphate, the Ottomans secured the title of keeper of the two holy shrines in Mecca and Medina. An Ottoman decree was issued confirming Sharif Barakat of the House of Hashem as Emir of Mecca. The Ottomans ruled the Hejaz through the Hashemites for 400 years until Sharif Hussein, great-grandfather of the late King Hussein of Jordan, rose in rebellion in 1916.

### Coffee, pearls, horses and thalers

Arabia's Ottoman era saw new economic developments. The coffee plant originates from the Horn of Africa but coffee cultivation was developed in southern Arabia. Arabs had a monopoly over its supply until the end of the 16th century. Mukha (Mocha) on Arabia's southern Red Sea coast was the principal coffee-bean export port. Cargoes were shipped to Suez where fast camels awaited news of the arrival, usually in September or October, of that season's coffee fleet. This information was taken to Cairo where there was a coffee futures exchange. European ships carried Chinese porcelain to Mukha and Jeddah where it would be sold to finance coffee exports back to China. The Dutch acquired coffee plant seeds in the early 17th century and started cultivating it in what is now Indonesia. There were coffee plantations across the world by the end of the 19th century.

The Gulf's still, shallow waters, intense light and high temperatures are among the best conditions for oysters with pearls. By the end of the 19th century, thousands of boats and tens of thousands of men worked in the Gulf pearling industry. The rise of Gulf pearls encouraged Bedouin tribes to move to the coast in the summer where the men worked on pearling boats. Many settled permanently, though they retained their tribal loyalties and attachment to the desert. Throughout the

Gulf, pearling was the initial source of wealth for some of the region's most influential business families. Pearling also produced mother of pearl, which is made from the inner shell of the finest oysters. The Gulf pearl economy peaked following the end of the First World War. It was ended by the development of cultured pearls. These were the life's work of Kichimatsu Mikimoto, a Japanese pearl-buyer born in 1858. Fearing natural oyster beds would be exhausted, he applied an old Chinese method of artificially promoting pearl production by introducing a piece of mother of pearl into each oyster. This irritated the mollusc and led to the creation of perfectly round pearls. The technique was perfected in 1916. Cultured pearls started to reach international markets in the mid-1920s. By the 1930s, the natural-pearl industry in the Gulf was in rapid and terminal decline.

Horses are another lasting Arabian contribution to the world. Through generations of specialist breeding, the Bedouin developed fast and light horses. By the beginning of the 14th century, Arabia was supplying buyers in India. Every thoroughbred on earth is descended from just three Arabian stallions: Beverly Turk, Godolphin Arabian and Darley Arabian. These horses were brought to England from Arabia around the start of the 18th century and bred with European mares. Thoroughbreds are unmatched for their speed, inherited from their Arabian antecedents, and stamina, derived from European horses.

The emergence of cash trade in high-value Arabian goods demanded an acceptable currency. The Portuguese brought the real. The word is the inspiration for the riyal, the name of the national currencies of Iran, Oman, Qatar and Saudi Arabia. For two centuries, it played the role of an international currency until it was replaced, in the 18th century, by the Maria Theresa thaler. The word *thaler* originated in the 16th century with the opening of silver deposits in Bohemia. These were used to make coins named after the region's St Joachim Valley; *thal* is the German word for valley. English speakers adapted the word to dollar and this name was adopted for the national currency of the US and many others since.

By the 17th century, *thaler* became a generic name for any large silver coin. Maria Theresa ruled Europe's Habsburg Empire based in Vienna, which used the thaler as its coinage. Her treasury head promoted the empire's currency as a form of international coin. To promote sales, the thaler was minted to the highest standards. By the time of Maria Theresa's death in 1780, the four Habsburg government mints had produced more than 30 million of them. They entered the Middle East through trade involving Europe, the Arab World and the Far East. Maria Theresa thalers, all dated 1780 regardless of when they were made, were minted in Vienna up to the 20th century. The coin was accepted until the coming of Gulf currencies in the 1960s.

Today, it is still used in Arabian jewellery, sometimes melted for its silver content.

## The advent of Shiite Persia

On June 24, 2005, Mahmoud Ahmadinejad was elected as president of the Islamic Republic of Iran. The former revolutionary guard had emerged late in the presidential election campaign to defeat the former Iranian head of state, Ali Akbar Rafsanjani, in the June run-off poll. Born in 1956, Ahmadinejad studied engineering at Tehran University and participated in the uprising that forced the Shah of Iran, Mohammed Reza Pahlavi, and his wife, Empress Farah, out and led to the triumph of the revolution in February 1979. It has been alleged that Ahmadinejad was among the radical students who seized the US embassy in November 1979 and held 52 Americans hostage. He fought in the war against Iraq, graduated with a doctorate in transport engineering and became a university teacher. He was an unknown when he was elected Tehran mayor in 2003.

Ahmadinejad's victory was unexpected and his subsequent actions startling. At a 'World Without Zionism' conference in Tehran on October 25, 2005, he said: "As the Imam (Khomeini) said, Israel must be wiped off the map." Ahmadinejad repeated the statement and refused to withdraw it. One of his first decisions was to announce Iran would resume work on highly enriched uranium, essential for nuclear power but also required to produce a nuclear bomb. In January 2006, Tehran notified the International Atomic Energy Agency (IAEA) that the work was to begin. Supreme religious leader Ali Khamenei declared on 18 January that Iran had no intention of producing a bomb. The IAEA was unconvinced and referred Iran to the UN Security Council, which voted for sanctions against Iran in December 2006. Further international anxiety about the Iranian regime has been caused by its support for the Shiite Hizbollah movement, the target of Israel's assault on south Lebanon in the summer of 2006.

Iran's oil, population and ambition make it a force to be reckoned with. Its recent actions revive memories of a past when nations trembled before Persian armies and marvelled at its creative genius. Independent Persian government was extinguished at the Battle of Qadisiya in 636. For almost 900 years, what is now Iran was divided among petty rulers. Initially, Shiite dynasties were dominant. In the 11th century, their states in the Levant and Mesopotamia were swept away by Sunni Muslim Turkish tribes. The Seljuks entered what is northern Iran in 1037 and made Isfahan their capital. They were replaced by other Turkish tribes who were, in turn, overwhelmed in the 13th and 14th centuries by the Mongols. Heirs of the Mongol Khans ruled most of what is now Iran but their system went quickly into decline.

This vacuum was filled by Safavid rulers who originated from a line of Sufi leaders from Azerbaijan. They founded a state in northern Iran in 1501. Shah Ismail I, founder of the Safavid Dynasty, adopted Twelver Shiism as the official religion of his state. It was imposed on his empire and exported into what is now Iraq and Afghanistan. The expansion of Safavid territory into the west brought it into contact with the Sunni Ottomans who were marching east at the same time. This precipitated war between the two empires that lasted for more than two centuries. Safavid Persia was brought low by rebellions, invasion from Afghanistan and pressure from Russia, which started to build a Middle Eastern empire in the 18th century. The final effective Safavid ruler was captured and executed by an Afghan rebel army in 1722.

Nader Shah, a commoner who seized power in 1736, restored Persian control in Afghanistan. He led an army through the Hindu Kush into northern India, defeated the Mughals and captured and looted Delhi in 1739. Nader Shah also invaded southeastern Arabia, capitalizing on conflict over the Ibadhi imamate. He was assassinated in 1747 and his empire collapsed. Chaos ensued until a new Persian dynasty was established in 1781 by members of the Qajar tribe from Azerbaijan. They restored order and made Tehran, which is in the Qajar homelands, their capital. But defeat in wars with Russia led to the loss of the Caucasus. With British support, Afghanistan absorbed Persian territory in the east. Turkmenistan and Uzbekistan were seized by Russia in 1881. Domestic demands for reform and pressure from tribes and ethnic groups mounted.

In 1906, the shah approved a constitution and the establishment of a *majlis* (parliament). Persian weakness was underlined the following year in the Anglo-Russian entente that effectively placed control of the country in the hands of London and St Petersburg. Foreigners dominated the economy. The oil industry was established by the British, who struck oil in 1908 and controlled its production through the Anglo-Persian Oil Company (APOC).

During the First World War, Reza Khan, the son of an officer, joined the Persian Army's Cossack Brigade, a unit trained by Russia. He was made an officer and promoted to colonel in 1915. By the end of the war, Reza Khan was a brigadier general. He came to the attention of the British who, together with Russia, had occupied Persia during the conflict. Reza Khan led a British-orchestrated coup against Ahmed Shah, the last Qajar ruler, in February 1921. He ended the Qajar Dynasty in October 1925 and was declared shah at the end of the year. Reza Khan changed his name to Reza Shah Pahlavi and renamed Persia Iran in 1935.

Reza Shah was deposed in September 1941 when he resisted British attempts to deploy troops in western Iran and tried to maintain Iran's neutrality. His son, Mohammed Reza Shah, then 21, was appointed in his place. In 1951, Mohammed Mosaddegh was made prime minister on a programme of reforms that included the nationalization of the oil industry. Constitutional government was overthrown in August 1953 in a coup fomented by the Central Intelligence Agency (CIA). The shah's rule continued for a further 25 years, but memories of the 1953 events lasted. Ahmadinejad, who was born three years after the coup, would have been raised on tales of the shah's treachery and weakness and British and American perfidy.

The shah followed in his father's modernizing footsteps. His attempts to reduce the power of the Shiite clergy and Westernize Iranian institutions were unpopular. The shah's pretensions and partnership with the West galvanized the opposition. Serious violence erupted across Iran in 1978. After months in which central government credibility was shredded, the shah left Iran on January 16, 1979. Ayatollah Khomeini, a Shiite cleric expelled to Iraq from Iran in 1964 because of his opposition to the shah's policies, returned to Tehran amid mass acclaim on February 1, 1979. The government that had been appointed by the shah before he left collapsed and power was transferred to the revolutionary regime on February 11. On November 4, students stormed the US embassy and held Americans hostage for more than a year. Anger in the US, fear in Moscow about the possible export of the Islamic revolution to its Muslim territories and anxiety among neighbouring states about Tehran's intentions set the scene for war.

Relations with Iraq degenerated. A failed attempt to assassinate Iraqi foreign minister Tariq Aziz was blamed on Iranian agents. Iranian and Iraqi forces clashed on the border. Iraq sent troops into Iranian territory on September 2, 1980. On September 17, Iraqi President Saddam Hussein abrogated the 1975 Iran-Iraq treaty that fixed the border between the two countries in the middle of the Shatt al-Arab and declared Iraqi control of the waterway. On September 22, he ordered an all-out invasion. After initial setbacks and the loss of Khorramshahr, the Iranian army recovered all captured territory by mid-1982. The conflict degenerated into stalemate. Iran came close to capturing Basra in 1985 and 1986, but the superpowers had thrown their weight behind Iraq. After an Iraqi offensive from April–August 1988, in which chemical weapons were deployed, Tehran announced it would accept a UN ceasefire plan. It came into effect on August 20, 1988.

Imam Khomeini died in June 1989. Ali Khamenei, previously president of the Islamic republic, was appointed supreme religious leader in his place. Iran has since been at peace, benefiting from the defeat of Iraq in the 1991 war for Kuwait and the deposition of Saddam Hussein by a US-led coalition in April 2003. The Taliban government in Afghanistan was seen as a threat. But this too was eliminated by a US-led coalition at the end of 2001. In 2004, Iranian *majlis* elections produced a conservative majority. The election of Ahmadinejad to replace Mohammed Khatami, the moderate but unsuccessful two-term head of state first elected in August 1997, appears to reflect the revival of Iranian revolutionary fervour.

Further shocks are in store. But in four centuries of change and turbulence, the adherence of the state to Shiism has never wavered. Schools of Shiite learning were established and missionaries were dispatched to the Shiite pilgrimage centres in Najaf, Karbala and elsewhere in what is now Iraq and beyond. The legacy is a system that threw up the Imam Khomeini, inspiration of the Iranian revolution and a movement that continues to compete for the hearts and minds of every Muslim.

Ahmadinejad in many respects is its logical inheritor.

### The Europeans come to the Gulf

In 1487, five years before the Genoan navigator Christopher Columbus set sail on a journey that was to lead to the European discovery of America, Bartholomew Diaz weighed anchor in Lisbon. He sailed down Africa's west coast and then around the Cape of Storms (now known as the Cape of Good Hope) to open up a sea route to Asia. Diaz was followed by Joao Peres de Covilhao, who aimed to reach the places of origination of the spices supplied to Europe through Arab intermediaries. The plan was to establish a direct and more profitable connection to their source.

The Portuguese were also in the grip of an ideologically motivated plan to continue the war against Islamic rule, which ended in the Iberian Peninsula in 1492. The Ottomans had captured Constantinople in May 1453. Trade routes through the Eastern Mediterranean to India and beyond were blocked. A new route was needed. Diaz showed the way. In 1497, Vasco da Gama sailed from Lisbon to Calicut in Kerala in south-west India. The Portuguese came into conflict with Arab navies that dominated the Indian Ocean. It became their goal to seize control of trade in the Gulf, the Arabian Sea and the western Indian Ocean. They called for a general to do the job.

Alfonso d'Albuquerque led a fleet of conquest from Portugal in 1506. The first target was Sohar in Oman, which was sacked, and then Khor Fakkan, which now lies in the UAE, which was pillaged and burnt. Muscat was attacked. The kingdom of Hormuz, a semi-independent Arab state based on the island of Hormuz in the lower Gulf, with domains on both sides of the waterway, was attacked in 1507. The island was occupied by the Portuguese from 1515 until 1622. D'Albuquerque also besieged Aden and led the first European fleet into the Red Sea. Among his wilder ideas were plans to divert the course of the Nile to break the power of Egypt, to steal the body of the Prophet (PBUH) and hold it for ransom until all Muslims had left the Holy Land.

The Portuguese built forts at Dibba, Khor Fakkan, Bidiya and Kalba, all in present-day UAE, and several in Oman, including at Muscat. In 1581, a Portuguese expedition tried to take Bahrain but was repulsed. Portuguese power was by then in decline. An army led by King Sebastian I had invaded North Africa and was effectively wiped out at the Battle of the Three Kings in 1578. Two years later, Portugal was absorbed into the kingdom of Spain.

But the Portuguese had stirred up a hornet's nest in southeastern Arabia, the heartland of the Ibadhi imamate. The Omani Yaariba family forged a national movement to expel the Portuguese. Spain, by then master of the Portuguese Empire, was distracted by its interests in the Americas and Europe. The British and Dutch were invited by Shah Abbas to help eject the Portuguese from Persia. After defeat at Bandar Abbas in 1625, they found refuge near Ra's al-Khaimah. A fort was built at Julfar in 1631, but Portuguese-Spanish influence in the region was effectively over.

On September 24, 1599, 24 merchants met in the City of London to found a company to trade in the Far East. At the end of the following year, the East India Company received a royal charter from Queen Elizabeth I. Its first vessel dropped anchor in Surat, north of Bombay. The Verenigde Oostindische Compagnie (VOC), known in English as the Dutch East India Company, was founded in 1602 to open up the eastern trades for the Dutch republic, which was then fighting for independence from Spain. In 1623, it secured the permission of Shah Abbas to set up a warehouse in Bandar Abbas, the port he'd founded and named after himself. Dutch interest focused on pearls. VOC established a base in Muscat in 1672 but not much came of it. It founded a warehouse in Basra, but this closed in 1754 when the Dutch resident quarrelled with the local governor. In retaliation Dutch ships blocked the Shatt al-Arab. A fort was built on Kharg Island, now part of Iran. This fell to the Persians in 1765.

The East India Company's influence, in contrast, expanded steadily. In 1616, it opened a warehouse at Ra's Jashk on the Persian side of the Strait of Hormuz. A British ambassador was appointed to the imperial court in Isfahan. Special treatment of British subjects was allowed in Persia. The partnership bore further fruit in 1622 when the company helped the shah expel the Portuguese from Hormuz. The following year, British merchants opened a warehouse in Bandar Abbas. Hormuz was allowed to decline. Similar outposts were opened at Isfahan, Shiraz and Basra.

The initial British East India Company route to India went round the Cape of Good Hope. But a faster route was established through the

Mediterranean, across Syria and Mesopotamia to Basra and from there down the Gulf. During the seven-year war between Britain and France that ended in 1763, a French fleet bombarded the British facilities in Bandar Abbas. The East India Company relocated to Bushire, which was to be the centre of British Gulf activities for the next 200 years. British contact with the southern Gulf coast began in the 1720s when the Al Qassimi ruler of Ra's al-Khaimah opened a trading centre on Qeshm Island. It competed with British concessions granted by the Persian government and was captured by the East India Company's agent in Bandar Abbas in 1727. But by 1760, the Al Qassimi were once again established on Qeshm.

By the end of the 18th century, the Al Qassimi controlled the southern coast of the Gulf from Ra's al-Khaimah to Dubai, most of the islands in the Strait of Hormuz and the area surrounding Lingah in what is now Iran. They had also embraced Wahhabism and were paying zakat to the Al Saud in Diriyah. After incidents involving Al Qassimi vessels and British ships, British India sent an expedition to the Gulf. In December 1819, the Al Qassimi were defeated and their fleet destroyed. Britain reached agreements with other Gulf rulers.

The first preliminary Gulf treaty was signed on January 6, 1820 with the ruler of Sharjah who also signed on behalf of the rulers of Ajman and Umm al-Qaiwain, pocket emirates on his northern border. Al Qassimi leader Hassan bin Rahmah relinquished control of Ra's al-Khaimah in an agreement signed on January 8. The port became the British Gulf garrison. The rulers of Dubai, Abu Dhabi and Bahrain signed preliminary agreements with Britain soon after. The General Treaty of Peace was signed at the end of January 1820 by nine rulers, including those who'd agreed to the earlier deals. They represented Ra's al-Khaimah, Jazirat al-Hamra, Rams, Abu Dhabi, Dubai, Bahrain, Ajman, Umm al-Qaiwain, and Sharjah. The ruler of Muscat, Sayyid Said, was present at some signings but was not party to the treaty.

The 1820 treaty outlawed piracy, forced sea captains to identify themselves as coming from one of the ports of the rulers that signed the agreement and vaguely promised Britain would act as policeman in the Gulf. It stipulated each ruler had to have a flag that their captains were obliged to fly. All were to be in white and red. In 1823, the British political resident in Bushire, the most senior official in the Gulf, visited all the treaty's signatories. The Royal Navy carried out a marine survey. By 1825, the British had appointed a local agent in Sharjah to represent their interests in the treaty states. The British started to suppress the slave trade and slavery in the region was largely abolished by the middle of the 19th century. Rulers covered by the treaty decided to focus on pearling and it quickly became their largest source of income.

The rise of the Gulf pearl industry led to rivalry at sea. Britain signed the first Maritime Truce with the rulers of Abu Dhabi, Dubai, Sharjah and Ajman in 1835. This banned hostilities at sea during the pearling season, which lasted from May to the end of November. Initially, the agreements were for one year only. In 1843, the truce was signed for 10 years. When this expired, all the rulers signed the Treaty of Perpetual Maritime Peace in May 1853. The geographical terms Trucial Oman, Trucial States and Trucial Coast refer to the territories controlled by the rulers who signed the 1853 agreement. The treaties imposed no obligation on Britain to become involved in the affairs of the Trucial rulers since none was sought. Nevertheless, it was sucked into onshore matters. Britain's House of Commons voted to ban the slave trade in 1807 and then, in 1833, to ban slavery anywhere in its empire. Royal Navy captains were given the right to search vessels and ports for slaves. A second cause for British involvement was the handling of debtors fleeing from one Trucial port to another. An agreement regulating the treatment of absconding debtors was signed by most Trucial rulers in 1879.

Britain's Gulf monopoly quickly came under pressure. Under Sultan Abdelaziz, who ruled from 1861–76, the Ottomans began to reassert themselves in the Gulf which they'd largely abandoned two centuries before. In May 1871, Ottoman troops seized Al Hasa and the Qatar Peninsula. Constantinople then laid claim to eight towns in the Trucial States. Around the same time, Persia, with Russian encouragement, was extending its influence in the southern Gulf. The last Al Qassimi sheikh on the Persian coast was expelled at the end of the 19th century.

French, German and Russian merchants and naval vessels started to appear. To counter the threat, the British secured in March 1892 the support of the Trucial rulers for an exclusive agreement that stated they and their heirs would not "enter into any agreement or correspondence with any power other than the British Government". It also barred them from providing facilities to any government except the British. In return, Britain promised to protect the Trucial States from foreign aggression. The Trucial rulers agreed in 1911 not to give rights for pearling and sponge collecting without reference to the political resident. Further agreements were reached covering a telephone cable laid through the Musandam Peninsula via Telegraph Island and a lighthouse on Greater Tunb Island. Sheikhs failing to comply with British wishes were threatened with naval bombardment. In extreme circumstances, British agents would organize the deposition of a leader.

British concerns were roused at the turn of the 19th century by German and Russian activities in the Gulf. St Petersburg asked Persia for a port concession in Bandar Abbas. In 1899, Britain signed an exclusive agreement with Kuwaiti ruler Sheikh Mubarak Al Sabah that required him to refuse to sell or rent any of his territory to any other power without prior consent. The same year, German engineers visited Kuwait to explore the possibility of building a harbour and a terminal for the proposed extension of the Ottoman railway they were building from Berlin to Baghdad and beyond. They were fobbed off.

In early 1900, a Russian warship sailed into the Gulf. Plans were drafted for a regular steamship link between Odessa in the Ukraine and Gulf ports. In 1901, Russian consuls were appointed in Basra and Bushire and a further tour by a Russian warship was made at the end of the year. In early 1903, another Russian warship carrying the Russian consul to Bushire called on Kuwait. British sources reported he had met Abdelaziz Al Saud who was on a visit to Kuwait. Abdelaziz had recovered Riyadh for his family two years earlier and was poised to launch a 30-year campaign that would lead to the creation of the Kingdom of Saudi Arabia.

Viscount Curzon, the Indian viceroy who almost became British prime minister after the First World War, was directed to make a tour to fend off growing competition from Russia and France, secret allies since 1894. The fleet that accompanied the viceroy was the largest seen in the Gulf since the Portuguese 400 years earlier. It began in November in Muscat, where Curzon invested Muscat's Sultan Faisal with the Grand Cross of the Order of the Indian Empire and announced all Oman's debts to Britain would be written off. Curzon then went on to visit all the emirs subject to British protection. His journey finished with a grand meeting with Kuwait's Sheikh Mubarak. The point was made. The Gulf was British. Russian prestige, wrecked by defeat in war with Japan and revolution in 1905, went into eclipse. A Russian scheme to build a railway from Kuwait to Tripoli in what is now Lebanon was stillborn. Its proposed terminus at Shuwaikh was handed to the British who turned it into a naval base.

## Arabia in the First World War

For more than a century before 1914, Britain supported the Ottoman Empire which extended from Morocco to the borders of Iran. Its polyglot population of Muslims of every sect, Jews and Christians, numbered no more than 25 million. London wanted the Ottomans as a buffer against Russia's expansionist drive south. But the second-class status assigned to Constantinople was unacceptable to the Young Turks who seized power in the Ottoman constitutional revolution of 1908. Their goal was to end the defeats that had reduced the Ottoman domain in the two previous centuries. They needed powerful partners. Britain's rising continental rival, Germany, was wooed but no military alliance had been formed by the time the First World War started in August 1914. Germany's early victories against Russia seemed to be an opportunity. The Young Turk defence minister, Enver Pasha, ordered an attack on Russian ships in the Black Sea in October 1914. The Ottoman navy under the command of a German admiral opened fire on the Russian coast and the British cabinet concluded there was Turkish-German collusion. On his own initiative, Winston Churchill, the civilian head of the Royal Navy, ordered the commencement of hostilities on October 31. London formally declared war on the Ottomans on November 5.

Herbert Kitchener, British viceroy in Egypt, had anticipated conflict with the Ottomans. He sent a letter to Sharif Hussein in September 1914 inquiring whether, in the case of war, he would support Britain or Constantinople. When the fighting started, Kitchener was recalled to London and made minister of war. The unsuccessful British amphibious invasion of the Dardanelles (Canakalle) was launched in the spring of 1915. While it was going wrong, British officials came up with the idea of promoting revolt within the Ottoman Empire.

An office for regional affairs, formed in Cairo when the war began, employed men who were to create the pattern of states in the Middle East we know today. They operated under a number of illusions about Arabia. One of them was that the ruler of the Asir, Mohammed bin Ali Al Idrisi, Yemen's Imam Yahya, Abdelaziz Al Saud, and his bitter rivals the Al Rashid of Hail, would unite in an anti-Ottoman Arab front under Sharif Hussein of Mecca. Not for the last time, Britain was woefully ill-informed. An exchange of letters between Sharif Hussein and Britain's high commissioner in Egypt from December 1914, Sir Henry McMahon, was interpreted by the Sharif and Arab nationalists as promising Britain would support the creation of an independent state encompassing all the Arab-speaking lands of the Ottoman Empire. The British were, in fact, reserving their options for the time the Ottomans had been expelled.

After weighing the odds and making promises to both Britain and the Ottomans, Sharif Hussein proclaimed the start of the Arab Revolt in June 1916. TE Lawrence, an orientalist and archaeologist, was dispatched to the Hejaz to find out what was happening. He set about galvanizing the Arab campaign in a guerrilla war. The Arab Revolt of 1916–18 is described in Lawrence's *Seven Pillars of Wisdom*. According to Lawrence, the army of Sharif Hussein, led by his third son Faisal, made a crucial contribution to the defeat of the Ottomans. This may be an exaggeration. It was armed and financed by Britain and played a secondary role in the British advance, from the Suez Canal into Palestine, that started in the spring of 1917. But the Arab army mattered and its achievements are proudly remembered.

Britain and France had already agreed about the division of the post-war spoils. The secret agreement of February 1916 – negotiated by George Picot, representing France, and Sir Mark Sykes for Britain

– divided the Arab lands of the Ottoman Empire into two, with the French promised the north and Britain getting the south. The agreement conflicted with any reasonable interpretation of Britain's deal with Sharif Hussein. It was made public after the 1917 Russian Revolution by the Bolshevik government which disclosed the contents of secret Tsarist files.

The third element of the contradictory pattern of agreements that was to turn the Middle East into a cockpit of conflict was the Balfour Declaration. Herbert Samuel, a Zionist and Liberal MP who was in the British cabinet as attorney general, drafted a plan for Ottoman Palestine to be set aside for a Jewish homeland. It was championed by Arthur Balfour, former leader of the Conservative Party who was British foreign secretary in the coalition government formed in December 1916.

At the end of October 1917, the British cabinet agreed a statement based on Samuel's idea. Balfour sent it on November 2 to Lord Rothschild, leader of the British Zionist movement. It comprised a single, 67-word sentence: "His Majesty's Government view with favour the establishment in Palestine of a national home for the Jewish people, and will use their best endeavours to facilitate the achievement of this object, it being clearly understood that nothing shall be done which may prejudice the civil and religious rights of existing non-Jewish communities in Palestine, or the rights and political status enjoyed by Jews in any other country."

Hundreds of books have been written about the Balfour Declaration, but there's no need to read more than one. By any objective assessment, the declaration is ambiguous, contradictory and arrogant. It was bound to create problems.

The war ended with the fighters of Sharif Hussein, led by his sons Faisal and Abdullah, scattered across former Ottoman territories and sharing the occupation of Damascus. Faisal, supported by Lawrence, led an Arab delegation to the Paris peace conference that opened in January 1919. On February 6, he addressed the supreme council of allied leaders. Faisal said the Arabs accepted there would be exceptions for Palestine and for Lebanon, where France was determined to establish a territory that would be controlled by local Christians. He declared the rest of the Arab World should have its independence and unity. His words had little effect.

Returning to Damascus, Faisal curried favour among Syrian nationalists and, reportedly, tried to stir up problems for Britain in Egypt and Mesopotamia. In Paris, Britain and France reached a deal. The Sykes-Picot Agreement would be applied. A French zone of influence was granted in the territory that now encompasses Lebanon and Syria. Britain would be responsible for Palestine, Transjordan and Mesopotamia. Both powers were to create a system of states which best combined the idea of local autonomy with French and British plans to keep control of the area they had so recently conquered.

Faisal was told in September 1919 that Britain would withdraw its troops from the French zone and that it was up to him to come to terms with Paris. This he apparently did, but Faisal's compromises outraged Arab nationalists. On March 7, 1920, the Syrian Congress, which had no standing in the eyes of the occupiers and acting against Faisal's advice, proclaimed Syria's independence 'within its natural boundaries, including Palestine'. The following day, Faisal was crowned king of Greater Syria. France, despite these developments, was given mandatory control of Lebanon and Syria in April. On July 21, French troops advanced east from Lebanon. Three days later, they defeated Faisal's poorly equipped army at Maisalun, west of Damascus. The next day Faisal fled Damascus. On July 28, he left Syria for good.

While Faisal was being kicked out of Syria, his elder brother, Abdullah, was preparing to stake a claim for a realm of his own. Abdullah had lost face in May 1919 when the army he'd led was defeated by the Saudis at the Battle of Khurma in the Hejaz. Up to then, he had been considered a possible candidate for the kingship of Mesopotamia under a British mandate. The self-styled Iraqi congress had in March 1920 proclaimed him king of Iraq, but this had no official standing.

British and French control of the Arab lands of the Ottoman Empire was formalized in the Treaty of Sevres signed by the Turkish government in August 1920.

At the end of September 1920, Abdullah led hundreds of tribesmen out of Mecca to Maan, an oasis town on the northern Hejaz frontier with the British-occupied territories that stretched from the West Bank of the Jordan to Mesopotamia. He arrived in mid-November and set up camp. In March 1921, at a meeting in Jerusalem with Winston Churchill, then British colonial secretary, Abdullah was told Britain had agreed to divide Transjordan from its Palestine mandate and run it as a separate administrative entity that he would be permitted to govern. Jordan became an independent kingdom in March 1946.

The Palestine mandate went into effect in 1922. But Britain's Middle East honeymoon was already over. There had been a rebellion in southern Iraq, anti-Zionist riots in Palestine, dissent in Egypt and a national revival in the Turkish heartlands of the former Ottoman Empire led by Kemal Ataturk.

Life in most of Arabia was largely unaffected by the First World War. The British expeditionary force to Mesopotamia was carried to Fao through the Gulf and there was an increased flow of goods and material through the waterway. But the fighting was distant. And the focus once the war ended was on oil.

## Arabia after 1945

The inter-war years were difficult ones for Gulf states, with the world-wide recession and the collapse of the market for natural pearls. During the Second World War, from 1939 to 1945, the Arab side of the Gulf started to become more important to Britain, particularly in the light of its potential for major oil finds. Britain's regional political resident was moved from Bushire to Bahrain. Following independence for India and Pakistan in 1947, control of the treaty arrangements governing the emirates of the lower Gulf passed to the foreign office in London. This placed the region's future in the hands of civil servants who were in-clined to sympathize with the aspirations of the people whose lives they directed more than the conservative imperialists of British India.

In 1948, a permanently resident British political officer was appoint-ed to sit in Sharjah to deal with the Trucial Coast. British officials press-ed for greater local involvement. In 1952, the UK established the Trucial States Council, a body comprising all the seven rulers of what was to become the UAE. One of the council's first steps was the crea-tion of a security force. In 1953, the Trucial Oman Levies were form-ed. They were later called the Trucial Oman Scouts. Most officers were British and some of its members came from Jordan. Increasingly, most of the force was locally recruited. The Scouts were financed by local rulers according to their financial capacity and were an important step towards the creation of the UAE 18 years later.

## Journeys around Arabia

Since the peninsula had become arid, only Bedouin seasoned by the demands of the desert made a home in Arabia's heartlands. For Eu-rope, Arabia until modern times was a place of fable and myth. But for Muslims, the land was known, without becoming familiar, from the time of the Prophet (PBUH) and before. Few of their stories were writ-ten down, but those that were shine through time. And, perhaps, the greatest travel story ever told is that of Shams Al Din Abu Abdallah Mohammed ibn Battuta, better known as Ibn Battuta, who journeyed across the Arab and Islamic World and beyond between 1325 and 1354. He is sometimes called the Arab World's Marco Polo, whose own account of his travels to the east includes a report of a sea journey along the Dhofar coast.

Ibn Battuta almost certainly travelled further and saw much more than the wandering Venetian. He probably never wrote a word but what he saw was dictated and taken down by scribes and, after editing, was recorded in *A Gift to Those Who Contemplate the Wonders of Cities and the Marvels of Travelling*. In the Arab World, the book is known simply as the *Rihla*. It is probably the largest travel guide ever written, extending to 1,000 pages in the English translation.

Ibn Battuta left his home in Tangier in the year Marco Polo died and headed east. His travels covered more than 112,000 km, included four Hajj pilgrimages and spanned what on a modern map is more than 40 countries, including Russia, Spain, Mali, Syria, Iraq, Persia, India, most of the coast of East Africa, India, Sri Lanka, Indonesia and China. Ibn Battuta finally returned to Fez to tell his matchless tale. He died in 1369 aged 65. Dubai has celebrated his memory in typical fashion by naming the world's largest single-floor shopping mall after him.

The first European visitor to Arabia to record his story was probably the 16th-century, Italian traveller, Ludovico di Varthema. An account of a journey he made to Medina disguised as a Muslim was published in 1510. A captured German soldier in the Hungarian army left a fuller account of being taken by his master on the Egyptian Hajj in 1607. A Danish mission of exploration in 1761 was the first scientific attempt to map the Arabian heartlands. It arrived in Jeddah, travelled openly as a Christian group and reached Sanaa in Yemen. Only one of the scientists on the journey, Carsten Niebuhr, returned to tell his story. His maps of the Red Sea and the Gulf were still being used by the Royal Navy a century after he drew them.

The German explorer and physician Ulrich Jasper Seetzen set out on a journey in 1802 that took him to Constantinople, Smyrna, Aleppo and from there to Cairo. Travelling in disguise, he sailed to Jeddah and reached Mecca in October 1809. In Arabia, he went to Medina, Lahak and then to Mukha. Seetzen recorded his experiences in letters sent from Mukha, the last one dispatched in November 1810. In September the following year, he left for Muscat. He was found dead two days later. It was believed he'd been poisoned on the orders of the Zaydi imam of Sanaa.

The first organized Arabian mission of the European enlightenment was conducted by the Swiss adventurer Johann Burckhardt. He regarded his journey to Mecca in 1812 as preparation for an expedition to Timbuktu in the Sahara. Travelling in disguise, Burckhardt wandered extensively, became the first European to record the existence of Petra, went to Cairo and joined the Egyptian Hajj mission to Mecca. It took him more than two years. Burckhardt returned to Cairo and died aged 31, never having managed to get to Timbuktu. He was the first European to report on the life of the Holy Cities.

Dutch administrators, seamen and adventurers were involved in the passage of Javan Muslims to the Holy Cities. The British, by virtue of their role in India, became responsible for transporting Indian Muslims to Jeddah. Western vessels started to call on Arabian ports. Horatio Nelson was a junior officer on a British ship that visited Omani ports.

In 1818, the Egyptian army mounted a campaign to suppress the Al Saud. As its army marched east, the Royal Navy in the Gulf was simultaneously preparing a campaign against the Al Qassimi. The British hope was that the Egyptians would complete the suppression of the followers of the Al Saud by marching to the Gulf and joining its campaign. The Egyptians, however, retired as soon as the Saudi capital Diriyah had been destroyed. The British sent Captain George Sadleir of the British army of India to convey the congratulations of King George III to Egypt's army for its victory. Sadleir landed on the east coast of what is now Saudi Arabia and arrived in Hofuf in June only to find the Egyptians had left. He set off in pursuit and reached Manfuhuh, which the Egyptians had also just evacuated, then Diriyah, Ra'ss and finally Medina, where the Egyptian commander Ibrahim Pasha, son of the Egyptian ruler Mohammed Ali, was camped. Ibrahim was unimpressed by the message and the messenger, who was dispatched to Yanbu on the Red Sea coast. The journey was the first time a European crossed Arabia from east coast to west. Sadleir completed the 1,600 km journey in 84 days. It was to be almost a century before the achievement was repeated.

Richard Burton, a former British India army officer, travelled in disguise to Mecca and Medina from Yanbu in 1853. Burton spent much of the rest of his life trying, and failing, to find the source of the Nile. In 1862, William Gifford Palgrave travelled from the Gulf to Riyadh via Hail in central Arabia disguised as an Arab doctor. Palgrave was of Jewish descent but born an Anglican. He converted to Catholicism, joined and then left the British army and became a secret agent of the French Emperor Napoleon III. Returning to England, he renounced Catholicism, returned to the Church of England and wrote an account of his Arabian adventure.

The first organized official British visit to central Arabia was conducted by Colonel Lewis Pelly, the first Gulf British resident in Bushire, who travelled to meet the Saudi ruler Faisal bin Turki in Riyadh in 1865. Charles Doughty began his Arabian journey in 1876 as a member of the Damascus Hajj mission, but went solo with Arab guides when he got to Madain Saleh. Doughty travelled to Hail and then journeyed to Buraidah and its sister town Unaizah. He was escorted west, skirting Mecca, to Taif. After two years, he arrived in Jeddah. His book *Travels in Arabia Deserta* is the first European record of the details of the Arabian interior.

Wilfred Scawen Blunt, who crossed the Nafud with his wife, Lady Anne Blunt, in a journey that began in Damascus in 1878, travelled to Hail before joining a Hajj caravan returning to Persia through Baghdad. The same route was followed later by Gertrude Bell, a liberal imperialist and feminist, who helped invent Iraq after the First World War. She spent 10 days in Hail in early 1914.

In 1902, Abdelaziz Al Saud recaptured Riyadh and declared the restoration of Saudi power in central Arabia after a 25-year hiatus. In 1910, Britain sent Captain William Henry Irvine Shakespear, then political agent in Kuwait, to find Abdelaziz and open a dialogue. Shakespear became the Saudi ruler's friend. He returned to Riyadh in January 1915 in the last of his six Arabian journeys of discovery. There, he drafted the document granting Abdelaziz British recognition as the independent ruler of the Najd. On his way back to Kuwait, Shakespear joined the Saudi campaign against the Al Rashid, who'd accepted the Ottoman mandate, but was killed in a skirmish at Jarrab in northern Arabia. In October 1916, TE Lawrence (who was to become known as Lawrence of Arabia) was sent to the Hejaz by the Arab Bureau based in Cairo to liaise with the Hashemites. Lawrence's war took him on an eventful Arabian journey from Jeddah along the Red Sea coast to Yanbu, Wejh and then through the Nafud to Aqaba and beyond.

As the age of exploration came to an end in the first half of the 20th century, one great challenge remained: the Empty Quarter. Three Britons are associated with its conquest by foreigners.

In 1931, Bertram Thomas, British representative in the government of Muscat and Oman, journeyed from Salalah in Oman, through the mountains of southern Arabia and then across the Empty Quarter to Doha. He was the first Westerner to record a journey across the great desert. In January 1932, Harry St John Philby – a former British India official who served in Iraq, resigned in 1925 and became an adviser to King Abdelaziz – set out from Hofuf and became the second foreigner to make the crossing. Philby followed this up with a voyage of discovery on behalf of the Saudi government in southern Arabia in the winter of 1936. This was in part inspired by Freya Stark's account of a journey through the Hadhramaut in 1935 that is detailed in her book *The Southern Gates of Arabia*.

Sir Wilfred Thesiger is the best-known desert traveller. His journeys across Arabia in the late 1940s are recorded in his book *Arabian Sands*. During 1935–39, Thesiger was an officer in the Sudan political service and was subsequently posted to Abyssinia, Syria and Palestine. Excited by the accounts of Thomas and Philby, he joined the Locust Research Organization that was trying to locate the origins of swarms that appeared to originate from southern Arabia. This led to two spells – one from 1946–47 and one in 1948 – in Oman, south Saudi Arabia and what is now the UAE. He became the first European to cross the Empty Quarter twice. But he was probably the first of all the Arabian discoverers to appreciate fully the qualities of the people who accompanied him.

"Those travels in the Empty Quarter would have been for me a pointless penance but for the comradeship of my Bedu companions," Thesiger wrote. "I knew their pride in themselves and their tribe; their regard for the dignity of others; their hospitality when they went short to feed chance-met strangers." Thesiger died on August 24, 2003. *Arabian Sands* is an epitaph for old Arabia, a glimpse of a time when most of the peninsula was trackless. Within a generation, highways created a new civilization in which acquiring desert skills was optional. *Arabian Sands* records when it was not.

### Travelling in the New Gulf

Today's Arabian travellers arrive by the million, and mainly by air. The first scheduled passenger air flights to the Gulf started in 1932 when Imperial Airways, forerunner of British Airways, began services linking London and British India with stops in Basra, Bahrain and Sharjah. The first national airline in the GCC was Saudia, which was born when President Roosevelt gave a twin-engined DC-3 Dakota aircraft to King Abdelaziz following their meeting in February 1945.

Regional services were launched by Gulf Aviation, forerunner of Gulf Air, in 1950. Kuwait Airways Corporation (KAC) started in 1955. Emirates was founded in Dubai in 1985, Qatar Airways in 1993, Oman Air in 1998 and Etihad Airways, founded by Abu Dhabi in 2003.

Today, the Gulf is the world's fastest-growing aviation market. Dubai is leading the way. The existing Dubai International Airport (DIA) is forecast to handle 70 million passengers in 2012. Dubai unveiled in January 2005 the biggest greenfield airport project in history at a site near Jebel Ali. To be known as the Al Maktoum International Airport, it will have up to six runways and capacity for 120 to 150 million passengers a year. If the plans are implemented in full, the two Dubai airports will be able to handle almost 200 million passengers by 2030. A new international airport is being built by Abu Dhabi. Work has begun on the new Doha International Airport, designed to handle up to 60 million passengers. Kuwait's international airport is being doubled. Bahrain is investing more modestly but could build a new runway in due course.

Jeddah's King Abdelaziz International Airport is being modernized and expanded. The kingdom has 26 other airports and intends to build at least three more. Capacity to cater for an additional 200 million passengers a year could be built in the GCC in less than two decades. This is more than double the number using Arabia's airports in 2006. The result may be too much airport capacity around the start of the next decade, intense competition for the shrinking number of international carriers and airport revenues lower than forecast in the investment proposals. It also means lower costs and much more choice for the growing multitudes of Middle East air travellers.

Gulf ports are expanding at a similar rate. Dubai's Port Rashid and Jebel Ali are together the busiest in the region and handled almost seven million containers in 2005. This figure will almost double by 2011. Abu Dhabi is building a new port at Taweelah. Kuwait is building a new port on Boubiyan Island near Iraq. A container terminal as big as Dubai's is to be constructed in Rabigh, north of Jeddah.

New railway lines are being planned, including one to cross the Arabian Peninsula from Jeddah to Riyadh where it will connect with an existing line to the Gulf coast. A high-speed railway line will link Mecca and Medina. A mineral railway from north Saudi Arabia will run to Riyadh and the Gulf. The UAE is planning a railway line from Khor Fakkan near Fujairah that will cut through the Hajar Mountains to Sharjah and run from there to Abu Dhabi and the Saudi border. This may be the first part of a line that will go through Saudi Arabia to Kuwait and Iraq. Dubai is building a light railway system. Riyadh, Medina, Kuwait and other Arabian cities are following its lead. With car ownership booming, new roads are being built at a record rate. Soon, no part of Arabia will be beyond easy reach of the casual traveller.

## The great Gulf oil boom

The huge increase in capital spending in the New Gulf is directly linked to the rise in oil prices. In May 2008, they rose above US$120 a barrel. Some forecast US$200 a barrel is possible World oil demand, despite higher prices, is continuing to grow by one to two million b/d a year. The GCC produced about 16 million b/d in 2006 and exported about 13 million b/d. No part of the world is benefiting more from higher oil prices and demand. It is forecast that the GCC Six will enjoy growth averaging 10 per cent a year and balance of payments surpluses amounting to US$500 billion during the next five years.

The big new worry is that the world is running out of oil. But there's little evidence this is the case. Oil reserves outside the Middle East are being depleted. But world reserves have never been higher thanks to the plentiful volumes still lying in the ground in the Gulf. The GCC Six account for about 40 per cent of world reserves, estimated in 2006 to be about 1,200 billion barrels. This figure is expected to rise during the next five years. To help keep supplies flowing, Gulf states are implementing history's biggest increase in oil- and gas-production capacity. The GCC Six will invest in the next five years more than US$100 billion to build wells, pipelines, processing plants, refineries and export terminals for oil and gas.

Saudi Arabia, the world's biggest oil exporter, is leading the way. It announced in April 2005 that the long-term plan is to lift capacity to 15 million b/d from about 9.4 million in 2005. The immediate target is 12.5 million b/d of sustainable capacity. Saudi Arabia's energy industry investment programme is being emulated across the Gulf. In Abu Dhabi, which owns the fifth-largest oil reserves on earth, the Abu Dhabi

National Oil Company (ADNOC) aims to raise production from about 2.5 million b/d to three million b/d by 2010. Kuwait, which produced not much more than two million b/d in 2004, plans to lift output to four million b/d by 2020. Oman, which suffered a fall in oil production to less than 600,000 b/d in 2005, aims to raise it back up to 800,000 b/d by the end of the present decade. Qatar is aiming for 1.1 million b/d of capacity by 2010. Only Bahrain, which produces about 40,000 b/d from its onshore fields, is unlikely to make much progress.

By 2015, combined oil production by the six states of the GCC could hit 20 million b/d. For those worrying about becoming overdependent on Gulf energy, there is further bad news. America is running out of gas and will need to import increasing amounts to meet demand from its electricity industry. By the end of the present decade, 90 per cent of all British power stations will have been converted to burn gas, most of which will have to be imported. A similar pattern is being repeated elsewhere in the world. Most of the gas required will come from Russia, Iran or Qatar, owner of the biggest non-associated gas field on earth. In 2006, Qatar became the world's leading supplier of liquefied natural gas (LNG).

## The history of oil in Arabia

The history of Middle East oil began with the Sumerians who used it to fix blades to handles, as a medicine for the sick and as a mortar in buildings. The Sumerians, Assyrians and Babylonians used asphalt from the pitch fountains of Hit about 150 km west of Baghdad. The Bible suggests Noah employed it to make the ark. The basket in which the infant Moses was cast adrift was waterproofed with asphalt. The Byzantines made Greek fire, a combustible oil-based mixture they poured on the surface of the sea or from city walls on invaders' heads. Early Muslim scientists described how to distil asphalt into a liquid similar to naphtha. A Baghdad caliph allocated revenues from natural naphtha wells near Baku on the Caspian Sea to local people. Marco Polo, who visited the area in 1271, said he saw an oil fountain.

A Pittsburgh chemist named Samuel Kier built what was probably the first oil refinery. Its most valuable products were lubricating grease and kerosene for heating and light. Another account claims that a Canadian called Abraham Gesner was first. But there's no dispute that the name kerosene, from the Greek words *keros* (wax) and *elaion* (oil), was coined by Gesner for distilled asphalt oil. The first oil-drilling rig was built in 1859 in north-west Pennsylvania, about 80 km from the south bank of Lake Erie. On August 27, a well drilled in the region to 21 m hit oil that had to be pumped up by hand. It started the first oil boom.

In 1866–67, the first oil bust bankrupted investors and made thousands jobless. The first oil pipeline was built and oil exchange established in Titusville in 1871. John D Rockefeller, the first oil mogul, set up a trading partnership in Cleveland, Ohio, near the Pennsylvania oil regions. When a new railroad link brought oil to Cleveland, refineries were built.

Rockefeller invested in them as a sideline. Rockefeller with four partners founded, on January 10, 1870, the Standard Oil Company (SO). It bought refineries, expanded production and sales and negotiated discounts from railway companies for freighting oil. By the end of the 1870s, SO controlled 90 per cent of American refining. A decade later, it started exploration in the Ohio-Indiana borderlands and later built the world's largest refinery at Whiting on Lake Michigan.

The Russian oil industry was born even before America's. Baku had been absorbed into the Russian empire in 1806. The region had been famous for oil seepages for thousands of years. By the middle of the 19th century there were dozens of hand-dug oil pits. The Russian government opened the region to competitive investment in the 1870s. Wells were drilled and more than 20 refineries were operating by the end of 1873.

The Nobel family, Swedes who had settled in Russia in the 1830s, bought a Baku refinery and established the region's first modern oil company. The Nobel Brothers Petroleum Producing Company built the first tankers to ship oil across the Caspian and appointed the first permanently employed professional geologists. A loan from the Rothschild family helped the Nobels build a railroad from Bakum to Batum on the east shore of the Black Sea. A legacy of the Nobel fortune are the Nobel Prizes, founded by Alfred Nobel, a weapons manufacturer. When his brother Ludwig died of a heart attack in 1888, newspapers wrongly printed obituaries about Alfred in which he was damned for making a fortune by finding ways to kill. He revised his will and established the prizes as a kinder memorial to his life and work.

SO and the Nobel company were the first two oil majors. The third was the Royal Dutch Shell Group. Shell was created, in London, by Marcus Samuel, born in 1853, and his brother Samuel. In 1891, Marcus won a contract to ship Russian oil supplied by the Rothschilds to world markets. He built storage tanks in Asian ports. The following year, the Suez Canal gave Samuel permission to sail his supertankers through the waterway. By 1902, 90 per cent of the oil passing through the canal was carried in Samuel tankers. The Royal Dutch Company, founded in 1890, discovered oil in what is now Indonesia, then part of the Dutch Asian empire.

Samuel's oil-shipping business was merged with Royal Dutch in 1907 to create the Royal Dutch/Shell Group, a holding company with Royal Dutch having 60 per cent of the stock in operating subsidiaries and Shell taking the rest. The business was run by a committee of managing directors comprising members of the boards of the two holding companies. This structure lasted until the group was rocked by a reserve revision scandal in 2004. The two firms were merged into a single entity in 2005.

In the US, Union Oil of California, now the Chevron subsidiary Unocal, was the largest producer to emerge from the discovery of a large oil field near Los Angeles in 1892. The 1901 Texas oil boom produced Gulf Oil Corporation, Sun Oil Company and The Texas Company, better known as Texaco. Meanwhile, the chief engineer of the Edison Illuminating Company of Detroit had resigned to produce a vehicle powered by gasoline, a by-product of the refining process. His name was Henry Ford. The first Ford car hit the road in 1896.

SO's power attracted the attentions of Ida Tarbell, a journalist who published critical articles about Rockefeller and his company. These were subsequently compiled into a book called *The History of Standard Oil*, published in 1904. The public response to Tarbell's allegations was noted by President Theodore Roosevelt. He launched an investigation into SO and the US oil industry. In 1906, the federal government charged the company with restraining trade under the 1890 Sherman Antitrust Act. A federal court found against the firm in 1909 and ordered it to be dissolved. Two years later, SO announced plans to split. The biggest new business to emerge was Standard Oil of New Jersey, originally called Esso. It was later renamed Exxon. Standard Oil of New York, later Mobil, was the second largest part. Socal (Chevron) was separately incorporated, as was Standard Oil of Ohio (Sohio), bought by BP in the 1970s; Standard Oil of Indiana (Amoco), bought by BP in the 1990s; Continental Oil (Conoco), which used to operate Dubai's principal oil fields, and Atlantic, which later became part of Atlantic Richfield. It is now a BP subsidiary.

## The first Gulf oil discoveries

British Petroleum (BP) originated from a British exploration concession in Persia that struck oil in May 1908. In April 1909, APOC, the forerunner of BP, was incorporated in Glasgow. It was not a financial success. In the summer of 1914, the British government bought a 51 per cent stake. The First World War expanded the demand for oil but added little to production capacity. Energy planning for the first time became part of government policy for all combatants. Ten days after the war ended on November 11, 1918, Lord Curzon, the Tory former Viceroy of India who'd toured the Gulf 15 years earlier, attributed Germany's defeat to oil. "The Allied cause had floated to victory upon a wave of oil," he declared.

Britain and France wanted to use oil to make their post-war Middle East mandates pay. There were two obstacles. One was American resistance to the predatory methods of old Europe and the desire of American oil companies to get a piece of the action. The other was an Ottoman oil concession that had been awarded before the war when a group backed by Deutsche Bank and sponsored by Germany's Kaiser Wilhelm had contended for the concession with a British group led by APOC. In 1912, Deutsche Bank claimed it had won and assigned it to the Turkish Petroleum Company (TPC). The shareholders were Deutsche and Royal Dutch/Shell with 25 per cent each, and the Turkish National Bank, owned mainly by British investors. Calouste Gulbenkian, an Armenian businessman, had 30 per cent of the bank's shares. Gulbenkian, a King's College London engineering graduate, who represented Shell in Constantinople before the war, persuaded the oil company, Deutsche Bank and the other British investors to participate in TPC. The British government heard about the deal and hated it. It persuaded the German government in March 1914 to restructure TPC in APOC's favour. The British firm was allocated 50 per cent while Deutsche and Shell kept their 25 per cent. Gulbenkian managed to secure from both APOC and Shell the rights to 2.5 per cent of each one's TPC stake. Ever after, Gulbenkian was known as 'Mr Five Per Cent' in honour of the share he secured in TPC and its successor.

On June 28, 1914, the day Archduke Ferdinand of Austria was assassinated in Sarajevo, Constantinople promised it would award the Mesopotamian concession to TPC. The European conflict started in August and the Ottomans declared war against Britain three months later. The deal was never signed. The status of the TPC concession was complicated by the 1916 deal between Britain and France negotiated by Sir Mark Sykes and George Picot. Paris was assigned Mosul as part of the post-war division of Ottoman Arab lands. The city was at the heart of one of the most promising regions in the TPC concession. Mosul was subsequently incorporated into Britain's Iraq mandate granted by the League of Nations. TPC was assigned the role of oil developer in the country. Under the San Remo Agreement of 1920, France took over Deutsche Bank's 25 per cent stake. CFP, a private firm controlled by the French government which is now part of Total, was founded in 1924. It was allocated France's TPC shares.

Washington was haunted by forecasts that the US would run out of oil. During the Paris peace negotiations of 1919, American oil companies urged President Wilson to stop the Anglo-French Middle East oil carve-up. In 1925, TPC's concession was confirmed by the Iraqi government. In October 1927, the company struck oil at Baba Gurgur, north-west of Kirkuk in the Kurdish north. But American pressure soon paid off. Nine months later, a new TPC shareholding was agreed. Royal Dutch/Shell, APOC and France, represented by CFP, were each given 23.75 per cent of TPC's oil output. A further 23.75 per cent was allocated to the Near East Development Corporation, a consortium of American oil companies. Gulbenkian retained his 5 per cent.

TPC was renamed the Iraq Petroleum Company (IPC) in 1929. In 1938, IPC was awarded a concession for southern Iraq that it developed through Basrah Petroleum Company, a wholly owned subsidiary. In 1941, it took over an existing northern concession which it renamed the Mosul Petroleum Company. In 1934, a pipeline was completed from the Kirkuk fields to Al Hadithah. From there, a pipeline went to Tripoli in Lebanon and another to Jaffa in what is now Israel.

Central to the TPC/IPC agreement was a commitment that its shareholders would not operate independently. Gulbenkian said he took a red pencil and drew a line around what he believed was the territory of the Ottoman Empire before 1914. It encompassed Turkey, the Sinai, Palestine, Jordan, Syria, Iraq and Arabia with the exception of Kuwait. The 1928 Red Line Agreement stipulated IPC owners could only work in cooperation with each other in the area it enclosed.

The agreement, however, could not keep new entrants out. One was Frank Holmes. Born in New Zealand, Holmes had worked in mining in South Africa, Australia, the Far East, Latin America, Russia and Nigeria before the First World War. He joined the British Army and became a quartermaster, rising to the rank of major. While looking for provisions in Ethiopia in 1918, he heard from an Arab merchant that there were oil seepages in Eastern Arabia. After the war, Holmes set up the Eastern & General Syndicate (E&GS) to exploit business opportunities in Britain's Middle East empire. He opened a pharmacy in Aden but spent increasing time in eastern Arabia trying to convince rulers to give his firm rights to search for oil.

In the summer of 1922, Holmes made a concession proposal to Abdelaziz Al Saud at a meeting in Al Hasa. Persisting, Holmes appeared at the September 1922 conference in Uqair that had been arranged to fix the borders between Kuwait and the Najd. Early in 1923, Abdelaziz granted E&GS the exclusive right to explore Al Hasa province. In 1924, Holmes was awarded the concession for the neutral zone between Kuwait and Saudi Arabia created in the Uqair agreement. Holmes pitched for a concession for Kuwait and tried to put together a bid for Iraq against IPC. He based himself in Bahrain and sought a concession there. The Bahrain government said no, but contracted E&GS to drill 12–16 water wells. The success of the water project convinced Bahrain that Holmes was worth backing. On December 2, 1925, E&GS was awarded an exclusive exploration licence. Lacking money, E&GS put the licence up for sale. APOC, heavily committed in Iran and Iraq, was not interested but wanted to keep others out. Britain opposed US oil-company involvement. But Holmes eventually sold the rights to Gulf Oil. The Bahrain development company that

Gulf Oil formed was registered as a wholly owned Canadian subsidiary in December 1927 to avoid British objections. Gulf also bought E&GS's Kuwait concession. There was a further complication when the Red Line Agreement came into force in 1928. Gulf Oil, controlled by the Mellon banking family, had a 20 per cent stake in the Near East Development Corporation that in turn had a 23.75 per cent shareholding in IPC. Gulf decided to adhere to its IPC obligations in Iraq, retained the concession in Kuwait, which was outside the Red Line, and disposed of its Bahrain interest, which was not.

The only possible buyer was a non-IPC company. On December 21, 1928, Socal acquired the Bahrain concession. It registered the Bahrain Petroleum Company (Bapco) in Ottawa the following month. All British objections were addressed and the deal was finally sealed in June 1930. The first well was started on October 16, 1931 on Jebel Dukhan (Mountain of Smoke), a rock dome about 30 m high in the centre of Bahrain. On the morning of June 1, 1932, oil was struck. The first tanker of Bahraini oil was dispatched to Japan in June 1934. The discovery conclusively disproved previous assessments that there was no oil in east Arabia and brought American oil companies independently into the Middle East.

Socal started to show interest in the lands of the Al Saud. The Kingdom of Saudi Arabia had been declared in September 1932. King Abdelaziz needed money. Socal and APOC courted the kingdom. The Americans outbid the British and an exclusive 60-year concession was signed in Jeddah on 29 May 1933. After drilling six dry wells, Socal struck oil on Jebel Dhahran on March 3, 1938. The first tanker of Saudi oil left Ra's Tanura just less than one year later. Socal had in 1936 formed a joint-venture marketing company with the Texas Corporation called the California Texas Oil Company (Caltex) that held both companies' interests in the Middle East and Asia. This made Texaco a 50 per cent shareholder in the California Arab Standard Oil Company (Casoc), the special-purpose company Socal had set up to own and operate its Saudi concession.

The transfer of the E&GS Kuwait concession was opposed by Britain even though discoveries in Iran by APOC and in Iraq by IPC would provide sufficient oil to meet imperial needs. The nationality clause in its 1899 exclusive agreement with Kuwait was insisted upon. This prevented non-British involvement in Kuwait without British approval. Nevertheless, the foreign office agreed in April 1932 to set aside the clause. But the discovery of oil in Bahrain in May raised the stakes. APOC urged London to reassert its rights. APOC and Gulf Oil submitted bids for the Kuwait concession in January 1933. In the end, the two companies set up a 50:50 partnership in the Kuwait Oil Company (KOC), which was awarded a 75-year concession in December

1934. Exploration started in 1935. Oil was struck in the Burgan Field on February 23, 1938. Stymied in Saudi Arabia, IPC turned to the lower Gulf. It secured the concession for Dubai in 1935, for onshore Qatar the same year, for Oman and Dhofar in 1937 and for Abu Dhabi in 1939. But IPC's only success before the Second World War was when it discovered the Dukhan Field on the west coast of Qatar in 1939.

### Arabian oil after 1945

The Second World War underlined the future importance of Middle East oil. US geologist Everette Lee DeGoyler reported in early 1944 that the region could hold reserves of up to 300 billion barrels. A colleague declared: "The oil in this region is the greatest single prize in all history." The war changed the structure of Middle East oil. Britain took control of IPC shares held by CFP and Gulbenkian following the fall of France. Gulbenkian moved to Vichy and was accredited as commercial attaché to the Iranian mission, though he spent the final part of the war in neutral Lisbon. His IPC shares were returned after the conflict. Gulbenkian's war record was later used to prove that the Red Line Agreement had been made null and void.

During the war, King Abdelaziz received financial assistance from Britain. Casoc called on Washington to help Riyadh. In February 1943, President Roosevelt extended the lend-lease programme to Saudi Arabia. It allowed the US to provide money in return for airfield and other rights. Dhahran was developed as a US air base. The US even considered buying Casoc and the Gulf Oil stake in the Kuwait concession. One result of Washington's Middle East initiative was a plan for a pipeline linking the oil fields of Kuwait and Saudi Arabia with the eastern Mediterranean. Work on Saudi Arabia's Ra's Tanura refinery started in 1943. A submarine pipeline linking Saudi Arabia to the Bapco refinery in Bahrain was built. Casoc was renamed the Arabian American Oil Company (Aramco) on January 31, 1944.

In February 1945, on his way back to the US after the American-British-Soviet summit in Yalta in the Crimea, President Roosevelt met King Abdelaziz on an American warship in the Suez Canal. The result was an oil and security understanding that has lasted to this day. Aramco agreed to invest to lift Saudi oil production. Standard Oil of New Jersey (Exxon) and Standard Oil of New York (Mobil) were in turn invited to invest in Aramco. Claiming the Red Line Agreement was dead and brushing aside concerns that they'd be in breach of US anti-trust legislation, four American companies signed with Saudi approval a new Aramco shareholding agreement on March 12, 1947.

Exxon, the biggest of the four partners, obtained 30 per cent. Socal and Texaco had their holding reduced to the same proportion. Mobil accepted 10 per cent. The deal called for the new stakeholders to participate in Tapline, a company formed by Aramco in July 1945 to build a pipeline to Sidon on the Lebanese coast. The day of the new Aramco deal, President Truman addressed a joint session of the US congress and proposed financial aid to Greece and Turkey to resist communist subversion. The Truman Doctrine, as the concept of American engagement against communism was called, together with the reborn Aramco, set the scene for a new era in US Middle East policy.

American actions in Saudi Arabia and the new circumstances created by the war demanded a revision of the IPC agreement. In November 1948, a group agreement was signed which erased the Red Line but set higher production levels and a bigger crude allocation for Gulbenkian. The Armenian was to die one of the world's richest men five years later at the age of 85. Gulf Oil signed a long-term agreement for Royal Dutch/Shell to market all its Kuwaiti oil. In Iran, APOC signed a 20 year oil-marketing agreement with Exxon and Mobil in September 1947. These new deals led to a massive rise in Gulf production. Much would flow into Europe where America's Marshall Plan helped finance the switch from coal-burning to oil-burning power stations. The rise of the motor car and demand for central heating in European homes sealed oil's post-war dominance.

The partitioning of Palestine and the First Arab-Israel War of 1948–49 provided the final element of the post-war Middle East order. Saudi Arabia resisted pressure to use oil as a political weapon. Work on Tapline, which passed through areas where there was fighting, was completed in September 1950. The following month, President Truman wrote to King Abdelaziz and implicitly offered an American guarantee against threats to Saudi integrity. Technology was advancing. In 1947, an oil strike in the Gulf of Mexico proved offshore development was possible.

The oil deals of the pre-1939 period entailed up-front payments and, sometimes, loans plus a royalty paid for each barrel of oil pumped out of the ground. Normally, no more than 25 per cent of the value of oil produced was paid. This arrangement was to be replaced after 1945 by a much higher profit take for national governments. The first Middle East breakthrough came in the neutral zone between Saudi Arabia and Kuwait created by the 1922 Uqair treaty. Kuwait and the kingdom sought concession bids from new entrants. The 60-year concessions on offer involved production being shared between the two countries. Each had the right to appoint one concession-holder with the terms being independently negotiated. In June 1948, Kuwait awarded a concession to the American Oil Company (Aminoil), a consortium owned by small US companies including Phillips, Ashland Oil and Sinclair Oil. Kuwait received US$7.5 million in cash, a minimum annual royalty and 15 per cent of the profits.

The Saudi neutral zone concession was awarded to Pacific Western, a firm owned by Paul Getty, an oil speculator and former amateur boxer born in Minneapolis in 1891. Getty offered US$9.5 million in cash, a guaranteed payment of US$1 million a year plus 55 cents royalty a barrel. His concession was signed in early 1949. The agreements called for the two concession holders to amalgamate their operations. In March 1953, Aminoil finally struck oil. The zone was partitioned between Kuwait and Saudi Arabia on December 18, 1969 and is now known as the Divided Zone. The partition did not affect the concession arrangements, but Aminoil and Getty from that time ran completely separate businesses in the zone. Getty was taken over by Texaco, now part of Chevron, in 1984 and the concession expires in 2009.

The next blow to the Middle East oil status quo came as a result of new policies in Venezuela where a 50:50 profit split between concession-holders and government was imposed in 1943 and made more robust in 1945. At the end of December 1950, Aramco signed a revised concession agreement that effectively imposed a 50:50 profit split. A similar arrangement was adopted in Kuwait and in Iraq in early 1952.

## Iran and the first oil shock

Oil was at the heart of the 1953 Iranian political crisis. The 21-year-old shah had replaced his father in 1941. The immediate focus of his attentions was the oil industry. Under the terms of the revised 1933 concession agreement, APOC – renamed the Anglo-Iranian Oil Company (AIOC) in 1935 – was the sole oil producer. It paid royalties plus a share of worldwide profits. AIOC built the world's biggest refinery on Abadan Island at the mouth of the Shatt al-Arab. Oil production had risen to 660,000 b/d in 1950. Money was flowing, but it was not enough. AIOC conceded a 50:50 arrangement in early 1951 but there was a rising demand for the company to be nationalized. The National Iranian Oil Company (NIOC), the vehicle for the takeover, was formed on March 19, 1951. In April, the Iranian parliament (majlis) selected Mohammed Mossadegh as prime minister with the mandate to take over AIOC. The nationalization law went into effect on May 1. Declaring the act illegal, the British Labour government imposed an embargo on Iranian oil exports and planned military intervention. Iranian oil exports stopped that autumn following the departure of AIOC staff.

The Labour Party was defeated by the Conservatives in the general election of October 1951. The new British government was headed by Winston Churchill, Zionist, imperialist and instigator of London's purchase in 1914 of a 51 per cent AIOC stake. Churchill approved action against Iran. He was supported by the Republican administration of President Eisenhower who was elected in November 1952. The CIA, believing Mossadegh was a communist tool, initiated in July 1953 a plot that, after a false start, led to anti-Mossadegh demonstrations, the dismissal of the prime minister and the return of the shah from Paris at the end of the month. The hapless monarch had fled to France when the Mossadegh coup seemed to be misfiring.

The new, loyalist government did not reverse the nationalization of AIOC. NIOC retained ownership of reserves but signed an agreement with a new consortium called Iranian Oil Participants Limited. In the new consortium, approved in October 1954, AIOC had 40 per cent, Royal Dutch/Shell 14 per cent and Exxon, Mobil, Socal, Texaco and Gulf had eight per cent each. The remaining six per cent went to CFP. Later in the year, each of the five US companies gave up one per cent to the Iricon Agency which was owned by nine independents: Richfield Oil Corporation, Signal Oil & Gas, Aminoil, Sohio, Getty, Atlantic Oil, Tidewater Oil and San Jacinto Petroleum Corporation. This arrangement was to last until the Iranian Revolution.

### Suez and the second oil shock

In July 1952, Egyptian army officers deposed King Farouk and declared a republic. In February 1954, the coup's leader, General Neguib, was replaced by Colonel Gamal Abdel Nasser. Two years later, Nasser was made president. Nasser blasted foreign control of the region and called for Arab unity and the defeat of Israel. The concession for the Suez Canal, owned since 1875 by Britain and France, was scheduled to expire in 1968. London planned to withdraw troops from the zone by the end of June 1956. After failing to secure weapons from the US and Britain, Nasser announced in September 1955 that Egypt was to receive Soviet-made military equipment from Czechoslovakia. He told the British he wanted a 50:50 profit split from the canal but drew no response. The last British troops left the canal zone on June 13, 1956.

A little more than a month later, the US rejected a request for financial support for the planned Aswan Dam, which Nasser believed was crucial to Egypt's development. In a speech in Alexandria on July 26, Nasser denounced foreign imperialists. Acting as previously agreed when Nasser said the word 'De Lesseps', the Egyptian army seized the canal. Nasser completed the speech by announcing it had been nationalized. There was domestic delight and a formidable international response. France regarded the move as a threat to its position in North Africa where it was under pressure from nationalists in Tunisia and Algeria. Britain believed Nasser was a threat equivalent to Hitler in the 1930s. Israel itched to hit Egypt as it was interfering with shipping in the Gulf of Aqaba.

On October 24, the three countries hatched a plan. Israel would strike across the Sinai. Britain and France would issue an ultimatum and then invade the canal zone, ostensibly to keep the waterway open.

On October 29, Israel attacked and seized the Sinai and the Gaza Strip within a week. The following day, London and Paris issued their ultimatum. On November 5, British and French forces launched an airborne assault on the canal zone. The Egyptians blocked the canal and Riyadh announced an oil embargo against the UK. Sabotage shut down Kuwait's oil-supply system. Syria blocked oil supplies through the IPC pipeline to the Mediterranean. On November 7, Britain announced plans to cut oil consumption in anticipation of shortages. A run against sterling began. Britain and France had announced a ceasefire but the US demanded a complete withdrawal. UK prime minister Anthony Eden, ill and blamed for the shambles, resigned in January 1957 and was replaced by Harold Macmillan. All invading troops withdrew by March 1957. The canal was reopened the following month.

The Suez Crisis confirmed the US was the principal foreign power in the Middle East. The West's dependence on Middle East oil was highlighted. The first co-ordinated programme to make up for lost oil supplies had been effective. But the canal stayed in Egyptian hands. Republican movements across the region were inspired. In July 1958, Iraq's Hashemite monarchy was deposed. Republican Iraq nationalized most IPC concession areas and formed the Iraqi National Oil Company (INOC). The Suez Crisis created opportunities for new players. Ente Nazionale Idrocarburi (ENI), a conglomerate of Italian oil businesses including Azienda Generali Italiana Petroli (Agip), was formed in 1953 under the leadership of Enrico Mattei. ENI signed an exploration and production agreement with Iran's NIOC in 1957 on the best terms yet secured by a Middle East country. The business was nationalized, with all other foreign oil activities, following the Iranian Revolution of 1979.

The Japanese, also capitalizing on their neutral status, bid for the offshore rights in the Neutral Zone between Kuwait and Saudi Arabia. In 1957, Saudi Arabia awarded a concession to Japan Petroleum Trading Company. In February 1958, it was transferred to the Arabian Oil Company (AOC) consortium of Japanese companies. In July, AOC was awarded a similar concession by Kuwait. AOC started drilling in 1959. It discovered the Al Khafji Oil Field in 1960 and the Al Hout Field in 1963. Saudi Arabia and Kuwait had each bought 10 per cent ownership of AOC soon after its formation. This was raised to 60 per cent in January 1974. By the end of the 1960s, AOC was accounting for 15 per cent of Japan's oil needs. All AOC oil was landed at Ra's al-Khafji where an operational centre, including a refinery, was built. The complex was knocked out in January 1991 during fighting between coalition and Iraqi forces. AOC's Saudi concession expired in 2000 and its Kuwaiti concession ended on February 3, 2003. Aramco Gulf Operations Company (AGOC), a Saudi Aramco subsidiary, took over

AOC operations in its territorial waters and the Kuwait Gulf Oil Company (KGOC), a subsidiary of Kuwait Petroleum Corporation (KPC), did the same in the Kuwaiti section.

The Mossadegh and Suez crises, the 50:50 Campaign and the rise of the independents coupled with rising world demand inspired the foundation of the Organization of Petroleum Exporting Countries (OPEC). The key figures behind its creation were Venezuela's minister of mines and hydrocarbons, Perez Alfonzo, one of the driving forces behind the 50:50 concept, and Abdullah Tariki, Saudi Arabia's director of petroleum and mineral affairs. The trigger was an oil price war between Russia and Western producers that led to unilateral cuts in the posted oil price paid to producing countries in 1959 and 1960. Tariki, Alfonzo and representatives from Kuwait, Iran and Iraq met in Baghdad in September 1960 and formed OPEC to restore prices and regulate global production. Its initial impact was modest. New discoveries in Algeria in 1956 and in Libya in 1959 increased supplies. Oil was discovered offshore in Abu Dhabi in 1958 and in Oman and in Dubai in 1966. At the end of 1967, a massive field was discovered in Prudhoe Bay, Alaska.

## The Six Day War and the third oil shock

In May 1967, Egypt ordered UN observers, in place since the end of the Suez Crisis, to leave Sinai. It started a blockade of Israeli shipping in the Gulf of Aqaba. This set in train events that culminated on June 5, in an Israeli dawn attack on Egypt, Syria and Jordan. Within a week, Israel had captured the Sinai Peninsula, Syria's Golan Heights, East Jerusalem and the West Bank of the Palestine mandatory area which had been held by Jordan since the end of the 1948/49 Arab-Israel War.

On June 6, Arab oil ministers called for an oil embargo against countries supporting Israel. Algeria, Iraq, Kuwait, Libya and Saudi Arabia banned deliveries to the US, Britain and, more selectively, to Germany. The Suez Canal and pipelines from Iraq and Saudi Arabia were closed. Civil war in Nigeria in June 1967 compounded the supply disruption. Action by other producers and consuming countries contained the shortages. The Arab summit in Khartoum in August 1967 sanctioned the resumption of Arab oil exports. That month, Arab oil production was higher than it was before the war. The Arab defeat of 1967 was to have profound effects, provoking fury in the Arab World, the rise of the Palestine Liberation Organization (PLO) under the leadership, from February 1969, of Yasser Arafat, and polarization between moderate and radical Arab states. A by-product was the July 1968 coup that restored the Arab Baath Socialist Party to power in Iraq with Saddam Hussein among its leaders.

On the night of August 31, 1969, young Libyan officers, led by the

29-year-old Muammar Qadaffi, deposed King Idris I, who had reigned since independence in 1951. In January 1970, the new Libyan government called for an increase in the posted prices paid by the 21 oil companies operating in Libya. Rebuffed by Exxon and the majors, Qadaffi shifted his attention to Occidental Petroleum, a Californian independent owned by Armand Hammer. It had won a concession and then struck oil in Libya in 1966. Hammer personally conducted negotiations and agreed, in September 1970, to a 20 per cent increase in tax and royalty payments. By the end of the month, most other oil companies had followed Occidental's lead. They also agreed to a sharp increase in the Libyan posted price and granted a 55 per cent profit share to the government.

Competing with Libya, Iran secured a 55 per cent profit share from the Iran consortium in November. In December, OPEC approved a 55:45 profit-sharing arrangement as a minimum and called for posted prices to be adjusted to reflect exchange rate movements. During the next 12 months, OPEC comprehensively outmanoeuvred the oil companies. In meetings in Tehran involving 22 oil companies and six Gulf oil-exporting countries in January and February 1971, a 55 per cent profit tax take and a 35 cent increase in posted prices were agreed. In separate negotiations in Tripoli between the companies and Mediterranean producers, including Iraq and Saudi Arabia because they had terminals in the region, the price was raised by 90 cents from US$2.55 to US$3.45 a barrel. The Tripoli deal in April had the additional provision of a 2.5 per cent annual price increase plus inflation. It also raised the tax rate to 60 per cent of the posted price. OPEC said the 1971 Tehran and Tripoli agreements would hold for five years. They lasted less than three.

With the oil companies on the run, a new objective emerged: national control of producing assets. Algeria took a 51 per cent stake in French oil concessions in February 1971. Libya nationalized the BP concession on December 5, 1971. The IPC concession in Iraq was nationalized in June 1972. Libya took a 50 per cent stake in two concessions owned by ENI in September. Bunker Hunt's Libyan operations were expropriated in June 1973 and a 51 per cent stake was subsequently taken in all other Western oil company interests in Libya. OPEC approved a plan for 25 per cent government ownership of all Western oil interests in Kuwait, Qatar, Abu Dhabi and Saudi Arabia beginning January 1, 1973. The plan also called for 51 per cent participation by January 1, 1983. The shah announced in January 1973 that the 1954 consortium agreement would not be renewed on expiry in 1979 and that the foreign firms would set up a company to act as a service contractor to NIOC. This was followed in March with an agreement in which Iran nationalized all oil assets in return for a 20 year oil-supply guarantee.

## The October War and the fourth oil shock

OPEC met in Vienna in September 1973 to prepare for a new deal with the oil companies to replace the 1971 Tehran and Tripoli agreements. The companies were summoned to hammer out a fresh deal with an OPEC team led by Saudi Arabia's petroleum and mineral resources minister, Ahmed Zaki Yamani, who'd replaced Tariki in 1962. The meeting was fixed for October 8. On the evening of October 5, Egyptian and Syrian forces attacked Israeli positions in Sinai and the Golan Heights.

Amid extraordinary tension at the Vienna meeting, the companies offered a 15 per cent rise in the posted price. OPEC demanded 100 per cent. The talks deadlocked and broke up on October 12. The US openly delivered weapons to Israel on October 14, outraging Arab opinion. Two days later, representatives from Iran and five Gulf oil-exporting states met in Kuwait City. Iraq demanded an all-out economic war against the US. This was rejected as impractical and the Iraqi delegate walked out. Those remaining announced they'd raise the posted price by 70 per cent to US$5.11 a barrel. The Iranian representative left and the meeting was then joined by non-OPEC Arab ministers. The following day, on October 17, the Arab oil states announced they'd cut production by five per cent from the September level and would continue reducing output by five per cent each succeeding month until their demands were met. Friendly states, however, would continue to receive supplies at the original levels. The nine ministers also approved a secret resolution that the US should be subjected to the most severe cuts leading eventually to a total embargo.

Following the meeting, some states immediately implemented a 10 per cent initial cut. Sheikh Zayed, president of the UAE, was the first ruler to give effect to the ultimatum delivered to President Nixon, calling for the US to end weapon supplies to Israel or face an embargo. On October 18, he authorized the cessation of all UAE supplies to the US. At this time, they amounted to 15–20 per cent of the volume coming from the Gulf. On October 19, President Nixon proposed military aid worth US$2,200 million to Israel. Libya announced a total embargo on supplies to the US. Saudi Arabia announced on October 20 that it would end oil shipments to the US as well. A ceasefire came into effect on October 23 but, at the end of the month, other Arab states joined the embargo that was extended to the Netherlands.

The Algiers Arab summit on November 27 approved the open and secret embargo resolutions and extended them to include Portugal, Rhodesia and South Africa. Following an EU ministerial resolution passed in November, which expressed support for the Arab position, the planned five per cent cut in supplies to Europe for December was waived. OPEC ministers met in Tehran in December and agreed to a further rise in the posted price to US$11.65 a barrel, with Arab Light as the marker. This was more than twice the level announced at OPEC's October gathering and four times the level before the October War. Convinced their point had been made, most leading Arab oil producers began to relax their embargos. OPEC met in January 1974 and agreed to freeze prices until April 1. Arab ministers, with the exception of the Libyan representative, met in March and agreed to lift the embargo entirely.

Nationalizations continued. At the end of January 1974, Kuwait announced it was taking 60 per cent of the BP-Gulf concession. Qatar took the same step with IPC on February 20. In June, Saudi Arabia announced 60 per cent participation in Aramco backdated to January 1. Abu Dhabi followed in September. Piling on the pressure, Saudi Arabia announced in the autumn that the tax rate on Aramco profits would rise to 85 per cent and royalty payments to 20 per cent. Iraq completed its nationalization measures. Kuwait agreed full takeover terms with BP and Gulf Oil at the end of 1975. In the spring of 1976, Saudi Arabia and the four Aramco partners sealed the full nationalization of the oil company. It came into effect in 1980, but Saudi control was only formalized in 1988 when Saudi Aramco was created.

OPEC's moment quickly passed. By the end of 1976, a division had emerged between the price hawks, led by Algeria, Iraq and Libya, and the doves, led by Saudi Arabia. At its meeting in December, OPEC split. The UAE and Saudi Arabia applied a five per cent price rise while the rest opted for 10 per cent. At the July 1977 OPEC meeting in Stockholm, the pricing system was unified. Nationalization and high oil prices stimulated the search for alternative energy sources. A major find was made in Mexico in 1972. The North Sea became one of the world's biggest oil provinces. The influence of non-OPEC producers began to grow.

## Khomeini and the fifth oil shock

Ruhollah Mussawi Khomeini was born in central Iran in September 1902. His father, a leading Shiite cleric in the town of Khomeini, was murdered when the future revolutionary leader was five. He was raised by his mother and his aunt but both of them had died by the time he was 15. Aged about 19, Khomeini was sent for religious training in Qom. He was an outstanding student, scholar and teacher, writing philosophical works that remain Shiite standards. In his private life, Khomeini was enlightened. His wife was the daughter of a cleric and they had seven children, though two died in infancy. The girls were educated and his granddaughter Zahra Eshragi has been an advocate of women's and human rights within the terms defined by the Islamic revolution her grandfather led.

Khomeini was to stay in Qom until he was deported to Turkey on November 4, 1964 for leading protests against the shah's secularization programme (known as the White Revolution) launched the previous year. In September 1965, Khomeini moved to Najaf in Iraq where he began to develop the theory of government that was to follow the triumph of the Islamic revolution.

Khomeini's influence threatened the secular Iraqi Baath Socialist Party, which had seized power in July 1968. His attitude hardened in October 1977 when his son Mustafa Khomeini was murdered, probably by Savak, Iran's secret police. In January 1978, an Iranian newspaper published an article attacking Khomeini, sparking riots in Qom, the principal centre of Iranian Shiism. The deaths were followed by a 40-day mourning period that was in turn followed by more demonstrations, deaths and mourning. By the autumn, Iran was in uproar. Encouraged by the shah, Iraq expelled Khomeini in October 1978 as Iran descended into chaos. Khomeini found refuge in a Paris suburb where he became the symbol of resistance to the shah. Strikes spread to the oil industry. By the start of November 1978, Iranian oil exports had fallen to less than one million b/d from their peak of 4.5 million b/d. By the end of the year, production had effectively ceased. On January 16, 1979, the shah left Iran, travelling first to Egypt and finally to Panama where he died in July of a previously undisclosed form of leukemia. On February 1, Khomeini arrived in Tehran from Paris. By February 11, his supporters controlled Iran.

Saudi Arabia lifted production to 10.5 million b/d at the end of 1978. Others raised output, but the world was still suffering a net loss of about two million b/d in the first quarter of 1979. The impact on prices was amplified by force majeure provisions invoked first by BP, which had heavily depended on Iranian oil, and then by most of the oil industry. Suppliers bid up the price of the limited supplies available on the spot market. By the end of February 1979, the spot price was close to US$30 a barrel. Aiming to close the gap between official and free market prices, OPEC met in Geneva in March and agreed to lift the marker oil price to US$14.56 a barrel, effective April 1. It also allowed members to apply premiums and surcharges. Iranian oil supplies resumed in March but Saudi Arabia reduced production to 8.5 million b/d for the second quarter, a move that offset the impact on prices of rising Iranian exports. Fuel shortages in the West compounded the misery caused by accelerating inflation. Responding to American calls, Saudi Arabia lifted production to 9.5 million b/d in July. Spot prices softened, but did not return to pre-Iranian crisis levels. Iraq announced it was extending its oil embargo, which it had maintained against the US since 1973, to Egypt for signing a peace treaty with Israel in March 1979. A measure of order was restored to OPEC's pricing system in

June when members agreed to narrow their price range with Saudi Arabia's marker Arab Light being raised to US$18 a barrel. Nevertheless, oil prices continued to leapfrog. Saudi Light was lifted to US$24 a barrel at the OPEC meeting in Caracas in December 1979 and to US$28 a barrel effective April 1, 1980.

## Saddam Hussein and the sixth oil shock

The 192 km-long Shatt al-Arab has been the border between Iran and the Arab World since the Treaty of Erzurum of 1847. It allocated Khorramshahr, Abadan Island and the east bank of the Shatt to Tehran. The Ottoman Empire was given sovereignty over the waterway itself. The border was never properly delineated. The Shatt is wide and lazy with shifting mud banks and an uncertain course. In 1937 the boundary near Abadan was shifted to the thalweg, the waterway's deepest point. In the following decades, Iran pressed for the boundary to be the thalweg for the entire length of the Shatt. This claim was consistently rebutted by Iraq.

The issue rumbled but remained dormant for 30 years. Tensions between Iran and Iraq increased following the 1968 coup that brought the Baath Party to power in Baghdad. In 1972, Iraq signed a friendship agreement with the Soviet Union. President Nixon and the shah made a secret agreement to start covert actions against Baghdad that involved Iranian support for the Iraqi Kurdish autonomy movement. The shah proved to be the Kurds' fickle friend. Tehran's support was abruptly terminated following an Iran-Iraq agreement in Algiers in 1975. Baghdad accepted the thalweg. Iran stopped supporting the Iraqi Kurds who were quickly defeated. The agreement was negotiated by Iraqi vice-president Saddam Hussein. He never forgot the humiliation.

Saddam Hussein became president in July 1979. He was conscious of the Iranian revolution's appeal to Iraq's majority Shiite population. Khomeini denounced the Baath as tyrannical and Godless. Attacks on Baath officials by Shiite radicals were blamed on Tehran. In April 1980, Tariq Aziz, then Iraq's deputy prime minister, survived an assassination attempt attributed to Iranian agents. Amid increasing border clashes, Saddam Hussein appeared on Iraqi television on September 17, and tore up the 1975 Algiers Agreement. He declared the Shatt al-Arab belonged to Iraq. On September 22, Iraqi forces broke through the Iranian border. On September 23, Iraqi planes attacked the Abadan refinery complex. An Iranian counterattack stopped all Iraqi exports through the Shatt. By the end of September, four million b/d of oil exports had been stripped from the market.

The OPEC meeting in Bali in December 1980 was dominated by the war. No price agreement emerged. The Saudis refused to raise prices from the US$32 a barrel marker. The majority adjusted theirs based on a US$36 a barrel benchmark. With the spot market making the running, oil prices hit a peak in January 1981 of close to US$40 a barrel, equivalent to about US$100 a barrel in today's terms.

The war dragged on. In September 1981, Iran repelled Iraqi forces around Abadan and, at the end of November, launched a major offensive. Meanwhile, in October, OPEC agreed to unify prices around US$32 a barrel for 1982 with a ceiling of US$38 a barrel. Record oil prices and a new global recession hit oil demand. OPEC was unable to respond because of the war between two member states. Spot prices tumbled. In March 1982, OPEC for the first time set output limits, fixing it at 18 million b/d for the group and allocating a quota to each member state with the exception of Saudi Arabia. In London in March 1983, OPEC cut output to 17.5 million b/d, formalized the quota arrangement and reduced, for the first time ever, the marker price by US$5 to US$29 a barrel. Saudi Arabia accepted the role of swing producer that meant it could lift output to contain prices or, as it did for the next three years, cut it to stop a price slump.

But OPEC had lost control of the market. Two thirds of world oil was coming from non-OPEC sources. Prices continued to fall. In October 1984, OPEC agreed a further reduction in the combined ceiling to 16 million b/d. The following month, nine OPEC countries reduced price differentials between light and heavy crudes and Saudi Arabia reduced its marker price to US$29 a barrel. Demand for OPEC crude fell to a 20-year low of 13.7 million b/d in June 1985. Every oil-exporting country was suffering serious economic problems.

### The great oil slump of 1986
At the OPEC meeting in Taif in Saudi Arabia in June 1985, Yamani read out a letter from King Fahd criticizing quota cheating and price discounting by other OPEC members. The warning had little effect. That summer, Saudi oil production fell to 2.2 million b/d. Without informing OPEC, Saudi Arabia dropped fixed oil pricing and adopted a netback system which involved purchasers paying an agreed margin on top of the price of refined products. Orders for Saudi oil began to increase. Other countries followed the Saudi lead.

In November 1985, futures prices rose to more than US$30 a barrel suggesting the worst was over. So there was no immediate reaction to the official communiqué issued on December 9 following OPEC's winter meeting that said the organization was abandoning the policy of defending prices. The chase for market share turned into a free-for-all among OPEC states, the divisions intensified by Iran's capture of the Fao Peninsula on the Iraqi side of the Shatt al-Arab in February 1986. In April, Vice-President Bush went to Saudi Arabia to argue for price stability. In July, Brent blend crude fell to US$9 a barrel. This more than offset the positive impact of demand for OPEC oil rising to 20 million b/d. A consensus emerged around a new price level based on US$18 a barrel for marker crude. In Geneva in December 1986, OPEC set a reference price at this level and fixed a new combined production target for all 13 members of 17.3 million b/d.

Military collaboration between the US and Iraq helped deliver victories to Baghdad on the ground. Iran announced in August 1988 that it would accept UN Security Council ceasefire resolution 598. No final peace treaty was agreed, but the eight-year war was over. Saddam Hussein claimed Iraq had won. But his country was economically crippled. The US and Iraq's other allies questioned the need to continue the support provided to Baghdad during the war. Pressure on Iraq grew as evidence emerged of attempts to develop weapons of mass destruction.

## Kuwait and the seventh oil shock

In the spring of 1990, Saddam Hussein's ire turned towards Kuwait and Abu Dhabi. He accused them of increasing oil production to depress prices and put financial pressure on Baghdad. Saddam Hussein charged the Kuwaitis with stealing Iraq's share from the Rumaila Field that straddles the two countries' border. Baghdad called for forgiveness for loans provided by Gulf states during the war with Iran.

In a speech on the anniversary of the Baathist coup on July 17, Saddam Hussein accused Gulf states of harming Iraq by pushing down oil prices. He charged the US with conspiring to lower oil prices and threatened "action will have to be taken to restore matters to their normal course". The next day, Iraq's deputy prime minister and foreign minister, Tariq Aziz, sent a memorandum to Kuwait stating it was encroaching on Iraqi territory, draining oil from the Rumaila Field and colluding with the UAE to depress oil prices. The memorandum decribed Kuwait's actions as "tantamount to military aggression". Kuwait denied the charges. The climax came at a Jeddah meeting under the sponsorship of King Fahd at the end of July between Kuwait, represented by Crown Prince Saad, and Iraq, represented by Izzat Ibrahim and Saadoun Hammadi. The bad-tempered encounter ended on the evening of July 31.

Saddam Hussein heard his demands had been rejected and ordered the two Iraqis to return to Baghdad. At 2 am local time on August 2, Iraqi troops smashed through the Kuwaiti frontier. By the end of that day, they had control of the country. The UN Security Council passed resolutions condemning the invasion, demanding Iraqi withdrawal and applying draconian sanctions. Iraqi and Kuwaiti oil production stopped. At the end of August, OPEC pledged to pump up to four million b/d of additional oil to make up for lost supplies. Oil prices, which had risen well above US$30 a barrel on the invasion, fell sharply.

On the evening of January 17, 1991, coalition forces began bombing targets in Iraq. After an initial spike, oil prices fell. The land attack launched on February 24, was quick and successful. On February 28, President Bush announced a ceasefire. But as it retreated, the Iraqi army set alight Kuwaiti oil fields. The last oil fire was extinguished in November. The elimination of Iraqi and Kuwaiti oil production allowed other OPEC states to lift output without depressing prices. Saudi production was raised to more than eight million b/d and held at that level for most of the rest of the 1990s. The collapse of the Soviet Union was an additional factor helping to keep prices up. Global economic recovery led to a revival in demand.

By the end of 1992, OPEC production was more than 25 million b/d for the first time in more than a decade. Kuwaiti oil production was restored to pre-war levels in 1993. In 1996, the UN Security Council passed resolution 986 which allowed Iraq to sell oil to pay for humanitarian goods. Qatar embarked on a programme to build world-scale LNG plants aimed at international markets. Its first Qatargas project opened in late 1996. US President Clinton approved the Iran Libya Sanctions Act (ILSA) banning US companies from investing in the Iranian oil and gas sector. It had little impact on Iranian behaviour.

OPEC decided at its Djakarta meeting in November 1997 to raise its target to 27.5 million b/d, an increase of 10 per cent. But the organization had underestimated the impact of the Asian financial crisis. Prices tumbled again. At meetings in March and June 1998, it introduced quota cuts, and secured the promise of similar action from Mexico, Oman and Russia. But oil prices fell to below US$10 a barrel in early 1999.

With profits under pressure, major companies agreed to the biggest mergers in oil history during 1998–2002. BP took over Amoco and then Arco. Exxon merged with Mobil. Chevron merged with Texaco. Phillips merged with Conoco. Total merged with Elf Aquitaine.

The oil-price turning point came in March 1999 when OPEC and non-OPEC states agreed to cut combined output by more than two million b/d, effective April 1. Prices doubled in the next 12 months. By the end of 2000, spot prices were more than US$30 a barrel. The administration of President George W Bush, elected in 2000, initially adopted a cautious approach to Middle East affairs. Joining with the UK, it attempted, but failed, to revise the oil-for-food programme to make it more effective and humane. The key policy departure of Bush's first year was the announcement that he would not ratify the 1997 Kyoto Protocol on climate change agreed by President Clinton.

For OPEC, fresh worries about an oil-price slump emerged as recession in the US led to slackening oil demand. Quotas were cut in March and July 2000, but downward price pressure continued for most of the rest of the year. OPEC production restraint intensified following the 9/11 attacks. After spiking initially, spot prices fell on fears that the attacks would deepen the American recession. Big production cuts for 2002 agreed by OPEC convinced the market that the organization was serious. Oil prices began an upward march helped by industrial action in Venezuela that led to cuts in the country's oil exports. In May 2002, President Bush and President Putin agreed on an energy partnership that would increase US investment in Russian oil and gas. They approved plans to raise Russian oil sales to North America. Moscow also announced it would suspend production cutbacks agreed with OPEC.

## President Bush and the eighth oil shock

The alliance between the world's largest oil consumer and the second largest oil producer was fractured by the White House's decision to press for action against Iraq. On September 12, Bush addressed the UN and charged Iraq with breaches of UN Security Council resolutions, particularly with regard to weapons of mass destruction. The US secured UN Security Council support for resolution 1441 which called on Iraq to comply within 30 days with all previous resolutions about banned weapons. The Iraqi response was incomplete.

US pressure for action continued to build, raising worries about oil security. In December 2002, OPEC lifted its combined quota to 23 million b/d and then to 24.5 million b/d effective February 1, 2003. On March 19, 2003, the US-led coalition began its invasion of Iraq. Exports of Iraqi crude were immediately halted and OPEC stepped in to make up the shortfall. Spot prices rose to US$30 a barrel by the end of major military operations in the middle of April. The Iraq-Syria pipeline, which had been used to sell oil outside the oil-for-food programme, was shut by the US military on April 15. At the end of the month, OPEC restored quotas but raised the combined ceiling to more than 25 million b/d.

Violence slowed the Iraqi oil-industry reconstruction programme. Exports through Turkey were resumed in June 2003, but pre-war levels of Iraqi production were not reached until the start of 2004. OPEC decided in March 2004 to go ahead with a previously agreed cut in its combined output ceiling to 23.5 million b/d. It quickly recognized it had misjudged trends and lifted the combined quota in two stages to 26 million b/d in August. Prices rose to more than US$40 a barrel in September. OPEC raised the combined ceiling to 27 million b/d from November 1, 2004.

Speculation about possible supply interruptions and buoyant demand pushed prices to more than US$50 for the first time in October 2004. Higher OPEC production coupled with President Bush's re-election reversed the trend. By the start of the second week of November, the OPEC basket price had fallen to about US$37 a barrel. But this was a temporary dip. In December 2004, oil prices started to move up again. In January 2005, the average price of OPEC crude oils moved to more than US$40 a barrel. It crossed US$50 in April. The death of King Fahd on August 1 prompted speculation of political problems in the kingdom. Iraqi oil production was still being hindered by sabotage. Venezuela looked restive.

On August 30, 2005, oil prices on US spot markets hit US$70 a barrel. Despite higher prices, world demand continued to grow. A new price spike occurred in January 2006 when the deadlock between Iran and the International Atomic Energy Agency (IAEA) provoked speculation that oil sanctions might be in prospect. The spot oil price, reflecting new concerns caused by Israel's war with Hizbollah in south Lebanon, rose in July 2006 to a new record high and has been more than US$60 a barrel ever since. The consensus is the oil boom will last at least five years. Some believe oil prices will remain high for at least a generation.

# CHAPTER 2

# IN THE KINGDOM

Riyadh is a sprawling city of more than five million people, occupying 1,500 km² of desert plateau at Arabia's heart. Lying 1,550 m above the sea, Saudi Arabia's capital scorches in summer and chills in the heatless winter sun. Its centre lies in the Wadi Hanifa, the dry bed of a river that once drained into the Gulf at the foot of the Qatar Peninsula. The water disappeared from the surface, but seeps invisibly eastwards in aquifers below the wadi floor. It fed springs and wells that sustained a faithful band that, less than a century ago, conquered the peninsula and made a kingdom.

This is the homeland of the Al Saud and their people. *Ar Riyadh* means 'The Garden' or 'The Meadow', a tribute to its original role as an oasis haven. In winter, its air is fresh and clear. Even in high summer, the surrounding desert is a cool retreat at night. Only 16 km away are the cliffs of the Tuwaiq Escarpment, a limestone ridge that rises hundreds of metres from the desert floor and runs in a north–south line west of the city. To the east, a broad band of sand desert separates the Saudi capital from the great palm city of Hofuf.

Riyadh is the locomotive of a nation looking to the future with growing optimism. Capital of the largest economy in the Middle East and seat of government of the region's most powerful state, the city is being transformed by the new wave of prosperity caused by high oil prices and mounting world energy demand. The figures are not precise, but Riyadh's population could be growing by as much as 10 per cent a year. The heart of modern Riyadh is the Olaya district, once the retreat for King Faisal who ruled the kingdom from 1964 to 1975. The road running north out of Riyadh towards the airport passes through Olaya, now the site of the two most striking icons of contemporary Saudi Arabia: the Faisaliah Tower, built by the children of King Faisal, and the Kingdom Centre, where Prince Alwaleed bin Talal labours into the night on Arabia's greatest private fortune.

Saudi Arabia is embracing the future, but its history still echoes. From this region, 250 years before, fighters and missionaries carried the purified message of Islam across the peninsula. The kingdom created in 1932 defined the limits to this mission of faith. Within its borders, peace came while the region and the world was wracked by war and revolution.

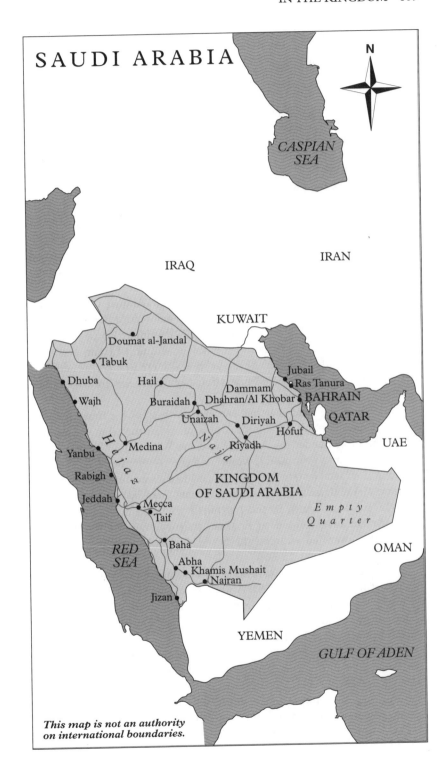

This map is not an authority
on international boundaries.

Saudi Arabia could not insulate itself from the new tide of radical Islam that swept the region and seized power in Iran in February 1979. Its first eruption inside the kingdom came in November 1979 when militants captured the Great Mosque of Mecca (Makkah) at the start of Islam's 15th century. After a two-week siege in which more than 100 died, the Holy Haram was regained but the comfort of half a century's domestic calm was lost. The rebel leaders, tried and sentenced, were executed according to Sharia law. The flash of the headsman's blade marked the beginning of a new time of rage at an intrusive world hostile to God's final word.

That month, Shiite rioting in Qatif in the kingdom's oil-rich Eastern Province, which was repeated in 1980, drew inspiration, it seemed, from the new Islamic Republic of Iran. It was fuelled by divisions between rich and poor, the rulers and the rest, and the centre and the periphery in Saudi Arabia's first age of prosperity. As oil income fell in the 1980s, discontent smouldered.

For Saudi Arabia, the occupation of Kuwait in August 1990 exposed the tension at the centre of the kingdom's policies since King Abdelaziz Al Saud, founder of Saudi Arabia, met US President Roosevelt in the Suez Canal in 1945. Guardian of the holiest shrines of Islam and leader of an Arab state that had never been conquered or controlled by a foreign power, the king sealed a relationship that seems to be based on the attraction of opposites.

The glue in the deal that has satisfied both sides for more than six decades is implicit but real. Saudi Arabia provided the oil in the amount and at the price needed by America and the West. The US guaranteed the status quo and promised it would end the conflict between the Arab World and an Israeli state America helped to deliver, finance and arm.

Since 1945, Riyadh and Washington have marched in step on practically every issue. And, in the partnership's finest hour, the US and Saudi Arabia collaborated to finance, train and supply thousands of fighters that eventually forced the Soviet Union to withdraw from Afghanistan in 1989.

But America's inability to impose the comprehensive settlement of the Palestine tragedy that Saudi Arabia, since King Abdelaziz, demanded was a festering sore. Iraq's invasion of Kuwait in 1990 was as unwelcome in Riyadh as it was in Washington. The differences about Palestine complicated the Saudi response.

As the Iraqis dug in, it became clear that the US wanted complete Iraqi withdrawal, not talk. The Saudi leadership debated Riyadh's options. King Fahd favoured supporting President Bush. His condition was that America should make a commitment that, this time, it would use its powers to bring peace and justice to Palestine.

On August 3, 1990, US Defence Secretary, Dick Cheney, invited

Saudi Arabia's Washington envoy, Prince Bandar bin Sultan, to a meeting with Colin Powell, then chairman of the US joint chiefs of staff; Paul Wolfowitz, then under-secretary in the defence department; and Richard Haas, a member of staff in the national security council. Prince Bandar was shown aerial photographs of Iraqi divisions moving through Kuwait and heading for Saudi Arabia. Saddam Hussein, Prince Bandar was told, planned to strike at the kingdom.

On August 5, Cheney travelled to the kingdom for talks. The following day, he called President Bush to report that Saudi Arabia was prepared to accept US troops. The conventional wisdom had been turned upside down. Saudi Arabia would allow foreign armies into the land of Islam's holiest cities and join a war against another Arab country.

Criticisms of the decision to join the US-led coalition were voiced in mosques and universities. Petitions signed by Saudis who'd previously been impeccably loyal to the regime were circulated. The regime's enemies connected its dependence on America with the difficulties of a barely-solvent government. One critic stood out from the rest.

A head taller than his contemporaries and an Afghan War veteran, Osama bin Laden had something none of his comrades could match: a fortune that made him independent of the Saudi state. In September 1990, Bin Laden met Saudi officials and presented a plan to raise an international force of Islamic militants to defend the kingdom. The offer was rejected.

After a tense autumn and winter, Iraq was tossed out of Kuwait in a six-week bombing campaign followed by a 100-hour land war. For some, Riyadh had become a collaborator with Islam's enemies. Seeds that were to produce violent fruit were sown in soil made fertile by the emotions provoked by the Kuwait War.

Bin Laden fled the kingdom in 1991. He initially found haven in Sudan and then in Afghanistan when it was about to fall to the Taliban (the students), a Sunni Muslim movement backed by Pakistan, a Saudi ally. Bin Laden's unbending attitude, charisma and wealth, combined with the assistance of a sympathetic regime, produced the atrocity of 9/11. It subsequently emerged that 15 of the 19 hijackers were Saudi Arabian. The FBI complained it was not getting full cooperation from the Saudi authorities. Saudi Arabia's antagonists were in full cry. The evacuation of dozens of Saudi business people and royals after 9/11 was the final public act of sympathy towards a regime that was to be systematically denigrated in the US. In Crawford in May 2002, Crown Prince Abdullah and his delegation were cordially greeted by President Bush but the wheels of war were turning.

In July 2002, Laurent Murawiec, an American neo-conservative, told a meeting of the Defense Policy Board, a Pentagon think-tank, that the kingdom was the kernel of evil. Saudi Arabia, nevertheless, shrugged off the insult, maintained its traditional position and became a member of what President Bush called the 'Coalition of the Willing'.

On April 9, 2003, the statue of Saddam Hussein in the centre of Baghdad was tumbled into the dust by American armoured vehicles. Most Saudi Arabians were pleased to see the removal of Saddam Hussein. But the occupation of Afghanistan and the fall of Iraq were the triggers for terrible events.

The remnants of the Al Qaeda leadership in hiding on the border between Afghanistan and Pakistan ordered their Saudi supporters to attack Western targets in the kingdom. The Saudi Al Qaeda, including Afghan War veterans, argued that a campaign in the kingdom would, in the words of a top diplomat, "foul its own nest".

They were overruled by Al Qaeda's leadership. On May 7, 2003, the Interior Ministry released a list of 19 top Al Qaeda operatives wanted for plotting a major terrorist attack in the kingdom. This set the scene for horror. Late at night on May 12, residents in the Al Hamra housing compound in Riyadh heard unfamiliar noises. "I had no idea what it was," says a banker who lived there. "But my wife had lived in Lebanon during the invasion and recognized the sound immediately. 'Get up and look after the children. It's shooting.'"

Two cars had broken through the compound's security, their occupants dressed as policemen. They raced to the centre of the compound and detonated enormous bombs. That same night, two other attacks were launched against Riyadh compounds used by Westerners and a bomb was detonated outside the office of a Saudi-US joint venture. A total of 32 people died and hundreds were injured.

Ten days later, a German businessman was shot dead outside a Riyadh supermarket. A second compound attack on November 8, 2003, killed 17 and injured more than 100, many of them Saudis and Muslims. Gunfights between militants and Saudi security were by this time happening almost weekly. On April 21, 2004, a suicide bomber outside a government building in Riyadh killed five people. In Yanbu on May 1, gunmen killed seven people, including six Westerners, in an attack on the office of ABB Lummus Global.

A greater horror followed. The morning of May 29, 2004 was the start of another working day for the Gulf port of Al Khobar, gateway to Dhahran, the Saudi Aramco oil city. For Scottish banker Michael Hamilton, 61, the city had been home for a decade. He had spent almost 20 years in the Gulf, the previous 15 working at Dammam-based Apicorp. It was Saturday and the first day of the week. Foreigners were aware they were potential targets but the danger seemed to centre on Riyadh, not easy-going Al Khobar, just an hour's drive across the King Fahd Causeway from Bahrain's hotels and restaurants. It is unlikely that any worries about safety were passing through Hamilton's mind as he approached the Apicorp building. As he did so, gunmen sprayed bullets into the driver's seat. Hamilton died instantly.

The killers moved on to the Oasis Residential Resorts compound. Working their way through the complex, men were quizzed about their religious affiliation. Those deemed to be non-Muslims were slaughtered, some with knives. Celebrating the murders as a gift to God, the murderers even at one point stopped for a meal before continuing the killing. A second group entered the Petroleum Centre, which is used for local and foreign companies. There were more murders. The carnage lasted hours. The final death toll was 22.

The savagery continued. On 6 June, BBC television reporter Frank Gardner and his cameraman Simon Cumbers were attacked while filming in southern Riyadh. Gardner was repeatedly shot by Jihadist militants. Cumbers was shot and died instantly. Gardner's spine was damaged but he has resumed his duties with the BBC. Two days after that attack, US military instructor Robert Jacob was shot dead. Four days later, Kenneth Scroggs, another American, was shot dead in Riyadh. On June 18, Paul Johnson, an American engineer, was beheaded after he'd been kidnapped six days earlier and filmed wearing a blindfold. President Bush, visibly furious, went on American television to condemn the killing and called for effective action against militants. Hundreds of police and National Guardsmen flooded southern Riyadh. All the kidnappers, including the suspected top Al Qaeda leader in Saudi Arabia, Abdelaziz Al Muqrin, were claimed to have been killed by the end of the day of Johnson's murder.

On June 24, 2004, the crown prince, now king, Abdullah, issued an ultimatum to the militants, demanding they surrender within one month in order to save their lives. His offer was that only those who committed acts that hurt others would be prosecuted and that no one who turned themselves in would face the death penalty. But the mood remained fragile.

In August, Tony Higgins, an Irishman working for a Saudi construction firm, was shot dead in his office. Higgins had lived in Saudi Arabia for 20 years and came from a distinguished Irish family. But the security crackdown was by then delivering results. At the start of 2005, the government stated 23 of the 26 most wanted men had been put out of action. In June, it announced one of the last remaining wanted men had been killed in Iraq. The leader of the group, Younus Mohammad Al Hayari, was shot dead in a gun battle in east Riyadh in July 2005. The impression that the war was being won was corrected when the government issued a new list of 36 suspects believed to be linked to attacks in the kingdom. Rewards of up to US$1.8 million were offered for those giving information leading to their arrest or providing help in preventing terror attacks.

After months of calm, a new shock was delivered when militants driving two car bombs penetrated the Abqaiq oil complex in eastern Saudi Arabia on February 24, 2006, in an apparent attempt to knock out one of the kingdom's most important energy centres. The two drivers and two guards were killed in the incident. On February 27, five militants who were said to have been involved in planning the attack were killed in a shoot-out with Saudi security in Riyadh. In February 2007, the killers struck out again. Four French and Belgian tourists where killed during a visit to Madain Saleh, site of Nabataean ruins in north-west Saudi Arabia. It is probable that Jihadists were responsible. At the end of April 2007, the Saudi authorities announced they had arrested 172 people who they said were planning to attack the kingdom's oil facilities. Weapons caches and US$30 million were seized.

None of the other five GCC states have endured terror attacks and attempts on such a scale. Nevertheless, with the terror threats under control, Saudi Arabia is trying to return to normal. Reassured by the government's crackdown on Jihadists, Westerners are returning and the number living in the kingdom is close to that before 2003. But Saudi Arabia is still wary. Roads to the capital have checkpoints where National Guardsmen scan the faces of drivers and passengers for terrorists. Hotels have armed guards, concrete barriers and heavy machine-gun emplacements. Getting into the offices of leading Western firms involves navigating electronic screening, security guards and electronically sealable doors. Long-term residents live in compounds enveloped in security and some continue to travel to and from work by different routes each day in the back of chauffeured cars with darkened windows. Wives and families had been dispatched to safe havens in Dubai or back home.

Convincing people to return to the kingdom remains a challenge. It was a task energetically tackled by Sir Sherard Cowper-Coles, a UK career diplomat and former ambassador to Israel who arrived to take over the British embassy in the kingdom in October 2003. It was a delicate moment for British relations with Saudi Arabia as Whitehall stepped up pressure for the release or proper trial of six Britons arrested, charged and convicted of carrying out bomb attacks that began with the killing of Christopher Rodway, a British expatriate, in November 2000.

The six were televised confessing to organizing the attacks. The Saudi claim they were involved in a war between competing syndicates of illegal alcohol suppliers was, initially at least, not entirely incredible. But after 9/11 and the Riyadh bombings in the spring and summer of 2003, the real culprits were obvious. Britain refused to accept Saudi assertions that the convictions were fair and that torture had not been used to extract confessions. By the end of spring 2003, London, which had organized more than 60 missions at ministerial level or higher to plead for the men's release, was poised to back up its demands with action. But a breakthrough finally came, perhaps as the result of the diligent diplomacy of Saudi Arabia's ambassador to the UK until the summer of 2006, Prince Turki bin Faisal, nephew of the king, who subsequently served as the kingdom's envoy to the US. The six were released on August 8, 2003.

The relationship was tested again in early 2005 when BA's departing chief executive, Rod Eddington, announced the airline planned to end all flights to the kingdom. Since the attacks of 2004, BA staff had refused to stopover in Saudi Arabia so all flights went to Saudi Arabia via Kuwait for a crew change. BA reported a loss on the routes. Saudis suspected this was further evidence of British ill will.

Saudi-British relations took a turn for the better in the summer of 2005. UK prime minister Tony Blair, on his way to Singapore in July to back London's successful 2012 Olympics bid, stopped over in Riyadh for a four-hour chat with Prince Abdullah, who was to become king the following month. This was Blair's first trip to the kingdom since the autumn of 2001. It signalled that London, at last, was back in Riyadh's good books. The prime minister called afterwards for efforts to be made to keep oil prices down, but added, appropriately, that Saudi Arabia was doing everything it could.

On August 1, the death of King Fahd and the succession of Prince Abdullah were announced in Riyadh. That week, Prince Charles and Tony Blair flew to the Saudi capital to express Britain's sympathy and salute the new king. But the Saudi-British locomotive was still not quite on track. On August 10, *The Times* of London published an interview with Saudi Arabia's UK ambassador, Turki bin Faisal, his last before leaving for Washington. The UK had not done enough to tackle Islamic militants living in Britain, he complained.

But London was working hard to rebuild relations. At the end of the summer, it was reported that it had won a contract to upgrade Tornado jets supplied to the Royal Saudi Air Force (RSAF). In December 2005, UK Defence Secretary, John Reid, visited Riyadh to sign a memorandum of understanding with the kingdom that called for Saudi Arabia to buy Eurofighter jets. BMI started direct services to Riyadh in September 2005 and to Jeddah in May 2006. Work is now under way on the Eurofighter project. Cowper-Coles, job largely done, left Riyadh and was appointed UK ambassador to Afghanistan in March 2007.

### The succession of King Abdullah
Of all the countries of the Gulf, Saudi Arabia is the most difficult to know. Its religion is severe. The ruling Al Saud family is enormous and private. The country is 1,600 km from its northern extremity to its southern one and almost 1,500 km from east to west. More than half its 24

million people live outside the three big conurbations, many in remote parts. Two large cities, Mecca and Medina, are out of bounds to non-Muslims. There's no press freedom. Foreigners need a visa in advance to get in.

The death of a Saudi Arabian king is a moment when the unseen becomes public. A system that survived everything the 20th century threw at it briefly opened the door to its inner places. Light and insight were temporarily increased. The life of King Fahd, the first Saudi leader completely in tune with the 20th century, who died on August 1, 2005, was an Arabian epic. Born in 1923, he was the 11th of the many sons of King Abdelaziz, founder of the Kingdom of Saudi Arabia. His mother Hassa bint Ahmed Al Sudairi, an educated and enlightened woman, was reputedly the king's favourite wife. King Fahd was the eldest of her seven boys, popularly known as the Sudairi Seven. Bright, charming and resourceful, King Fahd was given demanding duties at a young age and exposed to the outside world to a greater extent than most of King Abdelaziz's elder sons. In 1945, he attended with his elder brother Prince Faisal, later Saudi Arabia's third king, the UN's inaugural conference in San Francisco. Prince Fahd represented the kingdom at the coronation of Britain's Queen Elizabeth II in 1953.

Just before his father's death that November, Prince Fahd joined the first Saudi council of ministers as the kingdom's education minister. In his time, thousands of schools and Saudi Arabia's first university were opened. He was appointed minister of the interior in 1962, a post he held until becoming crown prince and first deputy premier in 1975. He was a cabinet minister for almost 52 years and king from 1982.

The sons of the late King Fahd, who've adopted the family name Al Fahd in honour of their father, include significant figures in Saudi government. The eldest, Prince Faisal, who was born in 1946, served as director general of youth welfare until his death in 1999. Prince Sultan took over the job when his elder brother died. Prince Mohammed, born in 1950 and governor of the Eastern Province, was an investor in Aitken Hume, a merchant bank led by Jonathan Aitken that financed TV AM, the first British commercial breakfast television station, launched in 1983. Prince Abdelaziz, who was born in 1974, accompanied his father on state visits and GCC summits when he was a youth. He was appointed minister of state in 1998 and sits in the cabinet.

On August 2, 2005, King Fahd's family and representatives of almost every Islamic country gathered in Riyadh to pay their final respects at Riyadh's Imam Turki Mosque. Just before the funeral began, the new king arrived to receive the condolences of the mourners. A pace behind was Prince Salman bin Abdelaziz, full brother of the late king, governor of Riyadh city and province, and one of the kingdom's most powerful men.

At the stroke of 3.30 pm, an ambulance bearing the king's body backed into the mosque entrance. King Fahd's remains were carried on a stretcher and laid on the carpet at the eastern end of the mosque. The imam called *Allahu Akbar*, God is Great! The worshippers muttered the requisite passage of the Koran that forms the first part of Muslim prayers for the dead. Three more times the assertion of divine omnipotence was made and followed by the recitation of Koranic verses. *Assalaam Alaykum*, said the imam. The words were repeated by a thousand voices. A dozen men, including the king's sons, carried King Fahd back to the ambulance. It was a 10-minute drive to the Oud Cemetery. There, in a grave marked only with a headstone, the king's body was laid to rest, his face turned to Mecca.

The funeral marked the end of an era, but did it represent the start of a new one? King Fahd was sophisticated and cosmopolitan. King Abdullah is most comfortable with Bedouin recruited into the Saudi Arabian National Guard he commands. King Fahd enjoyed the company of educated men and foreigners. King Abdullah is quiet and even introspective. King Fahd until his middle years had a taste for the high life. King Abdullah is more conservative. But both have large families. King Fahd had eight sons and several daughters. King Abdullah has seven sons and 15 daughters.

King Abdullah's sons have tended to be connected with the National Guard. Miteb bin Abdullah is assistant deputy commander for military affairs. His brother, Abdelaziz, is an adviser in his father's court.

King Abdullah is little known outside the kingdom. There are, however, clues to his priorities. As effective ruler since 1995, when King Fahd was incapacitated by strokes, he signalled a new openness by launching public campaigns that acknowledged some of the issues facing the kingdom, including urban and rural poverty, the high mortality rate on Saudi roads and the troubling incidence of drug abuse.

He has a reputation for being principled and uncorrupt. He ended the Al Saud family's free use of the national airline, Saudia, and its exemption from paying electricity and water bills. King Abdullah's style is direct to the point of bluntness, but he's warmly regarded by people who know him. A stammer has been largely overcome and, like all senior Al Saud, King Abdullah understands English, though he prefers to speak only in Arabic. His mother's only son, he has built close connections with the Al Faisal, sons of the late king, and younger princes who previously felt excluded from the inner circles of Saudi power.

The municipal elections held in early 2005, the first national ballot in modern times, were the most important achievement of his period as crown prince. He has also held four unprecedented meetings in what was called the National Dialogue that involved conservative clergymen and members of the Shiite minority.

In January 2004, King Abdullah met reformers who presented demands for wider political discourse, an independent judiciary and constitutional limits to government powers. "Your demands are my project," he told them. Encouraged, they pressed ahead with their campaign. In March 2004, 13 reformers were arrested, including some who'd met the crown prince. The final four were eventually pardoned and they were released from prison at King Abdullah's direction on August 8, 2005.

King Abdullah has enjoyed a honeymoon as Saudi Arabia's undisputed leader. He ordered at the end of August 2005 a 15 per cent increase in public salaries, the first across-the-board pay rise in more than two decades. He has banned Saudi visitors from kissing his hand. The king has introduced new blood at the top of the system of government. Prince Bandar, a modernizer who was previously Saudi ambassador to the US, has been appointed secretary-general of the Saudi National Security Council (SNSC), a new body modelled on the US National Security Council. Saudi foreign policy has become more robust. King Abdullah brokered a deal between Hamas and Fatah Palestinian factions in February 2007. In March, he hosted an Arab summit in Riyadh and described US troops in Iraq as "illegitimate occupiers".

King Abdullah was interviewed for US television by Barbara Walters and came across as tolerant and reasonable, even suggesting equal rights for women may come in due course. Insiders recognize he is treading a fine line. "Someone was arrested for publishing a letter criticizing Ghazi Algosaibi (Saudi Arabia's reforming labour minister)," a Saudi Arabian official with ministerial rank said in Riyadh in March 2006. "When liberals complain change is too slow and conservatives say it is too fast, the government has it about right."

King Abdullah is extraordinarily robust for a man of his years, but is over 80. His brother Prince Sultan, the second of the Sudairi Seven and now crown prince and heir to the throne, is no more than two years younger. Perhaps next in line is Prince Naif, Saudi Arabia's interior minister and the fourth of the Sudairi Seven. Salman is the sixth of the Sudairis. The three other Sudairis are Abdulrahman, Turki and Ahmed. They are all influential.

King Abdelaziz, founder of the kingdom, had an estimated 45 sons. Most are still living and healthy. Many hold important government posts. Those that don't are wealthy and influential. The youngest, Hamud, is not yet 60.

The succession is defined yet still vague. The kingdom's 1992 basic law, a form of written constitution, states the king should be selected from the sons and grandsons of King Abdelaziz. That means dozens of Saudi royals are potential contenders for the throne.

There's no lack of talent in the Al Saud. The sons of King Faisal include the foreign minister, Prince Saud, born in 1940 and son of his father's esteemed and philanthropic wife Iffat. His full-brother Turki, born in 1945, who from 1978 until 2002 was director general of Saudi intelligence, studied at Georgetown University in Washington DC where he was a contemporary of Bill Clinton. Prince Turki's elder half-brother Khaled, an Oxford University graduate, was governor of the Asir. An artist and intellectual, he has established a bond of shared interests with Prince Charles, the Prince of Wales, and is president of the Riyadh-based Arab Thought Foundation. Mohammed Al Faisal is one of the fathers of the Islamic banking movement. The Al Faisal family runs the King Faisal Foundation, a philanthropic body that's financed by the late king's estate and based in Riyadh's King Faisal Centre.

Among the sons of Prince Sultan are Prince Bandar and Prince Khaled, deputy defence minister and commander of joint forces during the war for Kuwait in 1990/91. Khaled trained at the Royal Military Academy, Sandhurst and at the US Army Command General Staff College, the Naval Postgraduate School, and the Air War College and spent more than a decade in private business before returning to government earlier in the decade.

Prince Naif's sons include Prince Mohammed bin Naif, deputy interior minister, who has the day-to-day responsibility for the domestic counter-terrorism campaign. His brother Saud built the SNAS/DHL business, the largest courier company operating in the kingdom, before becoming deputy governor of the Eastern Province in the 1990s. In 2003, he was appointed Saudi Arabia's ambassador to Spain.

Prince Salman's sons include Prince Sultan, head of the Supreme Commission for Tourism, who made his name in 1985 when he was a member of the crew of the space shuttle *Discovery*. Prince Faisal is chairman of Saudi Research & Marketing Company, the Jeddah-based media company that publishes the London daily *Asharq al-Awsat*, the English daily *Arab News* and the Jeddah business daily *Al Eqtisadiah*.

The richest of the grandchildren is Prince Alwaleed bin Talal, born in 1955, who is chairman of Kingdom Holding. His personal wealth is estimated at more than US$20 billion and his investments include major stakes in international service company brands. Alwaleed is the son of Prince Talal bin Abdelaziz, who in the late 1950s was considered to be a potential future king. His mother Mona is the daughter of independent Lebanon's first prime minister, Riad Al Soulh. Extraordinarily driven and energetic, Prince Alwaleed endeavours to straddle the divide within the region between old and new Arabia, the Gulf and the Lebanon, and between the Middle East and the US, where he's an investor through his shares in News Corporation in Fox Broadcasting Company, one of President Bush's firmest media supporters.

There are many other Saudi princes with experience, skills and a following. The implication is that Saudi Arabia is heading for a period when there'll be a rapid succession of elderly men and increasing jockeying for position among their sons and grandsons. Around them is an extended family that numbers in total more than 5,000 males. A common conclusion is that the kingdom is heading for a period of uncertainty that could become hazardous.

## Elections in Saudi Arabia

History suggests, however, that what keeps the kingdom going is stronger than what might make it stop. But the Saudi system will need to adapt to the new world of the New Gulf of instant communications, where the individual, not the group or tribe, is master.

Some answers about the kingdom's future came in the 10 weeks between February and April, 2005, in elections for 890 seats on Saudi Arabia's 178 municipal councils. Elected Saudi Arabian municipal councils have existed since the early 1950s, and in some places before that. In 2005, voting was for half of the 10 members that sit on each council. The other half was appointed.

By Western standards, the initiative was modest. Municipalities govern the way the cities and towns of the kingdom are managed, kept clean and provided with water and sewerage. High policy is not yet open to public debate. No political parties were allowed, but Islamists presented themselves as the Golden List. They used grassroots campaigning, e-mail and endorsements from religious leaders to win most seats. The only place that Islamists did not sweep the board was the province of Qassim, the heartlands of religious conservatism. The elections raised hopes among the kingdom's Shiites, estimated to account for 15 per cent of the total Saudi population. About 40 per cent of eligible voters in Qatif, the largest Shiite town, registered to vote, twice the percentage in Riyadh. About 150 candidates, including veteran civil-rights campaigners, competed for seats on Qatif's council. Despite their limited scope, the elections were widely welcomed.

The winners appear to be practical men who intend to focus on local issues. The defeated candidates are realistic about the limits to the pace of political change. Said one: "I think the government was happy with the result for three reasons: the elections were something to show the Americans. Secondly, it slapped the wrists of the most radical liberals. Thirdly, it is involving the religious people without giving them much power." Modernizers hope women will have a vote the next time.

Municipal elections are cited as evidence that the kingdom will introduce direct elections of the Majlis al-Shoura (Consultative Council), an appointed parliamentary body that acts as loyal adviser to the Saudi government. The third, four-year *majlis* was formed in May 2005 and its membership increased to 150 from 120. Mainly comprising technical experts and credible public figures, the *majlis*, which was first formed in 1993, is robust and lively. Ministers, when they present themselves before it, are subjected to rigorous questioning.

Direct elections are still a distant prospect but not an impossible dream. The successful municipal elections added buoyancy to the feel-good atmosphere sweeping the kingdom. Most Saudis are ambivalent about America's war against terror and suspect it is a cloak for self-serving actions in the region. But they back the authorities' campaign against the Jihadists and are pleased to see the end of violent extremists.

King Abdullah, seen as a sincere man of integrity with a common touch, is popular. Government steps to modernize the country are quickening. Even small steps, such as permitting singing on Saudi terrestrial television, are interpreted as evidence of welcome progress. But above all, it is the economy. In early 2008, Saudi oil production averaged more than 9 million b/d, near its maximum sustainable production. Oil prices were in excess of US$100 a barrel, in the longest price boom in oil history.

The government is solvent and spending on vital public services. Saudi businesses are profitable and liquid. Many Saudi households are better off than ever. The new wealth has converted the Saudi government in less than a decade from being one of the most indebted in the world to one of the most affluent.

The Saudi share market, now the world's largest emerging stock exchange, rose by more than 120 per cent from the start of 2004 until it experienced a sharp reverse from February–May 2006. Up to 500,000 have been financially damaged. As this book was being written, the economic and social implications of the share slump were top of King Abdullah's agenda. But the verdict by the summer of 2007 was that the damage was limited and containable. This was a bump in the road for the Saudi economy, not its end.

### The making of Saudi Arabia
"Come and fight us, you pagans, you beard-shavers, who glorify in libertinism and sodomy, you drunkards who have forgotten prayers, you usurers and murderers who permit yourselves forbidden deeds." This eloquent abuse was shouted by Saudi fighters in December 1811 at an Egyptian army sent to conquer central Arabia, restore order and tear out by the roots a religious movement that threatened the status quo.

The Egyptians had modern weapons and Western advisers. They were better fed and equipped than the Bedouin irregulars they encountered on their march from Jeddah into inner Arabia. They were confident in the inferiority of their opponents, in a swift victory and an early return home. Their arrogance was misplaced. Marching through a parched landscape where the wells were blocked or fouled, their morale collapsed as heat and thirst took its toll. The Saudi army attacked, the Egyptians broke and the invaders hurriedly retreated to the Red Sea coast.

Saudi Arabia has since changed unrecognizably. Most of its 24 million population live in towns and cities. The majority can read. Life expectancy is more than 70. Millions passably speak at least one foreign language. More than one million Saudi Arabians have been to university and there are more women in higher education than men. Yet every modern Saudi Arabian would recognize the insults hurled at the Egyptians almost 200 years ago.

The people of Saudi Arabia remain in many respects what they were before the world came knocking. And, because of its refusal to give up tradition and established beliefs, the kingdom is probably the most misunderstood country on earth. Some foreigners dislike it. Others are fearful. There are many perspectives on Saudi Arabia and few accepted truths. But as the 21st century unfolds, the kingdom's significance is ascending. It will be critical for at least a quarter century to the world economy and its influence as a moderating influence in the Islamic World has never been so necessary. But rising affluence and influence is accompanied by a growing number of challenges. To address them, Saudi Arabia is seeking help from a wider range of partners.

The kingdom's most powerful friend for more than 60 years has been the US. But it is a relationship that is constantly under scrutiny. Saudi Arabia is a country where power resides in the hands of the sons and grandsons of the kingdom's astonishing founder, King Abdelaziz. It has a system of consultation among its people based on Islamic principles and the traditions of the tribal Bedouin. People's rights are protected, the government listens and the system works. The Sharia is supreme. There is a basic law, but no constitution.

Practically everything about the Saudi system of government and law conflicts with what every American considers to be normal. Relations between Riyadh and Washington bridge a chasm in religious beliefs. In the kingdom, the officially recognized branch of Islam is its most conservative form. The kingdom's Shiite majority face disadvantages. Most Saudi Arabians respect the beliefs of others, including non-Muslims. But the centre of Saudi Arabia's intellectual gravity is some distance from liberalism. Saudi Arabian religious leaders assert that nothing should be allowed to prevent humanity from contemplating God and his works. This affects the character of Saudi cities since it limits the depiction of the human form, many leisure activities, singing and music, films (there are no cinemas open to the public in the kingdom) and dancing. This is not to mention the conventional Muslim proscription on consuming alcohol and eating pork.

*Call to prayer: the faithful head towards a Dubai mosque for* Isha *(evening prayer). Islam remains at the centre of life across Arabia.*

DAVID STEELE

*In the Empty Quarter: dunes in the world's greatest sand desert rise to 500 m. The area of south-east Arabia it occupies was once a lake.*

*The Hajar Mountains: running for almost 350 km, the Hajar Mountains in eastern Arabia rise to more than 2,000 m in Oman's Jebel Akhdar.*

*Sunset over the Gulf: shallow and saline, the Gulf is perfect for oysters, which supplied the region's pearling industry for centuries.*

*New Jeddah: ancient Red Sea gateway to the Muslim holy cities of Mecca and Medina, Jeddah is also Saudi Arabia's principal sea port.*

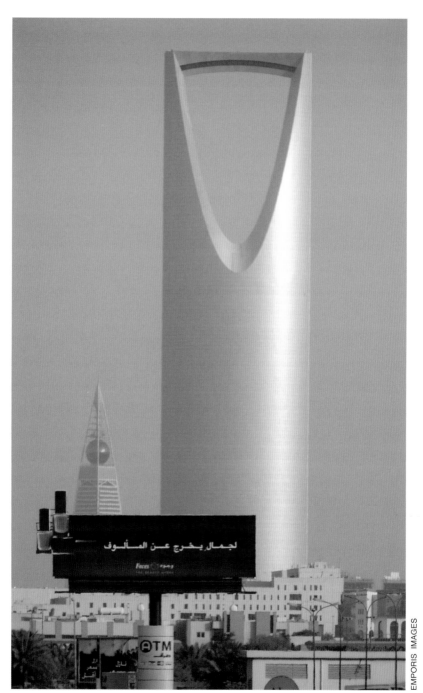

*Twin towers: Prince Al Waleed Bin Talal's Kingdom Centre and the Faisaliah Tower in the background are Riyadh's tallest skyscrapers.*

*Liberation Tower: built to celebrate the end of the Iraqi occupation, Kuwait City's most striking landmark symbolises Kuwait's hopes for the future.*

*Kuwait at night: the first GCC state to become fully independent, Kuwait was the original template for the New Gulf.*

From the orthodox Saudi perspective, individual freedom of choice is balanced by heavy obligations. God's rules have been written down in the Koran, the Sunna and authentic Hadith. Some things are simply haram or forbidden. Nothing, including reason, can make them acceptable. It is the job of a righteous ruler working through a Muslim government to ensure that God's rules are firmly applied.

Few Americans understand Saudi Arabia's record on women's rights. According to conservative interpretations of the Koran, the Sunna of the Prophet (PBUH) and the Hadith, women have been put on earth to provide company for men, supply and raise children and live virtuous lives to the glory of God. Men are susceptible to sexual desire. To minimize temptation, women should be kept apart from men who are not their husbands or family.

For the same reason, when women appear in public, all their 'private' parts, which include hair, arms, legs, lips and even eyes, should be concealed. It is a sign of modesty, good for society and in line with God's instructions.

The practical impact is that Saudi women are barred from most types of work since it inevitably leads to gender mixing. Driving is probably, though not definitely, acceptable. The problem is that it could lead to women having contact with men who are not their husbands or family and this could promote sin.

Defenders of the Saudi way say that this does not amount to discrimination. They argue women are freer than in Western society. They are protected from sexual harassment and allowed within the family to lead complete and fulfilling lives. They can work in appropriate jobs. And women in Islam are allowed to own their own property, like Khadija, the wealthy widow who was Mohammed's (PBUH) first and most influential wife. The reality, however, is that some Saudi men believe women should know their place and keep it.

In Saudi Arabia, capital punishment is applied with a rigour few other countries now find acceptable. Murder, sexual misconduct, drug dealing and apostasy, or the renunciation of the Islamic faith, if proven in court, can in principle lead to a death sentence. Decapitation in Saudi Arabia, a penalty solely for men, is carried out in public. The number of executions in the kingdom has recently been on the decline. But they are still comparatively frequent.

So why does the West find it hard to like Saudi Arabia? In summary, Saudi Arabia is a conservative Islamic country where political power is inherited within a single family, that allows women a limited role in public life, where no one can vote for or against the government and criticizing the regime publicly can get you into trouble and people have their heads chopped off for offences that in the West do not even lead to imprisonment.

And yet there are other facets. It's a land of extraordinary natural variety, including towering mountains and golden desert. Thousands of Westerners and millions from every part of the world contentedly live and work in the kingdom, raise families, save money and leave with happy memories of Saudi friends and a warm society.

Saudi people are good-humoured, kind and hospitable. The kingdom is run by a government of men with open minds and high achievements. Saudi Arabia has more women with university degrees than men. And it has, per capita of the population, the largest and most sophisticated business, professional and intellectual class outside the Organization for Economic Cooperation and Development (OECD). Among the kingdom's many secrets, these are some of the best kept.

## The rise of the Al Saud

Before tarmac roads and the passenger jet, central Arabia was difficult to reach, almost impossible to rule and largely economically valueless. Nomadic groups subsisted in oasis settlements in a sea of desert. But evidence is emerging of ancient civilizations before Arabia became arid.

Near Jawf in the kingdom's far north is Dumat al-Jandal (Duma of the Stone), named after its first settler, Duma, son of Ismail and grandson of Abraham. Flints shaped by humans have been found in the area that could be tens of thousands of years old. About 6,000 years ago, the people of Jawf erected groups of squared-off pillars up to three metres in height. At the time of the Assyrian Empire, the town was one of northern Arabia's most important trading centres. The Nabataeans incorporated it into their domain. The first Muslim campaign against the Byzantines passed through the town. The second caliph, Omar, is believed to have visited it on his historic journey from Medina to Jerusalem and ordered the construction of its first mosque.

In Dumat al-Jandal in February 658, the Prophet's (PBUH) son-in-law and the fourth caliph, Ali, the first Shiite imam, met his rival Muawiya in what is known as The Arbitration. This was a vain attempt to settle differences between the two men. Three years later, Ali was assassinated and Muawiya became the fifth caliph.

Set in Wadi Sirhan that descends towards the Tigris and Euphrates basin from the Hejaz, Jawf was a natural route for travellers. In the 9th century, Zubayda bint Jafar, wife of the Abbasid ruler, Harun Al Rashid, financed the construction of a road between Baghdad and Mecca that passed through Jawf province but avoided Dumat al-Jandal. The town then disappeared from history until the 19th century when it became the preferred entry point into Arabia for foreign travellers, including Ulrich Jasper Seetzen, Charles Doughty and Lady Anne Blunt.

The coastal plain to the west of the Hejaz and the desert hinterland to its east were highways for caravan trade between the ports and frankincense lands of south Arabia and Egypt, Persia, Greece and Rome. On the low coast of east Arabia, humanity began to settle about 7,500 years ago. By the time of Sumer, more than 5,000 years ago, small towns had developed and the area was named Dilmun. About 50,000 tumuli dating from this era have been counted around Dhahran. Others have been found inland. Discoveries dating from the early Sumerian period have been made on Tarut Island and in Al Hasa.

With the coming of Islam, Arabia was unified under a single ruler for the first time. But divisions soon followed. The Muslim capital was moved from Arabia to Damascus, Baghdad and then Cairo. Central Arabia was subsequently dominated by petty rulers who were technically subservient to the distant caliphs but in effect were totally autonomous.

The Hejaz continued to be attractive to Muslim rulers and was governed in succession by the Abbasids of Baghdad, the Fatimids of Cairo, the Seljuks and the Ayyubids and Mamluks of Egypt. In 1517, the Ottoman Turks captured Cairo and claimed the Hejaz. They were to hold it until 1918. The Ottomans were recognized as sovereigns in 1550 by the rulers of Al Hasa, east Arabia's only significant settlement. They were driven out in 1670 and did not return until 1871.

The Najd, which is Arabic for the high land, is an area occupying more than 130,000 km² of high plateau in central Arabia. With the coming of the desert climate, life contracted to the oases and springs found in wadis that run from west to east into the Dahna sands. Protected by desert on all sides, the people of the Najd were secure from outside intruders. Its settlements were ruled by independent emirs.

The Najd town of Diriyah was typical of the area. It had farmers, merchants, skilled craftsmen, religious leaders (or ulema) and slaves. One estimate is that there were no more than 70 households by the middle of the 18th century. Diriyah had fallen under the control of the Al Saud family, an offshoot of the Anaizah confederation who claim descent from Adnan, one of two parent lines from which all Arabian Bedouin are said to originate. The Al Saud had long given up nomadic life and founded Diriyah when they settled.

According to legend, the original founder of the house of Saud was Mani Al Muraidi, a sheikh from the Duru tribe of southern Arabia who were celebrated for breeding riding camels known as *Daraiya* or *Diriyah*. Mani took his family to central Arabia sometime in the 16th century and named Diriyah after his livestock.

One of Mani's descendants was called Saud. He has bequeathed his name to his descendants and, since 1932, to an entire country. The Al Saud are of pure Arab stock and were connected to the region before recorded time. This fact endows legitimacy to their continuing supremacy and helps to explain why no one for more than 70 years has seriously suggested another clan has greater right to rule than they.

The emir of Diriyah from 1726 was Mohammed bin Saud, a land-owner and trader who financed merchant expeditions across Arabia. He raised taxes to finance a small military force. Mohammed bin Saud formed a partnership with Mohammed Abdul Wahhab, who was born in Uyaynah in the Najd. His father was a judge and his family belonged to the Bani Tameem, another sedentary Bedouin tribe. Abdul Wahhab is said to have travelled to Medina, Basra and Al Hasa to pursue religious studies. In his journeys, Abdul Wahhab conformed to the conservative Hanbali school of Islam.

He returned to Uyaynah and urged the town to return to pure Islam, reject barriers between man and God, such as shrines and hymns, and rigidly apply the principle of zakat, or charitable giving. He was particularly firm about the need for communal prayer and declared it was the obligation of all Muslims to wage holy war (jihad) against those who did not follow these principles. His followers called themselves Muwahhidun (Unitarians) because they believed in the absolute oneness of God. The Muwahhidun have been named Wahhabis after Abdul Wahhab. It is a term that they themselves reject.

After initially endorsing Abdul Wahhab's reforms, the emir of Uyaynah turned against him. He was expelled and travelled 64 km to Diriyah where he was granted protection. There is rare precision about when Mohammed bin Saud and Mohammed bin Abdul Wahhab forged their missionary alliance. In 1744, they swore an oath in which they pledged to campaign for a state run on Islamic principles. Abdul Wahhab, then aged 42, is reported to have said: "I want you to grant me an oath that you will perform jihad against the unbelievers. In return, you will be imam, leader of the Muslim community and I will be leader in religious matters."

Mohammed bin Saud began by suppressing unacceptable, mainly Shiite, practices. His message gained adherents. In the following years, Saudi power was extended by armies comprising volunteers from the towns and Bedouin tribesmen. By Mohammed bin Saud's death in 1765, central Arabia was under Saudi control.

His successor, Abdelaziz, extended the Al Saud realm to the Red Sea, the Gulf and the Indian Ocean. Al Hasa fell in 1780. Qatar accepted Saudi authority in 1797. Bahrain followed soon after. Al Saud power was projected along the Gulf coast to Ra's al-Khaimah and into the Buraimi Oasis and the foothills of the Hajar Mountains. In 1801, they attacked and sacked Karbala, a Euphrates town less than 160 km from Baghdad. Wahhabi raids into Mesopotamia continued until 1812. Taif, the mountain town that overlooks Mecca, was taken in 1802 amid much bloodshed. In 1803, Mecca fell and Medina was captured the following year. Shrines and grave markers were destroyed.

The Saudi campaign into Yemen foundered. But practically everywhere else in Arabia, local rulers submitted. The Wahhabis began to attract international attention. The British, then the rising foreign power in the Gulf, heard that tribes were fleeing to the coast.

The capture of the Holy Cities was a challenge the Ottoman sultan, Mahmud II, could not ignore. He delegated the recapture of the Hejaz to Mohammed Ali, Ottoman viceroy in Cairo and effective ruler of Egypt. Abdelaziz, Mohammed bin Saud's successor, had died before the Saudi capture of Mecca in 1803. His son, Saud, was struggling with family divisions, attacks in the east by the ruler of Muscat supported by Britain and drought in the interior.

Mohammed Ali appointed his 17-year-old second son Tusun to lead the expedition. He landed in Yanbu in 1811. His first taste of battle was the defeat at the Battle of Safra, half way between Yanbu and Medina. The Egyptians captured Jeddah, Mecca and Medina and secured control of the Hejaz. By 1814, the Saudis had also been expelled from Bahrain, the interior of what is now Oman and part of the Tihama, the coastal region extending from the Hejaz into Yemen.

Saud died in 1814 and was succeeded by his son, Abdullah bin Saud. Tusun launched a new campaign and took more land. In 1816, Mohammed Ali replaced him with his eldest son Ibrahim. By the spring of 1818, Ibrahim had surrounded the Saudi capital with a force of more than 8,000 men. After a heavy bombardment, the Saudis surrendered on September 11, 1818. The invaders plundered the town. The remaining Saudi leaders, including Abdullah, were taken to Cairo.

The Egyptian army destroyed settlements, killed and captured livestock, cut down palms in the Najd and then withdrew to the west. Abdullah was sent to Constantinople where he was beheaded in front of the Hagia Sofia. After three days on display, his head under his arm, Abdullah's body was thrown into the sea. The first Saudi empire was over. But the message of Abdul Wahhab could not be extinguished.

Missionaries won over north Indian Muslim princes. In 1824, jihad was declared against infidels. The Sikhs were defeated in the Punjab. Peshawar was seized in 1830 and became the capital of a Wahhabi state. Wahhabi Indians played a role in the rebellion against British rule from 1857–59. The message was taken to Sumatra in what is now Indonesia and led to a rebellion against Dutch rule that lasted for 15 years until the middle of the 1830s. Throughout the Islamic World, the movement won adherents and challenged the status quo.

Some Al Saud family members had avoided the annihilation of 1818. Turki bin Abdullah, son of the Saudi leader beheaded in Constantinople, escaped, built an army and recaptured Diriyah in 1821. He recovered Saudi domains in the centre of Arabia but abandoned the ruined former capital. In 1824, he set up base in Riyadh, an oasis town a few miles to the south. Al Hasa was recovered and Saudi dominance restored in Bahrain by 1830. Control over part of the Buraimi Oasis was established soon after.

Turki was assassinated by a cousin in 1834. Nine years of internecine conflict followed in which four members of the Al Saud family held power. The chaos was compounded by the final Egyptian attempt to impose control on the region. An army under Ismail Bey, Mohammed Ali's grandson, entered Riyadh in May 1837. Faisal, then emir of the Al Saud, was taken prisoner. Riyadh and the Najd were ruled by Khurshid Bey, Mohammed Ali's regional vice-regent until Egypt's final withdrawal in 1840.

Faisal returned from Egypt in 1843. After winning a struggle with a family rival, he became the undisputed Al Saud leader. Faisal restored Saudi dominion across Arabia. Bahrain was brought to heel and Qatar was occupied by 1850. Muscat, Sohar and the Buraimi Oasis agreed to pay tribute. This time, no attempt was made to capture the Hejaz. Faisal died in December 1865. His sons battled for supremacy. Abdullah succeeded but was challenged by his half-brothers Saud, Mohammed and Abdulrahman.

Abdullah was deposed by Saud in 1871. When he died four years later, Abdulrahman became Al Saud leader but was quickly challenged by Abdullah. In the power struggle that ensued, Abdullah sought help from Mohammed Al Rashid, ruler of Hail. In the end, all the Al Saud lost. Abdulrahman was defeated at the Battle of Mulayda in central Najd in 1891. He settled in Kuwait two years later under the protection of the Al Sabah family. Mohammed Al Rashid became master of central Arabia. Power shifted to the Al Rashid capital in Hail. When Mohammed Al Rashid died, leadership passed to his son Abdelaziz, then aged 30.

### Abdelaziz rebuilds the Al Saud domain

Abdelaziz bin Mohammed's namesake and strong rival, Abdelaziz bin Abdulrahman bin Faisal Al Saud (later King Abdelaziz) entered the world as the sun was setting on the second Saudi empire. His mother Sarah was the daughter of Ahmed Al Sudairi, a member of a Najdi family closely connected with the Al Saud. He spent his teenage years living in the tents of the Murrah, the Al Saud's most loyal Bedouin allies, and in the home provided by the Al Sabah in Kuwait.

Dazzlingly handsome and taller by a head than most of his contemporaries, Abdelaziz nursed the Al Saud dream of recovering their lands. At the end of 1901, he led 40 followers in a mission to recapture Riyadh, the Saudi capital. They spent months on the northern edges of the Empty Quarter seeking to win over tribes near the Jabrin and Haradh oases. Abdelaziz gathered a further 20 fighters and set off in early January 1902. On January 14, while still more than an hour from

Riyadh, he left a third of his men with the camels and instructed them to return to Kuwait if they heard nothing in the next 24 hours. He advanced on foot with the rest and waited for nightfall. Leaving his brother Mohammed and 33 others as a backup, Abdelaziz and his companions scaled Riyadh's walls.

Their target was the house of Ajlan bin Mohammed, the Al Rashid governor of Riyadh. The house was entered, but Ajlan was not there. He had taken to spending his nights in Riyadh's Masmak Fort. The new plan was to wait for the Masmak gate to be opened and to take Ajlan alive if possible.

With the rise of the sun, the fort's gates opened and Ajlan walked out with 10 bodyguards. Abdelaziz sprang into action. Ajlan's guards fled and left the governor facing the attackers. Abdallah bin Jiluwi, cousin of Abdelaziz, threw a spear at Ajlan and missed. It embedded itself in the fort's gate and its tip remained there until the 1970s. Ajlan lunged at Abdelaziz, who covered his face and shot at the governor with his gun. Wounded, Ajlan dropped his sword and tried to retreat back into the fort. Abdelaziz grabbed his legs while the guards tried to drag Ajlan through the gate by his arms. Abdelaziz relaxed his grip and Ajlan escaped into the fort.

Bin Jiluwi charged after him, followed by 10 other Saudi fighters. The gates were flung open and Abdelaziz and his followers entered. In the fight that followed, the Saudis killed half the 80 defenders. Bin Jiluwi killed Ajlan with his own hands. Abdelaziz seems to have been welcomed by the town's inhabitants. He improved defences and won over neighbouring tribes. He sent for his father Abdulrahman who was still in Kuwait. Riyadh has remained under Al Saud control ever since.

In the next four years, the Al Saud challenged the Al Rashid for supremacy in the Najd. At the Battle of Rawdat Muhanna in 1906, the Al Rashid enjoyed the support of some members of the Al Saud family who disputed Abdelaziz's right to rule. They were decisively defeated and Abdelaziz Al Rashid was killed.

The sheikhs of Hail were weakened but continued to challenge the Al Saud for 14 more years. A rebellion was launched by dissidents in 1910. The same year, Sharif Hussein of Mecca demanded an annual tribute in cash. The Saudi leader's brother Saad was captured. Abdelaziz secured Saad's release by declaring the supremacy of the Ottomans and paying an annual tribute to Sharif Hussein. Abdelaziz repudiated the deal when Saad was released – it was a slight he never forgot.

Perhaps as early as 1912, an evangelical movement known as the Brotherhood, the Ikhwan, emerged. Their first settlement was in Artawiyah, 500 km north of Riyadh. It grew into a town of 10,000 people. The Ikhwan rejected the nomadic life and made a living from farming. Abdelaziz formed a close bond, and ordered, in 1916, all tribes allied to him to join the Ikhwan. He provided them with cash. They accepted him as their imam.

In 1913, Abdelaziz captured Hofuf from the Ottomans who had held the town since 1871. He was recognized as Ottoman governor of the territories he controlled but the Al Saud assert they made no formal pledge of allegiance to the sultan. Soon after the start of the First World War, Britain dispatched Captain Shakespear, its political agent in Kuwait, to secure a treaty modelled on ones already signed with Gulf states.

Captain Shakespear died during the Battle of Jarrab fought between the Al Saud and the Al Rashid in 1915. However, as a result of his work, an Anglo-Saudi treaty was signed on December 26. It provided a British security guarantee plus cash and weapons. In return, Abdelaziz promised to avoid dealings with foreign powers and refrain from attacks on Kuwait, Bahrain, Qatar, the emirs of Trucial Oman and the Omani coast.

Sharif Hussein, appointed emir of Mecca and Custodian of the Holy Places by the Ottomans in 1908, rebelled against Constantinople on June 5, 1916 and became a British ally. When the First World War ended in November 1918, he was disappointed that his ambition to become head of a large, independent Arab state was not supported by London or Paris. The Sharif also began to clash with the Al Saud. In May 1919, a Sharifian force of 5,000 men, led by his son Abdullah, was destroyed by the Ikhwan at Turaba, east of Taif. King Hussein had himself declared Sunni caliph in March 1924 following Kemal Ataturk's decision to abolish the Ottoman caliphate. The news alienated the Islamic World and incited Abdelaziz to strike the fatal blow. His call for a jihad against King Hussein was supported by the Ikhwan.

In September 1924, Abdelaziz captured Taif. The notables of the Hejaz forced King Hussein to abdicate in favour of his eldest son Ali. He was dispatched to Jeddah and from there to Aqaba and finally to Cyprus where he died in 1931. In mid-October, the Ikhwan took Mecca. Abdelaziz entered the city for the first time in December at the invitation of its citizens.

In January 1925, the Ikhwan appeared before Jeddah. The city surrendered after an 11-month siege on December 22, a month after the fall of Medina. King Ali left the Hejaz, eventually to live out his life in Amman. Abdelaziz was declared king of the Hejaz and sultan of the Najd and its dependencies. But there was unfinished business in the north and the south.

In the north, an attempt by the Kuwaitis to extend their territory had been rebuffed in 1920. In the south, the Asir was ruled by Sayyid Mohammed bin Ali, who was known as Al Idrisi. He was the heir to a dynasty that could trace his origins to Moroccan Arabs who had come to Mecca on pilgrimage in the 18th century and established themselves rulers of the region. Al Idrisi declared independence from the Ottomans in 1906 but had been defeated. During the First World War, he was supported by Italy and Britain and received an allowance to rebel against Imam Yahya of Yemen, an ally of the Ottomans. An enemy of Sharif Hussein, Al Idrisi also fell foul of the Al Saud. Abdelaziz took Abha, capital of the Asir, in 1922.

The Ikhwan defeated the last Al Rashid forces the following year. Hail was surrounded, the Al Rashid surrendered and its surviving members were taken to Riyadh. Abdelaziz married an Al Rashid widow. The single product of that union is King Abdullah.

The northern campaign brought the Saudis into contact with British mandates in Transjordan and Iraq. At the September 1922 Uqair Conference, Abdelaziz and representatives of Iraq's King Faisal I, under the supervision of Britain's high commissioner to Baghdad, Sir Percy Cox, agreed on a border that survives to this day. The frontier was drawn with a red pencil by Cox himself. It transferred to the Saudis territory claimed by Kuwait and to Iraq a portion of domains claimed by Abdelaziz. To meet the needs of Bedouin tribes who crossed over what was now an international boundary, Cox delineated two neutral enclaves, one in a diamond shape between Iraq and the lands of the Al Saud and the second with Kuwait.

Once the rule of Abdelaziz extended beyond the Najd heartlands, compromises became inevitable. His concessions conflicted with the Ikhwan's desire to purge Arabia of unbelief. During the Hajj of 1926, they attacked the pilgrim caravan from Cairo. Ikhwan raids across the northern border continued. One came within 16 km of Amman. They risked confrontation with Britain.

At an Ikhwan conference in January 1927, the ulema heard their grievances about the first telegraph lines and inaction against Shiites and tribes from Iraq and Transjordan who were grazing on Saudi land. The ulema ruled that only the imam, who was Abdelaziz, could declare jihad, but this failed to prevent an attack on a police post built inside the Iraqi border in September.

At a Bedouin congress in Riyadh in November 1928, Abdelaziz used the threat of abdication to secure support for a campaign against Ikhwan rebels led by Faisal Al Duwish. Abdelaziz defeated the rebels at Zilfi on March 20, 1929. Al Duwish fled to Kuwait in January 1930 and surrendered to the British. He was eventually handed over to Abdelaziz on the condition of clemency. Abdelaziz imprisoned Al Duwish and the Ikhwan leaders for the rest of their lives.

Abdelaziz turned his attention once more to the south. Al Idrisi had died in 1923. Three years later, his successor recognized King Abdelaziz as protector of his domains. The Asir was annexed in 1930. Imam

Yahya of Yemen, seeking to expand his territories, backed a rebellion against the kingdom in 1933 but was defeated by the Saudis in a campaign lasting from March to May. Imam Yahya invited Abdelaziz to define a new frontier with the kingdom.

The Taif Treaty of May 13, 1934 provided a generous settlement, handing back almost half the territories the Saudis had seized. The campaigns in the south-west delivered a rich prize. The capital of the Asir is the city of Abha, once a strategic point in the spice route. The province is the Alps of Arabia. Mount Soodah, the kingdom's highest peak, rises some 3,000 m. Less than an hour's drive down the east flank of the mountains takes you to Khamis Mushait, Asir's second city. Three hours from Abha lies Najran, which sits on the frontier of the Empty Quarter. The city was the site of a Christian bishopric at the time of the Islamic revelation. One of its bishops, Quss bin Saida, composed prayers and orations that earned him the title of the Cicero of the Arabs.

An Abyssinian army launched an attack on Mecca from Najran, using elephants, in 570. Their route through the Asir is known as Darb al-Fil, the route of the elephant. The Asir is famous for the friendliness of its people, good-quality coffee and the glories of its honey. The Yemen campaign defined the territory of Saudi Arabia as we know it today. There were to be no more wars of conquest. On September 18, 1932, Abdelaziz, then aged 52, was declared king of the unified kingdom of Saudi Arabia. The date is Saudi Arabia's national day.

### Americans make the greatest oil discovery

Charles R Crane, a Chicago sanitaryware millionaire, had been appointed by US President Wilson to an advisory commission on the Levant with Henry King, president of Oberlin College in Ohio. He co-authored the 1919 King-Crane Commission report that warned of the consequences of allowing unlimited Jewish immigration into Palestine. Crane maintained his interest in the Arab World. He financed water exploration and roads in Yemen during 1927–28 and commissioned a new translation of the Koran into English. Crane's work had come to Abdelaziz's attention.

A meeting was organized in February 1931 by Harry St John Philby. Crane offered a geologist to look for minerals and water. The man selected was Karl S Twitchell, an engineer who'd worked on Crane's Yemen projects. Twitchell arrived in Jeddah in 1931 and travelled across the Hejaz looking for water (there was none) and gold (there was not much). Abdelaziz summoned Twitchell to Riyadh to discuss the possibility of finding oil in east Arabia. The American suggested Abdelaziz wait until there were results from Socal's Bahrain concession where exploration had begun earlier that year.

Over lunch in London in May 1932, Francis Loomis, a Socal consultant, asked Philby whether there was any chance of an oil concession from Abdelaziz. He was told that Riyadh would welcome an approach. Philby agreed to act for Socal but had also offered his services to APOC. The Americans hired Twitchell and sent him with Lloyd N Hamilton, a lawyer, to open talks.

They assembled in Jeddah in February 1933. Negotiations lasted three months. The Saudis were represented by Abdullah Al Sulaiman, the Saudi finance minister; APOC was represented by Stephen Longrigg, who refused to meet the kingdom's demands. On May 29, 1933, the concession was signed in Jeddah's Kazma Palace by Al Sulaiman and Socal. It gave the Americans the right to explore in an area four times the size of the UK. For this, Socal provided an immediate loan of £30,000 sterling in gold with a further credit instalment of £20,000 sterling 18 months later. The annual rental was fixed at £5,000 sterling in gold. A secret addition to the agreement gave Socal preferential rights to the Najd and the neutral zone for a £100,000 sterling loan if oil was found in commercial quantities.

In September 1933, Socal geologists landed in Jubail, 100 km north of Dammam, and travelled south to a hill they'd previously glimpsed from Bahrain that resembled Jebel Dukhan, site of the 1932 Bahrain oil strike. The first Dammam well was started on April 30, 1935. On December 7, 1936, Dammam Well Number 7 was sunk on Jebel Dhahran. It struck oil on March 4, 1938. The presence of oil in commercial quantities was declared in October 1938. The following spring, King Abdelaziz, with a retinue of 2,000 people in 500 cars, travelled to the oil camp at Well 7 that had been named Dhahran. A 69 km pipeline to the port of Ra's Tanura had already been completed. On May 1, King Abdelaziz turned the valve that released oil into a pipeline to Ra's Tanura, where a tanker was loaded.

The Second World War placed Arabia near the front line of a global conflict between distant powers. Dhahran was mistakenly bombed in October 1940 by Italian flyers dispatched from the Horn of Africa, at that point still in Italian hands, to destroy Bahrain oil facilities. With America's entry into the war in December 1941 and the start of the Pacific war, the Gulf acquired new strategic importance. The Americans opened their first Saudi mission in the spring of 1942. President Roosevelt in 1943 approved lend-lease funds for the kingdom. Prince Faisal travelled to Washington in September that year, accompanied by Prince Khaled, also a future king. A refinery was built in Ra's Tanura by Bechtel, a San Francisco firm introduced to the kingdom by Socal.

Anticipating the end of the war, Roosevelt; UK prime minister, Winston Churchill; and Soviet leader, Stalin, met in Yalta in the Crimea to agree on plans for post-war Europe. Roosevelt departed from his original return itinerary for a meeting with King Abdelaziz on board a US warship in the Great Bitter Lake of the Suez Canal. The two leaders talked for five hours. The Saudi Arabians believed Roosevelt promised he would never do anything hostile to the Arabs and that the US would make no change to its Palestine policy without full and prior consultation with both Jews and Arabs. The US failed to live up to both commitments. In March 1945, Saudi Arabia declared war against Germany and Japan, becoming an ally and securing membership of the UN when it was founded three months later. Prince Fahd, Saudi king from 1982–2005, represented Saudi Arabia at the first UN conference in San Francisco later that year.

Three days after the talks with Roosevelt, King Abdelaziz met Winston Churchill at the Grand Hotel du Lac in the Fayoum Oasis, south of Cairo. At dinner, King Abdelaziz noted his religion's prohibition of alcohol and tobacco. Churchill declared that: "If it was the religion of His Majesty to deprive himself of smoking and alcohol, I must point out that my rule of life prescribed as an absolutely sacred rite smoking cigars and also the drinking of alcohol before, after and, if need be, during all meals and in the intervals in between them."

The king returned to Jeddah on a British cruiser, a journey he enjoyed less than being carried to the meeting on a US destroyer. Churchill, apparently embarrassed by the modest gift of perfume he delivered at Fayoum, said that he would present the Saudi king with a Rolls Royce. It did not arrive until 1946. Since its driving wheel was on the right and the king was, by convention, used to sitting in the front seat, this implied he would have to occupy the dishonoured place on the left of the driver. He never used it. The Americans on the other hand sent a twin-engined Douglas DC-3 Dakota airliner with an American crew on free loan for a year. It became the first aircraft of Saudi Arabia's national airline, Saudia.

In the spring of 1953, three new ministries were created. Prince Fahd was appointed as the kingdom's first education minister. Prince Sultan was made minister of agriculture. Prince Talal, then in his early 20s, was made minister of communications. The Ministry of Finance and National Economy was founded under Abdullah Al Sulaiman. Despite these changes, the kingdom was still run inefficiently. The government had come close to insolvency in 1949 and was to be financially embarrassed on several further occasions.

The first Saudi Arabian riyal was minted in silver, but British gold sovereigns, Indian rupees and Egyptian pounds still circulated. In 1950, gold riyals were minted. The Saudi Arabian Monetary Agency (SAMA), which acted as a central bank, was founded in 1952. Paper riyals were printed for the first time in 1953.

Society was changing. Football was legalized in 1951. In 1953, there was a strike in Saudi Aramco about pay and conditions. Problems associated with the growing number of foreigners in the kingdom started to emerge. The trade and consumption of alcohol was banned in 1952 after one of the sons of King Abdelaziz shot and killed British national Cyril Ousman in Jeddah the previous November during an argument.

King Abdelaziz by this time was weak and infirm. Anticipating generational change, a council of ministers was created on October 10, 1953. Crown Prince Saud became Saudi Arabia's effective chief executive. On November 9, King Abdelaziz's health collapsed while he was in Taif and he died in the arms of Prince Faisal. He was 72.

## The reign of King Saud

Crown Prince Saud was proclaimed king at the age of 51. Faisal became crown prince. King Saud's first disadvantage was that he was selected by his father rather than in the Saudi tradition of consensus. He was in poor physical shape. His eyesight was weak and he suffered from fallen arches. His first actions, however, were encouraging.

The Health Ministry was established under Rashad Pharaon, a doctor of Syrian origin who'd ministered to King Abdelaziz. Mohammed Abdullah Alireza, president of the Union of Chambers of Commerce, was made commerce minister. King Saud declared Riyadh as the kingdom's capital and launched a building programme in the city. Riyadh University, now King Khaled University, was opened in 1957. Scholarships were awarded to young Saudis to pursue education overseas. In 1955, King Saud ordered the first expansion of the Great Mosque of Mecca in more than 1,000 years. The project was one of the biggest in Saudi history. One of its heroes was Mohammed bin Laden, a businessman from the Hadhramaut who made his name with the quality of his work on the mosque. Further improvements were completed in 1959.

There were controversial business deals. Aristotle Onassis was given an effective monopoly over Saudi oil exports from the kingdom and Tapline's Mediterranean terminal. Aramco, which was then US owned, disputed the contract with Onassis' firm, the Saudi Arabian Tanker Company, and it was referred to independent arbitration in Paris and Geneva from 1956–58. This ruled in favour of Aramco which wanted to choose its own oil carriers. As a result, the Saudi government refused for decades to accept any contractual clause providing for international arbitration.

King Saud's foreign policy was initially based on a partnership with Egypt. He visited Cairo in the spring of 1954 and met Gamal Abdel Nasser, who'd emerged as the dominant figure in the republican Egyptian government. The new king's enthusiasm for a policy of positive neutrality went so far as to precipitate the expulsion of the US mission in October. The Saudi claim to the Buraimi/Al Ain area was rebutted in October 1955. Saudi Arabia responded by supporting the imam of Nizwa against the sultan of Muscat. The rebellion was quashed in 1959, but Saudi support for the imamate continued until the early 1970s. Abu Dhabi's control over its side of the Buraimi Oasis was only recognized by Saudi Arabia in 1974.

King Saud's ally, President Nasser, became an Arab hero by announcing the nationalization of the Suez Canal in July 1956. When Britain, France and Israel combined against Egypt, Saudi Arabia broke diplomatic relations with London and Paris and announced oil shipments to Britain and France would be banned in the first Arab oil embargo.

Soviet support for Egypt altered Saudi Arabia's attitude. In January 1957, King Saud visited Washington where he was met on arrival by President Eisenhower. The result was a deal in which the kingdom bought advanced American weaponry and adopted the anti-communist Eisenhower doctrine. In April, King Saud agreed to a five-year extension of the rent-free lease of Dhahran air base to the United States Air Force.

The policy shift was underlined in King Saud's state visit, in the spring of 1957, to Baghdad, where old rivalries with the Hashemites were set aside. The process was accelerated by charges that a plot to assassinate King Saud had been masterminded by Egypt. Syria, which had signed accords with the Soviet Union in 1956, agreed to merge with Egypt in the United Arab Republic on February 1, 1958. The Arab World was split between conservative, pro-Western Middle East regimes and radical governments supported by the Eastern Bloc.

Financial difficulties and King Saud's poor health created a domestic crisis. In March 1958, he agreed to hand executive powers to Prince Faisal, who quickly repaired the damage done to relations with Egypt and sought to reach détente with Britain and France.

Prince Faisal's hand was evident in the calm way Saudi Arabia reacted to the deposition of the Iraqi monarchy in July 1958. He stabilized the kingdom's finances and appointed capable younger men to key posts. But King Saud still held ultimate power. After a disagreement about the 1960 budget, Prince Faisal stepped down from government. King Saud appointed a new cabinet that included some of the most progressive members of the Al Saud family. The most dynamic was Prince Talal, the 23rd son of King Abdelaziz, who was then aged 28. Prince Talal presented a plan for a constitution that called for a national assembly and limits on the king's powers.

King Saud ignored it. But Prince Talal was impatient. At a press conference in Beirut in August 1961, he confirmed a national assembly was under consideration and acknowledged he had differences with Prince Faisal. King Saud recalled Prince Talal and demoted him. He turned once more to Prince Faisal who demanded the cabinet's resignation. King Saud refused, but his health was declining.

In November, King Saud collapsed and was sent to the US for medical treatment. Prince Faisal reasserted himself. On the king's return in March 1962, a new cabinet was formed with Prince Faisal taking over as finance minister as well as prime minister. Ahmed Zaki Yamani became minister of petroleum and minerals, replacing Abdullah Tariki who'd helped set up OPEC in 1960.

Prince Talal burnt his bridges with his family by announcing he and his half-brothers, Abdul Mohsen and Nawwaf, had freed their concubines and slaves. His passport was withdrawn in August 1962 while he was still in the Lebanon. His half-brothers Fawwaz and Badr, together with a cousin, Saud bin Fahd, handed in their passports in sympathy. They all settled in Cairo where they were later joined by Prince Abdul Mohsen. They were given the title of the League of Free Princes and used in Egypt's propaganda war with Riyadh.

Restraint between Riyadh and Cairo finally evaporated in September 1962 when the Yemeni monarchy was deposed by army officers with Egyptian support. Saudi Arabia backed Yemeni monarchists in a civil war that lasted until 1970. After Egyptian air raids on Najran and Jizan, Riyadh broke relations with Cairo. King Saud was incapacitated by ill-health and Prince Faisal was effectively in charge. He was mortified when President Kennedy recognized the republican Yemeni regime, but Saudi diplomacy always has an alternative. Relations with the UK, broken since the Suez Crisis, were restored in early 1963. Britain began to sell weapons to the kingdom.

Prince Faisal was appointed Saudi prime minister in October 1962 and implemented domestic reforms. The following month, he announced a 10-point plan that included the abolition of slavery, the promise of a fundamental law and an expansion of the defunct consultative council that had originally been set up in 1926. A year later, regulations were published for a system of provincial government, including the creation of local councils.

Relations between King Saud and the crown prince meanwhile reached breaking point. In March 1964, the ailing king was deprived of all executive powers. On November 2, King Saud abdicated and Prince Faisal succeeded. Early in 1965, Saud left for exile in Greece, having recognized his brother as king. He died there four years later. His immediate family were to remain exiles until the 1980s. Prince Khaled bin Abdelaziz, Faisal's half-brother, was named crown prince.

## The reign of King Faisal

King Faisal, a descendent from Mohammed bin Abdul Wahhab on his mother's side, was a moderniser and a conservative, a peacemaker who went to war, and a friend of the West who imposed an oil embargo during the last great Arab-Israel military confrontation. He put Saudi Arabia on the world map yet failed to deliver a single meaningful domestic political reform. His wife, Iffat, opened the door of opportunity to Saudi Arabian women. King Faisal's sons are among Arabia's most accomplished men. Without King Faisal, there'd be no New Gulf.

The first three years of King Faisal's reign were comparatively relaxed. But regional tensions were on the rise in 1966. In February, Britain announced its intention to withdraw from Aden by 1968. Palestinian guerrilla attacks on Israeli border settlements raised the stakes. Anger in the Arab World mounted after an Israeli punitive assault on the West Bank town of Samu in November. President Nasser increased the rhetoric against Israel, ordered UN forces out of the Sinai, and closed the Gulf of Aqaba to Israeli shipping.

At dawn on June 5, the Israeli air force attacked Egyptian fighters while they were still on the ground and seized, in a six-day campaign, the Sinai Peninsula, most of the West Bank of Jordan, east Jerusalem and Syria's Golan Heights. At least 100,000 Palestinians became refugees. It is said that King Faisal never smiled again.

At an Arab summit in Khartoum in August, Saudi Arabia, Kuwait and Libya agreed to make payments to the frontline Arab states of Egypt, Jordan and Syria. The summit also cleared the way for Egypt and Saudi Arabia to reach an agreement leading to the departure of Egyptian troops from Yemen. At the end of 1967, Yemen's pro-Egyptian president was deposed. Saudi Arabia recognized the Yemen Arab Republic in 1970, ending the civil war.

Discontent with the Arab response to the 1967 disaster manifested itself in the kingdom. In August 1969, reports emerged of a failed coup by junior army officers. To remind the Arab World where Saudi Arabia stood, King Faisal on August 22, 1969 delivered a speech, prompted by a fire at the Al Aqsa Mosque, calling on Muslim leaders and people to liberate the Islamic shrines in Jerusalem. It was the start of Saudi efforts to build an anti-communist international Islamic movement.

President Nasser died of a heart attack in September 1970 after a crisis Arab summit following the expulsion of Palestinian fighters from Jordan. He was replaced by vice-president, Anwar Sadat, who continued the rapprochement with Riyadh. Encouraged by the Saudis, President Sadat expelled Soviet advisers in 1972. President Sadat helped convince King Faisal that Hafez Asad, previously Syrian minister of defence, who'd become president in a coup in November 1970, was a man the Saudis could do business with.

King Faisal was initially unimpressed by the UAE and pressed a territorial claim against Abu Dhabi that was settled in 1974 when it secured territory between the new federation and the border with Qatar. Relations with Iran, despite Shah Mohammed Reza Pahlavi's regional ambitions, were generally sound.

To break the American oil companies' stranglehold on the oil sector, Saudi Arabia created Petromin, a 100 per cent Saudi firm, in 1962. Petromin granted a concession in the Empty Quarter to Saipem and Agip of Italy's ENI Group in partnership with Phillips Petroleum of the US. Concessions in the Red Sea area were awarded to foreign companies but oil was not found in commercial quantities.

In March 1972, the four American companies that owned Aramco – Exxon, Mobil, Chevron and Texaco – agreed to the kingdom's demand for a 20 per cent stake. Saudi oil income rose by almost 100 per cent in 1972. As Saudi oil income soared, President Sadat prepared for war. King Faisal sent Yamani to Washington in April 1973 to see Secretary of State William Rogers and National Security Adviser Henry Kissinger. Yamani said in an interview that the kingdom was ready to raise oil production from 7.2 million b/d to 20 million b/d to address American requirements, provided the US created "the right political atmosphere". He also stated Saudi Arabia could easily get much higher oil prices by reducing production by 25 per cent. There was no American response.

In May 1973, King Faisal went to Cairo for two days of talks, followed by a visit to France and then to Geneva to see the chief executives of the four Aramco partners. In Switzerland, he once again called on the US to break the Arab-Israel deadlock. On June 1, King Faisal sent a personal cable to President Nixon that emphasized the kingdom was serious about a possible production freeze. His last two appeals were made in interviews with NBC in August and *Newsweek* in September, in which he stated Saudi cooperation in raising oil production depended upon action about Israel and the Palestinians.

The Egyptian-Syrian assault began in the afternoon of October 6. King Faisal had hoped military action would be unnecessary and had advised President Sadat against the use of force. The kingdom, nevertheless, sent a motorised infantry brigade that arrived on the Golan Heights and engaged in one day's action on October 19.

The war coincided with negotiations between OPEC and major oil companies. The kingdom joined an oil embargo on the US. Oil prices in 1973/74 rose by 400 per cent. Flush with cash and seen as the key influence over oil prices, Saudi Arabia was lionized. In June 1974, it signed economic, technical and military agreements that at the time were the most comprehensive ever agreed between Washington and a developing country.

Later the same month, President Richard Nixon visited the kingdom to celebrate progress in Arab-Israeli military disengagement talks. US weapons sales quadrupled in 1974/75. By the summer of 1975, the US Army Corps of Engineers was managing more than US$10 billion worth of defence-related projects.

Saudi Arabia also placed defence orders with the UK and France. The boom in weapons deals created opportunities for middlemen. Adnan Khashoggi, the son of one of King Abdelaziz's doctors, made himself a key factor in practically every contract. Working for a number of foreign defence firms, he amassed a fortune. His influence continued into the 1980s when he was one of the middlemen in the Iran-Contra weapons deal.

Ghaith Pharaon, the son of King Abdelaziz's physician Rashad, also rose to fame and fortune. He'd studied at Stanford University and Harvard Business School. After returning to Saudi Arabia, Pharaon operated in many sectors and had an estimated income of US$300 million in 1974. Pharaon's business, Redec, started to experience financial difficulties in the early 1980s and he has since faded from public view.

The kingdom started systematically to invest in US government debt, increased its contributions to the IMF and the World Bank and provided a total of US$2,500 million in aid to Egypt, Syria and Jordan. New financial institutions were founded and money was pumped into infrastructure and industry. And still it had cash left over. This allowed the kingdom to emerge in 1974 as the leading price moderate in OPEC.

King Faisal was a ruler in the Bedouin mould and accessible to his people. This was to prove fatal. On the morning of March 25, 1975, his 28-year-old nephew, Prince Faisal bin Musaid, entered Al Raisa Palace. Previously convicted on charges of conspiring to sell LSD while he was a student in the University of Colorado in 1970, Prince Faisal perhaps nurtured a lasting grievance against the king for the death of his brother Khaled, who'd been shot dead by a policeman as he led an attempt to destroy a television transmitter in Riyadh in 1965.

Prince Faisal followed the Kuwaiti oil minister, Abdul Mutaleb Kazimi, into King Faisal's audience room. As the Kuwaiti was being introduced, the prince fired three shots at the king. Two were off target but one hit King Faisal in the throat. He died in a Riyadh hospital soon afterwards. Crown Prince Khaled was named king and Prince Fahd appointed crown prince. Prince Faisal was questioned about his motives amid speculation that blamed everyone from the CIA to the KGB. No evidence of a conspiracy has ever been made public. The assassin was beheaded in Riyadh on June 18 before a vast crowd estimated at 20,000 people.

### The reign of King Khaled

King Khaled, aged 62 at his accession, was seen as conservative. He had had a heart operation in 1972 and, despite surgery on his leg and hip, needed a stick to walk. But his sincerity, honesty and concern for ordinary Saudi Arabians won his people's affection. Recognizing Prince Fahd's skills, King Khaled empowered the crown prince to become, in effect, chief executive. Prince Fahd turned to his full brothers, the other six of the Sudairi Seven. A cabinet was formed in October 1975. Prince Sultan was named deputy premier. Prince Naif was made interior minister. Prince Ahmed was appointed deputy interior minister. Prince Salman continued as governor of Riyadh, a post he had held since 1962.

The first of the third generation of King Abdelaziz entered the cabinet in the form of Prince Saud Al Faisal who became foreign affairs minister. Capable commoners were given top jobs. Hisham Nazer, former head boy at the elite English-language Victoria College in Alexandria, was put in charge of the new planning ministry. Ghazi Algosaibi was appointed to lead the new Industry and Electricity Ministry. Mohammed Abalkhail, aged 35 and previously deputy finance minister, took over the top job. About 25 per cent of the kingdom's ministers and deputy ministers had doctorates.

The start of Khaled's reign coincided with dramatic signs of the impact of the massive increase in the kingdom's oil wealth. The second five-year plan, launched in July 1975, called for an economic revolution. Its centrepiece was a programme of investment in new domestic industries and refineries that would capture more of the value-added in the hydrocarbons supply chain, displace imports, promote exports and diversify the economy. They would be supplied with gas produced with the kingdom's oil that would be captured, rather than flared.

Most new industries would be built in two new cities: Jubail industrial city north of Dhahran on the Gulf coast and Yanbu industrial city on the Red Sea. Aramco would build a gas-gathering system and trans-peninsular gas and oil pipelines from the east to Yanbu. To accelerate progress, a separate executive agency named the Royal Commission for Jubail and Yanbu was created.

To promote inward investment and technology transfer, foreign corporations were offered a 50 per cent stake in new refineries and industries. They'd benefit from incentives including the right to lift Saudi oil in proportion to the amount they invested. Their Saudi partner would be Sabic, now the Middle East's largest manufacturing corporation. Every area of the economy was to be transformed. Total investment was put at US$141 billion over five years.

But the kingdom was trying to do too much, too quickly. The ports became congested. Its cities struggled to cope with the influx of people, goods and cars. Foreign business people could not get a flight into the kingdom, found no hotel rooms when they arrived, had difficulty travelling within the country and often suffered delays getting out. Inflation rocketed. Hundreds of thousands of foreign workers flooded into Saudi Arabia, many more than were envisaged in the plan. By the end of 1978, it was estimated they numbered 1.3 million (there are now about eight million) compared with a local labour force of just one million. But the pace of economic change was amazing. In the five years ending 1976, the Saudi economy grew by more than 600 per cent.

Saudi Arabia's wealth and moderation made it a desirable partner for the US and the West. Under Prince Fahd, the kingdom was open to dialogue. He visited France in July 1975 to sign an economic-collaboration agreement modelled on the one reached with the US the previous year. The UK government-to-government, air-defence agreement was renewed in 1973. James Callaghan, then British foreign secretary, visited Riyadh in November 1975 and signed a memorandum of understanding on economic, technical and industrial initiatives.

The Saudis also financed the frontline Arab states. In May 1975, it agreed with Kuwait, the United Arab Emirates and Qatar to contribute US$1 billion as the initial capital for a joint venture in Egypt to make weapons for the Arab World. The Suez Canal was reopened in June 1975. King Khaled visited Cairo the following month to give his blessing to the second Egypt-Israel disengagement agreement, which was signed in Geneva in September 1975. A further US$600 million in budgetary aid was announced.

The second disengagement, however, confirmed Syrian suspicions that Egypt was aiming for a bilateral accord with Israel in breach of Arab League policy. The divide in the Arab World deepened with the first violent incidents in the Lebanese civil war in April 1975. The kingdom tried to mend bridges with the Iraqi Baathist regime. Riyadh helped broker an agreement between Baghdad and Syria about sharing water from the Euphrates, but failed to persuade Iraq to drop its territorial claims on Kuwait. An agreement, however, was reached about dividing the neutral zone between Iraq and Saudi Arabia. A dialogue was opened with Iran to regularize relations. Financial aid was delivered to North Yemen for ending its military connection with the Soviet Union. Riyadh attempted to win over Marxist South Yemen, with which diplomatic relations were established in March 1976.

In Lebanon, all-out civil war erupted in 1976. Syria, supported by Saudi Arabia, was given a dominant role in the country in a ceasefire agreement reached in Riyadh in October 1976. It went some way to ease Syrian displeasure about Egypt's second disengagement deal but antagonized most Palestinians. Saudi Arabia insisted at OPEC's Doha meeting in December 1976 that it would not increase oil prices by more than five per cent. The UAE was its only supporter. The rest opted for a 10 per cent increase and scorned the kingdom's moderation.

The US, where Jimmy Carter had won the 1976 presidential election, applauded the kingdom's regional policies. But Saudi Arabia wanted something back in the form of action to deal with the Arab-Israel confrontation. President Carter seemed amenable. Prince Fahd visited Washington in May 1977 amid hopes that the kingdom and the US would work together on a comprehensive Middle East peace agreement despite the Likud bloc's victory that month in Israeli parliamentary elections. But Cairo broke ranks.

Without previously informing Riyadh, President Sadat told the Egyptian national assembly on November 9, 1977 that he would be prepared to go to Israel "to the Knesset itself" to talk peace. On November 21, he travelled to the Jewish state and delivered a speech to the Israeli parliament. In Israel, President Sadat adhered to the Arab position that there should be no bilateral deals, no argument about withdrawing from occupied territories including Arab Jerusalem, and no settlement without a resolution allowing for Palestinian claims. He did not, however, mention the PLO, recognized by the Arab League as the sole representative of the Palestinian people since 1974.

President Sadat's journey was condemned in the Arab World. Saudi Arabia withheld its support. King Khaled and Prince Fahd argued sanctions against Egypt would be a mistake and feared it would divide the Arab World. This happened almost immediately. An Arab League meeting in Tripoli in December, which Saudi Arabia, Jordan and Gulf Arab states did not attend, froze relations with Egypt. Cairo responded by breaking off diplomatic relations with the five states at the meeting; these were: Libya, Syria, Iraq, Algeria and South Yemen. These developments ensured America's plans to reconvene the multilateral Geneva Conference about the Arab-Israel confrontation were stillborn. Washington instead threw its weight behind a bilateral Egyptian-Israeli deal. This raised questions about America's attitude to Saudi priorities. These intensified when the Shah of Iran, following a visit to Washington in November 1977, suddenly converted to moderation about oil prices. His objective was White House agreement for weapons supplies and American silence about domestic human rights' violations.

Disillusionment with the US set in following a request by Prince Fahd during his visit in 1977 for six F-15 fighters. In February 1978, Carter approved the sale as part of a package that included aircraft deliveries to Egypt and Israel. After heavy lobbying by Israeli supporters and concessions about how Saudi Arabia would deploy the aircraft, congress finally approved the deal in May. But injury had been inflicted on the kingdom's relations with the Carter administration.

An Arab summit in November 1978 refused to endorse the Camp David accords between Egypt and Israel and appealed to President Sadat, who did not attend, to renounce his signature on them. A total of US$3,500 million in financial aid, of which one billion dollars was pledged by the kingdom, was promised if he did so. President Sadat denounced the proposal. The Arab-Israel peace treaty was signed in Washington on March 26, 1979.

The radicalization of the region was highlighted at the OPEC meeting in Geneva from 26–27 March. A multi-tier pricing system emerged with Saudi Arabia setting a base price of US$14.54 a barrel and the North African states charging more than US$18 a barrel. The kingdom separately imposed an 8.5 million b/d ceiling on Aramco production for the second quarter of the year. In June at a further OPEC meeting, also in Geneva, the kingdom raised its price to US$18 a barrel and other producers agreed a ceiling of US$23.50 a barrel with a US$2 a barrel surcharge. None of this had much impact on a market running out of control. In an effort to contain price trends, Saudi Arabia lifted production to 9.5 million b/d in July.

The most turbulent year in Saudi history since the Ikhwan rebellion in 1927 reached a dreadful climax in the Grand Mosque in Mecca at 5.20 am on November 20. Juhaiman bin Mohammed Utaibi and Mohammed bin Abdullah Al Qathani, a self-proclaimed Mahdi, or messiah, and several hundred followers interrupted dawn prayers, seized the Holy Haram and called for the overthrow of the Saudi government.

Juhaiman was born in an Ikhwan settlement in central Arabia. After serving briefly in the National Guard, he studied at Medina's Islamic University. His followers came from the Arab World, Pakistan and even America. Many of them had been at the same university. The seizure of the mosque was timed to coincide with the start of 1400 in the Islamic calendar, a moment forecast by some to be when a Mahdi would appear to purify Islam. The siege was ended on December 5. On January 9, 1980, 63 of the surviving members of the group, including Juhaiman, were executed by public decapitation in eight towns across Saudi Arabia. The siege of Mecca shocked the Muslim World and rocked Saudi Arabia.

Shiite Ashura celebrations in the Eastern Province, also in November, led to riots. Further riots took place in the Eastern Province in February 1980, the anniversary of the Iranian revolution. A challenging year closed with the arrival in Afghanistan in December of Soviet troops to support a pro-Moscow faction that had seized power. Things got worse. Iraq's President Saddam Hussein ordered a full-scale invasion of the Iranian Khuzestan province on September 22, 1980. The war led to massive destruction, the loss of hundreds of thousands of lives and, initially, record oil prices. The kingdom supported Iraq, seen as the lesser of two evils, with money and intelligence.

In 1981, the administration of President Reagan, elected in a landslide the previous autumn, adopted a fresh approach to the region. Washington's Middle East policy was pragmatic. It would confront the Soviet Union. The US needed allies and money. CIA director William Casey set out to find both.

Saudi Arabia shared many of Washington's concerns. It believed the

Soviets were attempting to encircle it. Saudi Arabia matched US contributions to the Afghan resistance and about US$3 billion was poured
into the anti-Soviet campaign. The partnership between Washington
and Riyadh during the Reagan years was not without glitches. Saudi
Arabia was vulnerable to congressional scrutiny. This reached a climax
during hearings into the White House plan to sell advanced warning
and control system (AWACS) aircraft to the kingdom. The deal provoked another round of Saudi Arabia-bashing on Capitol Hill. The
AWACS sale was approved by congress on October 28, 1981, but the
kingdom decided it had to make a point.

In 1985, Riyadh contracted the UK to supply Tornado fighter-
bombers in the Al Yamamah contract, the largest defence deal in history, which reports in June 2007 said was secured using secret payments
of US$2 billion. France had already been selected to supply warships.
Despite these blows, the Saudi-American relationship was closer than
before or since. US-educated Prince Bandar bin Sultan, son of the defence minister and ambassador to the US, charmed Washington.

Saudi money financed the Nicaraguan Contras and went to Sudan
to pressure the pro-Soviet regime in Ethiopia. The kingdom assisted
Jonas Savimbi, the rebel leader fighting Angola's Marxist government.
Prince Bandar was outside the inner circle of Saudi high society. His
mother Khizaran was dark-skinned, from the south-west of Saudi
Arabia and not of a major Saudi family. A driven man who trained as a
pilot, Prince Bandar had just completed a master's degree at the Johns
Hopkins University in Washington when he was enlisted to help lobby
for the AWACS deal. In 1983, following the accession of King Fahd,
he was appointed ambassador to the US, a post he held until the summer of 2005.

The boom of the early 1980s threw up some fascinating characters.
By the start of the decade, Rafik Hariri had already accumulated a
massive fortune. Born in Sidon in south Lebanon, he'd trained as a
teacher and emigrated to Saudi Arabia in 1965. Hariri supplemented
his earnings by book-keeping. In 1970, he set up his own construction
company. Hariri's breakthrough came in 1978. Saudi Oger, a partnership between France's Oger International and Hariri's own firm, won
the contract to build for the Saudi government the 78-room Al Hada
hotel in Taif, the mountain town that was used until the reign of King
Fahd as the kingdom's summer capital. The job was completed in 169
days, two months ahead of schedule. Hariri's reputation was made.

In February 1979, he bought Oger's stake in Saudi Oger and, four
months later, took over the French firm itself. In the following three
years, his company won massive government contracts through private
negotiation rather than competition. By the summer of 1981, Saudi
Oger was probably the Middle East's largest construction firm.

The death of King Khaled in June 1982 marked the end of the boom years for Saudi Oger. Under the new regime, directly negotiated contracts ended. Hariri, meanwhile, was planning to return to Lebanon. In early 1981, a Lebanese government report recommended Hariri's firm for a 30-year concession to develop a new port in Sidon, where he'd been investing for three years. This was the start of Hariri's engagement in Lebanese affairs. He was to be Lebanon's prime minister twice in 10 tumultuous years. Hariri was killed by a massive car bomb in Beirut in February 2005. His son Saad has now taken up his father's mission as head of Saudi Oger and a player in Lebanese politics.

## The reign of King Fahd

While the Iran-Iraq War blazed, a crisis was brewing in Lebanon. Claiming the south was being used as a haven for Palestinian guerillas, Israel invaded in June 1982. It was the final blow to King Khaled's failing health. He died on June 13. Prince Fahd succeeded. Prince Abdullah was named crown prince. Prince Sultan was made second deputy premier. King Fahd was well qualified to be head of state. He'd already made his mark with the Fahd Plan which called for Israeli withdrawal from land occupied in 1967, the creation of a Palestinian state with Jerusalem as its capital and, implicitly, Arab recognition of Israel.

The proposal, which presaged the Abdullah Plan of 2002, was tabled at the interrupted 1981 Arab summit in Fez and adopted as Arab League policy, again in Fez, in September 1982. It was rejected by Israel and noted but not accepted by the US. King Fahd dropped the title of His Majesty for Khadim Al Haramain Al Sharifain (Custodian of the Two Holy Mosques) and approved spending on the Holy Mosque in Mecca and the Prophet's (PBUH) Mosque in Medina, amounting to almost US$19 billion.

King Fahd's accession coincided with problems on all fronts. Iran came close to capturing Basra and winning the war. In June 1984 Saudi jets shot down one, and possibly two, Iranian jets that entered Saudi airspace over the Gulf. The competition for Muslim hearts and minds was acted out in the annual Hajj pilgrimage when the Iranian delegation held demonstrations and insisted on ritual visits to places in the Holy Cities venerated by Shiite Muslims. More than 400 Iranian pilgrims died violently during the 1987 Hajj. The Arab World was divided with Syria backing the Iranians.

The assassination of President Sadat by Islamist radicals in the Egyptian army at a parade to mark the anniversary of the October War in 1981 had ushered in President Mubarak. He attempted to end the breach with Saudi Arabia over Camp David, but progress was glacial.

To defend the oil price, the kingdom reduced oil production until in 1985 it was producing less than three million b/d of crude. As government income plummeted, the economy slumped. In the five years until the end of 1986, the Saudi GDP contracted by almost 50 per cent. At the end of 1985, OPEC gave up defending the oil price and adopted a policy of pursuing market share. This degenerated into a price war that seemed to be in part designed to put pressure on Iran to end the war.

On October 29, 1986, King Fahd, seeking an end to the price slump, dismissed Yamani as oil minister and replaced him with Hisham Nazer. Soon after, OPEC reached a new agreement based on a marker price of US$18 a barrel. The long Saudi economic recession caused problems for most Saudi banks, major firms went out of business and there was a freeze on government wages. Investment in infrastructure was largely halted with lasting negative implications. Demand for Saudi oil, however, recovered to about five million b/d in 1988 and 1989.

In 1988, Aramco was incorporated as a 100 per cent Saudi company with the new name of Saudi Aramco. Its first act was to set up a joint-venture refining company in the US with Texaco, now merged with Chevron as ChevronTexaco. In 1988, Star Enterprise was taken over by Motiva, which was owned by the Saudi-Texaco joint venture, and Shell Oil. In 2001, Saudi Aramco took over the Texaco stake to become a 50:50 owner with Shell.

The 1987 revelation that the US financed Israeli weapons sales to Iran shook Riyadh's faith in America. In an effort to regain Arab confidence, the US increased support for Iraq, helping to bring about Iran's ceasefire call in August 1988. The following year, Khomeini died and was succeeded as spiritual leader by his protégé Ali Khamenei. The end of the war ushered in a brief period of hope that a lasting Gulf peace was in prospect.

All illusions were shattered when Iraq invaded Kuwait on the morning of August 2, 1990. Iraq's expulsion from Kuwait was followed by Kurdish and Shiite risings. Both were repressed and hundreds of thousands of Kurds fled to escape the advancing Iraqi army. This led to the establishment of no-fly zones in the north and south of Iraq policed by coalition aircraft, some based in Saudi Arabia. The kingdom responded to the UN Iraqi oil embargo by lifting output to more than eight million b/d. Oil prices rose. New money was injected into the Saudi economy, but most of it was accounted for by emergency spending during the Kuwait crisis and contributions to the cost to the US and the coalition of fighting the war. Saudi Arabia in 1991 had its largest ever current account deficit. Austerity continued.

The alliance with Christian countries against Iraq was resented. Petitions circulated calling for changes in government policy. The first, signed by 43 public figures, called for the formation of a consultative council, the revival of municipal councils, modernization of the judiciary, constraints on the Committee for the Propagation of Virtue and the Prohibition of Vice (the Mutaween), equal treatment of all citizens and more participation by women. This was followed in May 1991 by a petition signed by 52 Islamists calling for reforms within an Islamic framework. The petition led to a memorandum of advice being submitted to Abdelaziz bin Baz, head of the higher council of ulema and the kingdom's most distinguished cleric.

Its wide-ranging criticisms centred on the charge that it was not enforcing the Sharia with sufficient vigour. Bin Baz – sightless, sincere but naïve – initially indicated his support for the document but later declared it should not have been circulated. He was subsequently appointed as mufti.

Caught between liberals and Islamic conservatives, the government had few incentives to change course. But the criticisms accelerated the announcement of three fundamental domestic reforms: the publication in 1992 of the basic law of government which defines in broad terms the rights and obligations of the Saudi government under the rule of the descendants of King Abdelaziz; the law for the establishment of a Majlis al-Shoura (national consultative council) and the law for the establishment of appointed councils in the kingdom's 14 provinces.

The first Majlis al-Shoura, inaugurated in December 1993 with a four Hijra-year term, had 60 appointed members. This was increased to 90 in its second term that started in 1997. The figure was increased to 150 in 2005. It was also announced that cabinet members were to be appointed for renewable four-year terms to introduce more accountability at the highest levels of government.

The new cabinet of 1995 saw wholesale change. Ibrahim Al Assaf, previously the Saudi representative on the IMF board, became finance minister to replace Mohammed Ali Abalkhail. Hashem Yamani, who has a doctorate from Harvard University, was made industry minister. Ali Naimi, previously Saudi Aramco chief executive, was made oil minister to replace Hisham Nazer. All three were still in the cabinet in 2007.

Naimi's rise to the pinnacle of world oil is a remarkable tale. Born in August 1936, he was a member of a recently settled nomad family living on the coast of Saudi Arabia's Eastern Province. Aged about nine, Naimi signed up for Aramco's original Jabal school and stayed there two years. A black-and-white photograph in Saudi Aramco archives taken in the late 1940s captures the moment. The smallest of 11 boys pictured holds a baseball in his raised right hand. The intelligent eyes and cheeky smile are familiar. It is Naimi, probably not yet a teenager.

When his brother, Abdullah, died in 1947, Naimi, then aged 12, took over his job as office boy. A government ruling that no one less than 18 could work full-time forced him to give it up. Naimi exaggerated his age and obtained a new position, this time in the personnel department. Naimi's abilities were spotted. In 1956, he left Saudi Arabia for six years of higher education, first at the International College in Beirut and then at the American University of Beirut. After that, he went to Lehigh University in Pennsylvania to emerge with a degree in geology. In 1963, he earned a master's degree in hydrology and economic geology from Stanford University.

Returning to Saudi Arabia, Naimi rose through Aramco's ranks, working initially as a geologist and hydrologist and then joining Aramco's public relations team, a crucial step for rising Saudi stars. From 1972–75, Naimi successively held the posts of assistant manager for the producing department, manager of the southern-area producing department and then manager of the northern-area producing department. In mid-1975, he was made vice-president and in July 1978 was elevated to the post of senior vice-president for oil operations. Naimi was appointed to the Aramco board in 1980, the year that Aramco was effectively nationalized by the Saudi government. At the start of 1984, Naimi replaced Hugh Goerner, the last American Aramco president. He was the first Saudi Arabian to get the top job.

Naimi's progress continued when Saudi Aramco was incorporated as a 100 per cent Saudi-owned entity in 1988 and he became chief executive. It was not surprising when Naimi was made oil minister in the cabinet reshuffle of 1995. He played a crucial role in the OPEC ministers' meeting that led to the 1998 oil price slump. But no one has worked harder since to keep the oil price up. Some say that, without Naimi, OPEC would have died when oil crashed to below US$10 a barrel in early 1999.

One effect of the cabinet appointed in 1995 was a tightening in government fiscal policy. Al Assaf, the new finance minister, was determined to restore the kingdom's creditworthiness. The government declared it favoured privatization, but took few steps to put it into practice. The capacity to pursue vigorous new policy initiatives was also constrained by a drastic worsening in the health of King Fahd, who had his first serious stroke in 1995.

In regional affairs, the new development was the election of the unknown Arkansas governor Bill Clinton as US president in 1992. The kingdom had banked on President George H Bush living up to promises that Saudi cooperation in the war for Kuwait would be rewarded by a new initiative in the Arab-Israel confrontation. This commitment was partly delivered in the October 1991 Madrid peace conference which for the first time involved all parties to the dispute sitting together in the same room at the same time. The momentum behind the Madrid process evaporated as American attention shifted to the 1992 presidential election. Clinton stood as a firm supporter of Israel and critic of the pressure being applied on the Jewish state. He won handily and launched US Middle East policy in a new direction.

In the summer of 1993, Palestinian and Israeli surrogates secretly meeting in Oslo reached an agreement. The news shocked most Palestinians who were dismayed that the longstanding policy of aiming for a comprehensive rather than a bilateral settlement had been breached. Many Israelis opposed negotiations with the PLO, which was still treated by Tel Aviv as an illegitimate terror organization.

Nevertheless, the Oslo accords were greeted with euphoria in Washington and the West. Israel and the PLO signed an interim agreement in 1994 and Jordan recognized Israel the following year. Progress with the details was slow. In December 1995, Rabin was assassinated and replaced by his deputy Shimon Peres. Peres launched an attack on southern Lebanon in the spring of 1996. Peres lost to the Likud's Benjamin Netanyahu in Israel's first direct elections for prime minister in May 1996. By the end of that year, Oslo was effectively dead.

Saudi Arabia regarded the Oslo approach as inadequate. It asserted there could be no peace without a comprehensive settlement encompassing land seized by the Israelis in 1967, the question regarding Palestinian refugees, and the establishment of a Palestinian state with Jerusalem as its capital. Saudi Arabia was also dismayed by the effects of UN sanctions against Iraq and welcomed the 1996 UN oil-for-food programme that allowed humanitarian good imports to be paid for through supervised oil sales.

Oslo's last gasp came following the election in May 1999 of Ehud Barak, Labour Party leader, as prime minister of a centre-left One Israel coalition. Barak said he aimed to achieve a comprehensive settlement with the Arab World in 2000. Barak asked Clinton to call a summit with Arafat. The meetings at Camp David ended on July 25, 2000 without agreement. At its conclusion, a trilateral statement was issued defining the agreed principles to guide future negotiations. Clinton blamed Arafat for failing to accept an Israeli offer. Arafat stated it fell short of his minimum aspirations and would have been unacceptable to the Palestinian people and the Arab World.

In September 2000, Likud leader, Ariel Sharon, visited the Haram al-Sharif, the sacred sanctuary surrounding the Dome of the Rock and Al Aqsa mosques. The Palestinians launched the second intifada. With a new Palestinian rising grabbing the headlines, last-ditch attempts were made to follow up on the Camp David negotiations in meetings in Washington and Taba in early 2001. But the Clinton administration was a lame duck following the victory of George W Bush in US presidential elections in November 2000. Sharon, reviled in the Arab World for his responsibility for the 1982 massacre by Phalangist militia of Palestinian civilians in Beirut's Sabra and Chatila refugee camps, was elected prime minister in February 2001. The Arab passion about

Palestine was shared by King Abdullah. This was expressed in a remarkable way in 2001 during the first year of the presidency of George W Bush. Abdullah, then crown prince, was dismayed by developments in the second intifada. According to a report in *The Washington Post*, he was outraged by a television report he'd seen at the end of August 2001 that showed an Israeli soldier holding an elderly Palestinian woman to the ground by putting his boot on her head.

His temper was worsened the following day when he heard Bush call for the Palestinians to halt "terrorist violence". The crown prince called Prince Bandar and ordered him to confront the White House. On August 27, the Saudi ambassador met Condoleezza Rice, then national security adviser, in her office in the White House. He used as a script a 25-page document sent from Riyadh that denounced the US as being hopelessly pro-Israeli. Prince Bandar told Rice he'd been told he was to have no further discussions with Washington. Rice agreed to take the message to the president.

The showdown produced a result. Two days later, Prince Bandar flew to Riyadh with a message from President Bush stating he believed the Palestinian people had a right to live in their own state. In what appeared to be a giant breakthrough for Saudi diplomacy, the White House secretly prepared a new Middle East peace initiative based on the idea of a Palestinian state. President Bush said he was willing to meet Palestinian leader Yasser Arafat at the UN at the end of September. Prince Bandar was invited to the White House on September 13 to work on the details. Anticipating a busy day, he called his office and said he would be taking the next day – Tuesday September 11 – off.

Prince Bandar's response to the 9/11 attacks was energetic. He denounced the atrocity and dismissed suggestions that Saudi Arabia was responsible. The meeting with Bush took place on September 13 as planned, but Washington's priorities had been radically altered. In the storm that followed 9/11, Saudi Arabia attempted to occupy neutral ground between the US and militants in the Arab and Islamic worlds.

The 2002 Abdullah Plan, almost identical to the 1982 Fahd plan, was accepted by an Arab League summit in March 2002, but the Israelis did not even bother to reject it. Saudi Arabians say it has been incorporated in the Road Map for Middle East Peace, a new peace initiative that in turn has made little progress and was made redundant by Israel's war against Hizbollah in Lebanon in the summer of 2006.

## Osama bin Laden and Al Qaeda
Osama bin Laden, his father's 17th son, was born in Riyadh on March 10, 1957 into a religious yet worldly family. The Bin Laden fortune had been created by the energy of Osama's father, Mohammed bin Laden, who'd been born near Tarim in the Hadhramaut. A bricklayer

turned builder, he set up in 1932 what would become the Middle East's largest construction company. Bin Laden senior initially made his mark by building roads, including a highway that climbed almost 1,500 m from the foot of the Asir Escarpment, south of Jeddah, to Taif. Commissions followed for government buildings and palaces for the Al Saud family. Bin Laden's reputation was sealed in contracts to rebuild and expand the Holy Mosques of Mecca and Medina.

Bin Laden produced an enormous family comprising 54 children, including 25 sons. He was devoutly religious, but his daughters as well as his sons were given excellent educations. In 1968, Bin Laden died when his private jet crashed in Saudi Arabia. King Faisal placed Bin Laden's company in government trust. Leadership eventually went to Mohammed's eldest son Salem, who'd been educated at an English school and married an English woman. He died in a plane crash in Texas in May 1988.

Osama's mother, Hamida Ghanoum, was the educated daughter of a Syrian trader. He was a quiet but charismatic boy and his father's only son to be educated entirely in the Middle East. During 1968–69, he learned English at Jeddah's Al Thagh school. Tales of his time at Lebanon's Broumanna High School, that portray him as a wayward youth, are false – as is the myth that he's an Arsenal fan.

Osama is a diligent Muslim. This was confirmed by Prince Turki Al Faisal, ambassador to the US since the summer of 2005, in an interview published with *The New York Times* magazine in August that year. "I met him five times," Al Faisal said. "At that time, which was in the mid and late 80s, he was a very shy person, very self-effacing, extremely sparse in his words and generally a do-gooder, someone who brought financial, medical and other support to the Afghan Mujahideen."

Osama started a degree in the management and economics faculty at Jeddah's King Abdelaziz University. He's believed to have married for the first time the same year, aged 17. He has an unknown number of children, although five are reported to be living in the kingdom. Osama is said at the age of 20 to have visited the cave on Mount Hira near Mecca, where the Prophet (PBUH) received his first revelation. The experience was profound.

Osama sold his luxury car, grew his beard and threw himself into Islamic studies. He graduated in 1979. The Islamic World was in turmoil. The government of the Shah of Iran was finally brought down in February 1979. Many Muslims were inspired by the destruction of the rule of what they considered to be an unbelieving tyrant. The Iranian Revolution influenced the militants that seized the Holy Haram in Mecca in November later that year.

Bin Laden joined the Afghan Mujahideen just before Soviet troops arrived. In the next two years, he played a role in recruiting, training, leading and financing volunteers for the Afghan War. In 1982, Bin Laden set up base in Peshawar, historically a centre of Wahhabism. His mentor was Abdullah Azzam, a Palestinian born in 1941. Azzam was a graduate of Islamic jurisprudence from Damascus University and had a doctorate from Al Azhar University in Cairo. He had taught Bin Laden at university.

By the end of the 1980s, the US was providing almost US$700 million a year to the Afghan resistance. More than 25,000 Mujahideen fighters were in action. Soviet leader Mikhail Gorbachev recognized the war as one that would not be won. A withdrawal of Soviet troops was negotiated. The last Soviet soldier left in February 1989. A pro-Soviet regime continued to hold power until it was deposed in 1990.

Bin Laden is reported to have taken part in only one battle but gave generously to the Afghan resistance. He was crucial in a network in the Muslim World that raised money and volunteers. Bin Laden and Azzam formed a Bureau of Services (Mektab al-Khidmat) to send recruits to Afghanistan. Following the Soviet withdrawal, they established a base or foundation (Al Qaeda) as a potential head office for future holy wars. Bin Laden became its effective leader.

Azzam and both his sons were killed in Peshawar in November 1989 by a car bomb that his followers attributed to US agents. Ayman Al Zawahiri, a doctor and Egyptian Islamic jihad member who'd been born in Cairo in June 1951, became Bin Laden's deputy when his militant group merged with Bin Laden's in 1998. Bin Laden returned to Saudi Arabia at the end of 1989. Around the same time, his agents began buying property in Sudan following an invitation from Hassan Al Turabi, head of the National Islamic Front, for his movement to transplant to Sudan where an Islamic regime supported by the army had seized power. Little more than a month after Saddam Hussein had seized Kuwait, Bin Laden met senior Saudi officials and presented his plan to raise an international force of Islamic militants to defend the kingdom.

The Saudis joined the anti-Iraq coalition. Bin Laden denounced the decision in taped speeches circulated to supporters and sympathizers after which his activities were restricted by the Saudi authorities. Bin Laden escaped the kingdom in April 1991 under the pretext of attending an Islamic gathering in Pakistan. The Saudi government froze his financial assets and revoked his citizenship in 1994.

Bin Laden moved to Sudan at the end of 1991 or early in 1992. According to *The 9/11 Commission Report to US Congress*, published in 2004, Bin Laden built his organization and constructed a highway from Khartoum to Sudan. Financial support was provided to Islamic movements in Bosnia, Azerbaijan and Chechnya. Links were established with sympathetic groups. Other versions say he spent his time trying to set up businesses and dreaming up pan-Islamic schemes.

According to *The 9/11 Commission Report to US Congress*, the Al
Qaeda leadership issued a fatwa, or divine judgement, calling for jihad
against the Western 'occupation' of Islamic Holy Lands in 1992.

The deployment of American troops to Somalia at the end of 1992
prompted what was probably Al Qaeda's first anti-US action. Bombs
were detonated in December in two Aden hotels used by US troops
stopping en route to Somalia. Two were killed, but no Americans. Al
Qaeda operatives are reported to have trained Somali militants that
downed two US Black Hawk helicopters in the Battle of Mogadishu in
October 1993 in which 18 American servicemen died. President
Clinton ordered US withdrawal from Somalia in early 1994.

In November 1995, a car bomb outside a Saudi National Guard
training base run with US assistance in Riyadh, killed five Americans
and two Indian nationals. Four men who said they were inspired by
Bin Laden were caught and executed. In June 1996, 19 Americans
were killed and 372 wounded in a truck bomb attack on the Al Khobar
Towers complex in Dhahran. The attack is usually blamed on Saudi
Hezbollah which draws its support from Shiite Muslims and had received help from Iran. It is uncertain whether Al Qaeda was involved.

An assassination attempt against Egypt's President Mubarak in
Ethiopia in June 1995 was blamed on a group with 'a haven in Sudan'.
In November, a bomb detonated outside the Egyptian embassy in
Islamabad left 16 dead and 60 injured. Sudan was blamed. Khartoum
was subjected to UN sanctions in April 1996.

*The Washington Post* reported in 2001 that Sudan had offered to
hand Bin Laden over to Riyadh, which had turned the proposal down
because of Saudi fears of domestic unrest. An unconfirmed report says
Sudan considered offering him to the US. This was rejected, according
to *Age of Sacred Terror*, written by two former Clinton administration
counter-terrorism experts, David Benjamin and Steven Simon, because
Washington then had no grounds to take him into custody. But Bin
Laden was no longer welcome in Sudan. He returned to Afghanistan.

Bin Laden arrived in Jalalabad in eastern Afghanistan in May 1996.
Three weeks later, Jalalabad fell to the Taliban, a conservative Islamic
movement founded in 1994 by Mullah Omar and 16 companions. On
August 23, he issued an 8,000-word declaration describing how Islamic rulers had been corrupted but focussed his attention on the need to
fight the US first.

The Taliban took Kabul in September, but Bin Laden, who
preached an international war, was out of tune with the Taliban leadership which wanted to restore a pure form of Islam to Afghanistan
only. He promised Taliban leaders he would adopt a low profile, but
appeared on CNN in March 1997 and made inflammatory remarks.
Mullah Omar encouraged Bin Laden to move to Kandahar in south-

west Afghanistan, where he could be more closely controlled.

On February 23, 1998, Bin Laden and Al Zawahiri issued a fatwa in the name of the World Islamic Front. It said the US had declared war against God and his messenger and that 'to kill Americans and their allies – civilians and military – is the individual duty for every Muslim who can do it in any country in which it is possible to do it, in order to liberate the Al Aqsa Mosque and the Holy Mosque (in Mecca) and in order for their armies to move out of all the lands of Islam, (to be) defeated and unable to threaten any Muslim.'

The Taliban were unhappy. According to Jason Burke in his book *Al Qaeda: The True Story of Radical Islam*, a US delegation was received in Kabul in 1998 and Mullah Omar offered to deliver Bin Laden to the Saudi Arabians. Bin Laden's call to arms was repeated. In an interview with ABC television in May 1998, he expanded on the nature of his campaign. "We do not differentiate between military or civilian," he was quoted as saying. "As far as we are concerned, they are all targets."

These statements set the scene for the first major attack attributed to Al Qaeda. On the morning of August 7, 1998, truck bombs were detonated outside US embassies in Nairobi in Kenya and Dar es-Salaam in Tanzania. A total of 12 Americans and 212 other people were killed. More than 5,000 were injured. President Clinton ordered retaliation. On the August 20, 1998, US Navy vessels in the Arabian Sea fired 80 cruise missiles at Bin Laden camps in Afghanistan and a factory in Sudan that the White House wrongly believed had been used by Al Qaeda to produce chemical weapons. Nothing significant was hit.

America's attacks transformed Bin Laden into a hero among impressionable Muslims. He is reported to have told Mullah Omar that he was not responsible for the East African attacks. The Taliban were not convinced. They dealt with the problem by claiming Bin Laden had disappeared. But the Taliban was losing the support of the government of Pakistan, unnerved by lawlessness on the North-West Frontier attributed to Taliban-inspired proselytizing. Bin Laden's money and influence was beginning to be useful. Taliban moderates were losing ground.

In July 1999, President Clinton issued an executive order effectively declaring the Taliban regime a state sponsor of terrorism. In a final effort to win international recognition, the Taliban announced the ban on opium trade, a crucial revenue source for Afghan farmers and the government. The gesture failed to win over the US. The following month, the UN imposed sanctions on Afghanistan for refusing to give up Bin Laden. Dismayed by the international response, the Taliban turned towards Bin Laden and increasingly adopted the rhetoric of international Islamic revolution.

The final full-scale Al Qaeda attack before 9/11 took place against the USS *Cole* off Aden on October 12, 2000. A total of 17 sailors were killed and at least 40 were injured when a motorboat packed with explosives slammed into the destroyer as it was refueling. The US government concluded the attack was masterminded by Bin Laden.

The events of September 11, 2001 are covered in detail by *The 9/11 Commission Report*. It shows how a small group of conspirators with no more than US$500,000 at its disposal carried out the most damaging attack on the American homeland since 1941.The report is often gripping. But it is not the final word. It tends to encourage the conclusion that Al Qaeda is an organized global conspiracy responsible for many outrages, including the three bomb attacks in Bali in October 2002 and the Madrid train bombings of March 2004. Some observers believe Al Qaeda is made up of independent militant groups with no central command structure.

In November 2001, US forces working with anti-Taliban elements invaded Afghanistan, deposed the Taliban and eliminated Al Qaeda safe havens. The US turned to Iraq. President Bush ordered a second invasion. Baghdad fell in April 2003 and Saddam Hussein was captured in December.

Osama is clearly the exception in the Bin Laden family. About 17 of his brothers are active within the Saudi Binladen Group. Its chairman and chief executive officer, Bakr, and other family members working in the business, are open-minded people aiming to build their company and pass it on to the next generation. About 70 of Mohammed's grandchildren are involved in the group and a separate company was set up in 2003 to allow them to learn how to run businesses.

The diversity in the Bin Laden family was underlined in early 2005 when one of Osama's many nieces announced she wanted to be a pop star. Wafah bin Laden was reported as describing herself as having a voice like Chrissie Hynde, the American singer who is the vocalist for The Pretenders.

The Saudi Binladen Group is one of Saudi Arabia's most successful and respected businesses. In 2005, it initiated a real-estate deal involving the construction of a tower in the Al Haram development in Mecca. It involved the groundbreaking use of Islamic finance. This confirms the actions of Osama are not blamed on his family, which disowned him in 1994. A new Bin Laden subsidiary called Al Rahim & Al Trahom has two divisions: one for men and one for women. There is no bar to women playing a full role in the group.

## Jeddah, bride of the Red Sea

Gateway to the Holy Cities, greatest Red Sea port and home to the liveliest business community in Saudi Arabia, Jeddah has a proud history, a beautiful coastal setting and a multiracial population of more than three million people. No one knows when it was founded, but the ancient Egyptians, Greeks and Romans knew it. Jeddah enters history around the start of the Islamic Hajj. Jeddah's prominence continued under Ottoman rule. European ships from Java and India began calling. By the 20th century, Jeddah was the region's busiest port. The city was entangled in the 15-year struggle between Sharif Hussein and the Al Saud. The kingdom of the Hejaz was declared by Sharif Hussein in 1917 and recognized by the victorious allies. Jeddah became the centre of the new Arab nationalist movement and had its own parliament.

At the end of the war, Britain withdrew its support for King Hussein, who was forced to abdicate in October 1924. His son King Ali was forced out at the end of 1925. Abdelaziz assumed sovereignty in the Hejaz. It lost its distinctive position when it was merged into the unified Kingdom of Saudi Arabia declared in September 1932.

Under the Al Saud, Jeddah lost some of its status, though its port remained the principal Saudi window to the outside world. The birth of the oil industry and the decision to make Riyadh the capital eroded Jeddah's prominence. Today, it is Saudi Arabia's second city with not much more than 60 per cent of the capital's population.

The first thing most visitors see is King Abdelaziz International Airport (KAIA). It took almost a decade to complete and was one of the Middle East's most costly projects. By the time it opened in the early 1980s, it was already out of date. The three terminals, each separated by miles of space, quickly made no sense. The KAIA is redeemed by the Hajj terminal, giant structures with no exterior walls and roofs shaped like Bedouin tents. It is designed to facilitate the disembarkation of thousands of pilgrims. The terminal is now being modernized.

The 35-kilometre corniche that runs to the beaches and villas of Obhur Creek to the north was one of the great Arabian urban achievements of the 1980s. The National Commercial Bank (NCB) headquarters in the heart of the old city was, when it opened in 1982, the Middle East's tallest building. Jeddah's mayor in the 1970s, Mohammed Farsi, commissioned 160 pieces of abstract sculpture from the world's most famous artists, including the late Henry Moore and Julio Lafuente. They adorn roundabouts and street corners and alone make Jeddah worth a visit. And yet, there is a sense of lost opportunities. In the 1980s, all embassies were obliged to move to Riyadh. Only two of the kingdom's banks are based in the city. The principal public agencies in Jeddah are Saudia, the national airline, and King Abdelaziz University.

But Jeddah is trying to rise again. The annual Jeddah Economic Forum has attracted star speakers, including former presidents George H Bush and Bill Clinton, Cherie Blair and Irish president Mary Macaleese. The management of the port has been privatized. Plans call for Jeddah to be the western terminus of a trans-peninsular rail link to Riyadh and Dhahran. A strategy to increase the number of pilgrims will boost the city. Plans include building a high-speed rail link through the city from Mecca to Medina. Jeddah is growing prodigiously. Its northern suburbs extend for more than 30 km and lap the airport's perimeter. But in the dash to build the new, the old is being lost. Traditional multi-storey houses built of coral have been preserved in central Jeddah. But not enough is being done to save the heritage of one of Islam's greatest cities. It is a pervasive problem. One of the features of the strict form of Islam dominant in Saudi Arabia is the rejection of the glorification of man and his works. There is uncertainty about what to make of humanity's achievements before the coming of Islam.

Buildings destroyed in Mecca include the mosque of the first caliph, Abu Bakr, and a site which some believe was where the Prophet Mohammed (PBUH) lived with his first wife, Khadija. A colonnaded courtyard in Medina called the Egyptian Monastery has been demolished. These echo the destruction over the decades of less well-known buildings and tombs.

Plans for Mecca that worry archaeologists include the creation of a huge avenue, into the city's heart, that will also accommodate the Mecca–Medina railway line. Architect Sami Angawi, one of about 3,000 people who've inherited the position of pilgrim guide or *mutawwaf* in the Holy Lands, told *The Wall Street Journal* in August 2004 that the destruction was already considerable. "We've done more damage to Mecca and Medina in the past 50 years than in the past 1,500," he lamented. It's estimated that there are no more than 20 buildings in Mecca that can be dated to the time of the Prophet (PBUH).

The official attitude is changing. The Supreme Commission for Tourism was founded at the start of the decade to quantify, develop and promote Saudi Arabia's potential as a tourism destination. It is also reporting on sites of outstanding archaeological interest. The commission has approved a plan to boost the annual number of visitors to Saudi Arabia to 21 million within two decades. Secretary-general of the commission, Prince Sultan bin Salman, son of Riyadh governor Prince Salman, says the kingdom will require an additional 50,000 hotel rooms and 75,000 furnished apartments by 2020. It is a striking affirmation of the new, open mood sweeping Saudi Arabia.

There is no shortage of Saudi Arabians willing to criticize government policy in private, but going public is hazardous. Saudi intellectuals opened a new chapter in 1991 when they published a 12-point petition calling for political reform. A year later, the same group circulated a 44-page reform programme.

In 1993, some of the authors of the original petition were arrested. All were subsequently released and some left the kingdom. They included Saad Faqih, a Saudi surgeon, who moved to London and initially formed a partnership with Mohammed Al Masari, another exiled

Saudi dissident and intellectual who quickly lost credibility because of the extremism of his statements. In 1996, Faqih formed the Movement for Islamic Reform in Arabia, an organization, despite its name, which calls for the liberalization of the kingdom, including the acceptance of freedom of expression and assembly.

In 2002, he launched a nightly three-hour radio broadcast from London called Islah (reform) Radio, which can be picked up by Saudi satellite television receivers. During one of the broadcasts, Faqih, who lives in the London suburb of Willesden, called for demonstrations in favour of reforms. Hundreds came out onto Saudi streets, but the demonstrations were dispersed by the police. There were many arrests.

The Saudi government calls Faqih a terrorist and accuses him of taking US$1.2 million from an agent of Libyan leader Muammar Qadaffi to help arrange the assassination of King Abdullah when he was crown prince. The Saudis have pressed the British government to detain Faqih on suspicion of terrorism and to shut down Islah.

Faqih denies the allegations and alleges that an attempt to kill him was made in June 2003 when two men claiming to be plumbers arrived at his home, sprayed him with gas and tried to drag him outside. Faqih was knifed in the leg. Saudi officials are reported by *The Washington Post* as saying it was an operation run by a rogue prince without the government's knowledge or consent.

Faqih continues to enrage. In his valedictory interview with *The Times* in August 2005, departing Saudi ambassador to the UK, Prince Turki Al Faisal, lingered over Al Masari, who runs a website criticizing the Saudi ruling family, and Faqih. "We have been urging your government to send them back since 1996, if not earlier," Al Faisal said. "During my two and a half years here, it was one of the most persistent and consistent topics."

According to Al Faisal, Blair told King Abdullah that new laws would be introduced to deal with Saudi Arabia's complaints. In September 2006, the London newspaper, *The Guardian*, reported that the expulsion of the two dissidents was a condition for Britain winning a Eurofighter deal from the kingdom. British officials dismissed suggestions of a link. The contract has since been confirmed.

The environment for Saudi Arabians speaking out continues to be challenging. In August 2004, the trial of three Saudi Arabians, who supported a petition circulated the previous December that called for a constitutional monarchy, opened. Ali Al Demaini, Matruk Al Faleh and Abdullah Al Hamed were charged with calling for this change and questioning the independence of the judicial system. Originally, 13 were arrested following the petition, but half were released after promising not to lobby publicly for reform. Two more were released later. The three were finally sentenced to up to nine years imprisonment by a court sitting in closed session in May 2005. In a June 19 speech advocating democratic reform across the Middle East, US secretary of state, Condoleezza Rice, complained that "many people pay an unfair price for exercising their basic rights" in Saudi Arabia. Speaking of the charges that sent the reform advocates to prison, Rice said, "That should not be a crime in any country." On August 9, eight days after he'd succeeded, King Abdullah pardoned and released all three.

Two years after King Abdullah's accession, there's growing confidence the kingdom has embarked upon a new era. Even the Saudi share price crash since February 2006 has been largely digested. The economy, driven by record oil prices and soaring demand for Saudi oil, grew more than 10 per cent in 2007 and has doubled in a decade. The boom, coupled with pressure from the government for more jobs for Saudis, is helping to contain the rise of youth unemployment, the kingdom's biggest challenge.

In Riyadh in the spring of 2006, Amr Dabbagh, the governor of the Saudi Arabian General Investment Authority (Sagia), described plans to radically expand the scope of the King Abdullah Economic City in Rabigh, a new conurbation being developed by Dubai's Emaar Properties that was unveiled the previous December. When complete, it will have a population of more than 500,000 people, a financial district for international banks, a large industrial estate, an airport and a port as big as in Dubai.

Five other economic zones are being established. The Saudi Railways Organization is implementing plans for a trans-peninsular rail link from Jeddah to Dammam that will service an Arabian equivalent to the Orient Express and a 500 km high-speed railway linking Mecca and Medina. Plans have been unveiled for the King Abdullah Financial District, a new development north of Riyadh that will accommodate banks and finance houses. Bauxite and phosphate mines in central and northern Arabia will be connected by rail to a metals manufacturing zone at Ra's al-Zour, north of Jubail, which is being doubled in extent. On the mineral rail line at Sudair, north of Riyadh, a huge industrial, commercial and residential city is planned. At least US$ 300 billion worth of projects are underway in the kingdom.

The direction for kingdom as a whole is clear. Modernization, resisted for so long by so many, is irresistible. Saudi Arabia has joined the march of the New Gulf and is, in fact, its most important component.

## Al Saud rulers
Saud

| | |
|---|---|
| Mohammed bin Saud ... ... ... ... ... ... ... ... ... ... ... | 1745–1765 |
| Abdelaziz bin Mohammed . ... ... ... ... ... ... ... ... ... | 1765–1803 |
| Saud bin Abdelaziz .. ... ... ... ... ... ... ... ... ... ... | 1803–1814 |

Abdullah bin Saud ... ... ... ... ... ... ... ... ... ... ... ...   1814–1818
Mishari bin Saud   ... ... ... ... ... ... ... ... ... ... ... ...   1820
Turki bin Abdullah .. ... ... ... ... ... ... ... ... ... ... ...   1824–1834
Faisal bin Turki .. ... ... ... ... ... ... ...first period of rule 1834–1838
Khalid bin Saud .. ... ... ... ... ... ... ... ... ... ... ... ...   1840–1841
Abdullah bin Thunayyan ... ... ... ... ... ... ... ... ... ...   1841–1843
Faisal bin Turki .. ... ... ... ... ... ...second period or rule 1843–1865
Abdullah bin Faisal .. ... ... ... ... ... ...first period of rule 1865–1871
Saud bin Faisal ... ... ... ... ... ... ... ... ... ... ... ...   1871–1875
Abdulrahman bin Faisal  ... ... ... ... ...first period of rule 1875
Abdullah bin Faisal .. ... ... ... ... ... .. second period of rule 1875–1889
Abdulrahman bin Faisal  ... ... ... ... .. second period of rule 1889–1891
Abdelaziz bin Faisal . ... ... ... ... ... ... ... ... ... ... ...   1902–1953
Saud bin Abdelaziz .. ... ... ... ... ... ... king of Saudi Arabia 1953–1964
Faisal bin Abdelaziz . ... ... ... ... ... ... king of Saudi Arabia 1964–1975
Khaled bin Abdelaziz ... ... ... ... ... ... king of Saudi Arabia 1975–1982
Fahd bin Abdelaziz .. ... ... ... ... ... ... king of Saudi Arabia 1982–2005
Abdullah bin Abdelaziz . ... ... ... ... ... king of Saudi Arabia 2005–

# CHAPTER 3

# KUWAIT AND THE
# FEMININE MYSTIQUE

In blazing heat on June 29, 2006, Kuwaiti women set their country on an accelerated path to the future in elections for the region's oldest parliamentary body. In wealthier parts of Kuwait City, women voters hurried from their chauffeured cars to polling stations. Elsewhere, they braved temperatures of more than 40 degrees and walked to vote enveloped in all-encompassing, black *abayas*.

The ballots were counted at the end of the day. They showed candidates supporting reform of Kuwait's political system had won more than half of the 50 seats open to election. No one will know whether women, allowed to vote for the first time in 2006, made the difference. What is certain however is that a political revolution had taken place. All Kuwaiti adults, with the exception of members of the armed forces, had been given the right for the first time to have a say in elections to the National Assembly. Most of Kuwait's estimated 340,000 electorate exercised it.

Although parliamentary life in Kuwait is almost 70 years old, 2006 was the moment when Kuwaiti democracy finally came of age. A legislative assembly had been formed in 1938. The government, dismayed by its radicalism, closed it after six months. A generation later, the 1962 independence constitution established the National Assembly that the government closed twice before its latest manifestation was given life after the end of the Iraqi occupation. In the summer of 2005, the assembly passed an important milestone. It had operated without indefinite suspension for the longest period since it first opened. Extending voting to all adult Kuwaitis including women was the logical way forward.

Previous attempts had been made to grant women votes. The first proposal went to the assembly in 1971. At least five further attempts followed and failed. The final push started in 1999 when the government temporarily dissolved the assembly. New elections to the body were called within the constitutionally prescribed 60 days. In this time, the emir, Sheikh Jaber Al Sabah, issued 63 decrees including one that conferred full political rights on women. But votes for women still required the assembly's approval. A bill finally clearing the way for the

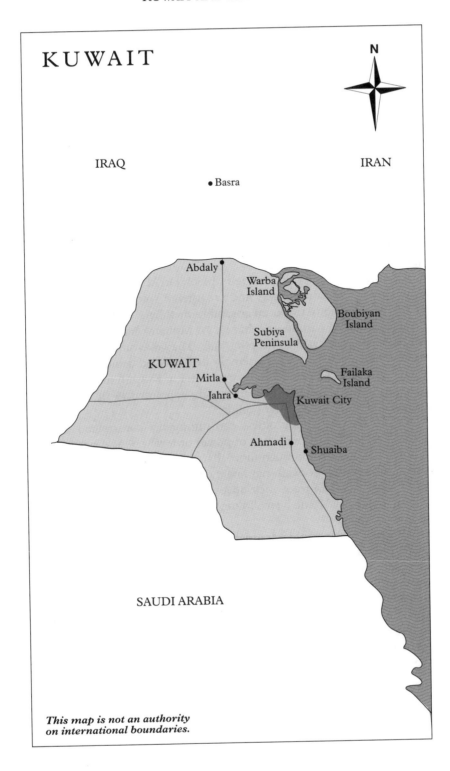

KUWAIT

N

IRAQ

IRAN

• Basra

Abdaly •

Warba
Island

Boubiyan
Island

Subiya
Peninsula

KUWAIT

Failaka
Island

Mitla •

Jahra •

Kuwait City

Ahmadi •

• Shuaiba

SAUDI ARABIA

*This map is not an authority
on international boundaries.*

amendment to be voted on was put to the assembly in April 2005.

Kuwait does not allow political parties, but assembly members have formed groups. The largest in 2005 was the Islamist bloc comprising 14 Sunnis and Shiites. Votes for women triggered their reflexive opposition. To get the amendment through, the government added a sentence stating that a woman voting and running for political office "should do so while fully adhering to the dictates of the Islamic Sharia".

Not everyone was appeased. After a heated debate, a vote was taken on May 16, 2005. The assembly divided by 35 to 23, with one abstention, in favour of the amendment. The votes of ministers sitting in the assembly were needed. Immediately afterwards, Dr Massouma Al Mubarak, a US-educated political-science teacher at Kuwait University, was appointed minister of planning and administrative development and became the first woman to sit in the assembly as ministers are entitled to do.

A last-ditch attempt was made to block Dr Al Mubarak's membership. Opponents said she was not a registered voter – a breach of one of the qualifications to be an assembly member. The objection was brushed aside. The irony was that Dr Al Mubarak had taught many of the MPs who had tried to keep her out. The government immediately set another precedent. The assembly had rejected a bill in April that would have allowed women to vote or stand in Kuwaiti municipal elections in June 2005, but two women were appointed to sit on the municipal council the week after polling.

Kuwait has the Gulf's oldest constitutionally constrained government. Yet, it has no circulation of power or legal political parties. The number of voters is not much more than 10 per cent of the people that live in the country. Kuwaiti nationality and the right to vote is restricted to those who can trace their ancestry to people who were native to Kuwait before 1921 and a small number who have been naturalized for at least 20 years.

A further demographic anomaly is the existence of 70,000 people called Bidoun (Arabic for without). They are Arabs who have been resident in Kuwait for generations who either do not have, or fail to produce, proof of nationality. The government says most entered Kuwait following the discovery of oil and it has, since 2000, deprived them of rights in an attempt to force them to disclose their original nationality. By the summer of 2006, 13,000 had been issued identity cards that allow them to work and obtain education and healthcare. The status of the rest is still unclear.

Kuwait's assembly has no power to initiate legislation and can only veto and revise proposed laws drafted by the government. The electoral system overstates some votes and understates others. For its first assembly elections in 1963, Kuwait had a 10-constituency system. In

1981, during the assembly's first suspension, the government issued a decree that divided the 10 constituencies into 25, with each one electing two members. There are substantial differences in the number of voters in each one and some of them are combinations of geographically disjointed neighbourhoods.

When the assembly was reconvened the following year, it had to ratify or reject laws decreed during its suspension. Since its members had been elected under the very system it was meant to scrutinize, there was no surprise that it voted to approve all the laws passed in this period, including the new constituency arrangements. The result is that some constituencies in 2006 had less than half the voters in others.

Critics allege votes are effectively bought in the smaller constituencies and the system is designed to appease sectional and tribal interests. The issue was the trigger for the June 2006 elections. The majority of elected members pressed for constituencies to be reduced to five of equal size, with each returning 10 members on a first-past-the-post basis, a measure that would radically increase the representation of low-income Kuwaitis.

The government countered by proposing a reduction to 10. The reformers said this would not change anything. The government then changed course and ministers decided to support a resolution moved on May 16, 2006, by tribal and conservative assembly members, to refer its 10-constituency proposal to the constitutional court. This move was interpreted as a delaying tactic that reflected the fact that ministers themselves were divided about the issue. Some said that the emir, Sheikh Sabah, who'd succeeded in January that year, preferred a single-constituency system.

With emotions rising, 28 of the 50 elected assembly members walked out when voting began on a referral motion. The session was abandoned and the opposition returned to the assembly to demand the cabinet's resignation. Demonstrations in support of the reformers were held outside the assembly building.

Two days later, three elected members used their constitutional right to call for the questioning in parliament of the prime minister, Sheikh Nasser Al Mohammed Al Sabah, about the constituency issue. This threatened to bring the row out into the open and might have led to a no-confidence motion, an unprecedented development that would have inevitably discredited more than the premier and his cabinet. On May 21, Sheikh Sabah nipped the issue in the bud, dissolved the assembly and called for elections a year earlier than constitutionally required. The reformers' subsequent victory has set the scene for a new era in Kuwaiti political life. The consensus is that change in the constituency arrangements will be only part of their agenda.

Kuwait was the first GCC state to establish a directly elected parliament. But in more than four decades since it was first formed, it has rarely been allowed to play a decisive role in the way Kuwait was governed. The result was frustration in the assembly and a record of obstructionism that's regularly hamstrung the nation.

The deadlock in the past decade between the assembly and the Kuwaiti government is linked to the declining powers of the generation of the ruling Al Sabah family that were at their prime at Kuwaiti independence in 1961. Sheikh Jaber, a popular and modernizing ruler who became emir in 1977, suffered a brain haemorrhage in September 2001 and he never recovered. The health of Crown Prince Sheikh Saad Al Abdullah Al Sabah had by then also collapsed. His condition was so poor that he was replaced as prime minister by the future emir, Sheikh Sabah, in July 2003.

At the start of 2006, Sheikh Saad was battling the effects of cancer and was largely incapacitated. Nevertheless, he was automatically declared emir of Kuwait when Sheikh Jaber's death was announced on the morning of January 15, 2006. The crown prince was unable to recite the oath of office, but a deeply-entrenched political convention came into play. For almost 85 years, with a single exception, rulership in Kuwait had alternated between two branches of the Al Sabah family: the Al Jaber and the Al Salem. Sheikh Jaber had been an Al Jaber. Sheikh Saad was an Al Salem. Partisans of his branch insisted that Sheikh Saad should become emir regardless of his physical competence. They lost the argument. In an unprecedented Arabian development, the assembly used its constitutional powers and voted on January 24 to depose Sheikh Saad on the grounds that he was medically unfit (he was to die in May 2008) just before a letter confirming his abdication had been received. The cabinet immediately asked Sheikh Sabah to take charge and he was elected emir by the assembly on January 29, 2006.

Sheikh Sabah, aged 75 when he succeeded, has held top government posts since 1955. He was deputy prime minister from 1978 until replacing Sheikh Saad in 2003. Sheikh Sabah is experienced, competent and respected. His career echoed that of his cousin, the late Sheikh Jaber, who was one of the original Gulf modernizers. Sheikh Jaber played a key role in every initiative following independence, initially as finance minister and deputy prime minister, then as prime minister and crown prince and, finally, as emir.

In this time, Kuwait shattered the Arabian mould. It was the first to break free from British control. It founded Arabia's first elected parliament. Independent Kuwait was impeccably non-aligned, establishing diplomatic relations with the Soviet Union, championing Palestinian rights and supporting the Arab cause in the 1967 and 1973 wars with Israel. Kuwait was one of the biggest beneficiaries of the 1973/74 oil price rises and set Gulf precedents with ambitious investments in international capital markets. Under Sheikh Jaber's leadership, Kuwait became one of the richest countries in the world. But splits in the Arab World and the degeneration in the regional environment took its toll. The Iran-Iraq War placed the country close to the front-line and Kuwait's support for Baghdad made it a target.

A stock-market bubble burst in 1982 and crippled the financial system. The 1986 oil price crash was a further blow. An attempt was made on Sheikh Jaber's life in a car bombing in May 1986. Hopes soared when the Iran-Iraq War ended in 1988, but Kuwait at the end of the 1980s was looking forlorn and vulnerable, particularly to its powerful northern neighbour.

## The 1990 invasion

On July 18, 2005, Saddam Hussein, still claiming to be president, sat in the dock in Baghdad to hear for the first time the full list of charges against him, nearly two years after he'd been found hiding in a hole near his home town in Tikrit in central Iraq. There were seven: killing Shiites in southern Iraq in 1991, waging war against Iran in 1980, gassing the people of Halabja in 1988, killing thousands of members of the Kurdish Barzani clan, assassinating Shiite clerics, mass murder and the 1990 invasion of Kuwait. The last upset him the most. "What a shame this charge is brought against an Iraqi by another Iraqi," he fumed. "The Kuwaitis wanted to make the Iraqi woman as cheap as 10 dinars . . . these dogs wanted to deny Iraq its historical right."

Saddam Hussein's courtroom insults repeated almost three decades of Baathist threats to Kuwait's independence and a claim that has challenged its autonomous existence for more than a century. But during his war with Iran, he projected himself as Kuwait's defender and an Arab moderate to win regional and international support. From 1984, when diplomatic relations were restored with Washington after a break of 17 years, the US accepted Iraq as a status quo power. Saddam Hussein even suggested he was prepared to normalize relations with Israel. But the need for moderation ended with the Iran War in August 1988.

James Baker, then US treasury secretary, visited the Iraqi president and told him Baghdad would get no more credit from Saudi Arabia, Kuwait or the West for its massive war debts unless Iraq gave up phosphate, sulphate, oil and other raw material rights as collateral. The proposal was rejected. Kuwait independently sought a fresh start in its relations.

Sheikh Saad, then crown prince, visited Baghdad in February 1989. The Iraqis raised a territorial claim that had been dormant during the conflict with Iran. Kuwait responded by demanding repayment of war loans. The Iraqis in outrage said the money was Kuwait's war contribution and that it was giving nothing back. It was an ominous development. Early in 1990, Kuwait and other Gulf states lifted oil production and sent prices tumbling. Kuwait started drilling in the Rumaila Field that extends across its northern border and was claimed by Iraq as part of its revived territorial claim.

Iraq by then was already rattling cages. In September 1989, Farzad Barzoft, an Iranian freelance reporter working for the London *Observer*, had been arrested after travelling to the Al Iskandari chemical plant where there had been a huge explosion. He confessed on Iraqi television to spying, was convicted and, despite calls for clemency, was hanged on March 15, 1990.

The affair roused international concern about Iraq's weapons programmes. During the Iran-Iraq War, Tehran persistently claimed Baghdad had used chemical weapons. When the war ended, Iraq's interest shifted to long-range weapons. In May 1989, it had displayed at a Baghdad exhibition a prototype of a supergun being developed in the Project Babylon programme inspired by Canadian weapons scientist Gerald Bull. Ostensibly, the 156-metre-long gun was for putting an Iraqi satellite into orbit but it could send projectiles hundreds of miles and had clear military uses.

This was, however, not the real issue. In return for supporting the supergun, Iraq had secured Bull's help to build a multi-stage missile made out of SCUDs, Soviet-designed, long-range, mobile ballistic missiles. Israel was relaxed about the supergun, which could not be hidden or moved and was vulnerable to bombing. But SCUDs, as the war for Kuwait proved, were a threat.

In March 1990, Bull was shot five times in the back of the head outside his Brussels apartment. The culprit was never caught, but official concern was stimulated. In April, British customs officials seized sections of the gun's barrels being made by Sheffield Engineering, a subsidiary of Sheffield Forgemasters, which had thought they were to be used in a petrochemicals complex. The British authorities investigated other companies supplying Iraq and decided to prosecute Matrix Churchill, another engineering firm. In February 1991, three of its executives were charged with illegally exporting munitions machinery to Iraq. Their trial began in October 1992 but the government's case was dismissed after four weeks when former UK defence minister, Alan Clark, was accused by the prosecution's own top lawyer of giving evidence under cross-examination that conflicted with previous statements made in support of the charges.

An inquiry was launched into alleged illicit weapons deals between British companies and Iraq. On February 15, 1996, the inquiry's chairman, Sir Richard Scott, published a three-volume report on the affair that criticized ministers and officials for failing to do more to stop defence equipment sales. It contributed to the decline in confidence in the Conservative government of prime minister John Major that was to be defeated in the general elections the following year.

All this was far in the future when Saddam Hussein played the Arab nationalist card in the spring of 1990. On April 2, he boasted Iraq had chemical weapons and would use them "to make fire to eat up half of Israel". The statement was condemned by the state department but the White House was reassured that it was just rhetoric.

In April 1990, US congressional leaders, including Bob Dole, who was to lose to Bill Clinton in the 1996 presidential election, visited Iraq and pressed Saddam Hussein to moderate his words and behaviour. But America continued to deliver mixed signals. The US shared military intelligence with Baghdad at least until May 1990. The White House announced further loans and stymied plans by the defence and commerce departments to impose restrictions on the sale of dual-use technology. At the end of July, President George H Bush opposed congressional sanctions moves against Iraq.

In June 1990, Iraq's deputy premier, Saadoun Hammadi, was dispatched to promote a rise in oil prices that had fallen from about US$20 a barrel in January to nearly US$15. At a press conference in Iraq's Kuwait embassy on June 26, Hammadi called for oil at US$25 a barrel. "I believe prices will go up to US$18 a barrel if there's a cut of 1.5-million b/d by Kuwait and the Emirates (UAE)," he declared. There was no Kuwaiti response. On July 17, Saddam Hussein, in a speech on the anniversary of the Baath Party's 1968 seizure of power, said the US was deliberately keeping oil prices down. The next day his foreign minister, Tariq Aziz, published a memorandum Iraq had presented earlier to the Arab League that accused Kuwait of stealing US$2,400 million worth of oil from Rumaila and suggested Iraq would not repay Kuwaiti and UAE war loans.

The US ambassador to Iraq, April Glaspie, was summoned by Saddam Hussein on July 25. Some suggest that Glaspie implicitly assented to his invasion plan, but transcripts of the meeting do not support this allegation. By July 31, Iraq had moved 100,000 troops to the border. The timing was calculated. Most Kuwaiti leaders were out of the country. A half-day public holiday to mark the Shiite Ashura festival had been declared for August 2. In the early hours of that day, Iraqi tanks crossed the border. By nightfall, Kuwait was occupied.

Saddam Hussein declared the occupation rectified a long-standing infringement of Iraqi rights and was part of a new effort to bring justice to the Palestinian people. He claimed the Kuwaiti people had revolted against their rulers and that Iraqi troops were there to support them. Some young Kuwaiti officers issued a communiqué saying Kuwait's unification with Iraq had been completed, but it had no credibility.

Tens of thousands fled. They included all the members of the Al Sabah family that were not out of the country at the time. Sheikh Jaber was persuaded to leave for Saudi Arabia by Sheikh Saad. The absence of the ruling family during Kuwait's darkest hour seriously damaged its legitimacy in the eyes of many who did not or could not leave the country. The occupation was tough and resistance was brutally repressed. On January 17, 1991, the US-led coalition began air attacks against targets in Iraq and Kuwait. On February 24, the ground offensive started.

The Iraqi evacuation was devastating. Saddam Hussein ordered the destruction of Kuwait's oil industry and most wells were set alight. By the end of February, hundreds were burning. Oil spilled uncontrollably, creating in one place a lake one kilometre in diameter. More than one billion barrels of oil were burnt in the seven months until the fires were extinguished. It added to pollution caused by up to 10 billion barrels of oil poured into the Gulf in an attempt to foul water desalination plants on Saudi Arabia's east coast. The fires were extinguished by the end of 1991 but mines are still being cleared.

Iraq announced it would accept all UN resolutions and US President George H Bush declared an end to the US advance on February 28. Iraq's seven-month occupation has left few visible scars. But there is psychological damage and lasting resentment towards Iraq that persists despite the deposition of Saddam Hussein. There are living reasons why Kuwait will have difficulty forgetting. In the atrium of the National Assembly building, a montage highlights the fate of 570 Kuwaitis who went missing during the occupation or were taken hostage by the Iraqis. The presumption is that all were killed, but a definitive answer about their fate has still not been provided.

Kuwait insists, despite the change in regime, that Iraq should continue to pay at least some of the reparations imposed on Baghdad when the 1990–91 war ended. A UN agency estimated the Iraqis caused a total loss to Kuwait, other countries and third-country nationals who fled the region at the time, amounting to US$354 billion, about 15 times Iraq's national income in 2007. No reparations were paid in the first five years following the end of the war during a total embargo that led to an estimated 60,000 Iraqi children dying in 1995 alone.

The 1996 UN oil-for-food resolution allowed Iraqi oil exports, and the proceeds were used to buy humanitarian goods and pay reparations. After the 2003 Iraq War, all restrictions on exports were lifted and compensation payments were reduced to five per cent of Iraqi oil revenues. In June 2005, Iraq called for reparations to be abolished. By that point, just under US$20 billion had been remitted, half of it to Kuwait. The proposal was ignored. Reparations are still being paid. The ghost of Saddam Hussein, hanged in December 2006, still haunts Iraq's relations with Kuwait.

## The fate of Boubiyan Island

The route taken in February 1991 by the retreating Iraqi army along Highway 80 towards the Mitla Ridge, rises about 30 m above Kuwait Bay. There, thousands of Iraqi soldiers may have been killed by coalition fighters and helicopter gunships. The carnage at Mitla remains one of the defining images of the Kuwait War.

About 65 km from Kuwait, Highway 80 rises up the desert escarpment towards Mitla and from there runs to Ardiya on the Iraqi border. At Mitla, Route 801 forks right and follows the sweep of Kuwait Bay's northern shore. The end of the journey is marked by the Subiya power station at the headland where the bay's coast meets the southern shore of the channel that leads to Umm Qasr in Iraq.

Access to the bridge to Boubiyan Island is still blocked by a security barrier near buildings destroyed in the last war, or perhaps the one before that. Kuwait City sits on the southern horizon almost 30 km away across the bay. The silence and peace is enhanced by bird song. Subiya figures in ambitious plans being implemented in a country flush with oil cash and free for the first time in decades from threats from its perplexing northern neighbour.

They call for a new city to cover what is now only sand and desert scrub. Perhaps by the start of the next decade Subiya will be linked to Kuwait by a 28-kilometre causeway. It will be almost 30 years late. The first Subiya masterplan was agreed in 1978. Two years later, Iraq invaded Iran and fighting erupted less than 80 km to the north. The plan was revived in the lost peace between the end of that conflict and Iraq's invasion and again in the 1990s. But Iraq still coveted all of Kuwait and claimed Boubiyan, Warba and the smaller Kuwaiti islands at the mouth of the Shatt.

Boubiyan is almost the size of greater London. Up to half of it sinks twice a day beneath six metre tides. In the island's north, the channel between Boubiyan and Iraq's Fao Peninsula is narrow enough at low tide for a person to be able to throw a stone from one country into another. During the Iran-Iraq War, it was hit by shells fired from Fao. Iraqi poison gas polluted the air. Grenades and sea-mines are still found rusting on its beaches. Concrete sea-defences erected by the Iraqis in the winter of 1990 are intact along its southern coast.

After the Kuwait War, the UN appointed a commission to define the Iraq-Kuwait border in accordance with 1991 UN Security Council ceasefire resolution 687. In April 1992, it fixed the Kuwaiti frontier near the Iraqi town of Safwan and pushed it north in the region of the contested Rumaila oil field to give Kuwait six oil wells and part of the Iraqi Umm Qasr naval base. Physical demarcation was completed in November 1992. Boubiyan and Warba were finally allocated to Kuwait. But the islands unpopulated might yet tempt Iraq. Something permanent to demonstrate Kuwaiti sovereignty was needed. In 2005, plans were approved for a container port on the island's north-west coast. A railway line will cut across the island, bridge the channel to the mainland and head north to Umm Qasr, the railhead of the existing railway line through Iraq to Turkey and Europe. When the Boubiyan line is complete, you'll be able to travel by train from Glasgow to the Gulf. It will be a route that will cross time as well as space.

## The creation of Kuwait

Kuwait City is the principal conurbation in a country that bears its name. Most nationals live there and it had a population in 2007 approaching two million people. The first town on the site was built in about 1716 when Bedouin from central Arabia settled to escape drought. The first written mention of Kuwait was in 1709 when it was described by a Syrian visitor. The Danish traveller, Carsten Niebuhr, was the first European to put the name Kuwait, the diminutive of the Arabic word *kut* (fortress), on a map, which he drew in 1765. Niebuhr also used the town's other name Grane. Grane, or *qurain*, is the diminutive of *qarn*, or hill.

Some 10,000 years ago, stone-age people inhabited the area. Around 7,500 years ago, a settlement was built on Kuwait Bay's northern shore. The only consistently settled spot is Failaka Island, which lies at the bay's entrance. During the Sumerian era, Failaka was part of the Dilmun civilization. It entered Western history when Alexander the Great ordered exploratory Gulf expeditions in preparation for an invasion of Arabia that was cancelled after he died.

Alexander is believed to have renamed Failaka as Ikaros because he was told it looked like Ikaria in the Aegean. The Greeks subsequently founded a colony on the island. It takes 30 minutes by fast boat for the 24 km journey from Salmiya Marina in Kuwait City to Failaka. A town that once accommodated as many as 5,000 people has been largely abandoned since its inhabitants left the island during the Iraqi occupation, when it was also bombed by coalition forces.

A holiday-chalet complex where you can hire bicycles and paddle on a boating lake is busy in season and on holy days and a new hotel is being built. But most of Failaka's 72 km² are empty. Visitors will find the remains of a 12-room house and a fortress from the Hellenic period, statues of Greek gods have been found, and a limestone plaque engraved with Greek writing suggests that Failaka in its Hellenic prime was a cultural centre.

The island also nurtures one of ancient Arabia's most obscure myths. It centres on the life of the Green Man (Al Khidr) who is said to have been the only soul to gain immortality by tasting the water of life (*Ma'ul Hayat*). Al Khidr lived on Failaka and transformed it into a green and pleasant land by sinking deep-water wells. According to the tale, Khidr became a companion of Alexander and Jesus. He witnessed the Prophet Mohammeds's (PBUH) ascension to heaven and conversation with God. Al Khidr may be the inspiration for the myth of George, patron saint of England and Georgia. The Green Man was memorialized in Failaka's Maqam Monument which was destroyed by puritanical Muslims in 1980. The island is destined for a renaissance. In June 2006, developers presented plans to convert it into a US$ 3,000 million leisure resort.

The Greeks and then the Parthians were followed by a new Persian empire under the Sasanians that absorbed what is now Kuwait. The coming of Islam in the 7th century brought a new political order, but this quickly dissolved.

For centuries, what is now Kuwait was no more than a stretch of desert separating the Shatt al-Arab and the valleys of the Tigris and the Euphrates from Arabia's oasis civilizations. Baghdad had not fully recovered from the Mongol invasion of 1258 when the Ottomans took the city in 1534 and Basra 12 years later.

By the middle of the 1600s, north-east Arabia was dominated by the Bani Khalid tribe. It was during their supremacy that the Al Utub, a division of the Anaizah confederation, arrived. The Al Khalifa segment of the Al Utub left in 1766 and eventually settled in Bahrain. In Kuwait, the Al Sabah emerged as tribal chiefs by about 1756, under Sheikh Sabah Al Jaber. They broke free of Bani Khalid control. Kuwait began to flourish as a consequence of pearl fishing and the Arabian caravan trade to Syria. Kuwait's first mud wall was probably built before 1770. It was a shipbuilding centre by 1800.

Kuwait's significance rose during the 1775–79 Persian siege and occupation of Basra. With access to the port blocked, ships carrying mail through the Gulf used Kuwait instead. In November 1777, the first East India Company vessel called. Kuwait was declared to have a suitable anchorage. Mail bound for Basra from India could cover the ground from Kuwait in three days compared with up to three weeks if it was sent by boat up the Shatt al-Arab. British merchants built a warehouse in the 1790s.

Kuwait encouraged trade by declaring itself neutral between the Ottomans and the Persians and it became a haven in a turbulent region. The Al Saud had seized much of Arabia. The Al Sabah under their second leader, Sheikh Abdullah bin Sabah, maintained Kuwait's autonomy by using diplomacy, defiance, British protection and blood ties to the Al Saud, who were also of the Anaizah people.

The fall of the first Saudi empire in 1818 marked the start of the rise of Britain's Gulf Arab dominion. The maritime treaty signed by lower Gulf rulers in 1820 was not extended to Kuwait which had no record of supporting piracy or having a central role in the slave trade. Kuwait's ruler, Sheikh Jaber, who succeeded Abdullah in 1814, was Britain's friend. No treaty seemed necessary, though Kuwait did sign up to the maritime truce for a year in 1841. The British link was strengthened in the 1820s when a British warehouse was again established during a dispute between the East India Company and Basra's Ottoman governor. Kuwait's autonomy during this period was cited more than a century later as evidence that it was independent long before the fall of the Ottomans in 1918.

Britain was again useful in the late 1830s when an Egyptian army marched across Arabia. It seized Al Hasa in what is now Saudi Arabia in preparation for an attack on Basra and Baghdad. The British agent in Bushire sent a letter warning the Egyptian commander, Khurshid Pasha, against seizing Kuwait. Sheikh Jaber took the additional protective step of secretly co-operating with him. The Egyptians withdrew from eastern Arabia in 1841. Trade increased and Kuwait's economy was boosted by the start of a fortnightly shipping service from Bombay by the British Indian Steam Navigation Company in 1862.

A new Al Saud threat after 1843 was countered through diplomacy under Sheikh Jaber – who died after 45 years as emir in 1859 – and his son Sheikh Sabah. The Kuwaitis co-operated with the 1871 Ottoman expedition that captured Al Hasa while the Al Saud were divided by civil war. Despite this, the Kuwaitis pragmatically accepted three Al Saud refugees later that decade. The British connection strengthened and, in the final years of the 19th century, Kuwait was a source of horses for the British Indian army and became the region's leading pearling centre.

Mubarak bin Sabah, known as Mubarak the Great, became Kuwait's seventh ruler in 1896 following the deposition and death of his brother Mohammed. His first test was an attempted coup by a local merchant allied to the family of his late brother. He continued to provide Kuwaiti protection to Abdulrahman bin Faisal Al Saud and his family, including his son Abdelaziz, the future king of Saudi Arabia, who'd been driven into exile by his rivals, the Al Rashid of Hail. Abdelaziz recaptured Riyadh with Kuwaiti backing in 1902.

A Kuwaiti army led by Sheikh Mubarak and Abdulrahman immediately marched on Hail to finish off the Al Rashid. It was ambushed at Al Sarif about 32 km north-east of Buraidah in central Arabia. The rout was so complete that Sheikh Mubarak abandoned his dream of establishing his own larger state.

The Middle East had by then been turned upside down. In 1869, the Suez Canal was completed. In 1882, Britain took control of Egypt. France was acting as guardian of the Christians of Lebanon. Germany wooed the Ottomans. Russia was consolidating its Central Asian empire, infiltrating Persia and testing Britain in north-west India. Concern

about the initial French monopoly over the Suez Canal prompted a report by Britain's parliament that called for a railway from Alexandretta,
on Syria's coast, to Kuwait, for transporting British troops to the Gulf
should Russia seize Persia. The project was dismissed as economically
unviable. News that the Ottomans had approved a German plan to extend the Berlin–Constantinople railway to Baghdad and reports that
Russia was planning to build a separate line from Tripoli in Lebanon
to Homs, Baghdad and Kuwait galvanized London. The final trigger
for British action was a report that a Russian named Adamoff, accompanied by two Russian doctors, had visited Kuwait.

The British political resident in the Gulf was directed to negotiate
an exclusive agreement modelled on treaties signed with other Gulf
Arab rulers. Mubarak secured a promise that it should include an ex-
plicit promise for British protection if Kuwait was attacked by a foreign
power. The treaty was signed on January 23, 1899. It defined Kuwait's
status until independence more than 62 years later. The following year,
Mubarak signed an agreement limiting weapons trafficking to Afghanistan and a further one in 1904 establishing a postal service.

Britain consolidated its influence with the appointment of a British
agent and in a secret 1907 agreement that allowed the Royal Navy to
use Shuwaikh. A British right of veto over foreign pearlers was accepted in 1911. Britain acquired first rights to oil exploration and production in an agreement signed in October 1913.

The exclusive agreement provided comfort. But Kuwait's border
with the velayet of Basra was never defined. Ottoman forces were stationed in Umm Qasr and Safwan and, in 1902, on Boubiyan Island.
Some uncertainty was removed by the 1913 agreement which divided
Arabia into British and Ottoman zones of influence. It recognized Safwan and Umm Qasr as part of the Basra region. But no permanent demarcation was in place by the time the war began in the Middle East in
November 1914.

Sheikh Mubarak died in 1915. He was succeeded by his son, Sheikh
Jaber, who died in 1917 and then by Sheikh Salem, another son of
Sheikh Mubarak. Kuwait served the British expedition that captured
Basra in early 1915. It benefited from trade with the British army as
well as from smuggling to the Ottomans. Sheikh Jaber, who declared
Kuwait's support for the allies, and Salem, a strict Muslim, were contrasting personalities. They bequeathed Kuwait's system of rotating the
emirship between their descendants that appears to have finally ended
with the succession of Sheikh Sabah in January 2006.

The Arabian power balance shifted with the end of the war. The Al
Saud, Britain's allies since December 1915, expanded west at the expense of the Hashemites and north east into Iraq. In the spring of
1920, Sheikh Salem sent a tribal force to Kuwait's southern border to

deter Saudi Ikhwan probes. It was surprised and wiped out on April 4 near Manifa. Sheikh Salem ordered the construction of a city wall and led a force to the fortified village of Al Jahra, where the Ikhwan were repulsed on October 10, 1920.

Britain helped by sending aircraft to drop warning leaflets among the invaders. It deployed warships in plain sight of the Ikhwan and landed marines in Kuwait City. Britain was by then master of Palestine and Mesopotamia and wanted an end to border wars. In May 1922, a meeting was convened in the Persian border town of Muhammara, now called Khorramshahr, to fix the border between the lands of Abdelaziz and Iraq, a new country under British mandated control. Abdelaziz signed an agreement but subsequently declared he'd been cheated and demanded fresh negotiations.

These were held in September 1922 at Uqair, a port on the coast of what is now Saudi Arabia. The British priority was to please the Saudis. Sir Percy Cox, British High Commissioner to Iraq, imposed an agreement that drastically extended the Al Saud domain at Kuwait's expense. Using a red pencil, he redrew the frontiers between Iraq, Kuwait and Saudi Arabia. The Saudi-Kuwait border was pushed north by 250 km. A neutral zone, now known as the Divided Zone, was established between Kuwait and the Al Hasa province controlled by the Al Saud that was to be open to Bedouin tribes regardless of nationality.

Cox presented the Uqair Treaty as a fait accompli to Kuwait's ruler, Sheikh Ahmed Al Jaber Al Sabah, who'd succeeded Sheikh Salem in 1921. The Al Saud were too strong for the Kuwaitis to resist, but Britain promised to guarantee Kuwait's northern border with Iraq. The deal was reluctantly accepted. Despite the concessions, relations with the Saudis remained bad. Abdelaziz claimed Bedouin from the Najd were evading zakat by trading in Kuwait's free markets. Sheikh Ahmed refused to act as an effective tax collector for Riyadh. The Saudis responded by preventing Bedouin from northern Arabia entering Kuwait to buy goods for 14 years and Ikhwan raids continued until Abdelaziz repressed the movement in 1930.

The slump of the 1930s hammered the Gulf and compounded the misery caused by the collapse in demand for natural pearls. In 1924, Frank Holmes, who'd secured an option to explore for oil in Al Hasa province the previous year, managed to win a similar commitment for the Neutral Zone. He tried unsuccessfully to get the concession for Kuwait proper.

Following the start of exploratory work in Bahrain in 1931, Sheikh Ahmed renewed contacts with Holmes who was then acting on behalf of Gulf Oil, the Texan oil firm. Kuwait was also being wooed by APOC, which was controlled by Britain. London, anxious to avoid a confrontation with America, did not insist on the application of the terms of the 1899 exclusive agreement that specified no business agreement could be made with a non-British entity. After months of negotiations, APOC and Gulf Oil established the Kuwait Oil Company (KOC) in December 1933. An agreement between Britain and KOC, signed in March 1934, stipulated KOC's management would be assigned exclusively to Britons.

Sheikh Ahmed finally awarded a 75-year concession to KOC on December 23, 1934. He appointed Holmes, who'd become a friend, as his KOC representative. Holmes held the position until he died in 1947. Exploration started in 1935. Oil was struck in the onshore Burgan Field on February 23, 1938. It was one of the greatest mineral discoveries of all time and Kuwait's proven oil reserves are now put at 100 billion barrels, almost nine per cent of the world total, although the real figure could be significantly lower. The Kuwait oil era was delayed by the start of the Second World War. The Allies ordered the suspension of operations. Kuwaiti wells were plugged.

In the 1930s, Kuwait felt the winds of political change caused by the Russian Revolution and the spread of radical ideas. This coalesced with growing frustration among the merchant class about the way Kuwait was being managed. The idea of creating some form of elected body was promoted by Britain's political agent in Kuwait, Gerald de Gaury, an Arabist who later formed the Druze legion to fight the Vichy French administration in Lebanon during the Second World War.

Sheikh Ahmed, who believed the political agitation was being fomented by Baghdad, relented and established a legislative council comprising appointed members. The council, which inspired a short-lived equivalent in Dubai around the same time, lasted six months before it was dissolved on December 21, 1938. A new council, formed in March 1939, was chaired by Sheikh Abdullah Al Salem, a cousin of Sheikh Ahmed who was to succeed as Kuwaiti ruler 11 years later. It comprised four members of the Al Sabah and nine reliable local notables. The war and the rise of the German threat to British control of Mesopotamia ended tolerance of nationalist and independence movements.

Kuwaiti oil exports began on June 30, 1946. Sheikh Ahmed used his first KOC oil payment to pay for the education of girls and women. When he died and was succeeded by Sheikh Abdullah Al Salem in 1950, Kuwait was well placed to capitalize on the new world order based on petroleum and the motor car. Educated, open-minded and innovative, Sheikh Abdullah defined a new Gulf template with social programmes, a willingness to accept foreign workers and a policy that placed Kuwait in line with the aspirations of the developing world. But plans for the future were consistently blighted by regional politics and the challenge presented by Iraq.

The border was first formally raised in July 1932 when Iraq, which had become independent in May, applied to become a member of the League of Nations. It needed to define its frontiers and this led to an exchange of letters between Kuwait and King Ghazi, the second king of Iraq. He called for territorial concessions and challenged Kuwait's right to exist based on the claim that it had been part of the Ottoman province of Basra and should have been transferred to Iraq, the successor state to the Ottoman system.

Baghdad argued that the 1913 Anglo-Ottoman Treaty had defined Mubarak the Great as a *qaimmaqam* (provincial sub-governor) under the Ottomans. The treaty had been declared null and void when war between Britain and the Ottomans broke out in November 1914. But Iraqi nationalists on both sides of the border asserted Britain had acknowledged in principle that Kuwait should have been part of Iraq. Sheikh Ahmed cited Iraqi mischief making as the main reason for replacing the 1938 legislative council.

The issue went into abeyance following King Ghazi's death in a car crash – which some believe was organized by Britain – in 1939. His son, King Faisal II, was three and too young to rule. Power was placed in the hands of his pro-British paternal uncle, Abdul Illah, who'd been a prominent figure in the Hashemite army during the 1916–18 Arab Revolt. Deposed as regent for two years during the Second World War, Abdul Illah was restored by Britain in 1943 and guided Iraq until Faisal's coronation in 1953.

By this time, Middle East politics had radically altered. Defeat in the first war with Israel in 1948–49 had discredited Arab leaders. In July 1952, the Egyptian monarchy was deposed. Under President Nasser, Egypt poured out anti-monarchist rhetoric. The Iraqi Hashemite monarchy was among its targets. On February 14, 1958, the Hashemite Arab Union was announced by King Faisal and his second cousin, King Hussein of Jordan, in response to the union between Syria and Egypt declared two weeks earlier. The Iraqi monarchy proposed recognizing the independence of Kuwait if it joined the new union. Sheikh Abdullah Al Salem turned the offer down and invasion threats ensued. On July 14, 1958, the Iraqi monarchy was deposed and replaced by military. The claim against Kuwaiti territory was revived by Baghdad's new republican regime.

Rising oil income, meanwhile, was lifting the Kuwaiti economy. One of the curiosities of Kuwait's history was the role of the Bush family in developing its oil industry. In 1954, George H Bush, president of the US from 1989–92, founded Zapata Offshore in Houston. The company developed international business. One of its customers was Kuwait, where Zapata drilled the country's first offshore oil well in 1963. The Bush connection with Kuwait was refreshed in December 2005 when the former president, accompanied by Brent Scowcroft, national security adviser in the Bush administration, visited to deliver a speech at a finance conference at Kuwait's Sheraton Hotel. An appreciative audience, grateful for Bush's determination to expel Iraq from Kuwait in 1990/91, warmly applauded his flattering comments about a country he'd known for more than four decades.

The growth of US business interests in Kuwait after 1945 reflected rising American influence in the Arab World as Britain's inexorably declined. The independent attitude of the ruling family, the competence of Kuwait's business class, increasing affluence and pressure from below for full self-government was irresistible. Agreement was reached with Britain that the 1899 exclusive agreement should be terminated in 1961 and that Kuwait would become fully self-governing. Independence was declared on June 19. Britain immediately signed a long-term defence agreement. Less than two weeks later, Iraq's prime minister, Abdel Karim Qassim, declared Kuwait was part of Iraq, announced he'd invade six days later and moved troops to the border. Sheikh Abdullah Al Salem called for support. On July 1, British troops were deployed on the border. They stayed until September when they were replaced by troops from other Arab countries.

Qassim was deposed and executed in 1963. Détente was reached with the new Iraqi regime headed by President Abdel Salam Arif, who died in a helicopter crash in April 1966, and then by his brother, Abdulrahman Arif. The first Arif recognized Kuwait's right to exist, basing his decision on correspondence between the two governments in 1932, but refused to accept any previous demarcations of the border. The issue continued to fester. There was a border incident in mid-1966, but no revival of the Iraqi claim to all of Kuwait. Boubiyan Island continued to crop up in Iraqi statements. Kuwait offered to rent the island to Iraq in the early 1960s for 99 years for a payment of KD1 a year. Baghdad turned the proposal down.

The Baathists deposed Abdulrahman Arif in 1968. The new regime occupied the Kuwait border outpost at Al Samtah in 1973 and penetrated three kilometres into Kuwaiti territory under the pretext of wanting land beyond Umm Qasr. After being pressured by the Soviet Union, Saudi Arabia and Iran, Iraq withdrew in 1977. A new border agreement was signed in July.

Kuwait's 1962 independence constitution called for the creation of an elected legislative body. It was accepted by the Al Sabah as a means of legitimizing its rule at a time when the family's position was threatened by Iraq's claim. The electorate was restricted to adult males whose ancestors were present in Kuwait in 1921. The constitution gave the emir the power to dissolve the body almost at will. Elections on January 27, 1963 produced a majority opposition in the form of the National Bloc. It challenged government policy in many areas. Independent Kuwait defined a new template for Gulf governments. The Kuwait Fund for Arab Economic Development (KFAED), the prototype for Arab aid agencies, was founded. Kuwait established diplomatic relations with the Soviet Union in August 1963 and started doing business with Poland, East Germany and other Soviet-bloc countries.

In the third Arab-Israel War of June 1967, it ordered an embargo on oil sales to the UK, the US and West Germany for supporting Israel. But a call by the assembly for Kuwait to withdraw reserves from British banks and pull out of the sterling area was ignored. By the end of 1967, it had the world's highest per capita income.

Kuwait championed Arab rights and became a refuge for Palestinian exiles. One was a Palestinian engineer named Yasser Arafat who settled in Kuwait at the end of the 1950s. In 1958, Arafat and Palestinian friends founded the mainstream Fatah guerrilla movement that in 1959 began to publish a magazine advocating armed struggle against Israel. At the end of 1964, Arafat left Kuwait to become a full-time revolutionary. He was elected chairman of the Palestine Liberation Organisation (PLO) in 1969. By the end of the 1980s, more than 300,000 Palestinians were living in the state. Arafat and the PLO supported Saddam Hussein during the Kuwait crisis. The consequences were disastrous. After the war, all Palestinians were ejected. There was no mourning in Kuwait at Arafat's death in Paris on November 11, 2004.

Sheikh Sabah Al Salem succeeded Sheikh Abdullah Al Salem who died in December 1965. This was, until January 2006, the sole exception in the rotation between the Al Jaber and Al Salem branches of the Al Sabah. Sheikh Sabah Al Salem had spent most of his working life as head of the police force. His cousin, Sheikh Jaber Al Ahmed, was appointed prime minister and named crown prince on May 31, 1966.

The second assembly elections were held on January 25, 1967 with 220 candidates contesting 50 seats. Most winners were loyal to the Al Sabah family. The opposition alleged election rigging. In January 1969, bombs were detonated outside government buildings. Hundreds of expatriate Arabs were arrested and some expelled. Later in the year, a group of Palestinians was arrested, charged and convicted of perpetrating the attacks.

The third poll in 1971 produced an assembly that focused on the demand for full nationalization of the oil industry. The fourth elections in 1975 produced an even more militant assembly. It pressed for Kuwaiti finance to be provided liberally to other Arab states. The government's track record was already established. It was supplying money to Palestinian guerrillas and had cut financial support to Jordan following its crackdown on Palestinian fighters in September 1970. In 1971, it recognized the People's Republic of China. Kuwait led calls for Arab action against the US and other countries providing military assistance to Israel in the 1973 war. It announced the nationalization of KOC in phases, starting with 60-per-cent participation leading to full state control that was agreed at the end of 1975 and made retroactive to March that year.

Kuwait's support for Arab radicalism was highlighted at that time when Oman's foreign affairs minister, Qais Zawawi, publicly accused Kuwait and Iraq of backing the Dhofar rebellion by financing Marxist-Leninist South Yemen. It announced plans, never implemented, to build a nuclear-power industry and suggested in 1976 that it would buy weapons from the Soviet Union.

Kuwait after the 1973/74 oil-price rises set the pace for the region with forays into Western capital and property markets. The London-based Kuwait Investment Office (KIO) bid for St Martin's Property in London in the teeth of strong local opposition. In late 1974, it bought almost 15 per cent of German car marker Daimler-Benz. By the end of the 1970s, the KIO was one of the world's biggest institutional investors.

Despite rising affluence, Kuwait in the mid-1970s was unsettled. The assembly was consistently at odds with the government. It embarrassed Kuwait's neighbours with criticisms of their failure to support Arab causes. In 1976, the assembly blocked a trade agreement with Romania because of that country's relations with Israel. Syria was attacked for intervening in support of the Christian-dominated government during the Lebanese civil war. The government in turn charged assembly members with destabilizing Kuwait in the interests of unnamed foreign countries, the standard code for Iraq. Amid mounting tension, the prime minister, Crown Prince Sheikh Jaber, resigned with his cabinet on August 29, 1976, and said that assembly members were making running the country impossible by blocking key legislation. The same day, the emir, Sheikh Sabah, dissolved the assembly and vested its powers in himself and the council of ministers.

Sheikh Jaber addressed the nation and claimed the crisis was the result of the 1962 constitution; he also accused unnamed people of exploiting the freedom it granted to undermine the country and charged some newspapers with acting as "obedient tools in the service of objectives alien to our country". The government was empowered to suspend newspapers for two years. In the following months, newspapers and associations were closed.

Domestic tensions escalated following President Sadat's visit to Israel in November 1977, a move that led to Egypt being boycotted by most Arab states. Demonstrations against the visit at Kuwait University led to clashes with police and arrests. Newspapers and magazines were suspended for attacking the Egyptian president. Sheikh Sabah died of a heart attack on December 31, 1977 aged 62. He was immediately succeeded by Sheikh Jaber. Sheikh Saad, the former police chief and interior minister, was named crown prince.

The oil-price increases of 1979–81 and the trans-shipment boom following the closure of Iraqi ports during the Iran-Iraq War lifted the economy to new heights. In a mad bout of speculation, hundreds would gather in the Souk al-Manakh near the official stock exchange, which had opened in 1977, to trade in shares free of the regulations applied to deals done on the approved market. Share prices were driven to fantastic levels on the promise of quick capital gains. The bubble burst and, by the start of October 1982, the unofficial market had collapsed. Most trading on the Souk had been done using post-dated cheques. A government inquiry showed that at the end of October 1982 almost 29,000 such cheques were in circulation with a face value of more than US$92 billion, equivalent in today's money to almost US$500 billion. Every Kuwaiti bank, with the exception of the National Bank of Kuwait, had lent money to the Souk and had to be propped up by the state.

The Kuwaiti cabinet split about how the issue should be addressed. Finance minister Abdel-Latif Al Hamad wanted the big debtors to go bust. Others in the cabinet wanted a bail-out. It was rumoured ministers favouring a benign approach had been involved in the Souk. The crisis rumbled on for 10 months. Al Hamad resigned in September 1983 and was replaced by Sheikh Ali Al Khalifa, Kuwait's oil minister. It took another decade and the Iraqi invasion for the consequences of the Souk al-Manakh to be resolved. The affair shaped the attitudes of a generation of Kuwaiti business people and served as a warning to the region.

Seeking support following the Iranian Revolution and the start of the Iran-Iraq War, Sheikh Jaber decided to reconvene the assembly and called elections in February 1981. The fifth assembly was fractious. Attacks on the government intensified following the election in 1985 of the most radical assembly ever. History repeated itself. Sheikh Jaber announced the assembly's second dissolution on July 3, 1986 and implied some members had been involved in a conspiracy designed to destabilize the country. Strict press censorship was introduced.

Free from parliamentary restraints, the government pressed ahead with measures to boost the economy. But its most important initiative was inviting the Soviet Union and China in 1997 to re-flag Kuwaiti oil tankers. This followed Iranian attacks against shipping in the Gulf and America's initial refusal to provide protection. Stung by the Kuwaiti move, Washington quickly agreed to re-flag 11 Kuwaiti vessels and provide more military protection.

US involvement in the Gulf was eventually to culminate in a confrontation with the Iranian air force and navy. On July 3, 1988, the US warship *Vincennes* shot down a civilian Iranian airliner flying from Iran to Dubai, killing all 290 people aboard. Realizing that a new front had been opened against it by the world's greatest military power, Tehran sued for peace. The war ended on August 25, 1988.

These dramas almost overshadowed Kuwait's greatest financial coup. The previous autumn, in a delicious reversal of historical fortunes, the KIO had acquired nearly 20 per cent of BP in the flotation of the remaining British government stake in the oil firm. Following an investigation, the KIO was instructed in October 1988 to reduce its ownership to less than 10 per cent. The KIO complied and sold its shares at a handsome profit.

The Iran-Iraq War was over, but political frustrations were once again on the rise. In 1989, members of the dissolved assembly began calling for its restitution and the application of the articles of the constitution suspended in 1986. The movement was supported by a business community suffering from the recession caused by low oil prices. The government announced in early 1990 that it would not restore the assembly but instead establish a national council, essentially advisory in nature, comprising 50 elected members and 25 appointed ones. The opposition boycotted the process. The council was constituted following a vote for the electable seats in June 1990. Its activities were interrupted by the Iraqi invasion. The council was abolished when a new assembly was elected in October 1992.

Kuwait recovered quickly from the occupation. The oil-price rise resulting from the elimination of Iraqi production helped the country regain its pre-war level of economic activity by 1995. The stock market soared and was given a further lift by the sale of shares in companies taken over by the government following the collapse of the Souk al-Manakh and Iraqi reparations payments after 1996.

The assembly resumed its pressure on the government. In March 1998, it forced the resignation of information minister, Sheikh Saud Nasser Al Sabah, for allowing more than 160 books critical of Islamic orthodoxy and related matters to be displayed at Kuwait's Arab book fair. There was a temporary suspension of the assembly in 1999. When it reassembled later in the year, the campaign against the government began again. In February 2000, Sheikh Jaber appointed a new cabinet that included younger members of the ruling Al Sabah family.

In the months leading to the 2003 invasion of Iraq, life in Kuwait was increasingly dominated by the arrival of tens of thousands of US and other coalition troops. Iraqi missiles fired at Kuwait City in the early stages of the war did little damage. When Saddam Hussein's statue was torn down in the centre of Iraq in April, there was joy in the hearts of most Kuwaitis. It remains the only Arab country wholly positive about the war's justification and results.

Saddam Hussein was finished and was hanged in degrading circumstances on December 30, 2006. But new enemies had emerged. In

October 2002, two gunmen fired on US marines conducting war games on Failaka Island. They killed one and injured another. The authorities later said one of the two extremists, who were killed when the Marines returned fire, had sworn allegiance to Osama bin Laden. There was another shooting involving US troops a week later. On January 21, 2003, a gunman shot dead an American civilian and wounded a second at a crossroads near a McDonald's restaurant near Camp Doha, the main US Army base in Kuwait.

The presence of Al Qaeda elements was unambiguously confirmed in January 2005 in gun battles between Kuwaiti security forces and militants believed to be plotting attacks on government and Western targets. Four police officers died and 10 others were wounded. In a shoot-out at the end of the month, eight militants, including a Saudi, were killed and two Kuwaiti security officers wounded. The authorities blamed the attacks on radicals fleeing Saudi Arabia and Kuwaitis returning from fighting coalition troops in Iraq. Security was tightened. The militants' alleged leader, Amer Khlaif Al Enezi, died suddenly in police custody eight days after his arrest in January. A total of 37 suspected militants were charged in June 2005 with carrying out the attacks. Of those charged, 34 face the death penalty. There have been no further attacks.

The New Gulf's most vulnerable nation continues to face great challenges. Restless Iran and tormented Iraq are immediate neighbours. The struggle between the assembly and government hinders long-term thinking. Society's dependence upon government jobs, state hand-outs and the labour of foreigners who outnumber nationals by almost three to one is a persistent source of concern. There are even worries about depleting oil reserves and shortages of natural gas.

The government and KOC believe Kuwait urgently needs the assistance of IOCs to make the most of what has been found. But soaring oil revenues and rising living standards are laying the foundations for a new era of progress and prosperity. The economy grew by 20 per cent in 2006 and expanded by at least 10 per cent in 2007. Huge new projects, including Subiya's City of Silk, with 750,000 residents, reflect a new mood of optimism in Kuwait's business community.

The impact of the assembly elections of 2006 is as yet unclear. The cabinet resigned to avoid a 'no confidence' vote and a new one was appointed in March 2007. A year later, the parliament was dissolved and fresh elections called, based on a five-constituency system. Sceptics argue Kuwait's bloated state bureaucracy is beyond redemption and conflict between parliament and the ruling family can never be resolved. But there is an alternative route for a country that was once the New Gulf's role model that the optimists believe will eventually be taken as rising affluence dilutes old resentments.

**Al Sabah rulers of Kuwait**

| | |
|---|---|
| Sheikh Sabah | died 1764 |
| Sheikh Abdullah Al Sabah | 1764–1815 |
| Sheikh Jaber bin Abdullah | 1815–1836 |
| Sheikh Sabah bin Jaber | 1836–1866 |
| Sheikh Abdullah bin Sabah | 1866–1892 |
| Sheikh Mohammed bin Sabah | 1892–1896 |
| Sheikh Mubarak bin Sabah | 1896–1915 |
| Sheikh Jaber bin Mubarak | 1915–1917 |
| Sheikh Salem bin Mubarak | 1917–1921 |
| Sheikh Ahmed Al Jaber | 1921–1950 |
| Sheikh Abdullah Al Salem | 1950–1965 |
| Sheikh Sabah Al Salem | 1965–1977 |
| Sheikh Jaber Al Ahmed Al Jaber | 1977–2006 |
| Sheikh Sabah Al Ahmed Al Jaber | 2006– |

# CHAPTER 4

# MAKING A NEW EDEN
# IN BAHRAIN

Just after sunset on May 2, 2007, Sheikh Khalifa bin Salman Al Khalifa, Bahrain's prime minister since independence more than 35 years before, declared the opening of the first phase of Bahrain Financial Harbour, a project some say is the most important in the country's modern history. The night sky over Manama exploded into a riot of fireworks and lasers played on the twin towers that are the harbour's centrepiece. It will be complete in 2011 and could accommodate the GCC central bank that will be set up after currency union, due to begin in the region in 2010.

It was a new beginning for a city first settled 5,000 years ago. Some argue that Bahrain was the site of the Biblical utopia where the first man Adam and his wife Eve lived. But the island state wears its history lightly. The future beckons as it seeks to define itself as a cornerstone of the New Gulf.

The author's first visit to Bahrain was in 1980 and he can still remember the thrill as the Gulf Air jet descended to Manama just after dawn. The flight path was close to the surface of a turquoise sea. Fishermen wearing sarongs were tending nets strung across the sandy shallows. A love affair was about to begin with the warmhearted people of the Middle East's smallest country. Perhaps it's the intimacy of the place that makes affection grow. Bahrain has a total land area of little more than 675 km², roughly the size of greater London. You can see it all in a day.

The rise and fall of the sea made Bahrain. At the peak of the last Great Ice Age, most of North America, Europe and Northern Asia lay buried beneath a thick glacial layer and the Gulf was mainly dry land. The sea level was more than 90 m lower than it is today. Jebel Dukhan, the limestone dome at the centre of Bahrain Island, where oil was struck in 1932, was then one of thousands of hills in a shallow valley that extended from Arabia to the mountains of south-west Iran. It was divided by the lazy meanderings of a river running from the Shatt al-Arab to the ocean lapping the Strait of Hormuz, 960 km to the south-east.

The retreat of the ice as global temperatures climbed caused a rise in the sea and Bahrain became an archipelago. Rainfall largely stopped

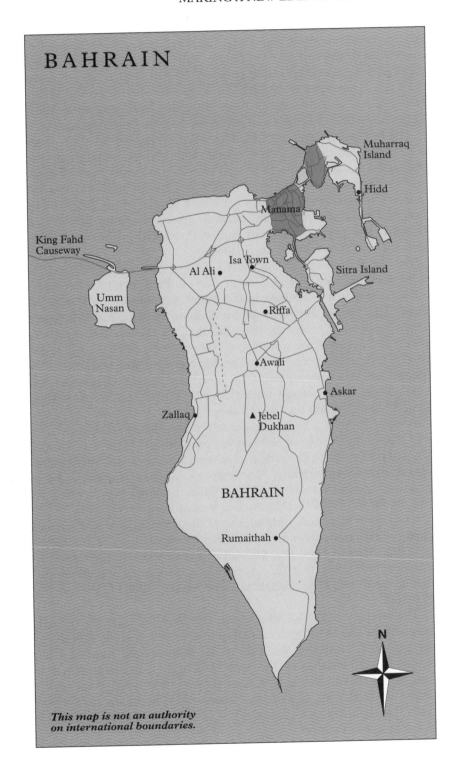

# BAHRAIN

Muharraq
Island

Hidd

Manama

King Fahd
Causeway

Isa Town

Al Ali

Sitra Island

Umm
Nasan

Riffa

Awali

Askar

Zallaq

▲ Jebel
Dukhan

## BAHRAIN

Rumaithah

N

*This map is not an authority
on international boundaries.*

and the archipelago became arid. But water trapped within aquifers was forced to the surface to make the island an oasis. Natural springs supplied irrigation water and attracted human settlers about 6,000 years ago. They survived by fishing in a sea rich with fish, crabs, turtles and dugongs and hunting on land for gazelle and migrating birds. There was a humid climate and mangrove swamps in coastal lagoons.

The first people that left their remains lived around 5000 BC. Pottery shards confirm they were in contact with Mesopotamia. Trade was conducted using boats made of reed coated in bitumen from oil seepages in Bahrain and Mesopotamia. Not long before 3000 BC, the Sumerian Civilization emerged in what is now southern Iraq. Bahrain and eastern Arabia were part of an economic system the Sumerians named Dilmun. The people of Dilmun buried their dead in tombs, creating almost 200,000 tumuli in Bahrain alone.

For the Sumerians, Dilmun was a land of milk and honey, rich in palm trees and wildlife and a key element in their own creation myth. Some believe it was adopted in the Bible's account of the Garden of Eden. The largest settlement of the Dilmun era is Qalat al-Bahrain, which lies west of Manama, Bahrain's modern capital. The town was walled and occupied an area of about one million square metres. It depended on trans-shipping and processing copper mined and smelted in Magan, an area encompassing the northern part of Oman and the UAE. There were probably trade links with settlements in east Arabia, Iran, Afghanistan and the Indus Valley.

Around 2000 BC, Failaka Island in the Bay of Kuwait emerged as a way station on the Mesopotamian sea route from Magan via Bahrain. Ur, Dilmun's principal market, was destroyed in a war of rebellion against Babylonian tyranny. New copper sources in Anatolia and Cyprus were developed and the Indus Valley declined. Trade dried up and, by about 1800 BC, Dilmun disappeared from the records.

The region reappears with the rise of the Kassites, a Mesopotamian dynasty that briefly dominated southern Mesopotamia and the northern Gulf. Around 1600 BC, Dilmun was absorbed into their domain. Their records show that they appointed a governor for Bahrain and that he ruled from Qalat al-Bahrain. The Kassites added to the number of tumuli.

The conquest of the Kassites by the Assyrians interrupts the records, this time for about 500 years. Dilmun re-emerged in about 709 BC in the bas-reliefs carved on the walls of the palace of the Assyrian King Sargon II in Khorsabad, on the north bank of the Tigris in what is now Iraq. Amid tales of battles won is an account, told seven times, of the defeat of Uperi, king of Dilmun "whose abode is situated like a fish, thirty double-hours away, in the midst of the sea where the sun rises." It was probably Bahrain.

It's believed Bahrain was seized by the Persians after the conquest of Babylon in 539 BC by Cyrus the Great. Alexander dispatched three expeditions along Arabia's east coast. At least one landed in Bahrain to inspect Qalat al-Bahrain. The Greeks gave the island of Bahrain the name Tylos, probably a corruption of its Semitic name Tilmun.

Tylos regularly figured in Greek literature as a place rich in vegetation, with date palms, vines and fig and other fruit trees where the people dived for pearls. Historians speculate Bahrain had a mint producing the Greek tetradrachma coin and was a base for the Greek Seleucid rulers of Persia.

Greek rule was swept away by the Parthians in the second century BC. Tylos disappeared from the records. The Roman historian Pliny, writing in the first century AD, mentions Tylos, using second-hand sources, as being 'famous for the vast number of its pearls'. Little has been found to link Bahrain to the Sasanian dynasty that replaced the Parthians in the third century AD. Christianity was joined by Judaism that was brought to Bahrain by Jews from south-western Arabia. Two bishoprics following the Nestorian Christian rite, which was tolerated by the Sasanians, were established in Bahrain in the third and fourth century AD.

### The coming of Islam

Attracted by its comparative prosperity, people from Arabia began to migrate to Bahrain. By the time the Prophet Mohammed (PBUH) launched his mission, Arabian tribes had settled. This increased the receptiveness to the Islamic message when it was brought to Bahrain in the form of a letter from the Prophet (PBUH), who was then living in Medina, in the seventh year after his flight from Mecca. The following year, Bahrain sent a mission to meet Mohammed (PBUH) and adopted Islam soon afterwards. The Greek name Tylos had by then been replaced by the Semitic one Awal.

With the coming of Islam, the word Bahrain, which means 'two seas' in Arabic, was adopted to describe the archipelago as well as the neighbouring areas of Arabia. Bahrain was caught up in the rivalries that enveloped the Islamic community after the death of Ali, the cousin and son-in-law of the Prophet (PBUH) and fountainhead of Shiism. It was probably held briefly by Kharijite forces that had split from the Muslim mainstream following the Battle of Siffin in 657.

Little more than 100 years later, Bahrain was taken over by the Qarmatians, a splinter group of Ismaili Muslims, a minority sect within Shiite Islam. The Qarmatians stole the black stone from the Ka'bah in Mecca and displayed it in their capital, Qatif, in what is now eastern Saudi Arabia. They were expelled from Bahrain and the island returned to Sunni Arab rule.

The connection with Persia was re-established with the emergence of the kingdom of Hormuz, a city-state owing allegiance to the Persian Empire that conquered Bahrain in the 14th century. Hormuz fell to the Portuguese in 1507. A joint Portuguese-Hormuz force temporarily captured Bahrain in 1521 and a Portuguese port with a warehouse and a protective fort was built in Manama.

A second, but unsuccessful, Portuguese attack was launched in 1529. Portuguese supremacy was eventually re-established and they used Bahrain as a base in 1545 in a campaign against the ruler of Al Hasa. The Persian Safavid Dynasty emerged at the start of the 16th century. Bahrain fell to the shah in 1603, an event that was to be used to support Iran's claim to the islands in the 20th century. It was eclipsed by Basra, the Ottoman port at the head of the Shatt al-Arab. But invaders continued to covet it. In the middle of the 18th century the Dutch, attracted by its rich pearl banks, even considered conquering the island.

Bahrain fell prey to rising powers on the Arabian mainland. It was besieged three times, the third successfully, by forces dispatched by the ruler of Muscat in 1717 or 1718. The Safavids paid off Muscat and recovered the island. Bahrain then fell under the control of Huwala Arabs who established positions on both sides of the Gulf. In 1736, Bahrain was once more in Persian hands.

Drought encouraged Bedouin tribes to move to the Gulf coast. One such group was the Al Utub, a branch of the Anaizah confederation. A division of the Al Utub under the leadership of Sheikh Mohammed bin Khalifa left Kuwait, where they'd settled earlier that century, headed south along the Gulf coast and, attracted by the rich oyster banks lying in the shallows between the Qatar Peninsula and Bahrain, moved into Qatar to found the town of Zubara.

Mohammed bin Khalifa established relations with the tribes of the region, but came into conflict with Al Nasr, the pro-Persian ruler of Bahrain. The Al Utub defeated a Persian invasion force at Zubara in 1782 and captured Bahrain the following year. The new rulers, capitalizing on Bahrain's pearls and date palms, started to trade in the Gulf and attracted the attentions of regional competitors. Once again, Muscat's interest was stimulated. In 1799, the ruler of Muscat defeated the Al Khalifa and forced them to pay duty on goods that were shipped to and through Bahrain and Zubara.

### The British connection

In 1801, Bahrain was threatened jointly by Muscat and Persia, supported by the Al Qassimi of what is now the UAE. Bahrain was seized and the Al Khalifa fled to Zubara where they formed an alliance with the Al Saud, then masters of east Arabia, and ejected the invaders.

Muscat tried to capture Bahrain for 20 more years and its forces destroyed the Murair fortress in Zubara in 1811. Britain imposed the General Treaty of Peace of January 1820 on the rulers of the lower Gulf, including Bahrain's Sheikh Abdullah bin Ahmed. The Royal Navy ended the threat from Persia, Muscat and the Al Qassimi and helped secure independence from the mainland of Arabia. The British connection also promoted trade between Bahrain and India.

By the middle of the 19th century, Bahrain was the most populous of the emirates of the lower Gulf and the region's biggest trading centre. Its ruler was not a signatory of the Treaty of Perpetual Maritime Peace signed by the emirs of the lower Gulf in 1853. But Bahrain became subject to many of its obligations in an agreement with Britain signed on May 31, 1861. External threats were ended but divisions within the Al Khalifa family led to almost 30 years of instability in which five rulers were deposed.

There was relief when Sheikh Isa bin Ali, then aged 21, was named joint ruler together with his brother in December 1869. Sheikh Isa was competent, conciliatory and sufficiently compliant to stay on Britain's side. He became sole ruler on the death of his brother in 1888 and governed for 63 years until his death in 1932, the year oil was discovered.

The divisions within the Al Khalifa promoted mutiny in Qatar where the Al Thani seized the opportunity to declare their allegiance to the Al Saud. In 1867, Bahrain, backed by Abu Dhabi, attacked Doha and Wakra on the Qatar Peninsula's west coast. A retaliatory attack was launched. The British dispatched a naval expedition to restore peace and imposed agreements on the two sides in September the following year.

Sheikh Mohamed bin Thani was recognized as the chief of Qatar, but the Al Khalifa refused to accept the Al Thani's right to rule. According to the Bahrainis, the Al Khalifa sheikhs traditionally resided in the islands of Bahrain during summer and in Zubara during winter. But, towards the end of the 18th century, they established their court on the main island of Bahrain and subsequently on the northern island of Muharraq.

The Al Khalifa appointed a governor to Zubara, evidence of their continuing claims. The connection was only broken following the destruction of Zubara by the Al Thani, by then rulers of Doha, in 1878. The Al Khalifa finally abandoned and evacuated Zubara in 1895. The argument about these incidents was to figure in the international court case that finally settled the maritime border between Bahrain and Qatar in 2001. Under Sheikh Isa, Bahrain became increasingly dependent on Britain. In December 1880, an initial exclusive agreement was signed. On March 13, 1892, a new agreement incorporated Bahrain into the security system established elsewhere in the Gulf. In 1904, Britain appointed a resident political agent, effectively an ambassador.

The final possibility of an Ottoman claim on Bahrain was dealt with in the 1913 Anglo-Ottoman agreement that divided Arabia between the two empires.

## The discovery of oil

The island's growing strategic role was underlined in the autumn of 1914 when an expeditionary force on its way to Abadan, in British-controlled Persia, to fight the Ottomans, anchored off Manama. Geologists believed there was oil in Bahrain, but APOC had more than enough to do in its Iranian concession and Iraq offered richer possibilities. In 1925, a concession was awarded to E&GS, a London-based trading firm represented in the Gulf by Frank Holmes. He won over Bahrain's deputy ruler, Sheikh Hamad bin Isa, by drilling successfully for water. The concession was eventually transferred to Socal and the Californians struck oil at Jebel Dukhan in 1932. The first tanker of Bahraini oil left for Japan in June 1934. In October the following year, work started on the Bapco refinery, the first on the Arabian side of the Gulf. It started operating in 1937. The 1932 oil discovery revived the smouldering dispute with the Al Thani. Three years later, Qatar signed a concession agreement with Petroleum Concessions Limited (PCL), a subsidiary of IPC. In March 1936, PCL bid for the areas in Bahrain that had not been awarded to Socal.

The following month, the government of Bahrain claimed the Hawar Islands, sandbanks that lie near Qatar's west coast, to maximize the potential area for oil exploration. In 1937, Qatar seized Zubara, expelled the population and permanently ended the Bahraini connection with the peninsula. Qatar's own Dukhan oil field was discovered two years later.

After Bahrain claimed the Hawar Islands, the British India government made a provisional decision in its favour. In 1937, the Bahrainis started building on the islands. The Al Thani submitted a counter-claim. In July 1939, Britain again ruled in favour of Bahrain. Qatar claimed this breached Qatari sovereignty. The dispute went into abeyance with the start of the Second World War.

Sheikh Isa died in 1932 and was succeeded by his son Sheikh Hamad, who'd been effective ruler since 1923. Stung by the failure to prevent the award of an oil concession to an independent oil developer with links to American oil, Britain's Gulf political resident imposed former British army officer Charles Belgrave as his adviser.

Belgrave retained this post for almost 30 years, eventually being seen as a reactionary holding back Bahrain's development. There are to this day Bahrainis who look back on British rule with anger. In *The House of Kanoo*, a history of Bahrain's leading business family published in 1997, Khalid Kanoo writes with animation about the clashes between

Hajji Yusuf Kanoo and Britain's representatives in the 1920s. "There is little doubt that the political agents had not met anyone like Hajji Yusuf and did not know how to deal with him," Kanoo writes. "If Hajji Yusuf did not follow their instructions, he was viewed as an 'intriguer'." The tension was compounded by commercial competition between the Kanoo family and Gray Mackenzie & Company, the principal UK shipping and trading firm operating in the Gulf.

The RAF made the first flights from Bahrain in the 1920s. Imperial Airways made its first landing in 1927. It started a twice-weekly service from London to Karachi via Basra, Bahrain and Sharjah in October 1932. In 1935, Britain built an RAF airfield on Muharraq Island and a naval base on Bahrain Island following the withdrawal of British forces from Basra on Iraqi independence in 1932.

The rise of Bahrain's economy was underlined by the opening in 1921 of the Eastern Bank, which was later taken over by Britain's Standard Chartered Bank. It was more than 20 years until the British Bank of the Middle East (BBME), now part of HSBC, opened a branch and not until 1957 that the forerunner of the National Bank of Bahrain, the first nationally owned bank, opened its doors.

## Bahrain and the Second World War

The start of the Second World War put Bahrain on the frontline. On the night of October 19, 1940, Italian planes dropped 84 bombs in a failed attempt to knock out Bahraini oil exports. Plans were drafted to destroy oil facilities if the island was captured by the Germans, who came close to seizing Cairo in the summer of 1942.

There were fears that Japanese paratroops could be dropped on the island to seize the refinery. Bapco cut production to 15,000 b/d in the middle of 1941. But the demands of the allied war in the Pacific began to mount. To keep the refinery supplied, oil from Saudi Arabia was shipped to the island from 1942. In March 1945, the Arabia–Bahrain pipeline was completed and a second line built in 1947. These pipelines continue to deliver most of the Bapco refinery's oil. Oil money financed development. The first government hospital was opened in 1940. A causeway between Muharraq and Manama was completed in December 1941. The following February, Sheikh Hamad died of a heart attack and was succeeded by his son, Sheikh Salman.

In 1947, India became independent. Responsibility for the Gulf was shifted to London from Delhi. In anticipation of the changes, the Gulf political resident moved from Bushire to Bahrain. Britain was under pressure from the US. The Dutch Reformed Church of America had established a station in Basra in 1892 and a smaller mission in Bahrain the same year. The missionaries opened the American Mission Hospital, the Gulf's first modern healthcare centre. Following the award of the Socal concession, the number of Americans increased.

During the Second World War, the flow of American servicemen and business people through Bahrain worried the British. They concluded their grip on the Gulf was about to be challenged. Sheikh Salman pushed for faster development. He negotiated a 50:50 profit-share arrangement with Bapco that came into effect on January 1, 1951.

The need for revenue continued to drive policy. Prospects were greatly enhanced in 1958 when, as part of a deal that demarcated the offshore border with Saudi Arabia, Bahrain was promised half the production of the Abu Safah Field which had been placed within Saudi territorial waters. Production from the field started in 1966 and Bahrain increased its Bapco profit share to 55 per cent in 1970. This was raised to 85 per cent in 1974. On January 1, 1973, the government took a 25 per cent stake in the Bahrain field and all Bapco assets. This was raised to 60 per cent in 1975. Full oil-industry nationalization was completed in 1997.

Development and the influx of new ideas exposed Bahrain to nationalist and socialist agitation. There had been anti-Israel riots in 1947 and an organized political movement had emerged. In 1954, the higher executive committee was formed to press for a legislative council, a labour law and civil and criminal codes, the legalization of trade unions and the replacement by trained judges of members of the ruling family who then presided over the courts. Strikes were organized.

The government, without recognizing the committee, made concessions, including a new labour law and health and education councils. Britain's foreign secretary, Selwyn Lloyd, was visiting Bahrain on March 2, 1956, the day King Hussein of Jordan announced the dismissal of General John Glubb, long-standing British adviser to the Jordanian government.

Demonstrators on Muharraq called for Belgrave to be sacked as well and threw stones at a car carrying Lloyd and Belgrave. Tensions on the island increased during the Suez Crisis in October. The higher executive committee, renamed the union committee, was allowed to organize a demonstration that turned into a riot. Its leaders were arrested, tried and sentenced to imprisonment on St Helena, a British-controlled island in the south Atlantic. They were released in 1961 but pressure for political reform was irresistible.

In 1957, Bahraini legal jurisdiction replaced British. The island introduced postage stamps in 1960 and its own currency, the dinar, in 1965. Politically inspired industrial strife persisted. In the spring of 1965, workers at Bapco struck against redundancy plans. The pressure took its toll on Sheikh Salman's health. In January 1958, he appointed his eldest son Sheikh Isa as heir. The ruler had his first major heart attack in June 1959. On November 2, 1961, he suffered a second heart attack and died. Sheikh Isa, then aged 28, immediately succeeded.

By 1965, three decades of development had made Bahrain the lower Gulf's most populous state. The population at the end of that year was 182,000 people, of whom almost 80 per cent were locals. Health care and education had been improved and illiteracy was effectively eliminated. By the end of the 1960s, Bahrainis were the Gulf's best-educated and healthiest people. Nevertheless, Sheikh Isa recognized Bahrain had to find new sources of income beyond oil that was forecast to run out within a generation. A 1967 study said its location between east and west offered opportunities. Its gas reserves could be used to create industries and jobs. A development bureau headed by Yousuf Al Shirawi was set up to promote manufacturing.

## Bahrain becomes independent

In 1969, two wells were drilled to tap natural gas in the Khuff geological structure that extends under much of Arabia. This was to be used to feed the first major industrial scheme. Aluminium Bahrain (Alba), currently the world's largest single-site aluminium smelter, started producing in 1971. A satellite earth station, the Middle East's first, was opened in July 1969. Oil production from the Bahrain field peaked at 77,000 b/d in 1970. It has since declined and averaged less than 40,000 b/d in 2006. Reserves will be exhausted within a generation unless there are new discoveries.

In early 1968, Britain announced its intention to withdraw military forces from east of the Suez Canal. The news was particularly disturbing to Bahrain. It had an organized labour movement and a sectarian division with about 70 per cent of the population being Shiite while the ruling family and the big merchant families were Sunni.

In November 1957, the Iranian *majlis*, or parliament, had asserted that Bahrain, which it called the Mishmahig Island, formed Iran's 14th province under a claim that originated in the Persian conquest of 1603. The Iranians cited the significant community of Shiites of Persian descent as further justification. Bahrain's response was to seek a federation involving Qatar and the seven emirates that were eventually to form the UAE.

Its enthusiasm evaporated when the other members of the proposed federation rejected Manama's proposal that its decision-making structures should reflect the population balance. A census at the time found that Bahrain's population was 216,000, compared with not much more than 110,000 in Qatar and about 217,000 in the seven other emirates combined. Bahrain prepared for independence. In January 1970, a council of state was formed with Sheikh Khalifa bin Salman, brother of the ruler, as its head. Bahrainis that were to shape the country's direction for a generation were appointed members. They included Ali

Fakhro, minister of health, and Yousuf Al Shirawi, development and engineering services minister.

The British Conservative government elected in June 1970 confirmed British withdrawal from the Gulf would go ahead by the end of 1971. The need to find a satisfactory arrangement became pressing. After Iran's claim to Bahrain had been referred to the UN, opinion on the island was tested by a UN mission. It concluded the majority wanted Bahrain to be independent. Iran accepted the UN report, but the shah opposed Bahraini membership of the federation. By the spring of 1971, the road to independence was being taken. Sheikh Isa went to Riyadh for King Faisal's blessing. An agreement was reached with Iran about the division of the continental shelf in June. With both Saudi Arabia and Iran mollified, Sheikh Isa broadcast the declaration of independence which went into effect on August 15, 1971.

### Gulf Air in Bahrain

The early years of independence were good ones. Oil price rises delivered unprecedented revenues to government and business. A key to Bahrain's early success was Gulf Aviation, the forerunner of Gulf Air, founded in Bahrain on March 24, 1950. The founder of the airline was Frederick Bosworth, a former RAF officer who initially tried to set up a charter airline in Iraq, where he'd been based, before moving to Bahrain in 1949.

The original investors were Hussein Yateem and Ahmed Kanoo, both from Bahrain, Abdullah Darwish and Saleh Al Manea from Qatar and Saudi Arabian businessman Khalifa Algosaibi. Bosworth was managing director and chief pilot.

The first scheduled service, from Bahrain to Sharjah via Doha, began in July. Gulf Aviation started to fly to Dhahran later the same month. Bosworth died in a flying accident in the UK in June 1951. Later that year, the British Overseas Airways Corporation (BOAC), predecessor to BA, took a 51 per cent stake in the airline. A new airport terminal was opened in 1961. In 1970, Gulf Aviation started direct flights from London to Bahrain, which became the hub for onward flights to other parts of the region.

In 1973, BOAC sold its shares to the governments of Bahrain, Abu Dhabi, Oman and Qatar and the airline was renamed Gulf Air. The following decade was the airline's golden era as Bahrain became the gateway to eastern Saudi Arabia. Big orders for modern passenger jets were placed. Gulf Air and the airport boom helped make aviation the largest employer of Bahrainis on the island.

For business travellers in the 1970s, sipping champagne served by Gulf Air's elegantly attired cabin crew in new Lockheed Tristars on the seven-hour flight from London to Manama was the height of sophistication. Capitalizing on the fact that its airport was the most modern in the region, Bahrain convinced international airlines to fly to the island or use it as a stop over. In 1976, Bahrain was selected by BA as one of the first destinations for Concorde flights. During 1976–77 and then from 1979–80, BA and Singapore Airlines jointly operated Concorde flights from Bahrain to Singapore. The start of Concorde services was the zenith of Bahrain's economic ascent.

The problems of Gulf Air's consortium ownership started to surface once the Gulf economic boom ended. The airline began to record losses and questions were asked about some of the jet-acquisition decisions. International airlines travelling through Bahrain to Asia began to compete for passengers on the profitable Europe–Far East routes.

The first major challenge came in 1985 with the launch of Emirates airline by the government of Dubai. Today, it has overtaken Gulf Air and is one of the world's fastest-growing airlines. Gulf Air faced a new problem in January 1994 when the Qatar government founded Qatar Airways. Oman Air, founded in 1991, unveiled plans to start intercontinental services by the end of the decade. In 2002, Qatar announced it was withdrawing from the airline.

James Hogan, an Australian airline manager, was appointed as Gulf Air's first non-GCC chief executive with a doctor's mandate. Despite the launch in November 2003 of Etihad Airways as the international airline of Abu Dhabi, Gulf Air started to recover its market position. Oman was persuaded to maintain its shareholding and Oman Air started to co-operate. But another blow fell in September 2005 when Abu Dhabi announced it was withdrawing to concentrate on Etihad. Gulf Air, nevertheless, continues to battle on, though without Hogan, who announced his resignation from the airline in July 2006. He is now chief executive of Etihad. In 2007, Bahrain raised its Gulf Air share to 100 per cent, even though the airline was still making a loss.

In 1973, the government converted the currency board set up by Britain into the Bahrain Monetary Agency (BMA), in effect the country's central bank. In 1975, it published offshore banking rules. Coupled with Bahrain's proximity to Saudi Arabia, they made Manama an attractive location for international banks seeking an alternative to Beirut, previously the preferred regional finance centre, which had been engulfed by the Lebanese civil war.

New banks including the Arab Banking Corporation (ABC) and the Gulf International Bank (GIB) were set up. A reclamation project to push out the corniche in front of Manama by nearly a kilometre was completed. Bahrain secured Arab industrial investment. ASRY, a shipyard to service the world's largest tankers, owned by members of the Organization of Arab Petroleum Exporting Countries (OAPEC), started operating in September 1977. A steel plant and a fertilizer factory financed by Arab governments were founded. By the mid-1980s, Bahrain was the most industrialized of the GCC six.

## Bahrain's first national assembly

Economic trends were exciting but Bahrain's political evolution was quickly halted. Following independence, a constitutional assembly was formed comprising 42 members, 22 of whom were elected. It was elected in December 1972 and approved, the following year, a 108-article constitution calling for a national assembly and an advisory legislative body comprising 30 elected members plus all the members of the council of ministers. Elections under a restricted franchise for the 30 places in the assembly took place in December 1973.

Political parties were banned but three groups were formed when the assembly opened. The People's Bloc, comprising eight members, advocated the legalization of unions and the abolition of security measures. The Religious Bloc, comprising six Shiites, supported labour reforms but wanted social restrictions including a ban on alcohol sales. The rest were pro-government independents.

The government soon became uneasy about the assembly's activities and this reached a peak in the spring of 1975 during a prolonged debate about a new state security decree issued the previous December. The assembly recessed for the summer in May 1975. In August, before it reconvened, Sheikh Isa dissolved the body, citing its inability to cooperate with the government. Some assembly members were arrested. In August 1976, Sheikh Isa announced that the assembly would remain dissolved indefinitely. The short life of Bahrain's first experiment in representative democracy left a lasting sense among sections of the population that their views were not welcomed. The feeling was strongly felt among Shiites and this dissatisfaction was to express itself following the Iranian revolution.

About 300 Bahrainis held a rally in Manama on February 23, 1979 in support of the new Tehran regime. During the Shiite feast of Ashura in November, a demonstration in Manama in support of Imam Khomeini was dispersed. There were public expressions of sympathy for Saudi Shiites following demonstrations in Saudi Arabia's Eastern Province in February 1980.

Bahrain's support for Iraq in its war with Iran polarized relations with Tehran. In 1981, a coup attempt supported by Iran was uncovered. In an interview with *MEED* in May 1982, Prime Minister Sheikh Khalifa blamed an unnamed "foreign power" and dismissed reports that thousands had been arrested in the aftermath. "We assure everybody that the whole prison population of Bahrain is less than 500," he said.

Bahrain's Arab neighbours increased their financial assistance. In

1982, the other members of the GCC gave Bahrain US$1,700 million to help improve security. Work on the King Fahd Causeway, a road linking Bahrain with Saudi Arabia, began in 1982 and was completed four years later.

Bahrain supported the US-led coalition formed to expel Iraq from Kuwait and it served as a base for air and naval operations. Bahrain and the US signed a defence cooperation agreement in October 1991 that granted US forces access to Bahraini facilities and ensured its right to pre-position material for future crises. It now accommodates the headquarters of the US Navy's Fifth Fleet. America designated the country as a major non-NATO ally in October 2001 and Bahrain played an important role in the US-led coalition's attack on Iraq in March 2003.

The 1986 oil price crash led to an extended recession. By the end of the decade unemployment was a source of growing discontent among Shiites who felt they were being discriminated against. An opposition movement had developed into three elements. Shiite, mainly religious, leaders in Bahrain focused on social and economic grievances. The Bahrain Freedom Movement was formed by exiles in London while other exiles established the Islamic Front for the Liberation of Bahrain in Tehran.

The trigger for five years of disturbances appears to have been the interruption of a memorial service at a Shiite mosque in the summer of 1994. There were demonstrations and arrests. A cleric named Sheikh Ali Salman was detained and had his passport confiscated. In November 1994, a petition with more than 20,000 signatures calling for the reinstatement of the national assembly was submitted to the emir. Runners in a marathon that passed through a Shiite village were stoned. Sheikh Ali was again arrested and this led to demonstrations in Shiite villages and Manama itself in which four demonstrators and one policeman are believed to have died.

Demonstrations in January 1995 led to arrests and another death. On January 15, Sheikh Ali Salman and two other Shiite religious leaders were expelled to Dubai and then made their way to London. Four more were expelled to Dubai later in the month. Further demonstrations in March and April set the scene for an unhappy summer. The government declared it would not start political reforms under duress.

In the late summer of 1995, Bahrain's interior minister, Sheikh Mohammed bin Khalifa, met jailed Shiite leaders and secured a commitment to an end to demonstrations in return for the release of detainees and the return of exiled opposition figures. This understanding soon broke down.

Further clashes with police, bombings of public buildings and arrests took place in January 1996. In March, a Molotov cocktail thrown into a restaurant caused a fire in which seven Bangladeshi workers died. Three Bahrainis were convicted of the crime and sentenced to death. At the end of the month, a Bahraini convicted of murdering a policeman was executed. Further arson attacks and demonstrations followed. The disturbances continued amid claims that detainees were being tortured and that at least one of them had died. In Kuwait, Bahrainis were arrested for plotting against the government.

In 1998, the retirement was announced of the director of public security, Ian Henderson, a former British special branch officer who'd run Bahrain's security services since 1966. Henderson's role was highlighted in a debate in the British House of Commons. George Galloway, then a Labour MP and now an independent parliamentary representative for an East London seat, described Henderson as "Britain's Klaus Barbie". On July 3, 2000, the Bahrain government announced Henderson, then aged 71, had retired completely.

## The accession of Sheikh Hamad

Sheikh Isa died of heart failure in March 1999. He was succeeded by his son the crown prince, Sheikh Hamad, who opened the door to an era of political amity. The emir, who was 57 in January 2007, is genial and popular with a family comprising seven sons, four daughters and a formidable wife: Sheikha Sabeeka bint Ibrahim Al Khalifa, who is a modernizer.

He immediately initiated constitutional reform and established, in November 2000, a committee to plan the transformation of Bahrain into a constitutional monarchy within two years. The resulting national action charter was put to the public in a referendum in which 95 per cent of voters were recorded as endorsing the charter.

That month, Sheikh Hamad pardoned all political prisoners and detainees, including those who had been imprisoned, exiled or detained on security charges. The state security law and the state security court, which allowed individuals to be detained without trial for up to three years, were abolished.

On February 14, 2002, the referendum's first anniversary, Sheikh Hamad unveiled what was in effect a new constitution that had previously not been discussed outside government. A decree declared that Bahrain would become a constitutional monarchy. Sheikh Hamad's status was changed from emir to king. The first municipal elections in 45 years were called in May 2002. Elections to a two-chamber parliament were announced for October 2002. This was not, however, a parliament in line with the 1973 constitution. In the new arrangements, an elected 40-member council of deputies (Majlis al-Nawwab) was to be balanced by a 40-member Majlis al-Shoura (consultative council) with equal rights whose members were to be appointed.

The elected council's powers were limited. In the event of the two councils taking opposite views, the appointed chamber's president had the deciding vote. The council of deputies could prepare draft laws, but only the cabinet, appointed by the king, could put them to a vote. Constitutional amendments required a two-thirds majority of the combined houses. The king retained the power to rule by decree, provided he did not violate the new constitution. He could suspend the elected council for four months without elections and had the right to postpone elections without time limit. The new constitution was immediately activated.

The opposition was dissatisfied. Their principal complaint was the constitution had not been discussed with opposition groups and that the 1973 constitution, including an elected parliament with power, had not been restored. The government's mind, however, had been made up. King Hamad issued a decree in July 2002 forbidding the council from deliberating any action taken by the government prior to its inaugural session on December 14 that year. Between the announcement of the constitution and the opening of parliament, King Hamad issued 56 decrees, including one that ensured control over financial affairs remained in his hands.

The new environment created opportunities for the opposition. The four largest political groups drawing support from Bahraini Shiites are the Al Wifaq National Islamic Society, led by Sheikh Ali Salman and the successor of the Bahrain Freedom Movement; the Islamic Action Society, which looks to Iraqi Shiite religious leaders for inspiration; the post-Baathist Progressive Democratic Forum Society; and the leftist National Democratic Action Society.

These groups organized a boycott of the municipal elections in May 2002 and the national elections in October in protest at the failure to restore the 1973 constitution and the decision to give the appointed upper house voting rights equal to the elected lower one. The turnout for the municipal poll was 51 per cent. In voting for the lower house, the turnout was 53 per cent in the first round and 43 per cent in the second. Sunni Islamists won 19 of the 40 seats in the council of deputies. No female candidates standing for election won a seat.

The expectations generated by the first years of King Hamad's rule proved difficult to contain. In April 2003, the council of deputies proved troublesome and formed a commission to investigate irregularities in two government pension funds that were in financial difficulties. In January 2004, the commission submitted a report that alleged mismanagement and corruption. It recommended ministers should be questioned by deputies. The government promised to rescue the two pension funds and make up the losses. The council stood its ground. Three ministers were quizzed and satellite television aired portions of the debate, after some editing. None of the three were forced to resign. Nevertheless, the questioning of ministers was unprecedented.

King Hamad tried to build bridges with the non-parliamentary opposition. On 19 May 2004, he met dissident Bahraini leaders and ordered the release of political prisoners. But events had a momentum of their own. On 21 May 2004, Bahrainis protesting against US troops in Iraq's Holy Cities clashed with security forces in Manama. The marchers carried portraits of Grand Ayatollah Ali Al Sistani, leader of Iraq's Shiites, and some wore white shrouds to indicate their willingness to die to defend the holy places. Tear gas and rubber bullets were fired.

Later that day, King Hamad sacked Interior Minister Sheikh Mohammed bin Khalifa and replaced him with Sheikh Rashid bin Abdullah Al Khalifa. A statement issued by the king indicated he was angry at the use of force against the demonstration.

A challenge from an entirely different direction emerged on June 22, 2004 when six men, reported to be Sunni Muslim radicals, were arrested on suspicion of planning an attack on US targets in Bahrain. The courts ordered the men to be released the following day. There was an immediate American reaction. On July 2, the US defence department ordered the evacuation of the families of US servicemen, a total of up to 900 people. The following day, the State Department advised Americans not to travel to Bahrain and suggested residents leave because of the threat of terror attacks. On July 4, the State Department authorized the voluntary departure of its employees' families. An advisory posted on the department's website declared 'extremists are planning attacks against US and other Western interests in the kingdom of Bahrain'. It was withdrawn at the end of the summer.

By the time Bahrain and the US signed the Free Trade Agreement (FTA) in Washington, the affair seemed to have been forgotten. The FTA was ratified by US congress in January 2006. But worries about security continue to drive government policy. In July 2006, a tough anti-terrorism law that provides for the death penalty, jail terms reaching life imprisonment, and house arrest for acts of terror or the establishment of terrorist groups was passed by both the council of deputies and the appointed consultative council. It was immediately criticized by Amnesty International.

In the more liberal environment that has prevailed since the start of the decade, public expressions of feeling about regional issues have been allowed. More than 10,000 marched in Manama in August 2004 to protest about American attacks in Shiite Holy Cities in Iraq. Tensions spread to the council of deputies and there were rows between representatives from each side of the sectarian divide.

Later, in August, Bahrainis staged a hunger strike to back some imprisoned Palestinians who'd begun a fast in support of demands for better treatment in Israeli prisons. On September 25, Abdul Hadi Al Khawaja, a human-rights activist and the brother of one of the leaders of the Islamic Action Society, was arrested the day after he'd criticized Bahrain's prime minister, Sheikh Khalifa.

A demonstration against Al Khawaja's arrest and the closure of his Bahrain Centre for Human Rights at the end of October attracted up to 4,000 people. There were clashes with police who fired rubber bullets and tear gas. The atmosphere was eventually calmed by Shiite leaders who called on the radicals to show restraint. Al Khawaja was convicted by a Bahrain court on November 22, but immediately released by King Hamad. His centre, though not authorized by the government, continues to function.

The politics of dissent continued to bubble. On March 25, 2005, Al Wifaq, which claims 65,000 members, defied a government ban and held a demonstration in Sitra in support of constitutional reform. The government in response attempted to ban the organization. The year ended with another unhappy incident. Ayatollah Mohammed Sanad, a Bahraini Shiite cleric, returned and was immediately detained for questioning at Bahrain International Airport. A demonstration within the terminal degenerated and there were clashes with the security forces, arrests and some damage.

The core challenge facing Bahrain remains the divided nature of its society. Some nationals came from the Arabian Peninsula. Bahrain's Huwala Arabs are Sunni Muslims who originated from the Iranian side of the Gulf. The largest group is the Al Baharina (singular Al Bahrani), Shiites who are descended from Bahrain's original Muslim inhabitants. The opposition says there's discrimination against Shiites. The government argues it's addressing Shiite grievances and charges some Shiites are supporters of the Islamic Republic of Iran. The opposition now discourages demonstrators from displaying portraits of Iranian and Shiite religious leaders.

A further opposition charge is that up to 60,000 Sunni Arabs have been granted citizenship in recent years to change Bahrain's demographic and political balance. The government dismisses the accusations of sharp practice and says it granted citizenship in 2001 to 1,000 Shiites who'd previously been known as the Al Bidoun (the withouts), because they were stateless. A further issue is the divide between modernizers and Muslim conservatives.

Addressing the sensitivities of the latter, the government restricted alcohol sales during Ramadan. Religious groups are pressing for gender separation to be extended to universities. Bahrain does not have a properly-codified family law. The rulings of Sharia courts can be unpredictable, particularly in matters involving divorce and the custody of children.

In October 2002, the government proposed the establishment of separate personal status laws for Shiites and Sunnis. This was attacked by liberals for failing to provide a uniform system of law and by conservatives for changing the status quo. The Bahrain Women's Union, an association of a dozen women's groups, finally secured official recognition in July 2006. It reflects the growing role of women in Bahrain's economy, a development religious conservatives find unacceptable. All these issues are bound to be acted out in the council that emerged from the elections held in November and December 2006. Al Wifaq is the largest party and 32 of the council's 40 seats were won by Shiite or Sunni Islamists.

The politics of personality also plays a role. Sheikh Khalifa, who was born in 1935, has held senior government positions since the 1950s and been prime minister since independence in 1971. Despite his fierce demeanour, Sheikh Khalifa is known to have charm and a lively sense of humour. He was behind many initiatives that made Bahrain a Gulf leader. But many believe the future lies with Sheikh Salman bin Hamad, the crown prince and King Hamad's eldest son.

Born on October 21, 1969, Sheikh Salman has a degree in politics from the American University in Washington and a master's degree in philosophy from Cambridge. He was undersecretary in Bahrain's Ministry of Defence before being made his father's heir in March 1999. Sheikh Salman is seen as a possible future prime minister.

Bahrain's future hangs in the balance. The Gulf oil boom is creating jobs and wealth. The fifth F1 Bahrain Grand Prix was held in April 2008 and further initiatives designed to attract tourists and investment have been launched. The new Bahrain Financial Harbour, a development in Manama designed to attract international and regional financial institutions, has opened. The airport is reporting record passenger numbers and is being expanded. Work has started on the US$20 billion North Shore project that will transform Manama and the surrounding areas. But fundamental challenges still need attention.

These include income distribution, youth unemployment, the need for more non-oil industries and, above all, further progress in engaging all Bahrainis in the programme of national renewal launched by King Hamad. The prize is considerable. Given the right domestic political environment, Bahrain is poised to recover its position as the linchpin of the New Gulf.

## Al Khalifa rulers of Bahrain

| | |
|---|---|
| Ahmed Al Khalifa ... ... ... ... ... ... ... ... ... ... ... ... | 1782–1796 |
| Abdullah bin Ahmed Al Khalifa ... ... ... ... ... ... ... ... | 1796–1843 |
| Salman bin Ahmed Al Khalifa.. ... ... ... ... ... ... ... ... | 1796–1825 |
| Khalifa bin Salman Al Khalifa.. ... ... ... ... ... ... ... ... | 1825–1834 |

Mohammed bin Khalifa Al Khalifa (deposed) ... ... ... ...   1843–1867
Ali bin Khalifa Al Khalifa (killed in battle) ... ... ... ... ...   1868–1869
Mohammed bin Abdullah Al Khalifa (deposed) ... ... ...   1869
Isa bin Ali Al Khalifa   ... ... ... ... ... ... ... ... ... ...   1869–1932
Hamad bin Isa Al Khalifa ... ... ... ... ... ... ... ... ...   1932–1942
Salman bin Hamad Al Khalifa . ... ... ... ... ... ... ...   1942–1961
Isa bin Salman Al Khalifa ... ... ... ... ... ... ... ... ...   1961–1999
Hamad bin Isa Al Khalifa ... ... ... ... ... ... ... ...   1999–

# CHAPTER 5

# GETTING RICH QUICKLY
# IN QATAR

Some of the New Gulf's most powerful figures gathered in a tent as big as a football pitch in May 2005 at Ra's Laffan, at the tip of the Qatar Peninsula, to launch the Gulf's boldest cross-border energy initiative. At the stroke of noon, Sheikh Tameem, Qatar's crown prince, joined the oil ministers of Qatar and the UAE. Together, they laid the foundation stone for the plant at the heart of the Dolphin Pipeline that will supply Qatari gas to Abu Dhabi, Dubai, Oman and Ra's al-Khaimah. In time, other pipelines may take Qatar's gas to Bahrain and Kuwait to create a steel bond that will encompass the Gulf.

Smaller than Wales with a population, including hundreds of thousands of foreigners, of less than a million people, Qatar is a winner in nature's energy lottery. The country has the world's largest reservoir of non-associated natural gas and this has been used to make Qatar the world's fastest-growing economy. Within a decade, the Qatari people will be among the richest on earth.

Sheikh Tameem, born in August 1980 and a product of Britain's Sherbourne College and Sandhurst, had been heir to his father Sheikh Hamad bin Khalifa Al Thani since August 2003, when he replaced his elder brother Sheikh Jassem who'd abdicated in frustration at the lack of responsibility he'd been given.

Sheikh Tameem and Sheikh Jassem are two of the seven children of Qatar's ruler by Sheikha Mozah bint Nasser Al Misned, co-pilot of Qatar's modernization drive and one of the first consorts of a Gulf ruler with a university degree. Their father, Sheikh Hamad, was born in Doha in 1952 and educated locally before being sent to Sandhurst where he graduated in July 1971, a month before Qatari independence. He joined the Qatari army with the rank of lieutenant colonel and commander of the first mobile regiment. Sheikh Hamad was subsequently appointed major general and commander-in-chief of the armed forces. On May 31, 1977, still just 25, he was named heir apparent and minister of defence.

During the next decade, Sheikh Hamad concentrated on developing Qatar's small, volunteer armed forces. Their moment came in 1990 when Qatar joined the anti-Iraq coalition and the country was used as

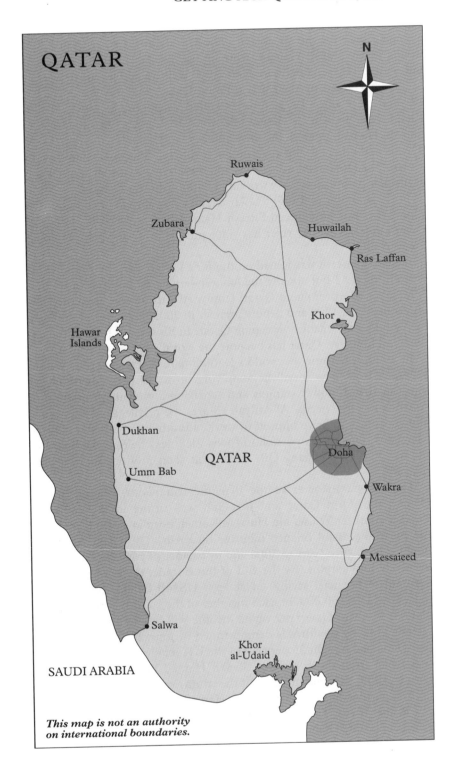

a staging base for the air assault. The US stationed more than 3,500 troops there. Sheikh Hamad, who speaks flawless English, impressed the coalition by sending more than 2,000 well-trained troops to war.

Sheikh Hamad by then was running Qatar while his father Sheikh Khalifa, ruler since 1972, took extended vacations. In 1992, Sheikh Khalifa left his son in charge and went to Cannes. In his absence, Sheikh Hamad purged the bureaucracy and appointed younger Al Thanis and others to top government positions. Sheikh Khalifa tried to reverse Sheikh Hamad's decisions and threatened to install another son as his heir before an uneasy working relationship was restored.

In the summer of 1995, Sheikh Khalifa was abroad once more. On June 27, it was announced Sheikh Hamad had replaced his father as Qatar's ruler. The new ruler has since put Qatar on the map. Dolphin is one result.

Sheikh Tameem was joined on the Ra's Laffan stage by Abdullah Al Attiyah, then 53 but already the longest-serving oil minister in OPEC. A member of a prominent Qatari family, Al Attiyah was appointed energy minister in 1992 and deputy premier in 2003. He is one of the three men guiding the changes sweeping Qatar. In his time as head of the national oil industry, Qatar has become the world's hottest energy story.

In 2006, it became the world's leading natural gas exporter. Within a decade from now it will be supplying up to 15 per cent of all gas burnt in British power stations and satisfying a growing proportion of American energy needs. Al Attiyah abjures the privileges of high office and continues to drive himself to work, admittedly in a better class of Mercedes. One of his portfolio of jobs includes chairing the board of the national oil company QP, which will soon produce more energy than BP.

The second member of the dynamic triumvirate helping Sheikh Hamad transform Qatar and the Gulf was sitting in the audience. Finance minister Yousef bin Hussein Kamal, born in 1948, is probably the most successful finance minister on earth. The Qatari economy doubled in the five years to 2006 and its balance of payments has swung massively into surplus. By the end of this decade, the government will accumulate financial savings of at least US$40 billion, equivalent to more than US$150,000 for each member of the country's national population. By then, Qatari per capita income will be more than $70,000. Qatar's growing wealth was demonstrated in June 2007 with the news that Doha had bought 25 per cent of the UK retailer Sainsbury's.

Missing from the event was Sheikh Hamad bin Jassem Al Thani, born in 1959, the final member of the triumvirate and the ruler's cousin. The partnership between the two Hamads, both physical giants, began in the 1970s. Having proven himself in junior government posts, he was appointed cabinet minister in 1989. Sheikh Hamad bin Jassem has been Qatar's foreign minister since 1992 and first deputy premier from 2003. In May 2007, he replaced Sheikh Abdullah bin Khalifa as prime minister. In the partnership of the two Hamads, the new premier is credited with supplying the intellectual ammunition needed to do the job and fortifying pep talks to the ruler when the going got tough.

Sheikh Hamad bin Jassem founded Al Jazeera, the 24-hour-a-day Arabic satellite television channel launched in Doha at the end of 1996. The station shook the Gulf information order with reporting and discussion programmes that broke Arab media taboos. The failings of Arab states were rigorously exposed.

In 2003, the interim government appointed by the US to run Iraq after the fall of Saddam Hussein was so exasperated by Al Jazeera's reporting that it was banned from the country. Former US Secretary of State, Colin Powell, suggested Al Jazeera's interviews with Osama bin Laden and Al Qaeda leaders might have contained secret messages for their Iraqi supporters. Bill O'Reilly of Fox News charged the station was supporting terrorists. It was reported in 2005 that President George W Bush even suggested in a conversation with UK prime minister Tony Blair that it should be bombed. The station started broadcasting in English in November 2006.

Two others joined the Dolphin ceremony. The slight figure of UAE energy minister Mohammed Al Hamili contrasted with the height of the crown prince and the burly frame of Al Attiyah. The fourth member of the stone-laying team was Ahmed Al Sayegh, an Abu Dhabi national and chief executive of Dolphin Energy. His company, which is owned by Abu Dhabi, Occidental and Total, had built the Dolphin Pipeline, currently the world's longest sub-sea energy pipeline. The crown prince and the two ministers smiled for the cameras and pushed the first brick into place.

The Dolphin launch in Ra's Laffan was just one of many amazing Qatar initiatives in 2005. In January, plans for two new giant LNG plants and two enormous petrochemical projects were announced on the same day Sheikh Hamad hosted the groundbreaking ceremony for the new Doha International Airport that had been designed to handle up to 60 million passengers.

Later that year, Shell started work on the world's largest gas-to-liquids (GTL) complex. Qatar is building a completely new plastics industry that could become one of the world's largest in a decade. With the money it's earning from gas, it is financing one of the region's biggest infrastructure modernization programmes.

In December 2006, Doha hosted the 15th Asian Games, featuring more sports and athletes than the Olympics itself. Education City, a project promoted by Sheikha Mozah, calls for one of the world's most advanced centres of higher learning. The new Lusail project north of

Doha involves building a town for 250,000 people. A railway line between the east and west coast is possible. More than US$130 billion in capital projects are planned during the next decade.

Political reform is taking place, though less swiftly than imagined when Sheikh Hamad took power. From the beginning, he asserted Qatar should be a democracy. One of his first measures was to abolish the information ministry and Qatar's censorship system. In 1998, elections, the first in Qatar's history, were held for a chamber of commerce and industry board previously appointed by the ruler. Voting was later extended to the central municipal council, in which all citizens over 18 years old, including women, could vote and run for office.

In July 1999, Sheikh Hamad formed a committee to draft a permanent constitution for a directly elected assembly and to define the role and powers of the legislature, judiciary and executive. It submitted its recommendations later in the year, but the next step took another four. Qatar's first written constitution was finally presented in a referendum to Qatar's 72,000 voters in April 2003. More than 90 per cent said yes. Sheikh Hamad approved the constitution in June 2004.

The constitution is weaker than the ruler's early statements had suggested. Its most important provision is the establishment of a parliamentary chamber. It will comprise 45 members but only two-thirds of them will be directly elected. Its powers are limited. Elections are yet to be held.

Nevertheless, the changes in the past decade have been remarkable. Qatar since 1995 has launched the Arab World's first uncensored television news service and welcomed Israelis to its capital. It supported the US in its wars in Afghanistan and Iraq, became the principal operational centre for the US military in the Gulf, approved a constitution and launched the world's most ambitious economic development plan. It hosts the weekly 'Doha Debates' chaired by British broadcaster Tim Sebastian that are shown unedited on BBC World television. No other Middle East country has done so much so quickly.

## How Qatar was made

Several times an island with the rise and fall of the sea over hundreds of millions of years, the Qatar Peninsula joined the Arabian mainland comparatively recently. The connection was created by silt and rocks washed east by a river that once flowed from the Hejaz Mountains, through central Arabia into what is now the Empty Quarter and finally into the Gulf. The lost river formed a marshy delta that has left the gravel plains and *sabkha* mudflats that lie between the coast of western Abu Dhabi and the Qatar border.

As Arabia became arid and the rivers disappeared from the surface, powdered rock and soil created enormous sand dunes that finally formed a bridge with Arabia and created the Qatar Peninsula. Humanity first came about 50,000 years ago. The carvings, or petroglyphs, they made have been found in exposed sandstone rocks and cliffs in more than 200 Qatari Stone Age sites. Evidence has been found of settlements made by the Ubaid people more than 5,000 years ago. A site at Shagra in the south-east has been dated to this period.

The civilization of Dilmun may have used ports on the Qatar Peninsula as trans-shipment centres. On the Al Khor Islands north of Doha, excavations have uncovered evidence of settlement during, before and after the Dilmun era and of a thriving dye-production centre dating from 1400–1200 BC. But evidence of settled life is sparse. One of Alexander the Great's admirals, dispatched to the Gulf to prepare for a Greek invasion of Arabia that never materialized, is reported to have stopped somewhere on the coast of Qatar. But the Greeks, who settled in Failaka in Kuwait Bay and knew Bahrain as Tylos, did not stay.

Arid and sandy, Qatar supported through the centuries a small population of nomadic Bedouin and a few coastal villages that depended on fishing and pearling. Qatar was nominally ruled by the Sasanian Empire when Islam came to eastern Arabia. The people converted immediately and are said to have acquitted themselves well in the Muslim wars against Persia. During the early Islamic period, its weavers were famous. The Prophet (PBUH) and his wife Aisha are said to have worn clothes made in Qatar. Qatar was captured by the island state of Hormuz and then by the Portuguese in or after 1515. The Portuguese were finally driven out by the sultan of Muscat. Regional chaos in the 17th century left the peninsula largely ungoverned.

### The Al Thani arrive

The Al Thani are descendants of Bedouin from central Arabia who migrated to the coast. According to the official Qatari account, the Al Maadhid, a section of the Tameem tribe which originated in Al Washm in the Najd, migrated to the south of the peninsula early in the 18th century, when the region was dominated by the Bani Khalid tribe. In the middle of the century, they moved to Zubara, Ruwais and Fuwairat in the north of the peninsula. The Al Thani moved from Zubara to Doha in 1847 and made it their capital.

A section of the Utub confederation under the leadership of Mohammed bin Khalifa separately left Kuwait around 1766 and settled in Zubara in north-west Qatar about six years later. A new Arabian order was established by the Al Saud, who claimed the allegiance of Qatar following their victory over the Bani Khalid of eastern Arabia in 1795.

This ushered in a period of government from the Saudi capital of Diriyah that lasted until an Egyptian army captured and destroyed the town in 1818. Al Khalifa rule was restored in Bahrain and this was confirmed in the General Treaty of Peace signed by the rulers of the southern Gulf with Britain in 1820. Qatar was treated as a de facto party to the treaty, though the people of Doha claimed they knew nothing of it. After infringements of its terms by vessels from Doha, British ships occupied the port and destroyed its dhows in 1821. Doha was bombarded again in 1840.

The people of Doha had conformed to Wahhabism and pro-Saudi sentiments remained strong. The Saudi leader, Faisal Al Saud, returned to Arabia in 1843 and started to build a new empire. Sheikh Mohammed bin Thani, the first ruling sheikh of Qatar, reached an understanding with Faisal, who visited Doha in 1851. The people of Doha, Wakra and Fuwairat declared their allegiance to the Al Saud.

In an attempt to recover control of the peninsula, the Al Khalifa, supported by Abu Dhabi, sacked Doha and Wakra in 1867. The Qataris counter-attacked and many lives were lost. At this point, the British intervened to impose a settlement. On September 12, 1868, six days after a similar deal was signed with the Al Khalifa, Britain's first political resident in the Gulf, Colonel Lewis Pelly, signed a treaty of maritime peace with Sheikh Mohammed bin Thani. Tribute was still paid to the Al Khalifa but at a reduced rate. The balance went to Riyadh to signify allegiance. The money was delivered through the British residency in Bushire, though this stopped after two years. Qatar maintained the money paid to Bahrain was due to the Saudis and did not represent an acceptance of Al Khalifa sovereignty, which the Al Khalifa maintained it did.

The Al Thani position was strengthened in 1871 when an Ottoman force arrived in Doha soon after occupying Al Hasa in Eastern Arabia. The ruler's son, Sheikh Jassem, accepted the Turkish flag against his father's advice. The move was prompted by fears that the decline in Saudi power following the death of Faisal six years earlier would expose Qatar once more to the Al Khalifa. Turkish influence was minimal but the initiative raised fears in British minds of a resurgence in the region of Ottoman power. The Ottomans made Sheikh Jassem *qaimmaqam* (governor) in 1876, a further indication of Doha's independence from the Al Khalifa.

Sheikh Mohammed bin Thani died in 1879. Sheikh Jassem succeeded. The new ruler quickly showed he was an independent figure and resisted Ottoman attempts to strengthen their control of Zubara, Doha, Wakra and Khor al-Udaid. Irritated by Sheikh Jassem, the Ottoman governor of Basra, accompanied by infantry and 300 cavalry, landed in Doha in 1893. Sheikh Jassem escaped to the interior but the Ottomans took his brother and 16 notables prisoner.

Despite the odds, Sheikh Jassem and his fighters defeated the Ottoman forces as they marched towards his base. The Ottomans decided the campaign was not worth the cost and reached a settlement. Sheikh Jassem, regarded as the founder of modern Qatar, accepted nominal Turkish control and a full pardon. He remained almost entirely independent. The Al Saud recovered Riyadh in 1902. Sheikh Jassem became an ally of Abdelaziz Al Saud. In July 1913, Sheikh Jassem died and was succeeded by his son, Sheikh Abdullah, who'd been governor of Doha since 1905.

The division of Arabia in the unratified 1913 agreement between the Ottomans and Britain, which placed Qatar in the British sphere of influence, passed unnoticed. The Ottomans withdrew their garrison from Doha in August 1915. Britain filled the gap. In November 1916, Sheikh Abdullah signed an exclusive agreement with Britain that put Qatar on the same footing as the states of the Trucial Coast, Bahrain and Kuwait. Uniquely, Sheikh Abdullah secured a promise of British protection from threats from land as well as sea. He was recognized as Qatar's independent ruler. The Al Thani were threatened by the expanding Al Saud state following the end of the First World War. Its southern border was undefined and indefensible. Britain was unwilling to honour the terms of the 1916 agreement. In the end, Qatar maintained its independence by making secret payments to Riyadh.

**The search for oil**
The possibility of discovering oil seemed to offer a solution to Qatar's poverty. But the work of oil companies required defining borders. Oil was struck in Bahrain in 1932 and exploration began in Saudi Arabia in 1933. In March 1934, discussions about oil were held between the British political resident in the Gulf and Qatar's Sheikh Abdullah.

On May 11, 1935, the resident wrote to the ruler reminding him about the protection which Britain was prepared to extend on land under the 1916 agreement. In return for this protection, Qatar was asked to award a concession to APOC. The deal was completed in two parts. Britain recognized Sheikh Hamad, Abdullah's second son, as heir. Six days later, the APOC concession was granted and subsequently transferred to Petroleum Development (Qatar), also known as PDQ and a subsidiary of IPC, the consortium oil company managed by Britons.

An article in the agreement stated the company could operate in any part of the state of Qatar. A map with borders, that had been agreed with no one, was attached. The lack of clarity about the border with Bahrain immediately caused problems. The adviser to Bahrain's ruler, Charles Belgrave, wrote a letter, dated April 28, 1936, to the British political agent based in Bahrain. The letter referred to the negotiations then in progress for an additional oil concession in the territory of Bahrain and declared the Hawar Islands near the Qatar coast were "indisputably" Bahrain's.

PDQ then wrote to the British India Office to ask which emirate owned the islands. The British political resident in the Gulf and the political agent in Bahrain supported Bahrain's claim to Hawar but no one told Qatar's Sheikh Abdullah. In 1937, Qatar attempted to impose taxation on the Al Naim inhabiting the Zubara region in north-west Qatar. Bahrain opposed the measure and claimed it had rights in the region.

Relations between the two emirates were broken off in July that year. According to the Bahrainis, Qatar took Zubara by force and illegally destroyed the houses of the Bahraini subjects living there. Qatar contended it was exercising its authority on its own territory over members of the Al Naim tribe that Doha accused of smuggling and other crimes and that Bahrain had clandestinely and illegally occupied the Hawar Islands. Bahrain maintained its actions were legitimate.

In July 1939, Britain again ruled in favour of Bahrain. Qatar claimed this breached Qatari sovereignty as established in the British-imposed 1868 peace treaty, its 1872 agreement with the Ottomans, the 1913 Anglo-Turkish agreement and the 1916 exclusive agreement with Britain. But it took no further action.

PDQ began drilling for oil in 1938 and struck the Dukhan structure in December 1939. APOC, which was operating the field, suspended activities for the duration of the Second World War. When it ended, the oil companies were eager to seize the opportunities offered in the southern Gulf. IPC wanted to start drilling in Qatar's western offshore waters but faced obstructions created by the Bahraini-Qatari dispute. On December 23, 1947, Britain unilaterally delimited the seabed boundary between the two countries. A line was drawn with Bahraini territory to the west and Qatari to the east.

There were two exceptions on the Qatari side: the Fasht al-Dibal and the Qitat Jaradah, which are shoals exposed at low tide, and the Hawar Islands. All of these were awarded to Bahrain. The decision was disputed by both sides. No progress was made with the dispute in the 1950s and 1960s. In 1978, Bahrain and Qatar agreed to Saudi mediation, though the first meeting did not take place until May 1983. It was held in Riyadh and solved nothing.

In April 1986, the Qataris, claiming Bahrain was building on Fasht al-Dibal in breach of the status quo, destroyed temporary structures that were being erected on the shoal. Bahrain and Qatar came close to war but were restrained by their larger neighbours. A fresh attempt to settle the dispute was made. In 1988, Bahrain refined its case, and, for the first time in the modern era, asserted a territorial claim on Zubara and the surrounding area. On July 1, 1991, Qatar filed an application for the issue to be settled by the International Court of Justice (ICJ) in The Hague.

In February 1995, the court rejected Bahraini objections and asserted it had jurisdiction. The ICJ finally ruled on March 16, 2001. It unanimously found that Qatar had sovereignty over Zubara and, by a majority, awarded sovereignty over the Hawar Islands to Bahrain. It also ruled by a majority that Qatar had sovereignty over Janan Island, including Hadd Janan, and that Bahrain had sovereignty over Qitat Jaradah as Britain had ruled in 1947. The low-tide elevation of Fasht al-Dibal was deemed to fall under the sovereignty of Qatar. The ICJ also ruled on the maritime border between the two countries. Bahrain claimed the ruling as a victory. The quiet way it was greeted in Doha suggested there was some truth in this assertion. In fact, it fell short of Bahrain's aspirations. Both parties had cause to be disappointed, but not seriously.

## Oil exports begin

After securing Zubara in 1937, Sheikh Abdullah gradually handed over control to his son, Sheikh Hamad. But Sheikh Hamad predeceased his father, dying in June 1948. Sheikh Hamad's eldest son, Sheikh Ali, succeeded as effective ruler but the ageing Sheikh Abdullah was still a force. His last act was to sign a seabed concession with Central Mining & Investment Corporation on August 5, 1949. The company and Superior Oil, also of the US, immediately began offshore exploration.

On December 31, 1949, the first shipment of onshore Qatari oil was made from the Mesaieed terminal south of Doha. After failing to find oil, the two American firms relinquished their offshore concessions and a new one was granted to Shell Company of Qatar, a 100 per cent subsidiary of Royal Dutch/Shell, in 1952.

Qatar established 50:50 revenue sharing with international oil companies in 1953. It joined OPEC in 1961. In 1963, the offshore field at Maydan Mahzam was discovered. A terminal was set up on the island of Halul, which remains a major oil centre. In 1964, Shell started full-scale production in the Idd al-Shargi Field, the first seabed oil reservoir to be operated entirely from offshore facilities. Exploration of the Bul Hanine Field started in 1965 and production got under way in 1977.

Full nationalization of the onshore concession operated by the state-owned Qatar Petroleum Company, now called Qatar Petroleum (QP), was achieved in September 1976. The offshore concession operated by a Royal Dutch/Shell Group company was fully taken over by the state in February 1977. Since that date, oil has been produced solely by QP or through production-sharing partnerships with foreign firms. No foreign oil company has a stake in Qatari oil reserves.

Sheikh Abdullah died on April 25, 1957. Sheikh Ali assumed the full powers of leadership and accepted a resident British political agent for the first time. Although the first hospital was opened by American missionaries in 1947 and Qatar's first primary school had opened in

1951, Sheikh Ali's accession marks the start of Qatar's modernization. The first power station started up in 1958. A national health service free at the point of use was established.

Qatar became a haven for Palestinian exiles. Many found employment in the oil sector and the booming construction industry. Some made fortunes. Sheikh Ali fell out with Britain and was deposed with London's connivance on October 24, 1960. He was replaced by his son, Sheikh Ahmed. Sheikh Khalifa bin Hamad, a cousin of the new ruler, was declared heir apparent and deputy ruler. Sheikh Ali died in August 1974 but lived long enough to see his deposer, Sheikh Ahmed, deposed by Sheikh Khalifa in February 1972.

## Qatar becomes independent

The 1960s saw the establishment of the key institutions of central government including the Finance Ministry under Sheikh Khalifa. The great challenge of the decade was Britain's decision to withdraw from the Gulf. Initially enthusiastic about the idea of a nine-member federation, including Bahrain and the seven emirates of what became the UAE, Qatar was influenced by Bahrain's decision to opt for independence following disagreements about how each state should be represented in the new country.

On April 2, 1970, the provisional Qatari constitution, which provided for a 33-member consultative council, including 20 elected members, was promulgated and the first council of ministers formed the following month. The Anglo-Qatari treaty of 1916 was terminated and independence declared on September 1, 1971, three weeks after a similar step by Bahrain. A treaty of friendship with Britain was signed in Geneva on September 3. The consultative council was selected through a process of limited voting.

The modernization process and federation negotiations had been led by Sheikh Khalifa. It became obvious that Sheikh Ahmed, then aged 55, was incapable of coping with the demands of being head of state in the era of independence. Meeting on February 22, 1972, the Al Thani family elected to replace Sheikh Ahmed, who was on holiday in Iran at the time, with Sheikh Khalifa, then aged about 40.

The new ruler's first act was to increase pay for civil servants and members of the armed forces. Sheikh Khalifa's son and the present emir, Sheikh Hamad, was appointed commander-in-chief of the armed forces in place of the Briton, Ronald Cochrane. He was named Qatari crown prince in June 1977. The deposed ruler, Sheikh Ahmed, lived quietly in exile in Dubai, hometown of his wife Mariam who is the elder sister of the present Dubai ruler, Sheikh Mohammed bin Rashid. He died on November 25, 1977.

The deposition of Sheikh Ahmed was the third Gulf shock after the replacement of Sultan Said of Oman by his son, Sultan Qaboos, in July 1970, and the assassination earlier in February 1972 of Sheikh Khalid bin Mohammed Al Qassimi, Sharjah's ruler. Suggestions that Britain was responsible were firmly and credibly dismissed.

A report in the *Financial Times* in March 1972 stated the deposition of Qatar's Sheikh Ahmed may have been triggered by the activities of his son, Sheikh Abdelaziz, who'd been plotting to replace Sheikh Khalifa as crown prince. Reports circulated that Sheikh Abdelaziz had installed an electric chair wired for 100 volts in his palace and that a list of 50 prominent Qataris and expatriate Arabs working for the government had been compiled. Sheikh Abdelaziz joined his father in exile.

Sheikh Khalifa took a new broom to government. He appointed a foreign minister and an adviser for day-to-day activities. The constitution was amended and more cabinet ministers appointed. The first production-sharing agreements were signed with the Standard Oil Company of Ohio (Sohio) in January 1985 and with Amoco in February 1986. A similar agreement was signed with Elf Aquitaine in January 1989. The biggest energy project of all, however, took almost 20 years to complete.

In 1974, Shell discovered a massive gas deposit in offshore Qatari waters. After further tests, it was declared to be the largest non-associated gas field on earth, a geological anomaly since gas and oil usually go together. It was called the North Field and is now estimated to have reserves of 25 trillion cubic metres, nearly 10 per cent of the world total.

Shell and Qatar wanted oil not gas, which was expensive to extract and difficult to transport. Nevertheless, by the end of the 1970s, plans had been devised for developing the North Field. In 1980, a programme was announced involving the investment of US$4 billion, about US$30 billion in 2007 prices. It called for the construction of an LNG terminal at Ra's Laffan at the tip of the peninsula. Gas production began in 1991 and LNG exports five years later. The turning point for the project was Exxon's decision in 1993 to back the scheme after BP pulled out two years earlier.

Relations with Saudi Arabia have been a persistent Qatari preoccupation. In 1935, the kingdom laid claim to much of the Qatar Peninsula, including the deep-sea inlet of Khor al-Udaid, and large areas of Abu Dhabi and Oman, including the Buraimi Oasis. Qatar and Saudi Arabia reached a preliminary agreement in 1965 that involved Doha giving up Khor al-Udaid. It divided the sea inlet of Dohat Salwa on Qatar's south-west coast between the two countries on the basis of equal distances measured from the two coasts. The land frontier was fixed. It should have been followed by the permanent delineation on the ground, but never was. The deal was not accepted by Abu Dhabi and the British government.

The conflicting territorial aspirations among the three states were further complicated in 1974 when Abu Dhabi's Sheikh Zayed conceded a slab of territory that included a stretch of coast between the UAE and Qatar. It encompassed the southern part of Khor al-Udaid. The deal resolved most of the differences between Saudi Arabia and Abu Dhabi, though it has been the subject of new attention in the UAE since the end of 2004, but did not involve Qatar.

The Qatar-Saudi border issue remained dormant for almost 20 years. In the early 1970s, other concerns, including the Arab-Israel confrontation, the oil price and the Iranian revolution, were a higher priority. Tehran's decision to end the war with Iraq signalled the start of a more pragmatic Iranian policy towards the region while the humbling in 1991 of Baathist Iraq removed a major threat. The collapse of the Soviet Union decisively eliminated the communist challenge.

In these conditions, inter-Arabian rivalries rose once more to the surface. The Qatari government believed the kingdom was infringing on its territory by building roads and facilities in the border region. On September 30, 1992, in an incident that was a throwback to previous centuries, Bedouin clashed at the Al Khofuous border post about 125 km from Doha. Two Qataris were killed and one was taken prisoner. The Qataris claimed the Saudi forces had attacked. The kingdom dismissed the accusation and said it was merely a clash between Bedouin from the two countries that signified nothing.

The clash excited international interest. Less than three months earlier, the US and Qatar had concluded a defence-cooperation agreement that provided for US access to Qatari bases, pre-positioning of US equipment and combined military exercises. It is possible that courting Washington without prior approval was seen by the Saudis as a challenge to its self-appointed role as guardian of Arabia. The border incident raised concern that a major confrontation was possible. In October 1992, a British naval task force docked in Doha in an apparently long-scheduled visit that undoubtedly had the additional effect of demonstrating Qatar had the support of the West.

Talks between Sheikh Khalifa and King Fahd in December 1992 seemed to have settled the issue. But another border incident in October 1993 caused more deaths. A further five incidents were reported in 1994 and Qatar protested by boycotting the November 1994 GCC summit. The following month, the leaders of Saudi Arabia and Qatar considered establishing a joint committee to resolve conflicts, but nothing was done. The Qataris presented the incidents as examples of bullying by its neighbour. The Saudis, in turn, accused the Qataris of provocation to get attention in the US and to put pressure on the kingdom to grant concessions, in this case territorial, which would not normally be available.

KEVIN PHILLIPS

*Capital city: modern Manama and Bahrain Financial Harbour – as photographed from the east in July 2007.*

*Built on reclaimed land, the Bahrain Financial Harbour will consolidate Bahrain's position as a leading regional banking centre.*

BAHRAIN FINANCIAL HARBOUR

*Fireworks over the Qatari capital on December 2006 mark the start of the Doha Asian Games, the biggest sporting event held in the Gulf.*

*Booming Muscat: the Omani capital is expanding rapidly into the Hajar Mountains, one of the sultanate's natural glories.*

*On the right is the new headquarters of the Abu Dhabi Investment Authority, which manages more than US$500 billion of foreign assets.*

*The Central Souk is one of the striking landmarks of Sharjah, named as the Cultural Capital of the Arab World by UNESCO in 1998.*

*Burj Al Arab: 'The Arab Tower', off Dubai's Jumeirah Beach, is designed in the shape of a sail. In 2006, Tiger Woods teed off from its helicopter pad.*

*New World in the New Gulf: Greenland (foreground) was the first island opened in The World archipelago being created by Dubai's Nakheel.*

The spectacle of two countries, ostensibly regional partners, arguing about what seemed to be very little may have been related to the tensions within the Al Thani family. Sheikh Khalifa had become inactive. Most years he spent months outside Qatar, leaving the management of the country to officials. By the end of the 1980s, Qatar had a reputation for being the most poorly managed Gulf state. In an attempt to modernize government, the *majlis* or advisory council, which had been in suspension for more than a decade, was reconstituted on December 4, 1990. Sheikh Khalifa appointed 19 new members and retained 11 of its old members. One of his last acts as ruler was to enlarge the council.

## The rule of Sheikh Hamad
Sheikh Khalifa's deposition in 1995 was accepted in Doha but others in the region were unhappy. Tensions with Riyadh boiled over in public in December 1995 when Qatar accused the kingdom of forcing Jamaal Al Hejailan, the former Saudi health minister and ambassador to France, upon the GCC as secretary general. The Qatari argument was that custom dictated that the secretary general should be chosen by alphabetical rotation. The previous incumbents had been from Kuwait and Oman and this seemed to suggest it was Qatar's turn. To emphasize their point, Sheikh Hamad and Sheikh Hamad bin Jassem walked out of the 1995 GCC summit.

Bahrain, which had its own issues with Qatar about the Hawar Islands, the UAE and Saudi Arabia all concluded the new regime was out of order. Sheikh Zayed, president of the UAE, was wounded since he had attempted to mediate between Doha and Riyadh. This set the scene for a piece of Arabian shadow-boxing in which Sheikh Khalifa, who was making it clear he was actively seeking to regain power, was received in Riyadh, Manama and finally in Abu Dhabi, where he arrived on December 21, 1995. He announced he would set up temporary quarters in the city until he was returned to power and could then restore brotherly relations with Qatar's neighbours. Sheikh Khalifa continued his restoration campaign with visits to Cairo and Damascus. Sheikh Hamad responded by visiting Cairo, Amman and Muscat and declared he too was seeking to repair the breach with other GCC states. The objection to the new GCC secretary general was dropped.

There is no consensus about what happened next. The government of Qatar says that some of its neighbours conspired with Sheikh Khalifa in a coup attempt on February 14, 1996 that involved a mercenary force of up to 2,000 Yemenis and other Arabs. Some accounts say the attackers came within a few miles of Doha before being halted and driven back. Oman denounced the coup attempt and Kuwait said nothing. The US supported a Qatari call for a special summit to resolve differences among the southern Gulf states while France and the

US carried out exercises with Qatar in a show of support. Meanwhile, the Qatar government settled its own internal account. A total of 33 people were eventually convicted, in 1999, of treason and sentenced to life in prison for their role in the 1996 affair.

The failed countercoup was embarrassing. Qatar and the other GCC states agreed that the secretary general should henceforth be selected in alphabetical order and should serve for a maximum of two three-year terms. Bahrain, Saudi Arabia and the UAE endorsed Sheikh Hamad as Qatari ruler. Bahrain accepted the jurisdiction of the ICJ over the Hawar Islands dispute. Doha restrained members of the Bahraini opposition based in Qatar. Saudi Arabia and Qatar appointed the French Institut Geographique National to demarcate their land and maritime borders.

Qatar continued to make waves. It opened talks with Enron Corporation about a possible LNG project that would involve supplying India, Islamic Pakistan's bitter rival, and Israel. Qatar also announced it was to allow the opening of an Israeli trade office in contravention of settled Arab policy. Saudi Arabia boycotted the Middle East economic summit held in Doha in November 1997 that was attended by an Israeli delegation that included former Israeli prime minister, Shimon Peres.

The start of the second Palestinian intifada in 2000 led to a closing of ranks within the Arab World. Enron, which was an investor in the Dolphin Pipeline scheme, pulled out of the project and subsequently collapsed. The rise of Crown Prince Abdullah, now Saudi Arabia's king, helped ease tensions. In 1999, the kingdom and Qatar initialled maps showing a new land border and the division of Dohat Salwa. It was more favourable to Qatar. A final border agreement with Saudi Arabia was signed in Doha on March 21, 2001, five days after the ICJ ruled on the Hawar Islands, awarding them to Bahrain.

But Al Jazeera continued to anger Riyadh and other Arab governments. Saudi Arabia withdrew its ambassador from Doha in response to a programme that criticized the late King Abdelaziz. Kuwait closed Al Jazeera's local offices following a report about a member of the Kuwaiti ruling family.

In 2002, Qatar reached an agreement for a pipeline to supply gas to Kuwait, which was facing a serious gas shortage. In March that year, the Qataris sent a letter to Saudi Arabia asking permission to build the line that would cross Saudi territorial waters. The kingdom declined and, more than five years later, still objects. The possibility of importing gas from Qatar in a liquefied form, which would involve building an expensive terminal in Kuwait, was investigated.

Fresh light was shed on the Saudi-Qatar row in May 2005 when members of the Al Ghafran clan, a division of the Murrah tribal confederation, wrote to US congressmen to complain they'd been stripped of their Qatari citizenship. It was reported by the *Financial Times* that about 6,000 people had been affected. The clan, which holds dual Saudi and Qatari nationality, is seen in Doha as supporters of the kingdom. Despite protests, they were expelled from Qatar to Saudi Arabia in June. Relations with Saudi Arabia have since radically improved.

Doha is a peaceful town but, on February 13, 2004, a car bomb was detonated in the city. It killed exiled Chechen leader Zelimkhan Yandarbiyev and injured his 13-year-old son as they were leaving a mosque. Yandarbiyev had been given refuge in Doha in 2001 after fleeing his homeland following the defeat of his separatist movement in the second Chechen war. Five days later, two Russians were arrested in their homes in Doha. On July 1, the men, who'd been identified as Russian intelligence agents, were sentenced to life imprisonment by a Qatari court. The judge said that the Russian leadership had ordered the assassination. The convicted assassins were extradited at the end of the year to serve their sentence in a Russian jail. Moscow has since stated neither are in prison.

## Qatar's role in the New Gulf

Qatar is breaking the Gulf mould in many areas. In May 2004, it hosted a conference led by the Vatican to discuss relations between Christians and Muslims. Since the start of January 2005, workers have been allowed to form unions under a new law that reflects Qatar's relatively liberal political environment and the country's desire to conform to international labour standards. The law also gives equal rights to men and women in wages, promotion and training opportunities.

In March 2005 there was dismay when a suicide bomb attack on the Doha national theatre, by an Egyptian living in Qatar, killed a British teacher and injured 12 others. A previously unknown group claimed responsibility and there is consensus that the attack was inspired by forces from outside Qatar. The tidal wave of affluence, modernizing policies and one of the most liberal political environments in the Middle East quickly made the event a distant memory.

There are questions about Sheikh Hamad's health following a kidney transplant in 1997. But at the start of 2006, Hamad was looking fit and well as he was photographed with Sheikha Mozah outside Number 10 Downing Street with UK prime minister Tony Blair and his wife Cherie and, again, accompanied by his wife, with President Chirac and his spouse in Paris in March. This is probably the first time the wife of a Gulf ruler has been recorded publicly and jointly meeting other heads of government.

Comfort can also be derived from the maturity and competence of Qatar's top men. The prime minister, Sheikh Hamad bin Jassem, is seen as headstrong, though there's evidence that a calmer approach has recently been adopted. Youssef bin Hussein Kamel, the cautious and vastly experienced finance minister, has the safest financial hands in the region. Energy minister Al Attiyah, who was made deputy premier in 2007, has built a strong team to run the oil and gas industry.

There are also new people on the rise and their ideas include the Qatar Financial Centre (QFC), an initiative designed to encourage major banks to set up offices in the country. But perhaps the greatest guarantee is provided by the forceful personality of Sheikha Mozah. Sheikh Hamad might not have done half the things he has without her.

The new spirit sweeping Qatar was reflected in the opening ceremony for the 15th Asian Games in Doha on December 1, 2006. As the start approached, winds buffeted Doha and rain started to fall. For a nervous couple of hours, the organizers weighed their options but pressed on with most of the original plan when they were advised the rain would stop soon after the ceremony began.

A few minutes past 6 pm, a four-hour pageant began in the Khalifa International Stadium. Orry the Oryx, the game's mascot, was introduced. Qatari girls and boys danced publicly together. A story about an Arab sailor seeking fortune and love was acted out with a cast of hundreds. It climaxed with 64 Arab horsemen charging into the stadium. To the pounding beat of thousands of drums, athletes from the 45 nations participating in the games marched by country into the stadium. Last in, to be greeted by a great roar, was the huge delegation from Qatar. The spotlight fell on the main podium where Qatar's crown prince Sheikh Tameem delivered a welcoming speech, in Arabic for the first time at a major world sports event. This was followed by songs from Hong Kong pop star Jacky Cheung and Indian Bollywood singer Sunidi Chauhan. Spanish operatic tenor Jose Carreras joined Lebanon's Magida Al Roumi to sing 'Light the Way', a hymn of hope in Arabic and English.

The event reached its climax with the arrival of the Games' torch which was carried around the stadium by a relay of Qatari sports stars. Then, rising into the stadium through a hidden trap door, Qatar's equestrian champion Sheikh Mohammed bin Hamad Al Thani, son of the ruler, appeared on his horse Malibu. In the opening ceremony's most dramatic moment, he took the Games' flame and rode Malibu to the top of the stadium where he transferred the flame to the giant cauldron. At that moment, the sky over Doha exploded with one of the world's largest firework displays.

Two weeks later, the Games came to a close. Qatar won nine golds and a total of 32 medals, the largest number won by an Arab country. The closing ceremony developed some of the themes of the opening and the pageant centred on a story from *A Thousand and One Nights*. Filipino Broadway star Lea Salonga performed 'Triumph of the One', a song written specifically for the games. Amid a further storm of fireworks, the biggest sporting event ever held in the Middle East came to an end.

More than 13,000 athletes participated in the games. There was a shortage of accommodation that was dealt with by hiring cruise liners. Rain at the opening ceremony led to delays in people leaving the Khalifa stadium. The attendance at some events was patchy. But it had all gone better than anyone could have imagined when Doha won the Games' mandate in 2000. They were declared to be the best ever.

Qatar immediately announced it planned to make Doha the sports centre for the Gulf. In early 2007, it notified the International Olympic Committee (IOC) that it intended to bid for the 2016 Olympics. Some in Doha are now contemplating the ultimate: bidding for the 2018 FIFA World Cup Finals.

### Al Thani rulers of Qatar

| | |
|---|---|
| Sheikh Mohammed bin Thani . ... ... ... ... ... ... ... ... | 1847–1879 |
| Sheikh Jassem bin Mohammed  ... ... ... ... ... ... ... ... | 1879–1913 |
| Sheikh Abdullah bin Jassem  ... ... ... ... ... ... ... ... | 1913–1957 |
| Sheikh Ali bin Hamad (deposed) .. ... ... ... ... ... ... ... | 1957–1960 |
| Sheikh Ahmed bin Ali (deposed)... ... ... ... ... ... ... ... | 1960–1972 |
| Sheikh Khalifa bin Hamad (deposed) . ... ... ... ... ... ... | 1972–1995 |
| Sheikh Hamad bin Khalifa .. ... ... ... ... ... ... ... ... | 1995– |

# CHAPTER 6

# THE LAST ARABIAN
# SULTANATE

At Muscat's Sultan Qaboos Stadium, Oman was celebrating national day. Some 40,000 Omanis and foreign guests enjoyed a military tattoo with an Arabian twist as sunset turned into a starry November night. A marching band opened the event. They were followed by soldiers, students, athletes and a squad of Firqa, the tribal fighters who'd helped defeat the Dhofar insurrection in the 1970s.

Sultan Qaboos bin Said Al Bu Said, 14th of his line, stood to attention to receive the salute. The band struck up the national anthem. The spectators rose and thousands of Omani boys and girls raised their voices in song. White doves were released and flapped around the terraces, narrowly escaping Omani hands reaching out to trap them.

The parade in a stadium bearing his name – and at which the sultan is the star – takes place annually to mark his birthday and the start of another year in the rule of the man whose vision has transformed a nation. Oman, once poor and divided, has come of age. Its people are healthier and better educated than ever. External threats and internal enemies have been vanquished. Since the sultan's accession in July 1970, Oman has broken the embrace of the past to seize the opportunities offered by the 21st century.

It is the work of many hands, some not Omani. But there is only one mastermind. And there was no doubt in the stadium that evening, or anywhere else in Oman, who that person is. This chapter is not solely about Sultan Qaboos. But it is impossible to write about modern Oman without acknowledging the achievements and aspirations of the last Arabian sultan. Sultan Qaboos is special even by the region's standards. No Arabian ruler had a more unusual route to the top. None has done more when he got there. And none has created more uncertainty about what happens when he is gone.

Oman advances before the benign gaze of its perfectionist ruler like a national-day parade. For the Omani majority, who were born after 1970, this is natural. The sultan is the only leader they've known. The sultanate in the fourth decade of his rule is Sultan Qaboos' country and the Omanis are, by definition, his people.

Oman has a population of 2.5 million people scattered across a

OMAN

N

Khasab
Musandam Peninsula
Dibba
Dubai
Shinas
GULF
OF OMAN
Abu
Dhabi
Sohar
Buraimi
Dimaaniyat
Islands
Hajar Mountains
Muscat
UNITED
ARAB
EMIRATES
Barka
Ibri
Bahla   Nizwa
Sur
Ras al-Hadd
KINGDOM
OF SAUDI ARABIA
OMAN
Empty Quarter
Masirah
Island
Hayma
Duqm
ARABIAN
SEA
YEMEN
Dhofar
Mirbat   Hallaniyat Islands
Salalah

*This map is not an authority
on international boundaries.*

country the size of the UK that occupies two-thirds of the coast of south Arabia. Omanis are a mixture. The sultanate has as many as 200 different tribes. In the north, these can be classified into Ghafiri and Hinawi factions, a split that emerged in the first half of the 18th century. In the far south, the tribes can be divided between non-Jabali and Jabali people, named after the Jebel Dhofar where a language that an Arabic speaker would not understand is spoken.

About 45 per cent of Omanis are Ibadhi Muslim, a distinctive Islamic group mainly concentrated in the north. Most of the rest are Sunni Muslims. There are distinct Omani minorities. The Baluch are found mainly in the Batinah and in the twin towns of Muscat and Muttrah. The Baluchi port of Gwadur was an Omani possession from 1784 until it was sold to Pakistan in 1958. A high proportion of the sultanate's first modern army originated from Baluchistan and Baluchi recruitment continued until the 1970s. There could be 250,000 Omani Baluchis. including a community that settled on the west side of the Hajar Mountains.

Associated with Omani Baluchis are the Zadjalis, a community that also originated in what is now Pakistan. They have their own language, which is similar to Kutchi, which is spoken by some Hindus, who in the Gulf are traditionally known as Banians. Some Baluchis and Zadjalis have risen to the top of government and business. An example is executive president of the Central Bank of Oman, Hamoud Al Zadjali.

The Lawatiyya or Khojas are the most numerous of Oman's three Shiite groups. It's believed they arrived from India more than three centuries ago. They concentrated in the ports and a section of Muttrah is known as Sur al-Lawatiyya (the Lawati area). All are Jafari Shiite, sometimes known as Fiver Shiites, since they recognize only the first five Shiite imams. The Lawatiyya have done well. Its most prominent business family is the Sultans, who own the WJ Towell Group, a Muscat firm originally founded in 1865 by a visiting American businessman. Maqbool Ali Sultan, son of the late head of the Sultan family, is minister of commerce and industry. Lawatiyya women have been groundbreakers in government and business.

Arab Shiites that originated from the northern Gulf, though not necessarily from Bahrain, are known as Baharina. Prominent representatives include the Makki family that provides Oman's finance minister and some top business people. There is a community of Omani Zanzibaris, many of whom speak English and Swahili better than Arabic. They originate from Omani communities who settled in East Africa. Zanzibaris have a liberal reputation. Many have risen in government, but, so far, none has entered the cabinet.

Dhofar, with a population of some 250,000 people, has its own social character. Many of its people are members of divisions of the large

Al Kathir tribe, but smaller tribes, such as the Al Qara, the Al Shahra and the Al Mahra, are represented throughout the province. Dhofar has many *Khadim*, or descendants of former slaves, and other people of African origin. Practically all are Sunni Muslims of the conservative Shafi school which also dominates the southern parts of Yemen. Various dialects of Jabali are spoken in Dhofar, but standard Arabic is taught in schools and is becoming the main language of the region.

Movement of people within the country for work and leisure is also beginning to break down the distinctiveness of the sultanate's many communities. The definitive dress item for Omani men is the *kummah* (cap). On formal occasions, it is wrapped in a woollen Kashmiri scarf. The *thawb* is normally white, but can be other colours. In the north of Oman, young men often wear a white *ghutrah* (headscarf) in a style seen in Dubai and the northern emirates of the UAE. Omani women traditionally dress colourfully, but the plain black *abaya* is common.

Illiteracy, pervasive a generation ago, has been effectively eliminated among people younger than 30 years of age. The sultanate's social mosaic is the result of thousands of years of settlement and migration. Of the nations of the Gulf, Oman has the most romantic history.

Covering an area of just a little less than 300,000 km$^2$, Oman is comprised mainly of sand and gravel desert and mountains stripped of topsoil. Most Omanis live in Muscat and in towns and villages along the coast of the Batinah Corridor. This is a plain, rarely more than 15 km wide, between mountain and sea, that stretches north from the Omani capital to the UAE border. Batinah takes its name from the Arabic word for belly, a reference to the fact it protrudes from the front of the Hajar Mountains.

The second major population centre is Salalah, the capital of Dhofar, more than 800 km by road to the south-west of Muscat. Oman's coastline is embellished with rocky outcrops and islands. Masirah Island is a military staging and listening post. The Al Hallaniyat, formerly the Kuria Muria Islands, are attracting tourists.

Among Oman's curiosities are two enclaves in the north separated from the rest of the country by the territory of the UAE. They are Al Mahda and most of the Musandam Peninsula, homeland of the Shihu people who have consistently been loyal to the Al Bu Said dynasty. American listening posts have been built in Khasab, Musandam's sole town of significance, and on Jazirat al-Ghanem in the Strait of Hormuz at the tip of the Musandam.

Oman has a delightful diversity of landscape from the peaks of the Jebel Akhdar to the symmetrical Wahiba Sands. But its glory is a 2,240 km coastline that's sheltered and fed the people of south Arabia since humanity first arrived more than 7,000 years ago. Fishing continues to be a major source of employment. Among the sea's many fruits is the abalone, a plant-eating marine shellfish that is prized as a delicacy, particularly in the Far East. In the spring of 2007, a kilo of abalone flesh was selling in Dhofar at US$150. Abalone's value is enhanced by the fact that its shells are a source of mother of pearl.

## The making of Oman

There were Stone Age settlements in what is now Oman. The region enters history with the Sumerians. Their records show that the city states of ancient Mesopotamia bought copper mined in Magan in what is now the Sultanate of Oman and the UAE. Ingots were taken by camel to the Omani coast or north through the Hajar Mountains to the Gulf for shipment to Sumer.

The ancient world loved Dhofar's frankincense and myrrh. The inhabitants of the Hajar region developed in around 1000 BC the *falaj* irrigation system to deliver spring water from the foothills to the farmlands. It is used to this day. Before the coming of Islam and under Sasanian rule, a Nestorian Christian bishopric is believed to have existed in Sohar. It has left no mark on the landscape, although there's an ancient Jewish graveyard in the town.

The people of Oman embraced Islam during the lifetime of the Prophet (PBUH). They became early missionaries and helped spread the faith to Indonesia, Malaysia, Sarawak, Brunei and the southern Philippines. The Omani navigator and missionary, Abu Ubaida bin Abdullah bin Al Qassim, completed the 1,000 km sea journey to Guangzho (Canton) in the 8th century, opening up a trading route that was for centuries the most profitable on earth. The legendary Arab sailor, Sinbad, embarked on many voyages from Sohar and other Omani ports.

The region's distinctiveness was enhanced by the role of Ibadhi Islam. Seeking to separate themselves from the Muslim majority, the Ibadhis found refuge in the Hajar Mountains. They established an imamate, or religious state, that endured to the middle of the last century. The first Ibadhi imam, Rashid bin Al Walid, was elected in 750. Despite its schismatic origins, the sole major difference between Ibadhism and mainstream Sunni Islam is the conviction that only Abu Bakr and Omar, the first two caliphs – successors of the Prophet (PBUH) – were legitimate.

The idea that spiritual leadership can be transferred within a single family, as Shiites contend, is rejected. In Ibadhism, the imam is the man best qualified to provide leadership. If no satisfactory candidate can be found, the post can be left vacant. Because of their elective approach to leadership, Ibadhis are often called the people of Consultation (*Ahl al-Shura*). The Ibadhis aimed to create a perfect Islamic community but remained open to the ways of the outside world. Self-contained but extrovert, Ibadhism provided an excellent intellectual context for trade coupled with missionary work.

Their mark on Islam is far larger than their present numbers would suggest. By the start of the 15th century, Omanis had established Muslim Arab communities around the Indian Ocean rim. They traded in spices, incense, gold, pearls, tortoiseshell, ivory and rhino horn. Omanis were civilized and cosmopolitan advocates of the Islamic faith, dazzling sailors and intercontinental entrepreneurs. Their legacy is impressive. Omani Arab settlements in East Africa include the island of Zanzibar. The mixture of the African Kiswahili language and Arabic spoken by Omani Arabs produced Swahili, which is still spoken in Oman.

Omanis were to play a critical role in the coming of the first North European imperialists to the Gulf. In 1497/98, Vasco da Gama found his way to India. He was guided round the Cape of Good Hope to his ultimate destination by an Arab familiar with the work of Ahmed bin Majid, a navigator probably based in Julfar near present-day Ra's al-Khaimah who sailed Indian Ocean routes.

The Portuguese seized Omani East African ports and decided to take control of the Gulf and Indian Ocean trade. Admiral Alfonso d'Albuquerque captured and sacked Sohar. Other ports, including Muscat, were attacked. The kingdom of Hormuz was beaten in 1507. The conquerors' violence provoked the sequence of events that would eventually produce the present government of Oman. In 1624, Nasr bin Murshid bin Sultan Al Yaarubi was elected Ibadhi imam at Rustaq, then the Ibadhi capital, which lies in a valley in the Jebel Akhdar. Imam Nasr forged a national movement that eventually drove out the Portuguese, who'd already been expelled from the Persian coast.

The Portuguese built many forts on the Gulf coast. But they are sometimes wrongly credited for all the 500 forts, castles and towers that can be found in Oman. The Al Jalali and Al Mirani forts that guard Muscat Bay were indeed built by the invaders for whom the port was an important naval base for 150 years. But most were erected by the Yaariba and succeeding Al Bu Said dynasties during and after the mid-17th century.

The fort in Sohar, once the greatest seaport in Islam, was probably originally built in the 13th century. The circular tower in Nizwa west of the Jebel Akhdar was constructed around 1660 during the rule of Imam Sultan bin Saif Al Yaarubi. The Al Khandaq and Al Hillah forts command the Buraimi Oasis. Ra's al-Hadd Fort occupies a site on Arabia's most eastern headland. In the far south-west, forts in Taqah, Mirbat and Sadah in Dhofar have been restored. An increasing number of Oman's forts are being properly investigated and dated.

The next wave of European visitors was welcomed. In February 1646, the (British) East India Company signed a treaty with Imam Nasr that granted the company, which had already established a station in Sohar, a monopoly over Omani trade. Imam Nasr died in April 1649 as his army laid siege to the remnants of Portugal's Muscat garrison.

His successor, Imam Sultan bin Saif, declared holy war against the Portuguese in January 1650, chased their ships to Goa, the main Portuguese colony in India, and bombarded their forts in East Africa. In 1659, Imam Sultan signed a further treaty with the East India Company. In the early years of the 18th century, the Omanis were having their ships built in the dockyards of British India. By 1668, Omanis were rulers of most of their East African possessions. In 1696, the Portuguese-supported sultan of the island of Zanzibar was expelled. In 1699, Pemba fell and Portuguese rule in East Africa north of Mozambique was ended.

From that time until the middle of the 19th century, Zanzibar was ruled by governors appointed by the rulers of Muscat. Gwadur in what is now Pakistan was a further pillar supporting the Omani trading empire that stretched across the Indian Ocean. The legacy of Oman's golden era was, nevertheless, a bitter one. Its economy depended on slavery. Omani slavers penetrated the African interior. They discovered the source of the Zambezi River more than a century before the Scottish missionary, David Livingstone. Most famous of them all was Tippu Tip, a Zanzibari Omani, properly known as Hamed bin Mohammed Al Marjebi, who was born in 1837. He struck fear into millions of African hearts until late in the 19th century.

Imam Sultan died in 1679 and was succeeded without election by his son Bil'Arab. The democratic tradition in Omani Ibadhism was temporarily extinguished. Bil'Arab, whose right to rule was consistently challenged, died by his own hand in 1692. He was succeeded by his brother, Imam Saif, an innovator who promoted well digging in the Batinah Corridor. Imam Saif's son, Imam Sultan, inherited and extended Omani rule into the Gulf. Bahrain was captured in 1717 or 1718 but later sold back to Persia. Islands off the coast of southern Persia were seized.

In 1718, Imam Sultan II died. His 12-year-old son, Imam Saif II, was manoeuvred into the imamate, provoking a split in the Ibadhi community. The strongest contender was Mohammed bin Nasser, the paramount sheikh of the Bani Ghafir, a tribe tracing its descent from the northern Adnani/Nizari division of the Arabian people. He deposed the young imam and was elected in his place. This development was contested by Khalaf bin Mubarak of the Bani Hinawi, the leading tribe in the confederation of the Qathani/Yamani people, who traced their origin from southern and western Arabia. They were mainly located in the Hajar. The Nizari were mainly settled on the Gulf coast and in the desert. Civil war erupted and divided the tribes of the region, including non-Ibadhi people in the west of what is now the UAE. Imam Saif II, who was supported by the Bani Hinawi, grew to maturity and asserted his claim to the Ibadhi leadership. In desperation, he called on Nader Shah of Persia, the conqueror of Delhi, for help. A Persian army landed in Julfar on the Gulf and Khor Fakkan on the Arabian Sea in 1737 and advanced from both east and west towards the Buraimi Oasis.

## The rise of the Al Bu Said

The Persians, ostensibly championing Imam Saif II, came close to complete victory. The civil war turned into a battle to resist Persian dominance. The governor of Sohar, Ahmed bin Said bin Mohammed Al Bu Said, a member of a small Hinawi tribe, forged a coalition that drove the Persians out by 1744. Ghafiri and Hinawi factions were unified and Ahmed bin Said became the Ibadhi imam. He established the dynasty from which Sultan Qaboos is descended.

After the civil war and the rise of the Al Bu Said, the power of the imamate declined. The new ruling family adopted secular rather than religious means to govern its domain and a system of hereditary rule was established. Imam Ahmed bin Said promoted sea-borne commerce, making Muscat an important trading centre. A standing army and navy were established. An English visitor in 1775 reported Muscat was one of the most prosperous ports in the Indian Ocean.

Imam Ahmed bin Said died in 1788 and was succeeded by his second son, Imam Said, a weak ruler who surrendered real control to his son Hamad. Hamad moved the seat of Omani government to Muscat from Rustaq and assumed the secular title of Sayyid, or Lord. He renamed his realm as the Sultanate of Muscat & Oman. Sayyid Hamad predeceased his father, dying of smallpox in 1792. His uncle, Sayyid Sultan bin Ahmed became ruler.

Prompted by the landing of a French army of invasion led by Napoleon Bonaparte in Egypt in July 1798, the East India Company signed, three months later, the first in a series of friendship treaties that have linked London and Muscat ever since. It involved an Omani undertaking to deny French and Dutch vessels entry to any of its ports or to allow them to set up any trading or manufacturing activity. In effect, Oman became an affiliate of the expanding British Empire. Two years later, a further treaty was signed that tied Oman even closer to Britain and provided for the appointment of a permanent representative of the British crown in Muscat. The site of his residence, opened in April 1800, was until recently occupied by the British embassy.

The opening years of the 19th century were dominated by the threat presented by the Al Saud, who were building an empire across Arabia. Rebuffed by the Omani forces in 1803, the Al Saud launched a fresh assault two years later and quickly seized control of most of Muscat's lands. Oman's ability to respond was crippled by internecine rivalry that followed Sayyid Sultan's death in 1804.

After a two-year power struggle, Sultan's son, Sayyid Said, assassinated his principal rival, his father's cousin named Badr. Supported by British gunboats and soldiers, supplied by British India and assisted by Persia, Sayyid Said expelled the Al Saud from his domains by 1820. In 1829, Sayyid Said annexed Dhofar, but firm control of the province was only established from 1879.

Sayyid Said set about establishing Oman as the dominant power in the lower Gulf, using a fleet of British-made gunboats. The 12-gun Omani battleship *Sultanah* was built in Bombay and later sailed to the Royal Naval Dockyard at Woolwich for repairs. In 1836, the 74-gun *Liverpool* was sent to Britain as a gift to King William IV. One of the English king's yachts, the *Prince Regent*, was dispatched to Oman and anchored in Muscat in 1837. The following year, Oman's first ambassador to the Court of St James arrived in London. Sayyid Said launched a programme of cultivating cloves, previously only produced in the Far East, on the islands of Zanzibar and Pemba. Enchanted by his wealthy East African possessions, Sayyid Said spent increasing time there. In 1853, he announced he was transferring his court to Zanzibar.

The British connection was a mixed blessing. Parliament voted in 1807 to ban the slave trade and, later, to emancipate all slaves in the British Empire in 1833. The British government, working through the East India Company government, pressured the Omanis into signing the Moresby Treaty of 1822 that banned the sales of slaves to subjects of Christian powers. The terms of the restrictions of the trade in slaves were tightened in the Convention of Commerce, signed in 1839. This was four years after the signing of the 1835 maritime truce treaty between Britain and the states of the lower Gulf, which also effectively ended slave trading, but not ownership, in the Trucial emirates. Since Oman was independent, it was compensated by being given most favoured nation status within the British Empire.

The following year, to demonstrate his autonomy and to buy weapons for a campaign to capture Mozambique from the Portuguese, Sayyid Said dispatched an emissary to New York. His flag ship *Sultanah* carried his envoy, Ahmed bin Naaman, and gifts of jewels, a Persian rug, a sword and two Arabian horses among other items for President Van Buren. The sultanate thus became the first Arab state to establish diplomatic relations with the US. The ship and Naaman stayed in New York until August 1841, causing a memorable stir. Sayyid Said never launched his Mozambique campaign and relations between Muscat and Washington lapsed for generations.

Two further treaties were signed with Britain. The Hamerton Treaty of 1845 ended the export of slaves from Oman's African possessions. The treaty of 1873, which finally ended the slave trade, was signed by the Omani rulers of what had by then become two states: one in Arabia and one in East Africa. The division was precipitated by the death of Sayyid Said at the age of 59 during a visit to the Seychelles in 1856. Sayyid Said willed a system of joint rule involving two of his sons. Thuwainy was to have Oman while Majid took over Zanzibar and the African territories. With their father's passing, the brothers fell out and were on the brink of war when the government of India intervened. In April 1861, British India's viceroy, Lord Canning, who'd repressed the Indian Rebellion three years earlier, confirmed Zanzibar and mainland Oman would henceforth be separate, each with its own sultan. Zanzibar, which became a British protectorate, agreed to pay Muscat 40,000 silver Maria Theresa thalers each year in what became known as the Canning Award. The payments soon fell into arrears and British India itself paid the levy from 1871 until 1956.

Muscat's Sultan Thuwainy died in 1868 and, after further family feuding, was replaced by his cousin, Sultan Azzan bin Qais, who also assumed the title of imam. Sultan Azzan tried to impose his rule on inner Oman and fell out with the British. Sayyid Turki bin Said, son of the previous ruler, rose in rebellion with British connivance and Sultan Azzan died fighting his rival in January 1871. The chaos did nothing to lift morale in Muscat and its hinterland as poverty spread and more people left. The final end of the slave trade brought about by the 1873 treaty sent the Omani economy into a slump. The tribes of the interior, for whom old loyalties were only a distant memory, came close to capturing Muscat. A fresh outflow of people to Zanzibar drained talent and energy from the sultanate.

Sultan Turki died in 1888 and was succeeded by Faisal, his second son. The new sultan, hemmed in by enemies and constrained by Britain, bankrupted the state by buying off the leaders of a further interior rebellion. Desperate for new sources of money, he started to cultivate the French, who were supplying weapons to rebel tribesmen on the north-west frontier of British India.

Britain responded in 1895 by providing a loan and another in 1897. Sultan Faisal, nevertheless, renewed relations with the French and granted them access to Barr al-Jissah, a port south of Muscat that today has been converted into a holiday resort. The British declared the deal with the French to be a breach of the agreement of 1798. They summoned Sultan Faisal to the deck of a British battleship in Muscat harbour to repudiate the deal publicly with the threat that the Royal Navy would open fire on his capital if he did not.

Despite these acts of bullying, British-Omani relations were restored, helped by the influence of Major Percy Cox, possibly the first genuine British Arabist, who was appointed imperial resident in 1899. Cox travelled to the interior and took Sultan Faisal's heir Sayyid Taimour, the present sultan's grandfather, to Delhi in January 1903 to witness the coronation durbar of King Edward VII.

In November that year, the viceroy of India, Lord Curzon, visited Oman as part of a Gulf tour, invested Sultan Faisal with the Grand Cross of the Order of the Indian Empire and announced all Oman's debts to Britain would be written off. The Omanis, nevertheless, were a divided people. Muscat and the port towns of Oman became accustomed to British dominance and foreign visitors while the tribes of the interior hankered after the egalitarian certainties of the imamate and resented the intrusion of infidels.

The festering discontent exploded into rebellion when the British insisted on ending the export of guns from Muscat and closer control over weapons held by the sultan's soldiers. The trade in rifles was an important source of income in the hinterland and a symbol of the independence of the tribes. Their leaders met in May 1913 in Tanuf, near the historic imamate capital of Nizwa, and declared an end to the rule by sultans and the restoration of the principle of election for the selection of leaders. Salim bin Rashid Al Kharusi was named imam. Plans were laid for an attack on Muscat and the deposition of the Al Bu Said.

**The rule of Sultan Taimour**
Sultan Faisal's eventful life and 30-year rule ended in October 1913. The new ruler, Sultan Taimour, Anglophile and sophisticated, had a dire legacy. For 18 months, he tried to reach an accommodation with the rebels. Led by Sheikh Isa bin Saleh of the influential Al Harthy family, Sultan Taimour's enemies launched an all-out attack on Muscat in early 1915. Only the intervention of a battalion of Baluchi soldiers led by British officers prevented Muscat's fall. The underlying grievances were not addressed. Distracted by the campaigns in Mesopotamia and the Levant, Britain sought only to preserve the status quo while the First World War lasted.

After 1918, the rulers of Britain's Middle East empire set about the task of regulating a vast land area which they could not afford to police. In September 1921, Sultan Taimour signed a treaty with Sheikh Isa at Seeb, about 15 km north of Muscat and now the site of Oman's principal airport. The Seeb agreement formalized what all knew to be true: there were now two states within the domain of Sultan Taimour. The tribes of the interior led by Imam Mohammed bin Abdallah Al Khalili, who'd succeeded Imam Salim bin Rashid when he was assassinated in 1920, were permitted to assume that they had achieved self-rule. Sultan Taimour in Muscat was allowed to behave as if they had not. The agreement lasted until 1954.

The Seeb agreement led to greater British involvement. In 1925, Bertram Thomas, an official who'd previously worked in the Palestine mandate, was seconded as financial adviser. His five-year term in Muscat is deemed to have been a failure. But his name lives in the records because he was the first European to complete a journey through the Empty Quarter, the greatest of Arabia's five sand deserts. Thomas' rival, Harry St John Philby, who was then adviser to the Saudi king, said British policy in Oman in that period was unsuccessful precisely because of the absence of desert journeys of the nominated British representative.

## The rule of Sultan Said

Sultan Taimour was the first Omani ruler to visit London. In 1932, four years after his trip to the imperial capital, he abdicated under pressure from British officials. He was succeeded by his son Sultan Said, then aged 21. The new sultan seemed to be the Omani ruler who'd take his people into the 20th century. He had been sent, after initial schooling in Baghdad, to Mayo College, the Eton of British India, founded in 1870 in Indian Rajastan by a British earl.

Taimour, stripped of power, travelled to Japan, his interest stimulated by the visit eight years earlier by Shigetaka Shiga, a geographer and map-maker. In 1936, on a journey to Kobe, he fell in love with a Japanese woman named Kiyoko Ohyama. They married and had a daughter. Kiyoko died prematurely and when the Second World War ended, Taimour took his daughter, Buthaina, back to Oman. She lives today in Muscat where she's respected and loved. The former sultan died in 1965.

Sultan Said's accession coincided with the world depression. It hit the Gulf and reduced the number of ships passing through Muscat, decimating government income from customs dues. Sultan Said balanced the government's books by slashing spending, including on his own household. Economy measures meant his rule was only effective in Muscat and its environs and in Salalah, where Sultan Said was to spend most of his time.

The sultan's attachment to Dhofar was reflected in his marriage to a daughter of a Jabali sheikh. She bore him a daughter. When she died, Sultan Said married her cousin, Mizoon bint Ahmed Al Mashaani, who was born in Taqah, a port west of Salalah. On November 18, 1940, Sayyida Mizoon gave birth to Qaboos, the sultan's only son and ruler of Oman since July 1970.

The main challenge was in the north. Supremacy over the interior was claimed by Imam Al Khalili and the leaders of the Hinawi and Ghafiri tribes. Sultan Said, nevertheless, insisted that sovereignty over the interior was still his. To make the point, passports were issued and duties were levied in Muscat on all Omani imports and exports.

The sultan's interest in the interior was enhanced by hopes that it contained hydrocarbon treasure. His father had awarded an exploration licence to the D'Arcy Exploration Company in 1924, but this lapsed after a geological survey found no conclusive evidence of oil.

Sultan Said was then approached by IPC. He granted it an exclusive 75-year concession for Oman and Dhofar in 1937. Exploration was run for IPC by Petroleum Development (Oman & Dhofar) Ltd, a special-purpose company with four shareholders, each with an interest of 23.75 per cent. These were Royal Dutch/Shell, APOC, Compagnie Française des Pétroles (CFP – now part of Total) and the Near East Development Company (owned by companies that are now part of ExxonMobil). The remaining five per cent stake was held by Partex, the holding company set up to represent the interests in IPC of Calouste Gulbenkian.

Because of the opposition of Imam Al Khalili, no attempts at exploration were made before the Second World War started in 1939. The war gave Oman a financial lift, elevating Muscat's significance and bringing more ships, flying boats and money to its ports. IPC mounted its first exploration campaign when the war ended. Entering the interior from Abu Dhabi in the winter of 1947, an IPC survey team led by Richard Bird attempted to contact Imam Al Khalili and make agreements with tribal leaders without Sultan Said's prior approval. The sultan was outraged and Bird and his explorers were ejected. Bird made another foray with the sultan's approval the following year, but it too was rebuffed.

The search for oil set in train a sequence of events that were to climax in the 1955 Buraimi Oasis Crisis. The Saudis, who claimed the oasis, sent in an armed force on August 31, 1952. Riyadh won over some local leaders. It also tried to get the support of Imam Al Khalili for a campaign to liberate the region from infidel British control.

The imam turned down Riyadh and called for action by Sultan Said who meanwhile had gathered an expeditionary force in Sohar to expel the Saudis. War was averted when Britain agreed that the issue should be referred to international arbitration. Sultan Said dispersed his eager army, creating a fresh source of discontent among those who believed that he was controlled by British imperialists.

A new crisis developed in May 1954 when Imam Al Khalili, who'd co-operated with Sultan Said, died in Nizwa. The leaders of the Hinawi and Ghafiri immediately voted for Ghalib bin Ali Hinai as imam. But the real power was with Ghalib's ambitious brother, Talib bin Ali Hinai. The brothers set about destroying the Seeb concord.

The change at the top in the imamate coincided with the first serious attempt to explore for oil in the interior. The IPC expedition of February 1954 was supported by 400 Omani soldiers. It landed at Duqm, a port town halfway between Muscat and Salalah, and waited for final permission from Sultan Said to enter the interior. It began its journey into the interior in October. Omani troops seized Ibri. By the end of November 1954, the power of the Omani government had been decisively projected into the interior.

Talib seized on the issue, claiming IPC activities breached the Seeb agreement. Fighting between the imamate, supported by Saudi money and weapons, and the sultan's army began at the end of 1954. Imam Ghalib responded by declaring the imamate's independence and applying for membership of the Arab League.

The chaos was settled in phases. In October 1955, the British-led Trucial Oman Scouts, supported by the sultan's armed forces, ended the Saudi presence in the Buraimi Oasis. In December, the sultanate's forces seized Rustaq and Nizwa in swift succession. Ghalib and Talib fled to Saudi Arabia. The interior was sufficiently under Omani control to permit Sultan Said to drive from Salalah to Nizwa and from there to Ibri, the Buraimi Oasis and then into Al Ain for a meeting with Sheikh Shakhbut, Abu Dhabi's ruler at the end of the year.

The imamate's final flourish came in April 1957 when Talib, based in Dammam, sent armed fighters into Oman through the sultanate's eastern coastline. Led by Talib, the rebels seized Bahla and Nizwa in June. Nizwa was recaptured in August by a combined force of Omanis, a detachment of the Scottish infantry regiment, The Cameronians, and the Trucial Oman Scouts supported by the RAF. An attempt to end the rebellion was made in June 1957 when the Omani army, supported by the British army and the RAF, hit rebel bases in the Jebel Akhdar. Nevertheless, a guerrilla war continued.

To formalize British military support against the insurgency, an agreement signed in London in July 1958 gave the RAF landing rights in Salalah and on Masirah Island. In January 1959, the UK's Special Air Service (SAS) working with the British Life Guards, a tank regiment, and the Omani army stormed the last rebel redoubt on Jebel Akhdar. Ghalib and Talib escaped to Saudi Arabia. Minor hit-and-run attacks continued until 1962, but the imamate was dead. It was a turning point. For the first time in almost 200 years, the ruler of Muscat was master of the hinterland, Salalah and Dhofar.

**Oil is discovered**

Oil exploration had already begun in the interior. The first well was sunk in 1956 in Fahud, but nothing was found. After IPC's failure to find oil, the IPC partners, with the exception of Royal Dutch/Shell and Partex, withdrew from the concession in 1960. Shell and Partex persisted and struck oil at Yibal in 1962, in Natih in 1963 and Fahud the following year. The first oil shipment left Oman's shores on July 27, 1967.

In June 1967, the oil partnership was revised. CFP rejoined the concession by taking over two-thirds of Partex's equity. The operating company was renamed as Petroleum Development (Oman) or PDO, with Shell owning 85 per cent, CFP 10 and Partex five per cent. The government took a 25 per cent stake in PDO on January 1, 1974. Six months later, this was raised to 60 per cent, backdated to the start of the year. Shell's share was reduced to 34 per cent, CFP's to four per cent and Partex's to two per cent. These arrangements remain unchanged although the company's name was changed to Petroleum Development Oman in 1980.

The rise of the unified Sultanate of Oman demanded an end of traditional administration practised by Sultan Said in his 30-year rule. Britain increased its involvement in developing the state it had paid money and blood to secure. A British development secretary arrived at the end of 1958, his department funded by the UK treasury. To raise money, Sultan Said sold the enclave of Gwadur to the Pakistan government for £3 million in 1958. But there was discontent resulting from Oman's poverty and disillusionment with a government that had ceded power to Britain and appeared to be disinterested in the dire condition in which the majority lived.

At the start of the 1960s, when the population was no more than 400,000 people, as many as 70,000 Omani men had left the country to find work in other parts of the Gulf. The disaffection was compounded by growing nationalist and anti-British sentiment across the region. The 1956 Suez Crisis exposed British and French mendacity. The deposition of the British-supported Iraqi monarchy in 1958 suggested the regional status quo was collapsing. In south Arabia, British rule was being challenged. In September 1962, the imamate government of North Yemen was deposed. This encouraged the demand for South Yemeni independence and the expulsion of Britain from south Arabia.

Signs of a new rebellion came in 1962 when minor acts of sabotage were reported outside Salalah. Serious violence began in April 1963 when rebels attacked an oil-company convoy in the desert. The assailants, led by a former gardener in Sultan Said's Salalah palace, Mussalim bin Nufl, fled to Saudi Arabia and made contact with Imam Ghalib bin Ali. Financed by the Saudis, Nufl went to Iraq for further training.

In 1964, Nufl's group returned to Dhofar. The rebels were supported by a curious combination of states: republican Egypt and Iraq and the independent traditional states of Saudi Arabia and Kuwait. They insisted that Dhofar's anti-government groups should merge. The result was the Dhofar Liberation Front (DLF), an umbrella organization that encompassed Marxists, Arab nationalists, supporters of the imamate and deserters from the Dhofar Defence Force.

On August 14, 1964, a Jeep in the sultan's armed forces hit a mine laid by the DLF. The driver was killed and the passenger wounded. This was followed by attacks on RAF vehicles and oil-exploration teams in different parts of Dhofar. The government made arrests and seized weapons. During 1–9 June 1965, the DLF held its first congress in the Dhofar Mountains. It issued a declaration calling for all-out war against sultanate and British forces in Dhofar and Oman. The rebels, trained in Iraq and Syria, turned much of Dhofar into a no-go area for government forces.

In the spring of 1966, Sultan Said decided to inspect the Dhofar Defence Force, a unit organized in 1955, first under British and then Pakistani officers. It was made up mainly of Khadim, Salalah people of slave stock, and Jabalis. As the inspection was taking place on April 26, three members of the force fired directly at the sultan but missed by a wide margin. A subsequent investigation showed that the force had been penetrated by the Arab Nationalist Movement (ANM), a leftist group that recruited from among Palestinians and Lebanese and had cells in Kuwait and Yemen.

The threat was compounded by Imam Ghalib who was welcomed in 1969 in Cairo, Damascus and Baghdad as the representative of the Omani people and recognized by the Arab League as rightful leader of Oman. The UN general assembly consistently voted in favour of resolutions that alleged Oman was under British colonial rule. London asserted the sultanate was independent but outside UN jurisdiction anyway.

The rebels were more than just nationalist romantics but had become, potentially, the vanguard of a radical Arabian revolution. King Faisal ordered a halt to Saudi support for the DLF. Oman's differences with the kingdom were largely settled in 1971, when Sultan Qaboos visited Riyadh, met King Faisal, and agreed to meet Imam Ghalib. The imam refused to see him but Saudi recognition of the sultanate came soon after.

Britain's withdrawal from Aden in 1967, and the triumph of the Marxist National Liberation Front (NLF) in what was to become the People's Democratic Republic of Yemen, inspired a further change in the character of the Dhofar rebellion. In September 1968, the DLF held its second congress and renamed itself the People's Front for the Liberation of the Occupied Arab Gulf (PFLOAG). Soon after, 30 of its members travelled to China via Aden for training in guerrilla tactics.

In 1969, 15 guerilla bands entered Dhofar from South Yemen, forcing the sultan's forces to withdraw from their positions on the border. In August, the town of Rakhyut in west Dhofar fell to the rebels. Following a hit-and-run attack on Habrut Fort, the sultan's air force bombed Hauf, a town in South Yemen that was being used as a base for the rebels. The PFLOAG at this point probably had some 5,000 fighters. The Soviet Union, competing with China for influence in the region, had started supplying Dhofar rebels by the end of 1969.

The violence in Dhofar overshadowed the first exports of Omani crude oil. The sultanate produced an average of almost 60,000 b/d in 1967, nearly 250,000 b/d in 1968 and more than 300,000 b/d in both 1969 and 1970.

The rebellion took a fresh turn on June 12, 1970 when a new group, calling itself the National Democratic Front for the Liberation of the Occupied Arab Gulf, and supported by the Iraqi Baath regime that had seized power two years earlier, attacked the Izki military camp near Muscat. The group was broken up when a weapons cache was discovered in Muttrah. It dissolved itself and joined the PFLOAG. But the spectre of an Arabian Vietnam started to haunt the Omani government and its British advisers.

### The succession of Sultan Qaboos

Rising oil exports, the Dhofar rebellion and the new attacks near Muscat ignited the fuse that was to lead to political change in 1970. Some believe that the trigger for the fall of Sultan Said was his decision to award an exploration concession in Dhofar to Cities Services Corporation of the US – a move that seemed to challenge British domination of the oil industry.

This allegation, citing an unnamed former British army officer as its source, is made in *Oman: The True Life Drama & Intrigue of an Arab State* by John Beasant, published in 2002. However, the timescale seems to be wrong. The Cities Services Corporation concession was awarded in 1953 and the company found oil in 1957, but not in enough quantities to justify commercial exploitation.

Beasant also reports the same source as saying that the US, worried that the Ethiopian monarchy might fall to a Marxist-inspired takeover, was looking for an alternative to Massawa on the coast of Ethiopia as the base for a major intelligence-gathering centre. A sympathetic regime open to greater Western involvement was required.

This charge is also unsubstantiated but there's no doubt that Sultan Said was a reactionary who openly questioned the idea of providing education and healthcare to his people. Omanis were in general forbidden from travelling abroad. The unauthorized wearing of sunglasses was punishable with a spell in jail while Muscat in 1970 was still a walled and gated city and locked up for the night at 9 pm.

On the afternoon of July 23, 1970, Sheikh Braik bin Hamood bin Hamid Al Ghafiri, son of the governor of Dhofar, arrived at the gates of Salalah Palace and demanded to see Sultan Said. Granted an audience, Sheikh Braik called for the sultan to abdicate. Sultan Said ordered Sheikh Braik to be ejected. There was a melee. Sultan Said drew a handgun and shot Braik in the stomach. There was further shooting and Sultan Said was himself shot four times, once in the abdomen. The sultan also accidentally shot his own right foot.

News spread beyond the walls. A British major named Spike Powell arrived at the palace after nightfall and appealed to Sultan Said to give up power. Later that evening, Lieutenant Colonel Edward Tunill, an-

other British officer, presented Sultan Said with two documents of abdication: one in English and one in Arabic. They were signed. The
sultan and Sheikh Braik were flown by the RAF to the RAF hospital in
Muharraq in Bahrain. Braik returned to Oman after medical treatment. Sultan Said was taken from Bahrain to Brize Norton airfield in
Oxfordshire and finally to an RAF hospital in Wroghton in Wiltshire.
After recovering from his wounds, he was delivered to the Dorchester
Hotel in London's Park Lane where he remained in a suite of rooms
until his death on October 19, 1972. He's buried in the Brookwood Islamic Cemetery in Woking, Surrey. News of these developments was
reported on July 26, three days after the event. On July 29, Britain announced it had recognized Sultan Qaboos, who had remained in the
Salalah palace throughout the affair, as ruler of Oman. The following
day, the new sultan flew to Muscat. The authorized version of these
events describes what happened as an abdication.

Then aged 29, Sultan Qaboos was master of a country where ne-
glect and insurgency had bequeathed a challenging legacy of poverty
and division. His solution was to reject his father's conservatism. A provisional government was formed with his uncle, Sheikh Tariq, brother
of the deposed sultan, as prime minister. The country was renamed the
Sultanate of Oman. A new national flag was designed. A development
programme was launched that emphasized education and health. And,
in an effort to end the Dhofar rebellion, an amnesty was announced for
all PFLOAG members.

The Dhofar rebels, meanwhile, had fallen out among themselves.
Hardline Marxists now dominated the movement. More than 300
PFLOAG members were summarily executed in September 1970 alone.
There was a rise in the number of defectors, including Bin Nufl, the
royal gardener turned guerrilla. Many took the option of joining the
Firqa, an irregular, tribal force organized by the sultanate. London dispatched the SAS to train the sultan's army. They quickly became involved in active operations, a fact never acknowledged by the British
government but confirmed by veterans of the Dhofar War including
the explorer and adventurer Sir Ranulph Fiennes.

The turning point came in July 1972 when PFLOAG fighters were
comprehensively defeated at the town of Mirbat. In the autumn of
1972, the Shah of Iran sent a special-force unit comprising 200 men
and a squadron of helicopters to support the sultanate's army. Three
battalions of Iranian special forces were dispatched with 30 helicopters
in December 1973. Jordanian troops had joined the campaign earlier
that year. A defensive barrier of barbed wire, mines and sensors was
built from the coast near the border with South Yemen to a point 64
km inland. At the end of 1974, the shah provided ground-to-air missiles. Jordan's King Hussein sent 31 Hawker Hunter fighter jets in the

spring of 1975 and a special forces unit later in the year. A major offensive was launched in western Dhofar in October. The rebel haven of Hauf in South Yemen was bombed. On December 2, Dhalkut, the last rebel-held town in Dhofar, fell to the sultanate's forces.

The Dhofar War was declared over on December 11, 1975 though attacks continued for several more years. In one of the rebellion's last gasps, the governor of Dhofar, Braik Al Ghafiri, a cabinet member and author of the 1970 deposition of Said, was assassinated in June 1979.

In May 1978, Oman became the second Gulf country after Kuwait to recognize the People's Republic of China that had been financing Dhofar rebels only four years earlier. The decision reflected concern about Soviet activities in the Red Sea region and the growing role of Cuban military trainers in South Yemen.

For six years before becoming Oman's ruler, Sultan Qaboos had lived in isolation in Oman, but he had tasted life outside the sultanate. In 1958, he'd been sent to stay with the Roman family in Felsham, in rural Suffolk, to prepare him for entry to the Royal Military Academy at Sandhurst. In September 1960, Qaboos entered Sandhurst where he formed friendships that last to this day. He graduated in August 1962 and was attached to the 1st Battalion of The Cameronians, the Scottish infantry regiment that had fought in the imamate war five years earlier. He had a tour in Germany and attachments to institutions of local government in Bedford and Warwick.

Returning to Salalah after leaving the British Army in 1964, Qaboos passed through and admired the bustling port of Aden. From then until July 1970, he was mainly confined to the town's royal palace, the isolation interrupted by visits from his mother, the delivery of *The Times* of London and tea and bridge parties with guests. He'd been kept in the dark about the state of the country. The system he inherited was archaic. There was not even a decent set of accounts.

Development accelerated. Welfare services were provided for the first time to much of the population. Muscat flourished. The new port in Muttrah, named Mina Sultan Qaboos, was built and Seeb international airport opened. At the end of 1971, Oman became a member of the UN.

Yet, the promised political reforms that some had hoped would include the advent of a constitutional monarchy never materialized. It was, and remained until the 1990s, one of the most difficult places in the Middle East for journalists to enter. In an atmosphere of secrecy, people connected with Oman were reported to be facilitating sanction-busting oil shipments to the illegal regime in Rhodesia. Oman became a major purchaser of British defence equipment. Critics believed it was being overcharged.

Following the Iranian Revolution, Oman gained fresh strategic importance. Masirah Island, which lies about 400 km south of Muscat, served as an RAF staging post and diplomatic telecommunications centre from 1929 to 1977. In 1969, the BBC opened a transmitter to broadcast its programmes in the Gulf region. This was closed when re-broadcasting began onshore in October 2002. Oman in 1980 concluded a 10-year facilities agreement that granted the US limited access to air bases on Masirah Island and at Thamarit and Seeb airports, as well as to the naval bases at Muscat, Salalah and Khasab in the Musandam.

At almost the same time, diplomatic relations were established with the Soviet Union, sponsors of the Dhofar rebellion. Masirah was the staging base for the failed American attempt to rescue hostages from the Tehran embassy in 1980. Omani air bases were used in the war for Kuwait in 1991 and the war for Iraq in 2003. More than 4,000 US servicemen are now permanently based on Masirah, which has also become popular with surfers and bird and turtle-watchers. In addition, the US National Security Agency (NSA) has four listening stations: one on Masirah, one each at Jazirat al-Ghanem and Khasab and the fourth at Abut.

The economic horizon in the early 1980s was bright. Major projects were approved, notably the Al Bustan Palace Hotel which overlooks a bay south of the capital. To build it, a village was evacuated, a mountain removed and as much as US$1 billion spent. Oman's special relationship with the UK was maintained in contracts with British companies.

In April 1981, UK Prime Minister Margaret Thatcher visited Oman. It is reliably reported that, during her visit, Sultan Qaboos gave her a diamond necklace said to be worth about £200,000 at the time. Under established rules, such gifts cannot be accepted by the recipient and remain the property of Her Majesty's government. Thatcher asked the sultan to meet representatives of Cementation, the British construction firm. Later that month, the meeting took place with Thatcher's son Mark in attendance.

The result of this diplomacy soon emerged. In March 1982, during a state visit to the UK by Sultan Qaboos, it was announced that Cementation had won the contract to build the Sultan Qaboos University. Rumours began to spread that Mark Thatcher had benefited from the deal. Nothing has ever been proved, but the affair marked the start of Thatcher's acquisition of massive wealth. As many forecast, it all ended in tears. In January 2004, he was charged in a South African court with conspiring to finance a coup in Equatorial Guinea. Thatcher was fined the equivalent of US$500,000 and given a four-year suspended sentence after he admitted unwitting involvement in the plot.

The annual GCC summit was held for the first time in Oman in the Al Bustan Palace Hotel on the final two days of 1985. It marked the end of Oman's first economic boom. In the next six months, oil prices slumped by more than two-thirds to less than US$10 a barrel. The age of austerity had begun.

The 1986 oil price slump wrecked the finances of Middle East oil-exporting nations. Oman had to get back to basics. The region was in turmoil. The sultanate maintained a neutral position between the protagonists in the Iran-Iraq War. The short peace that followed the end of the conflict raised hopes of a new era of regional cooperation. But a new crisis quickly developed. On August 2, 1990, Iraq seized Kuwait. The sultanate provided basing and logistic facilities for US-led coalition forces.

The end of the war for Kuwait marked the start of a new era in which economic and political reform was to be pushed higher up the Omani agenda. Oman was one of the region's most enthusiastic economic innovators. The Muscat Securities Market (MSM), the local stock exchange, was opened in 1988. In 1992, Oman was the first Middle East country in modern times to allow a privately owned power station. Rules were changed to make it easier for foreigners to invest. Doubts about allowing mass tourism were set aside. New hotels opened.

On the political front, the reforms were cautious. In November 1981, Sultan Qaboos formed the 55-member State Consultative Council (Al Majlis Al Istishari Lil-Dawlaj), an appointed body that was confined to making policy suggestions. In 1990, it was replaced by the more representative, 59-member Majlis al-Shoura, a national consultative council made up of men who were indirectly elected. Its remit remained limited. It could only advise and comment about legislation and was barred from discussing defence, foreign affairs and the oil and gas industry. In 1994, membership was expanded and women in Muscat were allowed to vote for members.

In 1997, the sultan issued a decree establishing the Basic Law of the State, a document akin to a written constitution. This signalled a more far-reaching attempt to modernize government institutions. The Basic Law called for the creation of the Council of Oman. This was to comprise the Majlis, which was to be henceforth elected every three years, and an appointed Majlis al-Dawla (State Council), which meets four times a year.

In the 1997 Majlis elections, the electorate was expanded to more than 50,000 people. A further extension of the electorate to 115,000 voters, about 30 per cent of them women, was introduced for the 2000 Majlis elections. The third Majlis elections were held at the end of 2003. The electorate was expanded and it's estimated that this was to more than 800,000 people, of whom 194,000 voted. Elections for the fifth Majlis in 2006 were based on a universal franchise for everyone aged over 21. Membership of the State Council was expanded in 2003 to 58 and now includes women.

The calm surface obscured inner tensions. Beginning in December 2004, dozens of Ibadhi Muslims were arrested and charged with belonging to an illegal organization and seeking to overthrow the government to establish an Ibadhi religious state. Most were convicted in May 2005 of possessing illegal weapons and sentenced to terms of one to 20 years. They were pardoned the following month.

The issue of greatest concern is what happens after Sultan Qaboos. This was underscored in August 1995 when Oman's finance minister, Qais Al Zawawi, was killed in a road accident involving a convoy of vehicles in which Sultan Qaboos was travelling. In March 1976, Sultan Qaboos had married his cousin, Nawwal, the daughter of his uncle, Tariq bin Taimour, who changed her name to Kamila. The marriage was short and he has no heirs. The family convention of the past 200 years, which involved the ruler appointing a son, is therefore likely to be broken.

The Basic Law provides guidance and states the succession should be confined to the male descendants of Sultan Turki bin Said, the 10th Al Bu Said ruler who died in 1888. When the throne becomes vacant, the Al Bu Said family council must assemble within three days to name the new sultan. If they do not agree, the Defence Council will confirm the person designated by the sultan. The Al Bu Said council is not required to accept the sultan's choice and can over-rule the Defence Council, a government body responsible for defence and security issues.

It is believed that Sultan Qaboos has named two family members as his successor and their identities have been consigned to documents in sealed envelopes kept in two secret locations. It's believed they are sons of Sheikh Tariq bin Taimour, who was prime minister in 1970 and held senior government posts until his death in December 1980.

What is clear is that there can be no going back, something that was in doubt the first time the author visited Oman in 1983. Despite the economic progress and the spreading benefits of a cradle-to-grave welfare state, Oman then was still largely closed to the outside world. Getting an entry visa was by no means automatic, particularly for journalists.

More than a decade later, at a conference about capital market development in Oman, there was still tight control over what was said by speakers who were drawn from the across the world. On the final night of the event, conference speakers were entertained at the home of Mohammed bin Musa Al Yousef, a businessman who'd been made development minister to bring in sweeping economic changes.

Sipping from crystal glasses and supping in restrained opulence, they were entertained with tales of Al Yousef's education in Britain at a time when it took several weeks, involving trains and boats, to get from London to Muscat. The tone of the evening spoke volumes about what the sultanate is and wants to be. Oman aims to join the modern world.

In 1999, following the fall in the oil price, the Omani stock market went into reverse, creating difficulties for business and government. New regulations have been brought in to control irrational exuberance among investors. Oil-industry expansion was slowed by the 1986 oil price fall, but subsequent OPEC agreements stabilized prices for most of the period since then and encouraged further production expansion.

By the end of 2000, reserves had been increased to five billion barrels, almost five per cent of the world total. Oil production rose from 500,000 b/d in 1985 to 840,000 b/d in 2000. Some said the one million b/d was within reach. Oman also started to use the growing volume of gas being produced as oil output soared. In 1996, PDO won government approval to develop central Oman gas fields and Shell built an LNG plant in Qalhat, near Sur. The first cargo of LNG was shipped to Korea in April 2000.

After reaching a peak of 849,000 b/d in June 2000, output began to decline despite attempts to halt the slide by the conventional method of drilling more wells. Injecting millions of gallons of water into the Burhaan and Musallim fields in an attempt to force oil out of the ground produced limited results. In January 2001, production dropped below 800,000 b/d and has continued to slump.

In August 2001, the Zauliyah-16 well in central Oman exploded, spilling tens of thousands of barrels of oil before it was capped in September. Output continued to fall. This was a serious challenge for Oman, which had based its economic strategy on high levels of oil and associated gas production. If the fall in output could not be reversed, the economy would be seriously damaged. Oil and gas were by then accounting for 40 per cent of GDP and more than 70 per cent of export revenues.

The fall in output was so striking that Shell was obliged to reduce its estimate of the amount of oil still left in the ground in the PDO concession. Since about one-third of this was Shell's, the downward revision was too large to conceal and was followed by other downgrades that amounted to 25 per cent of the previously stated Shell total. The news shook investor confidence. Shell chairman Sir Phil Watts quit in March 2004 and was quickly followed by its Dutch exploration director, Walter van de Vijer.

Oman's production fell to less than 600,000 b/d in 2005. But investment and new technology, including the process of pumping steam into underground reservoirs to liquidize otherwise immovably viscous oil, should get output back to target levels by the end of the decade. To help reverse the trend, the Omani government also took the unusual step of removing the Mukhaizna oil field, which was discovered in 1975, from the PDO concession and allocating it as part of a production-sharing agreement with a consortium led by Occidental in the summer of 2005. Occidental's partners include Liwa Petroleum, which is owned by Mubadala Development Company, an Abu Dhabi government investment company.

By this time, Oman was beginning to enjoy the fruits of the higher oil prices in existence since the end of 2003. A third LNG train opened at Qalhat in the spring of 2006 and a world-class fertilizer plant was completed nearby.

A new law allowing foreigners to buy land was passed. Work was finished on the Barr al-Jissah tourism complex south of Muscat. An even bigger project is on the horizon. Private investors, including the Dubai-based Majid Al Futtaim Group, are investing in a US$800 million combined tourism and commercial development near Seeb airport called The Wave. Work has also started on the US$15 billion Blue City on the Batinah Coast.

The highly successful container port in Salalah is being expanded. Sohar has been chosen to become the sultanate's largest industrial centre. A refinery and polypropylene plant opened in 2006 and plans have been devised for plastics plants, steel factories and an aluminium smelter. Total projected investment in Sohar is now about US$15 billion. The Sohar plan reflects a new flexibility at the highest levels of government. Officials promoting the project openly state that one of its advantages is its proximity to Dubai. Once seen as a rival, the Gulf's busiest business centre is now viewed as an inspiration. The overarching priority is creating jobs for Oman's young people; there is now no patience for pointless vanity.

Tourists are heading towards the last Arabian sultanate. Even in January at more than 1,000 m, it's warm enough to sunbathe on the plateau of Jebel Akhdar. From there, the hardy can park and complete the six-hour trek by foot to the top of Jebel Shams (mountain of the sun), Oman's highest peak at more than 2,000 m. For the rest, the best option is peering queasily over the edge of a cliff that falls 1,000 m to the wadi floor or sipping a drink at a new coffee shop.

Arabia's hidden places are for the first time being explored by the ordinary traveller rather than the soldier, adventurer or eccentric. Jebel Akhdar is among its most remarkable secrets. It extends about 20 km north to south and 30 km east to west. Its glory is in its violent ascent from the Rub al-Khali. From the east, there are only two access routes to and from the coast, one via Ibri and one via Nizwa.

Jebel Akhdar's impenetrability provided for more than 2,000 years a haven for the unorthodox and rebellious. Before modern times, the mountain was conquered only once – by the Persians in the 10th century. Its independence was finally ended when the rule of the sultan was extended into the interior in the late 1950s. But less than a decade ago, much of it was still out of bounds to foreigners.

Jebel Akhdar today is open for business. New roads guide growing numbers to one of Arabia's great natural wonders from Muscat, less than two hours' drive distant, and the cities of the UAE, about four hours away. Hamlets in hidden wadis are now receiving electricity and clean water, but life remains much as it was 100 years ago.

At the village of Masfut off the road to Jebel Shams, the village butcher slaughters goats before breakfast and leaves skin and guts on the roadside. Women in *abayas* carrying green wheat in bundles on their heads walk barefoot through the village. Change, nevertheless, is quickening as the sultanate focuses on tourism. Billboards invite visitors to leave the mountains as clean as they found them.

Among the jebel's western foothills, ancient caravan towns are reviving. Before the rise of sea routes along the Gulf and the Red Sea, frankincense from Dhofar and goods destined for Mesopotamian cities were taken by camel through the jebel to Nizwa and then north through Bahla, Jibrin, Ibri and the Buraimi Oasis to the Gulf. For almost 40 years after 1920, an independent imamate was run from Nizwa until its pretensions were finally extinguished with the capture of the jebel by government forces in January 1959.

Nizwa today is the pearl in Oman's tourism oyster. Its fort has been restored, complete with cannons. The top commands a view over one of south Arabia's largest palm oases, with the immensity of the jebel itself beyond. Bahla's fort, declared a World Heritage Site in 1987, probably originally dates from the 12th century. Set on a hill overlooking a wadi that drains winter rains from the jebel to the desert, the fort is being slowly restored though the walls that once enclosed Bahla are diminishing every time rain falls.

The fully restored fort at nearby Jibrin is, perhaps, a better place to imagine the wealth and culture that made the town and the region prosperous and proud. Oman remains irresistibly alluring. Its wadis, mountains and matchless coastline are among the most compelling of Arabia's natural wonders.

## Rulers of Oman since the 16th century

| | |
|---|---|
| Imam Nasr Al Yaarubi ... ... ... ... ... ... ... ... ... ... ... | 1624–1649 |
| Imam Sultan bin Saif ... ... ... ... ... ... ... ... ... ... ... | 1649–1679 |
| Imam Bil'Arab bin Sultan ... ... ... ... ... ... ... ... ... ... | 1679–1692 |
| Imam Saif bin Sultan ... ... ... ... ... ... ... ... ... ... ... | 1692–1711 |
| Imam Sultan bin Saif ... ... ... ... ... ... ... ... ... ... ... | 1711–1718 |
| Imam Saif bin Sultan II . ... ... ... ... ... ... ... ... ... ... | 1711–1744 |
| Imam Ahmed bin Said ... ... ... ... ... ... ... ... ... ... ... | 1744–1783 |
| Imam Said bin Ahmed ... ... ... ... ... ... ... ... ... ... ... | 1783–1785 |
| Sayyid Hamad bin Said .. ... ... ... ... ... ... ... ... ... ... | 1785–1792 |
| Sayyid Sultan bin Ahmed ... ... ... ... ... ... ... ... ... ... | 1792–1804 |

Sayyid Said bin Sultan ... ... ... ... ... ... ... ... ... ... ...   1806–1856
Sultan Thuwainy bin Said... ... ... ... ... ... ... ... ... ...   1856–1869
Sultan Azzan bin Qais ... ... ... ... ... ... ... ... ... ... ...   1869–1871
Sultan Turki bin Said ... ... ... ... ... ... ... ... ... ... ...   1871–1888
Sultan Faisal bin Turki .. ... ... ... ... ... ... ... ... ... ...   1888–1913
Sultan Taimour bin Faisal .. ... ... ... ... ... ... ... ... ...   1913–1932
Sulan Said bin Taimour. ... ... ... ... ... ... ... ... ... ...   1932–1970
Sultan Qaboos bin Said.. ... ... ... ... ... ... ... ... ... ...   1970–

# CHAPTER 7

# THE UAE AND
# THE NEW GULF

Shortly after noon on Tuesday April 17, 2007, more than 1,000 of the most powerful people in the United Arab Emirates (UAE) gathered in the conference hall of the Emirates Palace Hotel at the southern end of the Abu Dhabi corniche. Led by the president, Shaikh Khalifa bin Zayed Al Nahyan, the leaders of the seven emirates that make up the UAE filed in and took their seats. After the UAE national anthem and a short film about the country's achievements, the UAE's vice-president and prime minister, Sheikh Mohammed bin Rashid Al Maktoum, ruler of Dubai since January 2006, stepped up to the stage to deliver a 60-minute address about the government's long-term strategy.

It was a groundbreaking moment for the UAE, the Gulf and the Middle East. Addressing the gathering and a live national television audience, Sheikh Mohammed challenged his cabinet to make the federation one of the world's leading nations. Breaking the Arabian convention of always being polite in public, he criticized three federal ministries. Despite huge education spending increases, Sheikh Mohammed declared that the federation's schools weren't improving. The Justice Ministry wasn't delivering timely justice. The Labour Ministry was failing to get to grips with illegal immigration and the imbalance between nationals and foreigners in the workforce. Sheikh Mohammed noted some UAE homes had more house servants than family members. Federal ministers arrayed behind the rulers looked thoughtful. The position of several may have been made untenable.

Sheikh Mohammed's speech came to a stirring conclusion. "Life has taught us that the impossible is a matter of opinion and that there are no limits to excellence in the pioneering race," he said. "Life has taught us that clear vision, strong determination and devoted compatriots can turn dreams and visions into reality. I assure you that our vision is clear and our determination is strong.

"I can see the future UAE a while from today. I see the whole world looking up to the UAE. I see the UAE full of success stories in healthcare, education, public administration and other sectors that the world adopts as best practices. I see the future UAE, under your leadership, Your Highness, reaching the highest levels of science knowledge and

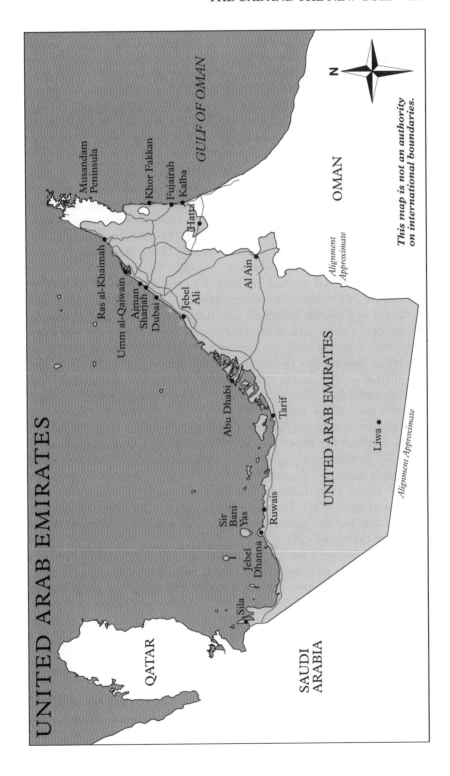

achieving progress and prosperity. I see the future UAE with its people enjoying the best quality of life. I can almost feel the size of our achievements 20 years from now. Walking down the streets, entering the schools and watching students learning modern sciences in the most advanced laboratories, and using cutting-edge technology. I can see myself strolling in the parks, entering the hospitals and seeing the look of satisfaction in the eyes of the patients and the look of determination and care in the eyes of the staff.

"I can see myself visiting government departments and seeing satisfied customers and employees with enthusiasm and passion to excel and overcome challenges. I can see our government departments as the hot spot for world delegations which come to learn from our experiences and follow our practices. I see myself passing by harbours, airports, factories and malls and see great achievements. I see international cities, throbbing with activity and vibrancy.

"I can see myself walking by houses to see residents living happily and honourably in beautiful homes, playing with their children in lush gardens. I can see the children's eyes full of love, peace and optimism. We are not of those who talk or indulge in dreams, for I can see and I know with certainty that the men and women of this great nation are capable of making this dream come true, sacrificing their lives to elevate their country's name, help achieve their leaders' vision, and conquer all challenges. The vision is clear and the goal is set. The future does not wait for the hesitant. We do not have the luxury of time. And we were never used to hesitating and waiting. This is a call to join hands, combine our efforts and set off to make this vision come true."

Sheikh Mohammed's speech was perhaps modelled on the State of the Union address US presidents make to joint sessions of congress and the senate every January. But there was nothing routine about his message in April 2007. It was the declaration of the start of a new era for the UAE and the region and the announcement to the world of the coming of the New Gulf.

The UAE is one of the world's most successful small nations. Thanks to oil and gas, it has the second largest economy in the Middle East. Per capita GDP, at more than US$30,000 and rising fast, is among the highest outside the OECD. The pace of federal development had quickened in the 30 months since Sheikh Khalifa bin Zayed succeeded his father Shaikh Zayed to become ruler of Abu Dhabi and federal head of state. In December 2006, national elections were held for the Federal National Council, a consultative body that was previously appointed. A new wave of investment is upgrading the federation's infrastructure. The UAE government is now committed to a programme of unprecedented structural and policy reform. Stable, prosperous and tolerant, the UAE provides a compelling vision of what the New Gulf might be.

But the challenges are coming almost as quickly as the reforms. The federation's friends welcome Sheikh Mohammed's robust leadership. And they share his anxiety that the pace of change and improvement needs to be faster and broader than ever.

The conference broke up for lunch hosted by Sheikh Khalifa. After, representatives of the local and international press assembled for a briefing. Sheikh Mohammed bustled in, followed by Sheikh Abdullah bin Zayed, brother of Sheikh Khalifa and the UAE's minister of foreign affairs, and Sheikh Mansour bin Zayed, another brother of the federal president and member of the cabinet. He is also the Dubai ruler's son-in-law. Sheikh Mohammed took off his gold-trimmed black cloak and stood to take questions. He was wearing, as is his convention on formal occasions, a gold-coloured *thobe*. "Your Highness, how would you summarize the goal of the new strategy?" was the first question.

"To make the UAE number one in the world," he replied. After 30 minutes of speaking in English and Arabic, Sheikh Mohammed declared the press conference over. "Speak to Abdullah," he said as he left.

Sheikh Abdullah bin Zayed is another leading figure behind the changes sweeping the UAE and the Gulf. He previously headed the federal information ministry, but the department was abolished as part of a cabinet reshuffle that followed Sheikh Mohammed's appointment as prime minister in February 2006. He now also heads the UAE's National Media Council, a new body set up to regulate the local press and broadcasting. Complete press freedom has not yet arrived in the UAE, but it has been given a huge push forward since the start of 2005.

Terrestrial radio and television, which are owned by federal and local governments, have been given greater freedom to report local and international issues. Even the advertisements have become more exciting. Since the end of 2004, four daily English newspapers and one new Arabic-language daily were launched in the UAE alone, as the federal government relaxed controls over the media. Not all of them lasted but more launches were expected. The UAE magazine industry is largely deregulated. In 2001, the Dubai government launched Dubai Media City, a free zone. By the summer of 2005, it was approving new magazine launches on a weekly basis, subject to final approval from the National Media Council. About 1,000 firms now have Media City licences and more than 400 magazines and journals are published in the zone. Its tenants include AFP, BBC World, CNBC Arabia, CNN, Dow Jones, MEED, Pearson, Reuters and the Middle East Broadcasting Centre (MBC) and its sister channel Al Arabiya Television News. More than 60 broadcasters operate there.

With all remaining Media City plots sold to investors, attention is shifting to two new media-industry free zones. Dubai Studio City, which is located in Dubailand, was launched in February 2005. Dubai has already started to develop location filming. *Syriana*, starring George Clooney, was partly filmed in Dubai. Two major Arabic films were set in Dubai in 2005. Work has also started on the International Media Production Zone, Dubai's third media zone, near Jebel Ali. It focuses on publishing, printing and packaging.

Sheikh Mohammed bin Rashid declared there would be freedom of expression within Media City and a complaints tribunal was set up in 2003, though it is yet to hear a complaint. The licence of one monthly was suspended in the summer of 2005 after it published a photograph of an underdressed woman, but this was a minor issue.

A more common complaint is that Media City has issued too many publishing licences and this has led to a flood of low-quality magazines. "I am not here to judge their quality," Dubai's media supremo Amina Al Rostamani said in 2006. "It is for their readers. If they can sustain their business, that means there is a demand for their services."

The new mood is also sweeping radio and television. Dubai Television has revamped its principal channel as The One. The Dubai Radio Network relaunched its 103.8 channel as a talk and music station, the first in the Middle East. Some of the most politically sensitive subjects in the Gulf, including the Arab-Israel conflict, the role of Islam and terrorism, have since been comprehensively aired. City7, a new channel focussing on local issues, was launched in the autumn of 2006.

But the UAE is part of a broader wave of change in the region's media industry. Throughout the Gulf, systems of censorship are being eroded by the demands of the people and the power of technology. Governments realize satellite television and broadband internet mean an end to their ability to control what is read, heard and seen.

The new media wave started with the launch at the end of 1996 of Al Jazeera, the Qatar-based, Arabic-language satellite television station. Al Jazeera brought television news and comment that was compelling to the viewer and impossible for governments to block from going into Gulf homes. It broadcast speeches by Saddam Hussein denouncing America and its regional allies, statements by Osama bin Laden after 9/11 and open political debate about Arab governments. For the first time, people who spoke nothing but Arabic were being addressed about issues that affected them in terms they understood. The station was a hit with viewers, disliked by most Middle East governments and boycotted by Saudi Arabian advertisers. Al Jazeera International, an English-language version of the original satellite channel, was launched in September 2006 with Sir David Frost as one of its star presenters.

Al Jazeera and subsequent satellite initiatives were made possible by the launch in 1985 of the Arabsat satellite that was initially used as a way for Arabic-language newspapers produced in London to be transmitted for printing in the Middle East.

It all began with the Middle East Broadcasting Centre (MBC), started in London with Saudi money in 1994. MBC was designed to provide an alternative, controlled by Riyadh, to Western satellite news. It moved its operations to Dubai at the start of this decade and now also broadcasts three other entertainment channels and, to compete with Al Jazeera, the news channel Al Arabiya. Other satellite initiatives followed, including the Egyptian Space Channel (ESC), Beirut-based Future TV, owned by the family of Lebanon's late prime minister, Rafik Hariri, and the Arab News Network (ANN), owned by a member of the family of President Asad. Today, the satellite television market of the Gulf is among the world's freest and most competitive.

**The geography of the UAE**
The Middle East media revolution is just one of the many changes shaping the New Gulf that have been embraced by the UAE, a federation of seven emirates with a combined land area of about 78,000 km$^2$, about the size of Scotland. It encompasses mountains, sandy desert and unspoilt beaches lapped by warm seas. You can in one day watch the sun rise over the east coast, have lunch in the Hajar Mountains, drive through giant dunes in the afternoon and toast the sun setting over the Gulf.

The UAE has three main natural environments; coastline, mountain and desert. Some 650 km of seashore extend from the Musandam Peninsula to the border with Saudi Arabia in the south-west. This is being increased by giant reclamation projects such as Dubai's Palm islands. The UAE also has 80 km of coast in the east that runs from the Musandam to Kalba, near Oman. Stands of mangrove are often extensive, particularly in Ra's al-Khaimah, the Khor Kalba creeks and along the Abu Dhabi coast. The UAE's Gulf coast sweeps east from the base of the Qatar Peninsula and then north in a crescent interrupted by salt flats, known as *sabkha*, that grow in size as the Saudi border is approached. Along the Abu Dhabi coastline there are more than 200 low, sandy islands, including the UAE's largest island, Abu al-Abyadh. The Abu Dhabi islands of Sir Bani Yas, Dalma, Mubarraz, Arzanah, Zirku and Das lie deeper in the Gulf. Most rest on salt plugs, columns that have risen through the earth's crust. Abu Dhabi city, capital of the federation, is itself built on one of the larger islands.

The second natural environment is the Hajar Mountains, the backbone of the UAE, that occupies about 20 per cent of federation's land. The mountains start at the tip of Musandam and run unbroken for about 640 km to Ra's al-Hadd in Oman. Their highest point in the UAE is about 1,000 m. Deep wadis have been carved into the mountains. The greatest in the UAE is the Wadi Bih, which drains west from the Hajar watershed towards Ra's al-Khaimah.

More than half the UAE is occupied by arid desert – consisting of sand, dunes and gravel plains – that run into the eastern fringes of the Empty Quarter. Deep in the desert south of Abu Dhabi is the Liwa Oasis, adjacent to massive sand dunes that can be as much as 100 m high, and on the edge of the Empty Quarter. Small lenses of water near the foot of the dunes have made it possible for little oases to be established, cultivated by nomadic tribesmen.

Abu Dhabi's second great artesian oasis is in Al Ain, about 160 km east of Abu Dhabi city in the Hajar Mountains' western foothills. Gardens and date plantations have been irrigated for at least 5,000 years with well water supplemented by spring water delivered to where people live by *falaj*, irrigation channels dug by hand and sometimes covered.

As mentioned earlier, Abu Dhabi city occupies an island. The cities of Dubai, Sharjah, Ajman, Umm al-Qaiwain and Ra's al-Khaimah on the UAE's northern Gulf coast are built around sea inlets or creeks (*khor* in Arabic). Over the centuries, these have been screened from the Gulf by sand spits created by powerful tides sweeping north up the coast. The creeks attracted settlers because they provided shelter from seas that can be violent, particularly when the north wind blows. East coast towns lived off Indian Ocean trade and rich fishing grounds. They are among the most ancient in Arabia and include Dibba, site in 633 of a deadly battle between Muslim armies and rebels; Khor Fakkan, which was old when the Portuguese arrived almost 500 years ago; and Fujairah and Kalba, both settled more than 3,000 years ago.

**The archaeology of the UAE**

The UAE has a rich archaeological and palaeontological heritage. In Abu Dhabi, it's being systematically explored. The earliest discoveries, from the coastal areas of Abu Dhabi's Western region, are of fossils from the Late Miocene period, some five to six million years ago, when the country had a climate that was much less arid than it is today. Among major discoveries have been elephant tusks, ribs and skulls and other remains from animals such as hippopotami, gazelles, giraffes and turtles, representing one of the most important areas for fossils of this period anywhere in the world. The earliest evidence of man is from the Lower Palaeolithic period, perhaps as much as 250,000 years ago, from Jebel Barakah, in the west of the emirate, although no settlements from this period have yet been identified.

The earliest settlements date to the Arabian Neolithic, or Late Stone Age, 7,500–6,000 years ago, including a village on the island of Marawah with well-built stone houses and pottery imported from Mesopotamia, and a well-preserved human skeleton. Other Neolithic sites have been found throughout the country, including the deep deserts, with the exception of the central part of the Hajar Mountains.

The local Bronze Age began around 3000 BC, with the discovery of how to exploit the reserves of copper ore found in the mountains. To this period date the earliest above-ground tombs found in the country, including many on Jebel Hafit near Al Ain, with others on Jebel al-Emalah, south of Dhaid, and many more widely scattered through the mountains. Those that have been excavated date from about 3000 BC and contained pottery imported from central Iraq during the Sumerian era. The rise of the desert climate caused a change in human settlement. Oasis towns sprang up across south-eastern Arabia. Their remains have been most fully explored in Hili, Tell Abraq between Sharjah and Umm al-Qaiwain, Bidiya in Fujairah and Kalba. Fortresses were built and the dead buried in round, stone tombs.

South-east Arabia was known as Magan when copper mining started in the Hajar Mountains and copper goods started flowing north from about 3000 BC. This export trade flourished, in particular, from around 2500 BC to 2000 BC, a time which is known as the Umm al-Nar period after a settlement dating from that period found on Umm al-Nar Island near Abu Dhabi city. It lasted to 2000 BC. In the Wadi Suq period (2000–1600 BC) and the Late Bronze Age (1600–1300 BC), the number of towns shrank as the climate became drier in the interior. Fishing became more important and there was change in burial customs. Long tombs from this period have been excavated at Shimal and at Ghalilah and Dhayah in Ra's al-Khaimah. They contained swords, bows and arrows, and bronze arrowheads.

The invention of the *falaj* system coupled with the domestication of the camel, both around the beginning of the Iron Age (1300–300 BC), encouraged the growth of date gardens and agricultural plots. Around the third century BC, Mleiha, near Dhaid, emerged as the region's largest settlement. Mud brick cysts that were used to bury the dead have been found. They are similar in design to funeral towers in Palmyra and in Petra in northern Arabia.

During the first three centuries of the Christian era, the largest port of south-east Arabia was Omana, a town which occupied a site north of the Dubai/Sharjah conurbation that has since disappeared. This has been linked to Al Door, a contemporary settlement in Umm al-Qaiwain that has been excavated. Some experts conclude Omana and Al Door were the same place, although others have argued that Dibba, on the East Coast, is another candidate.

Roman glass, brass and coins have been found in Al Door and Mleiha. The language of both these settlements appears to have been Aramaic, the tongue of the Assyrian empire that was spoken in Palestine during the life of Jesus. From the middle of the 3rd century AD, contacts resumed with the north under the Sasanians. Finds have been made of coins and ceramics from this period and subsequently at Kush in Ra's al-Khaimah, Umm al-Qaiwain and Fujairah. By the 4th or 5th century AD, there was at least one Christian monastery of the eastern Nestorian rite on the island of Sir Bani Yas in what is now Abu Dhabi.

The UAE is an Arab country, but this was not always so. Arab migration began with the movement of people of the southern Qahtani/ Yamani segment of Arabian peoples that got under way around 100 AD. There was a later movement of Adnani/Nizari Arab people from the north. By the time the Prophet (PBUH) was born in 570, Bedouin Arabs dominated the west of the Hajar Mountains and trekked to the Gulf, central Arabia and places further north. South-east Arabia quickly adopted Islam.

### The life of Sheikh Zayed

The oasis civilization, coastal towns depending upon fishing and sea trade, the Arabic language and the faith of Islam are the original foundations of UAE society. They shaped the personality of Sheikh Zayed, a towering figure in the history of Arabia. The official record says Sheikh Zayed was born in Al Ain in 1918 though it is widely believed he was more than 90 when he died. His early years were dominated by a struggle among his father's generation to secure the inheritance bequeathed by Sheikh Zayed the Great, Abu Dhabi ruler for 54 years until his death in 1909. In July 1926, Sheikh Zayed's father Sheikh Sultan, then ruler of Abu Dhabi, was killed. Sheikh Zayed and his mother Sheikha Salama bin Butti had previously been sent to Al Ain under the protection of Shakhbut, Sheikh Zayed's eldest brother. Two years later, Shakhbut was selected to be leader of the people of Abu Dhabi.

Sheikh Zayed spent much of his youth in the company of the Bedouin of the interior. In the 1930s, he led an initial exploratory foray into the interior by Western oil companies. His unconventional nature showed early. At the age of 25, Sheikh Zayed gave up hunting with a rifle in favour of falconry, about which he remained passionate until his death. At the beginning of 1946, Sheikh Zayed was appointed Sheikh Shakhbut's representative in Al Ain. It was then a frontier zone with nine villages and a mixture of tribes and families pledging loyalty to Abu Dhabi and Oman. Sheikh Zayed's status was boosted by his work to repair and expand the *falaj* system. This entailed engineering skill, hard work and the ability to convince leaders in the region that the benefits of the project were worth short-term sacrifices.

While in Al Ain, Sheikh Zayed played an important role in ending the border dispute between Abu Dhabi and Dubai in the post-1945 period. He also helped forge the partnership between Muscat, Britain and local tribesmen that was to lead to the expulsion of Saudi forces from the Buraimi Oasis in October 1955. The successful resolution of the Buraimi affair capped Sheikh Zayed's reputation.

Sheikh Zayed's first journey outside Arabia was in 1953. In Paris, he saw one of the city's public hospitals and decided Abu Dhabi should have a medical system too. By the end of the 1950s, Al Ain was better managed than Abu Dhabi and had more public facilities, including the emirate's only school. This was despite the amounts Sheikh Shakhbut had received for oil exploration rights since 1939. Sheikh Zayed's growing frustration with his elder brother's refusal to promote social improvements was never made public and the bond between the two remained strong until the end.

By the start of the 1960s, Sheikh Shakhbut was spending more time in Al Ain, which was relatively prosperous thanks to Sheikh Zayed's agricultural improvements, than in Abu Dhabi. The town was losing population and in decline. In 1952, the British formed the Trucial States Council, on which the rulers of all of the seven emirates that were to become the UAE were represented. Sheikh Zayed attended its meetings from 1953 and started to play an influential role. The council provided a means by which Sheikh Zayed and Sheikh Rashid, who was to become ruler of Dubai in 1958, could meet.

The circumstances surrounding Sheikh Zayed's accession to the leadership of Abu Dhabi have been finally clarified. According to Sheikh Zayed's official biography, *With United Strength*, Shakhbut suggested he would abdicate in favour of Sheikh Zayed twice: once in 1954 and again in 1962. Both times, Sheikh Zayed urged him to continue as ruler but to spend more time developing Abu Dhabi and promoting its people's welfare. At times, Sheikh Zayed acted unilaterally. Deputizing for his absent brother, he ordered the construction of Abu Dhabi's first road that ran across Al Maqta'a causeway between the island and the mainland to the airport.

After oil exports began, Sheikh Shakhbut became more active, but failed projects led to disillusionment. A crisis was reached in early 1965 when the ruler announced he wanted to disassociate himself from the other states participating in the Trucial States Council. Perhaps the final straw was Sheikh Shakhbut's decision, during a visit to Amman in the spring of 1966, to make a donation to Jordan that seemed to overshadow the amounts he was prepared to spend at home. At the time, the police and the Abu Dhabi army had not been paid for months.

Sheikh Zayed travelled to London in July and informed senior British officials that the Al Nahyan family was thinking about replacing Sheikh Shakhbut. The response was that Britain would not interfere. On the morning of August 6, 1966, Sheikh Shakhbut was told to step aside by Britain's acting political agent, Glen Balfour-Paul.

Shakhbut telephoned Sheikh Zayed. The brothers spoke for almost an hour. What was said is not recorded, but the outcome was clear. Shakhbut packed his bags and left Abu Dhabi on an RAF aircraft just before 3pm the same day. Sheikh Zayed was immediately declared Abu Dhabi's ruler.

Sheikh Zayed's first actions were on the domestic front. He ended the divisions between Abu Dhabi and the rulers of Qatar. Abu Dhabians who'd left for Doha during Sheikh Shakhbut's rule were welcomed back. Development accelerated. A five-year plan was unveiled in March 1968. It called for housing, a new port and a proper airport. Central markets were opened in 1969 to promote commerce. Young Abu Dhabians were sent overseas to study.

Modernization quickened following the UK announcement that it would withdraw from the Gulf. Britain wanted Sheikh Zayed to take a leading role in handling the consequences. Sheikh Zayed first dealt with a territorial dispute with Dubai in an agreement that benefited his neighbour and set the tone for what happened next. At a meeting at Al Semaih between Abu Dhabi and Dubai, on February 18, 1968, Sheikh Zayed and Sheikh Rashid agreed on the principle of union among the emirates of the lower Gulf. The UAE was finally declared on December 2, 1971, with Sheikh Zayed as its first head of state.

By the summer of 2004, it was clear that the final chapter of Sheikh Zayed's life was being written. He went to London for medical treatment in August. On his return in September, Sheikh Zayed was pictured being greeted by his family and making a tour of the city but quickly dropped from view. In early October, the UAE announced the 2004 GCC summit would not be held in Abu Dhabi and that Bahrain had agreed to host the event. It was a signal that all was not well. After sunset on November 2, the Emirates News Agency (WAM) announced Sheikh Zayed had died. The federation went into instant mourning. The following day, Sheikh Zayed was buried. The eldest of his 19 sons, Sheikh Khalifa bin Zayed, crown prince for 35 years, was elected by the UAE's rulers as president of the UAE.

## The life of Sheikh Khalifa bin Zayed

Sheikh Khalifa bin Zayed Al Nahyan has inherited the leadership of a prosperous, tolerant and strategically vital country with practically no enemies and an estimated US$750 billion or more in foreign investments and reserves. Born in 1948, Sheikh Khalifa is Sheikh Zayed's only son by Sheikha Hessa bin Mohammed Al Nahyan. He had a traditional education that involved learning as he travelled through the Al Nahyan domain in the company of his charismatic father.

Sheikh Khalifa bin Zayed's first official job was accepted in September 1966, a month after Sheikh Zayed became Abu Dhabi ruler, when he was appointed as his father's representative in the Eastern Region. He was named Abu Dhabi crown prince aged 20 on February 1, 1969. Immediately afterwards, he was made chief of the Abu Dhabi Defence

Force. In July 1971, as the emirate prepared for the creation of the UAE, Sheikh Khalifa, then just 23, was made Abu Dhabi prime minister and minister of defence and finance in the first Abu Dhabi cabinet. From January 1974 until the end of 2004, he chaired the Abu Dhabi Executive Council. When the armed forces of the individual emirates were merged to form a single federal army, Sheikh Khalifa became deputy supreme commander of the UAE armed forces, a post he held until November 2004.

One of Sheikh Khalifa's most important early decisions was to set up, in 1976, the department of social services and commercial buildings, usually known as the Khalifa Committee. It administered land given by Sheikh Zayed to Abu Dhabians. The committee designed, built and let buildings on behalf of the owners.

Sheikh Khalifa continues to occupy the emirate's most powerful posts, including the chairmanship of the Abu Dhabi Investment Authority (ADIA), the world's second-largest institutional investor. He also chairs the Supreme Petroleum Council of Abu Dhabi, which controls the emirate's booming oil industry, and the Abu Dhabi Fund for Development (ADFD), its development-aid agency.

Sheikh Khalifa faces three key challenges. The first is strengthening federal institutions. On the day his father's death was announced, he appointed a new cabinet, which included a woman for the first time. The salaries of all its employees were raised by one quarter in the spring of 2005, and again by 70 per cent in early 2008. Sheikh Khalifa is pressing the rulers of the emirates to raise standards of health, education and basic amenities and to ensure UAE nationals enjoy equal services regardless of where they live.

The second challenge is using the UAE's economic strength to shape the region's fate. The emirates' rising status is reflected in the number of world leaders making the journey to Abu Dhabi. The third challenge is strengthening representative forms of government. In December 2005, elections were held for the first time for the Abu Dhabi Chamber of Commerce & Industry, a body of which all local businesses are members. In his annual national day speech on December 1, 2005, Sheikh Khalifa announced indirect elections would be held for half of the 40-member Federal National Council (FNC), a body established by the UAE's constitution that had previously been appointed. These took place on schedule in December 2006. They involved appointing councils comprising at least 800 members each in Abu Dhabi and Dubai, 600 each in Ra's al-Khaimah and Sharjah and 400 each in Ajman, Umm al-Qaiwain and Fujairah. The councils in Abu Dhabi and Dubai elected four FNC members apiece. Ra's al-Khaimah and Sharjah elected three and the other three elected two. The other 20 members were appointed by the rulers of each emirate.

### Sheikh Zayed's sons

Most of Sheikh Zayed's other 18 sons have roles in government. Sheikh Sultan bin Zayed, the second eldest and his mother's only male child, is the federation's deputy prime minister. Crown Prince Sheikh Mohammed bin Zayed, born in 1960, has served a lengthy apprenticeship. A graduate of the Royal Military Academy in Sandhurst, Sheikh Mohammed was made chief-of-staff of the UAE armed forces in 1994. In December 2003, he was named deputy crown prince and became crown prince following Sheikh Khalifa's succession as Abu Dhabi ruler. On January 1, 2005, he was named deputy supreme commander of the UAE armed forces, a post previously held by his elder brother.

Since Sheikh Mohammed bin Zayed became chairman of the Abu Dhabi Executive Council, in effect the cabinet of Abu Dhabi, top officials have had little time for vacations. His impact has been immediate and pervasive. Since the start of 2005, Sheikh Mohammed has pushed ahead with the biggest real-estate projects in Abu Dhabi's history, public-service privatizations and eye-catching energy-industry forays. One of his first measures was rationalizing Abu Dhabi's government, merging departments and preparing others for privatization.

The Abu Dhabi urban structure framework plan unveiled on September 19, 2007, by Sheikh Mohammed bin Zayed, is the region's most ambitious city development programme and might well be the most coherent ever seen. The scale of change it envisages will be gigantic. The plan's baseline assumption is that the population of Abu Dhabi city will grow to 3.1 million residents by 2030 from the present figure of about one million. That is an annual growth rate of a little more than five per cent, making Abu Dhabi one of the world's fastest-growing conurbations. Office space is projected to grow by more than 400 per cent to 7.5 million square metres. The number of hotel rooms is forecast to increase more than sevenfold to 74,500 to cope with almost eight million tourists compared with 3.3 million in 1997.

The plan, however, goes well beyond coping with the expected population boom. It entails radically reorienting Abu Dhabi's centre of gravity by developing two main built-up areas about 20 kilometres apart, installing a comprehensive public transport system, and completing some of the world's most iconic buildings. And all this will be done without disturbing Abu Dhabi's delicate natural environment.

The urban structure framework report provides an early taste of a comprehensive Abu Dhabi plan that will be completed around the start of the next decade. Planning council officials say that investment in the UAE capital will amount to at least $135 billion in the period to 2030. Taking every private sector development into account, the figure is likely to be significantly higher.

Sheikh Mohammed is one of the Bani Fatima, or children of Fatima, who are named after their influential and educated mother, Sheikha Fatima bint Mubarak. Sheikh Hamdan bin Zayed, a Bani Fatima and his father's fourth son is, together with Sheikh Sultan bin Zayed, a deputy UAE prime minister. The ninth son, Major General Sheikh Saif bin Zayed, was made UAE interior minister in the 2004 cabinet and reappointed in the reshuffle that followed the death of the UAE vice-president and prime minister, and the Dubai ruler, Sheikh Maktoum, in January 2006. Sheikh Mansour bin Zayed, another son of Fatima and his father's 13th son, joined the UAE cabinet in 2004 to head the new ministry for presidential affairs. He had previously been director general of Sheikh Zayed's office. Sheikh Abdullah bin Zayed, the 18th son, was appointed UAE foreign minister in the January 2006 cabinet reshuffle in which the information and culture ministry, which he previously headed, was split into two, to create a Ministry of Culture and a separate body, the National Media Council, to handle media affairs. Sheikh Abdullah was subsequently appointed chairman of the National Media Council.

Outside the UAE cabinet, sons of Sheikh Zayed to watch include Sheikh Hazza bin Zayed, a Bani Fatima, who's responsible for state security. Sheikh Tahnoun bin Zayed is chair of Abu Dhabi's Amiri Flights aircraft fleet. Sheikh Saeed bin Zayed sits on the Abu Dhabi Executive Council. Sheikh Nahyan bin Zayed is commander of the presidential guard. Sheikh Ahmed bin Zayed works in the UAE Ministry of Finance and Industry. Sheikh Hamed bin Zayed is chairman of the Abu Dhabi crown prince's court. Sheikh Dhiyab bin Zayed chairs the Abu Dhabi Water & Electricity Authority (ADWEA), which has implemented the region's most complete power- and water-privatization programme. Sheikh Omar bin Zayed is a presidential aide de camp.

The second generation is maturing and accepting responsibility. Sheikh Khalifa's son Sultan, who has a PhD, is a member of the Abu Dhabi Executive Council and president of the Abu Dhabi Chamber of Commerce, while his younger brother, Sheikh Mohammed, is chairman of the Abu Dhabi Department of Finance.

Other prominent members of the Al Nahyan ruling family include Sheikh Tahnoun bin Mohammed, who recently stepped down as the ruler's representative in the Eastern Region. Sheikh Tahnoun's son, Sheikh Sultan, a member of the Abu Dhabi Executive Council, is chairman of the Abu Dhabi Authority for Culture and Heritage (ADACH) and of the Abu Dhabi Tourism Authority (ADTA), a body set up in 2004. His goals include increasing the visitors to Abu Dhabi from the present one million to three million in 2015.

Sheikh Nahyan bin Mubarak Al Nahyan, son of the former minister of interior, Sheikh Mubarak bin Mohammed, who studied at Magdalen College, Oxford, is federal minister of higher education. He created the higher colleges of technology that provide vocational and English-language training to young Emiratis. His younger brother, Sheikh Hamdan, is minister of public works.

## The rise of Abu Dhabi

Abu Dhabi's growing significance results from it having the world's fifth-largest reservoir of proven crude oil reserves. The national oil company, ADNOC, founded in 1976, is a giant, handling as much oil as BP. The conglomerate has joint ventures with some of the world's largest oil companies. It is lifting oil capacity from about 2.5 million b/d at present to three million b/d.

Onshore gas-gathering capacity is being expanded. In March 2006, ADNOC signed an agreement with ExxonMobil for a 28 per cent stake in the Upper Zakum oil field, one of the world's largest offshore crude reservoirs. And, in the summer of 2006, IOCs were invited to bid for a stake in a new Abu Dhabi company that is to increase the emirate's natural-gas production by 50 per cent in little more than five years.

ADNOC chief executive is Yousef Omair bin Yousef, who was UAE minister of oil in the early 1990s. Standing in the wings are experienced Abu Dhabi men destined for higher heights. ADNOC deputy chief executive Abdul Nasser Al Suwaidi is being groomed to take greater responsibility. Mohammed Sahoo is chief executive of Gasco, the ADNOC subsidiary responsible for expanding the gas network. Ahmed Al Sayegh is chief executive of Dolphin Energy and ALDAR Properties chairman.

Dolphin Energy is the product of the work of Abu Dhabi's Mubadala Development Company headed by Khaldoon Al Mubarak, an Abu Dhabi Executive Council member and chairman of the Executive Affairs Authority. Mubadala-owned Liwa Energy has a 10 per cent stake in five exploration blocks awarded by Libya in March 2005. In June that year, it signed a strategic agreement with Royal Dutch/Shell for joint oil projects. Seven months later, the Mubadala-Shell partnership announced plans to invest in the Algerian oil industry. Liwa also has a 15 per cent stake in the Occidental Petroleum consortium that signed a production-sharing agreement for Oman's Mukhaizna Field in June 2005. Mubadala is a 50 per cent shareholder in Emirates Aluminium, planned as the world's largest single-site smelter, which is being built at Taweelah, north of Abu Dhabi city.

Abu Dhabi government-owned International Petroleum Investment Company (IPIC) announced in June 2006 that it had raised its stake in Denmark's Borealis to 65 per cent and taken a 20 per cent share in a new petrochemicals project in Taiwan. Borealis is a partner with ADNOC in Borouge, the first petrochemicals to plastics plant in the UAE. The portfolio of international oil, gas and petrochemical assets is expected to grow.

The quickening pace of Abu Dhabi development is reflected in a series of initiatives outside the oil-and-gas sector. In December 2004, the formation was announced of ZonesCorp, an executive agency that is aiming to promote rapid industrial development by creating industrial and free zones within Abu Dhabi. ZonesCorp plans to build accommodation for about 500,000 industrial workers, most recruited from outside the region.

ADTA is pressing ahead with plans to make the emirate a high-class holiday destination. Dozens of hotels are planned and projects are being developed for some of Abu Dhabi's many coastal islands. Saadiyat and Reem islands, which lie east of the capital, are being transformed into integrated residential and tourism zones. The influx of visitors will be facilitated by the expanded Abu Dhabi International Airport that will have capacity to handle 20 million passengers by 2010. Etihad Airways, founded in 2003 and chaired by Abu Dhabi Executive Council member, Sheikh Ahmed bin Saif Al Nahyan, aims to have six million passengers in 2009 compared with fewer than one million in 2005. It started direct flights to New York in November 2006 and to Sydney in March 2007. In February 2007 it was announced that from 2009 a Formula One grand prix would be held at a new track to be built on Abu Dhabi's Yas Island.

ALDAR Properties, which carried out the most successful IPO for a start-up company in history in November 2004, has launched a US$15 billion development of Al Raha Beach on the approach road to Abu Dhabi. It will be joined in developing Abu Dhabi housing and tourism by Sorouh Real Estate, which launched the largest share offering in UAE history in May 2005. Sorouh's keynote project is Shams Abu Dhabi on Reem Island.

## The BCCI shock

Abu Dhabi's sole setback in recent times was its failure to get satisfaction for a grievance arising from the closure of the Bank of Credit & Commerce International (BCCI) in 1991. It had been founded in 1972, initially with Bank of America as a partner, by Pakistani businessman Hasan Abedi. His vision was to build a global financial institution serving developing countries. Sheikh Zayed, together with other Arab personalities, took a shareholding. The bank grew rapidly but by the mid-1980s was in financial difficulties. Saudi's Bin Mahfouz family, who then controlled Jeddah's National Commercial Bank, doubled its shareholding to 20 per cent in 1986. The BCCI group comprised two units, one registered in Luxembourg, and a separate but connected entity registered in the Cayman Islands. BCCI's operational headquarters was in London. The Bank of England became uneasy about a global financial institution that was outside its effective regulatory control.

After months of negotiations, a solution was found. On April 30, 1990, Abu Dhabi pumped US$400 million into new BCCI shares to deal with a major loss made the previous year, bought out the Bin Mahfouz family and increased its stake in the bank to 77 per cent. The next step was re-registering the bank under a single regulator, possibly in Abu Dhabi itself, where BCCI had a large subsidiary.

As this was happening, storm clouds were gathering in the US. The bank had branches in Panama and there were suggestions that they had been used to finance illegal activities in Central America. In 1989, executives in the bank's Florida branches were arrested for alleged drug-related money laundering. Federal authorities then charged the BCCI group of money laundering, but dropped the case in return for guilty pleas by two of its subsidiaries. The department of justice had meanwhile launched its own BCCI inquiry. A similar investigation by the Manhattan district attorney's office was also started. A congressional report at the end of the 1980s claimed BCCI was involved in criminal activities in Latin America.

In March 1991, BCCI confirmed it had bought 25 per cent of First American, a Washington-based bank, without regulatory approval in the late 1970s. The same month, the Bank of England asked Price Waterhouse, which had become BCCI's sole auditors in 1987, to carry out an inquiry into the bank's affairs. This was not disclosed to Abu Dhabi, which had been assured that its reconstruction plan had the Bank of England's blessing.

On June 24, 1991, Price Waterhouse handed the Bank of England a report that alleged BCCI was guilty of widespread fraud and manipulation. The report included details of how the organization headed by Abu Nidal, a renegade Palestinian militant backed by the Iraqi regime, had held accounts at BCCI's Sloane Street branch. The Bank of England decided to take BCCI out of business. On July 5, 1991, regulators in seven countries closed the bank and froze its activities. The Bank of England, prime mover behind the closure, declared it had been notified of enormous fraud. An initial assessment suggested almost US$10 billion had gone.

The bank's governor, Robin Leigh-Pemberton, quipped at a press conference that BCCI was better known as the 'bank for criminals and crooks international'. It was an old joke. The shut-down came as a complete shock to Abu Dhabi, which had by then invested US$2 billion in BCCI. It argued that it was unaware of wrongdoing and had taken over the bank in good faith. While liquidators wound up BCCI's operations, US litigators targeted those alleged to have been behind its activities. On July 1, 1992, Manhattan district attorney, Robert Morgenthau, indicted Khalid bin Mahfouz, then NCB chief operating officer, and others of having wrongfully obtained US$300 million from

BCCI depositors. Bin Mahfouz resigned from NCB and, in 1993, jointly agreed with another defendant to pay US$225 million in restitution without admission of guilt.

In January 2004, BCCI liquidators, acting on behalf of the bank's creditors, launched a claim for US$850 million in damages against the Bank of England for failing in its supervisory duties. In June 2004, the bank completed its opening statements which had occupied 119 days. The opening statements by the lawyers acting for the liquidators took 86 days. By then, the case has already cost about US$100 million and was set to become the most expensive private case in British legal history.

The argument pressed by the creditors was that BCCI was not insolvent when the Bank of England and other regulators acted in 1991. They cited the fact that the liquidators had recovered about 85 per cent of the bank's assets. If there was fraud, it was modest.

But the odds were loaded against them. The liquidators, recognizing defeat was likely, dropped their case on November 2, 2005. The bank's governor, Mervyn King, declared that "there had never been a shred of evidence" to support allegations that the bank and 22 of its present and former employees had acted in bad faith or dishonestly and knowingly failed to protect BCCI depositors.

Lord Justice Tomlinson, who heard the case, said that the allegations were wholly without foundation. The Bank of England announced it would seek indemnity costs of £70 million sterling from BCCI creditors who were already facing their own legal costs of £38 million sterling. It was a stinging result for Abu Dhabi, the principal BCCI creditor and its majority owner. It can easily bear the costs. This cannot be said about other BCCI creditors.

We now know that in 1990 BCCI was in a better financial condition than most UK banks. But was there Bank of England wrongdoing? The answer is no. But there was supervisory failure and a breach of promises made to the shareholders.

Despite the above, the balance sheet for Abu Dhabi in the first decade of the 21st century was overwhelmingly positive. The economy was booming, new government policies looked promising and a younger generation was taking the reins of power. Men of competence and energy, and some women, are rising through the ranks.

### The origins of Abu Dhabi

The source of the power of the Al Nahyans is a federation called the Bani Yas, a people tracing their origins to a charismatic Bedouin chief named Yas bin Amer. He was a member of a tribe of the northern Adnani/Nizari division of Arabian people. Historians believe the Bani Yas lived in central Arabia before moving to the mountains of Oman and then the desert areas of what is now the emirate of Abu Dhabi. A wadi in Yemen named Wadi Nahyan has been interpreted as indicating more precisely the tribe's origins.

Until the end of the 18th century, the Bani Yas were based in Liwa, which they shared with the Al Manasir tribe. Their leader around the end of the 17th century was Falah and his descendants are known as the Al Bu Falah. Falah's oldest son, Nahyan, in turn led the Bani Yas and established the dynasty that's produced all the leaders of the Bani Yas for more than 200 years.

The Bani Yas includes seven other leading clans. The Al Rumaithi traditionally spent most of their time in Abu Dhabi and the coast. The Al Qubeisi are well represented in areas frequented by the Al Bu Falah. The other leading Bani Yas families are the Al Muhairi, Al Mazrouie, Al Hamili, Al Suwaidi and the Mishaghin.

There is one further substantial branch of the Bani Yas: the Al Bu Falasah (descendants of Falasah). Its largest contemporary division is the Al Maktoum. The Al Bu Falasah seceded and moved to Dubai in 1833. In a region where there were no borders, the people of Abu Dhabi ranged widely. Members of the Al Suwaidi, Al Mazrouie, Al Rumaithi and Al Qubeisi migrated to Qatar in the 1950s. Some are now so well established in Doha that most newcomers think they have always been there.

After the Al Bu Falah, two Abu Dhabi tribal groups are recognized as first among equals in the emirate. The Al Manasir (individual members are known as Al Mansouri) are the second largest tribal grouping in Abu Dhabi. They have strong bonds of kinship with the Al Bu Falah. The second group, which originates in the Al Ain region, is the Al Dhawahir (Al Dhaheri in the singular form), which is an Arabic word for the people from behind the (Hajar) mountains.

The Bani Yas, Al Manasir and Al Dhawahir form the core of the Abu Dhabi tribal system. But other tribes were irregularly present in the Abu Dhabi domain and their descendants are prominent in the life of the emirate. The Awamir travelled over a huge area including what is now eastern Yemen and central Oman. The Afar and Manahil originated in the Hadhramaut. The Al Rashid, who were described by Wilfred Thesiger in the late 1940s as "the most authentic of the Bedu," traditionally ranged from the lands of the Bani Yas to Dhofar.

The Al Murrah (Al Marri or Al Merri in the singular form), a segment of the Anaizah federation, originate from Al Hasa Oasis, but there are branches in the territory of modern Abu Dhabi. The Al Shamsi, a division of the Al Naim tribal group that provides the ruling family of Ajman, became allies of the Al Bu Falah in the 19th century. The Bani Kaab traditionally moved in an area encompassing Buraimi, the Batinah coast of what is now Oman, and Hatta – the Dubai enclave

in the foothills of the Hajar. The Bani Qitab are based in the Hajar
Mountains and have representatives on both sides of the border with
Oman. Sheikha Fatima bint Mubarak, wife of the late Sheikh Zayed
and mother of Mohammed, Mansour, Hamdan, Hazza, Tahnoun and
Abdullah, is a daughter of the tribe.

## Abu Dhabi is founded

In 1793, Sheikh Shakhbut bin Diab, great-grandson of the founder of
the Al Nahyan, came to power. He moved the Bani Yas headquarters
from Liwa to the 10 km-long island of Abu Dhabi. The best-known
story is that, in 1761, a party of Bani Yas trailing a desert gazelle crossed from the mainland and found a fresh water spring where the animal
had stood. The spring became the basis of a settlement that was named
Abu Dhabi, or 'Father of the Gazelle'.

There are other reasons why Shakhbut may have moved. Around
that time, there was a drought in the Arabian interior and the Bani Yas
were under pressure from the west. The Al Saud had extended their
domain to the outskirts of Karbala and Najaf in Iraq, taken control of
the Arabian west coast including Mecca and Medina, mastered the Arabian east coast and penetrated into the interior of what is now Oman.
The followers of Al Saud were puritan Sunni Muslims known as Wahhabis. The Bani Yas, in contrast, followed a more moderate school of
Sunni Islam.

Abu Dhabi island was a defensible redoubt with water and access to
a new source of wealth: pearls found in the oysters that flourished in
the Gulf. The Bani Yas may also have been attracted to the Gulf coast
by the rise of a trading system based on the ports of British India. In
the 16th and 17th centuries, the Portuguese built forts along the Gulf
coast and along the UAE's East Coast as well as in Oman. They were
regarded as thugs and tribes retreated to the interior to escape their
depredations and taxes. The Portuguese were replaced by a new combination: the traders of the British East India Company in partnership
with the Persian Empire. The British competed with Dutch merchants
who set up their own trading centres in the region. But the newcomers
were not occupiers. In this more benign regional context, Sheikh
Shakhbut built Qasr al-Hosn, a fort that still stands in the heart of the
city of Abu Dhabi.

Many Bani Yas remained in Liwa, only travelling for work on the
pearling boats in the summer. Sheikh Shakhbut tried to take control of
part of the Buraimi Oasis in the foothills of the Hajar Mountains. There,
contact was made with Sayyid Sultan of Muscat, who had signed a
treaty with Britain in 1798. In Buraimi, there were Bani Yas and tribesmen who accepted the supremacy of Muscat. But people journeying
from central Arabia who were loyal to the Al Saud passed through and

stayed in Buraimi to graze their herds and trade. For most of the first half of the 19th century, Buraimi village, close to Al Ain but traditionally part of Oman, was intermittently held by tribes loyal to the Al Saud. The Abu Dhabians insist, however, that Saudi control never extended to Al Ain and other villages that are now part of Abu Dhabi. In any case, Saudi control of Buraimi finally ended in 1869.

Three brothers successively ruled Abu Dhabi after Sheikh Shakhbut, who stepped down in 1816. His son, Sheikh Mohammed bin Shakhbut Al Nahyan, ruled from 1816 until 1818 and consolidated the status of the Al Nahyan. Sheikh Mohammed bin Shakhbut Al Nahyan ruled from his father's death in 1816 until 1818, when he was deposed by his younger brother Sheikh Tahnoun, with support from Sheikh Shakhbut, who lived until the early 1840s. Sheikh Tahnoun was ruler for the next 15 years and was one of the signatories of the 1820 General Treaty of Peace with Britain. Signing a treaty that gave Britain the right to intervene at sea offered Abu Dhabi protection against the Wahhabis, crushed in 1818 by an Egyptian army but likely to rise again. This was to prove helpful in 1833 when the Wahhabis resumed their attacks into Buraimi.

Rivalry with the Al Qassimi of Ra's al-Khaimah and Sharjah had also degenerated into low-level war about territory that continued intermittently for more than half a century. At the end of 1833, Abu Dhabi was under attack from Sharjah and Dubai. Amid growing lawlessness, the Bani Yas war fleet attacked ships under the British flag, drawing sharp retribution. Exhausted by mutual depredations, the rulers of the coast finally signed the first maritime truce, again supervised by Britain, in 1835.

Sheikh Tahnoun had been murdered by an unrecorded assassin in 1833 and was succeeded by his younger brother, Sheikh Khalifa. The events surrounding Sheikh Khalifa's succession were the cause of the schism that led to the secession and departure to Dubai of the Al Bu Falasah. For a period, the Al Bu Falasah were allied with the Al Qassimi and provided asylum for breakaway Abu Dhabi subjects. The independence of the Al Bu Falasah was recognized in a truce with the Al Qassimi in 1834. Fighting between Dubai and Abu Dhabi continued until a settlement in 1843 laid the foundations for a modus vivendi between the two clans.

Abu Dhabi's tendency to dynastic dispute found a fresh expression in 1845 when Sheikh Khalifa, who'd signed the second Gulf treaty of maritime peace with Britain two years earlier, was deposed and he and his brother, Sheikh Sultan, were killed by a distant relative.

This was followed by a further breakdown in the regional order that was restored with the encouragement of British gunboats later that year when Sheikh Said, son of Sheikh Tahnoun, was recognized as ruler.

More fighting broke out with Abu Dhabi, Dubai and the Al Qassimi combining and fighting in a sequence of battles with Britain as the reluctant referee. In a final twist, Sheikh Said fled Abu Dhabi in 1855, being replaced by Sheikh Zayed, the son of Sheikh Khalifa, but attempted to recover the town the following year, dying with his brother in the process. Perversely, given the violence during his rule, Sheikh Said had signed in 1853 the third and most extensive agreement with Britain, known as the Treaty of Perpetual Maritime Peace since it was to last indefinitely.

### The rule of Zayed the Great

Sheikh Said's removal as ruler set the scene for the entrance of one of the greatest figures in Abu Dhabi history. Sheikh Zayed, whose father, Sheikh Khalifa, had been killed 10 years earlier, was also the first ruler whose image was captured in a photograph. Declared leader of the Al Bu Falah in 1855 when he was 20, Sheikh Zayed bin Khalifa was to govern Abu Dhabi for 54 years and is the great-grandfather of the present ruler, Sheikh Khalifa. Zayed the Great extended Abu Dhabi's authority south into Ibri (now in Oman) and the Dhahirah region of the Hajar Mountains.

His principal rivals were the Wahhabis and their allies the Al Qassimi. Capitalizing on the existence of rich pearling grounds between Dubai and the east coast of Qatar, Sheikh Zayed made Abu Dhabi the Gulf's leading pearling centre. As Abu Dhabi rose, it came into conflict with the Al Thani, the dominant family of Doha. Adherents to Wahhabism, the Al Thani challenged the Al Khalifa of Bahrain for control over Qatar. Rich pearl banks were also at stake.

In October 1867, Sheikh Zayed joined the Al Khalifa to attack towns south of Doha in breach of the 1853 Treaty of Perpetual Maritime Peace. Since the dissolution of the East India Company a decade earlier, the Royal Navy had been made responsible for policing the Gulf. Two British gunships were dispatched to Abu Dhabi. Under duress, Sheikh Zayed boarded a British ship and agreed to pay compensation to Doha, through Britain, for the damage done. Relations with the Al Thani were further damaged in 1869 when the Al Qubeisi defected for the third time in little more than 30 years and sought Doha's protection. They settled in Khor al-Udaid. Sheikh Zayed claimed the Al Qubeisi were absconding debtors.

The Ottoman Turks, who'd secured the submission of the Al Thani in 1871, subsequently offered the Al Qubeisi protection. The bulk of the Al Qubeisi returned to Abu Dhabi in 1880, but the region remained the target of conflicting claims between the emirate and Qatar. In May 1881, the Al Thani, encouraged by the Ottomans, asserted Khor al-Udaid was part of their territory. War with Abu Dhabi followed and reached a climax in Qatari attacks on Liwa and the Dhafrah area. Raids continued until 1893 when the Al Thani rebelled against the Ottomans and lost interest expanding their domains. The wounds were to be lasting. Relations with the Al Thani were only completely normalized in 1966.

Sheikh Zayed came into conflict with Britain. In 1895, the British, acting on a protest from the Ajman ruler, forced him to abandon an attempt to build a settlement on the island of Zora between Hamriyah and Ajman, which lie north of Dubai and Sharjah. A further confrontation came in 1896 when Sheikh Zayed offered France a port of call for Messageries Maritimes, the Marseilles-based shipping line. Britain deemed this to be in breach of the exclusive agreement, signed by Abu Dhabi and the other emirates in 1892, which prevented contact with foreign powers.

The issue rumbled on until a final showdown was precipitated when Sheikh Zayed, acting in his capacity as a peacekeeper in the lands of his ally the Sultan of Muscat, imposed a fine on the Bani Qitab, who were then in rebellion. Britain intervened to end the dispute and its control over traffic to and from the Trucial Coast was tightened. Sheikh Zayed died in 1909 and was succeeded by three sons. His heir Sheikh Tahnoun, who ruled until 1912, was paralysed below the waist. He was succeeded by his brother Sheikh Hamdan (grandfather, through his daughter Sheikha Latifa bint Hamdan Al Nahyan, of the present Dubai ruler Sheikh Mohammed). He was to rule for 10 years.

Sheikh Hamdan's 10-year reign encompassed the First World War, which had a devastating impact on the pearling industry, a major source of export income, and also saw the beginnings of major expansion by the new Al Saud state, with a combination of poverty and shifting tribal alliances leading to growing weakness and chaos in Abu Dhabi and to divisions among the sons of Sheikh Zayed bin Khalifa. Sheikh Hamdan was killed in 1922 by two of his brothers, one of whom, Sheikh Sultan, the father of the late UAE president Sheikh Zayed, took his place for four years before he, in turn, was killed by the second brother, Sheikh Saqr, who ruled for little more than a year, until January 1928, when he himself was killed by a retainer. During this uneasy period, some of the tribes on the periphery of the emirates, such as the Duru, fell firmly under the sway of Bin Jiluwi, the Al Saud governor of Al Hasa, whose authority stretched steadily deeper into the southern deserts.

In his account of these years, Mohammed Al Fahim in his book *From Rags to Riches* says the following: "This decade-long family strife, rooted for the most part in greed, was aided and abetted by British practices and policies at the time. When a British ship arrived in the Gulf, for example, the ruler would often visit it in a small boat and subsequently be seen bringing back a dispatch box given to him by the

Political Resident. Members of his family assumed wrongly that this box contained money and presents, whereas it probably held only papers . . . if family members suspected a ruler of deceit they frequently turned against him, causing infighting which sometimes resulted in death, or deaths, as it did in the 1920s."

## The rule of Sheikh Shakhbut

Order was restored when the Al Nahyan united to name Sheikh Shakhbut bin Sultan Al Nahyan, then just 24, as ruler. He ruled Abu Dhabi for 38 years, acquiring a reputation for charm and ruthlessness, coupled with thrift and a relentless distrust of the British. He had a difficult inheritance. Things did not improve. Abu Dhabi was immediately hit by world recession and the collapse in the natural pearl market that bankrupted Abu Dhabi's pearling vessel owners, who were indebted to Indian merchants resident in Trucial Oman. As British subjects they called on the authorities to act against Abu Dhabi in pursuit of unpaid debts. This led to confrontations with Sheikh Shakhbut. Abu Dhabi's poverty led to families leaving for Al Ain and Liwa, Dubai, Doha, Manama and Kuwait.

Sheikh Shakhbut opposed practically everything that would alter his people's way of life. He eventually agreed to the opening of Abu Dhabi's first bank, a branch of the British Bank of the Middle East (BBME), in February 1959, more than 13 years after Dubai opened its doors to the bank. In his autobiography *Wells of Memory*, Easa Al Gurg, UAE ambassador to the UK, described how Sheikh Shakhbut would take radical steps to prevent modernization. Al Gurg was asked by Dubai's British political agency to persuade Sheikh Sultan, son of Sheikh Shakhbut, to set up an office for the Abu Dhabi municipality, of which Sheikh Sultan was the head. Al Gurg managed to do so and an office with a filing cabinet was opened. Sheikh Shakhbut visited the office and ordered the files to be burned. Whether this was out of horror at a modern device, fury that his son had acted autonomously or a desire to irritate the British is not clear. It was probably all three.

Some financial problems were relieved in 1939 when Sheikh Shakhbut concluded an exploration agreement with Petroleum Development (Trucial Coast), a subsidiary of Petroleum Concessions Limited, which had been set up by London-based IPC, a consortium of BP, Shell, the companies that later became Total and ExxonMobil, and Partex. Oil was not discovered for almost 20 years but Shakhbut received a substantial signature fee plus an annual payment.

The prospect of oil strikes led to disputes among the Trucial rulers about territory. In 1936, Sheikh Shakhbut, the first to sign an oil concession, set out his claims in a letter to Dubai ruler Sheikh Saeed bin Maktoum Al Maktoum. He asserted Abu Dhabi's territory extended to

Jebel Ali. Sheikh Saeed's rejoinder was to claim Dubai ran to Khor Ghanadha, 80 km south of Dubai Creek. Exploration stopped during the Second World War, from 1939–45. The Abu Dhabi-Dubai truce dissolved when war ended and exploration resumed. At the end of 1945, Sheikh Saeed sent fighters by sea to Khor Ghanada and laid claim, as he had to 1936, to the land between there and Dubai. Sheikh Shakhbut protested that the 1892 exclusive agreement prohibited moving troops by sea. Britain intervened to force Dubai to withdraw and imposed a fine on Sheikh Saeed.

Following a major skirmish in early 1948 at Ruweihah, an oasis between Liwa and Abu Dhabi, in which 52 men of the Manasir tribe, allies of Sheikh Shakhbut, were killed, a truce was agreed. An agreement on the border between Abu Dhabi and Dubai was eventually made between Sheikh Rashid of Dubai and Sheikh Zayed of Abu Dhabi in the late 1960s, with the border running roughly half-way between Khor Ghanadha and Jebel Ali.

There were also border disputes between Abu Dhabi and Doha, prompted, in part, by traditional Abu Dhabi claims that its western border extended to Mesaieed and by disputes over the ownership of several offshore islands, in particular Halul, traditionally owned by Abu Dhabi. Sheikh Shakhbut, however, declined to present evidence of ownership to a court convened to settle the issue, and Halul was awarded to Qatar.

### The Buraimi Crisis and its consequences

The area known as the Buraimi Oasis in Oman and Al Ain in Abu Dhabi, lying some 300 m above sea level, is comprised of nine original villages, of which six, including Al Ain, were part of Abu Dhabi and three, including Buraimi, were part of Oman. It is blocked to the east by the Hajar Mountains and to the south by Jebel Hafit. In the west is the Empty Quarter that extends practically without settlement to Hofuf in eastern Saudi Arabia.

In 1800, the Al Saud captured Buraimi and the adjacent Omani villages, as well as, for a short period, much of Central Oman. Although they later were driven out of Buraimi, as the Al Saud state declined, during the next seven decades, the Al Saud temporarily re-established a presence in Buraimi on several occasions, before their final expulsion by Oman's Sultan Azzan bin Qais in 1869.

Buraimi acquired greater importance following the signing in May 1933 of an exploration agreement between Saudi Arabia and Socal. It specified the concession covered all eastern Saudi Arabia, but there was no international agreement about where the kingdom ended.

The US asked Britain, as guardians of Abu Dhabi, to state where they believed the border lay. Britain referred to the unratified Anglo-

Ottoman convention of July 1913 that defined the easternmost point of Ottoman influence. This was later referred to as the Blue Line, after its colour on an accompanying map. It ran directly south from Zakhuni-yah Island, which is west of the Qatar Peninsula, and ended in the heart of the Empty Quarter. The Blue Line had little legal standing and Riyadh rejected it. The border was the subject of negotiations between the UK and Saudi Arabia during 1935–38 but no agreement was reached by the start of the Second World War.

With the war over, the search for oil began in earnest. Edward Henderson has left a compelling account of what happened in his memoirs. He records that when he arrived in the region in 1948, as part of an IPC mission preparing for the start of prospecting, there was no evidence of allegiance to Saudi Arabia in Buraimi.

Aramco started sending survey units into Abu Dhabi emirate in 1949. Later that year, Riyadh made a claim that included Buraimi and the Abu Dhabi coast to Mirfa. In an agreement signed in 1951, Britain, on behalf of Abu Dhabi, and Saudi Arabia agreed not to put forces into the disputed area. Talks in Dammam in January and February the following year left the Buraimi issue unresolved.

In August 1952, the 'Buraimi Dispute' entered a new phase when the sheikh of Hamasa, one of the Omani villages in the Buraimi area, without the approval of the Government in Muscat, invited the Saudis to send a small military force to his village.

Abu Dhabi and Oman mobilized forces to expel the Saudis. Britain intervened. In October 1952, a standstill agreement between Britain and Saudi Arabia under US mediation was signed in Jeddah. The following month, London called for the issue to be referred to international arbitration.

An agreement about its terms was signed in Jeddah on July 30, 1954. It allowed each side to keep 15 men and one officer in the Buraimi area pending the outcome of the arbitration, which was held in Geneva. The tribunal opened on September 11, 1955. Five days later, the British tribunal member resigned and accused the Saudi representative of partiality and improper practices. Britain claimed the kingdom had been airlifting military supplies into Buraimi and attempting to suborn local leaders.

On the morning of October 29, 1955, Abu Dhabi and Omani forces, supported by British-officered Trucial Oman Scouts, entered the Omani villages of Buraimi and Hamasah. According to Henderson, the operation, with Sheikh Zayed and his brother Sheikh Hazza in attendance as observers, was completed mainly by negotiation. The Saudis and their local allies were flown out.

Anthony Eden, who'd replaced Winston Churchill as British prime minister in April that year, told the House of Commons the same day that the Riyadh line, which had been proposed by the British in 1935 and amended in 1937, would henceforward be the border. It placed the frontier deep in the Empty Quarter and encompassed Khor al-Udaid within Abu Dhabi. This set the scene for the definition of the border in Buraimi between Oman and Abu Dhabi. It was adjusted to Oman's benefit.

The 1955 Buraimi confrontation left a number of unresolved issues, including the final definition of the borders dividing south-east Arabia. This continued to rankle with Faisal, Saudi crown prince during the Buraimi affair, who succeeded to the Saudi throne in 1964. When Britain announced, in January 1968, its plans to withdraw from the Gulf, King Faisal insisted the Buraimi Oasis and a swathe of territory, including Liwa and much of the coastline stretching westwards from Abu Dhabi, was rightfully Saudi territory. An earlier claim that covered nearly 80 per cent of the emirate, including all its onshore oil fields, was dropped.

In July 1970, King Faisal told Sheikh Zayed he wanted a plebiscite among the people of Buraimi to determine whether they thought it lay in Saudi Arabia, Oman or Abu Dhabi. The Saudi king said he believed the border should run from Buraimi west to the Abu Dhabi coast at Jebel Dhanna. Sheikh Zayed opened border negotiations with Riyadh soon after the federation was formed in December 1971.

In 1974, the UAE and Saudi Arabia ratified the Treaty of Jeddah, designed to settle the border between the two states. This involved the ceding to Saudi Arabia of a land and sea corridor, west of the Sila'a Peninsula, that separated Abu Dhabi and the rest of the UAE from Qatar, and the cession of an area south of the Liwa Oasis that contained the larger part of the Zarrarah Oilfield (known to the Saudis as Shaybah), which had been discovered by IPC in 1968.

Some believe Sheikh Zayed was misled by his senior advisers. Others argue that he feared unilateral Saudi action. Sheikh Zayed asserted that the 1974 Jeddah treaty was not signed in good faith but that he would not raise the issue during his lifetime. Sheikh Khalifa brought the border up with Riyadh soon after his father's death in November 2004.

In early 2005, the UAE and Qatar announced they were considering plans to build a causeway that would cross the Gulf from Qatar to Abu Dhabi. This drew Saudi objections that were a reminder that the maritime border is also still undefined.

The Jeddah treaty was again raised with King Abdullah, then crown prince, during a visit he made to Abu Dhabi in early 2005. Top UAE officials were reported as saying they believed the Jeddah agreement was now no longer practical and that it should be amended.

On June 16, Prince Naif, Saudi Arabia's interior minister, returned to Saudi Arabia after a visit to Abu Dhabi and reported the border issue had been discussed. Less than a week later, the UAE issued its first definitive statement on the matter. The UAE news agency, WAM, quoted Sheikh Hamdan bin Zayed, then minister of foreign affairs, as saying his country considered parts of the 1974 agreement had become inapplicable. He said this position was not new and repeated the position expressed by the UAE since 1975. He stressed his country's desire to "reach a pleasing satisfactory (agreement) as soon as possible".

### Oil is discovered

The search for oil gathered momentum after 1945. An offshore concession was awarded in 1953 to Abu Dhabi Marine Areas (ADMA), a joint venture between BP and Total. It operated from Das Island. The first well on the Trucial Coast was spudded at Ra's al-Sadr in 1950. It was abandoned after 13 months. A second well was sunk on Jebel Ali in what is now Dubai. ADMA eventually struck oil in commercial quantities at Umm Shaif in September 1958. IPC struck oil in Murban about 125 km south-west of Abu Dhabi island in October 1960.

The first offshore oil shipment left Das Island on July 5, 1962. Onshore oil was shipped from Jebel Dhanna on December 14, 1963. The IPC subsidiary, Petroleum Development (Trucial Coast) became the Abu Dhabi Petroleum Company (ADPC) in 1962. In 1978, ADPC and ADNOC, by then the owner of 60 per cent of the onshore concession, transferred operating responsibility to the Abu Dhabi Company for Onshore Oil Operations (ADCO).

Oil provided the finance for modern infrastructure. The first non-religious school opened in Abu Dhabi in 1959 and the first water-desalination plant opened in 1961. In the spring and summer of 1961, Sheikh Zayed, acting on behalf of Sheikh Shakhbut, ordered the construction of a road from Abu Dhabi to the mainland at Al Maqta'a.

A British political officer reporting to the political agent in Dubai was appointed in 1955. At the end of 1961, Hugh Boustead was named Britain's first resident Abu Dhabi political agent. The BBME opened a branch and was followed by the Eastern Bank, which was eventually absorbed by Standard Chartered Bank, and the Ottoman Bank. The first international telegraph office opened around the same time. The first hotel was completed at the end of 1962. A telephone system and a post office were opened in 1963.

Development was slowed by Sheikh Shakhbut's ban on new construction in Abu Dhabi. The ruler was suspicious of Boustead and the activities of the UK-controlled oil developers. He reluctantly agreed to electricity being supplied to his palace but prevented power being supplied elsewhere. Immigrants arrived from other parts of the Arab World. Radio allowed people to listen to Radio Cairo. In the spring of 1963, oil workers went on strike over pay and conditions. Sheikh

Zayed replaced Sheikh Shakhbut in August 1966. Sheikh Shakhbut went into exile, first in Bahrain and then to Iran and finally to Lebanon. He returned in the late 1960s and lived in Al Ain until his death.

One of Sheikh Zayed's first actions was to announce that anyone in need could come to Abu Dhabi from anywhere on the Trucial Coast for a handout. A government structure was established. Electricity was supplied to Abu Dhabi in 1967. Mina Zayed port and the international airport were completed in 1969. A planning council was established the same year to promote ordered development. A policy of granting land to Abu Dhabians was begun and it helped to spread wealth and promote private-sector initiatives. Trade in land was quickly banned following the sale of worthless plots to Abu Dhabians. It was only lifted in 2005.

By the end of the 1960s, Abu Dhabi was one of the Middle East's boom capitals. In February 1970, John Butter, previously permanent secretary to the Kenyan treasury, was appointed financial adviser to help Abu Dhabi deal with its growing wealth. For the first time in decades, the emirate's future seemed secure. The political environment, however, was about to take a turn for the worse.

Britain dismayed Gulf rulers by precipitately withdrawing from Aden in November 1967. When London announced in January 1968 that it planned to end military involvement east of the Suez Canal, and would, therefore, terminate its old treaties with the seven emirates, the concern built.

The immediate response was a plan to forge a union. The key partner would be Abu Dhabi's old rival, Dubai.

## The Al Nahyan family tree

Yas

Falah

Nahyan bin Falah

Isa bin Nahyan

| | |
|---|---|
| Dhiyab bin Isa | 1793 |
| Shakhbut bin Dhiyab | 1793–1816 |
| Mohammed bin Shakhbut | 1816–1818 |
| Tahnoun bin Shakhbut | 1818–1833 |
| Khalifa bin Shakhbut | 1833–1845 |
| Saeed bin Tahnoun | 1845–1855 |
| Zayed bin Khalifa | 1855–1909 |
| Tahnoun bin Zayed | 1909–1912 |
| Hamdan bin Zayed | 1912–1922 |
| Sultan bin Zayed | 1922–1926 |
| Saqr bin Zayed | 1926–1928 |
| Shakhbut bin Sultan | 1928–1966 |

Zayed bin Sultan.. ... ... ... ... ... ... ... ... ... ... ... ...   1966–2004
Khalifa bin Zayed   ... ... ... ... ... ... ... ... ... ... ... ...   2004–

## The Al Maktoum and Modern Dubai

On the morning of January 4, 2006, the sudden death was announced of Sheikh Maktoum bin Rashid Al Maktoum, Dubai's ruler. He was 62 and had been Dubai ruler, and UAE vice-president, since he succeeded his father, Sheikh Rashid, in October 1990.

Sheikh Maktoum had been appointed the federation's first prime minister at the age of 29 on April 4, 1972. In April 1979, he'd given way to Sheikh Rashid as prime minister and became his father's deputy. He became UAE premier again when Sheikh Rashid fell ill in 1981. Sheikh Maktoum's death at the Palazzo Versace Hotel on Australia's Gold Coast was unexpected and a shock. The UAE immediately began 40 days of mourning.

Some of the most generous tributes came from people from the world of horse racing which he'd supported passionately. Sheikh Maktoum's principal wife was Alia bint Khalifa. They had two sons and three daughters. The eldest, Sheikh Saeed bin Maktoum, pursues mainly private interests. The second son, Sheikh Rashid bin Maktoum, was killed, aged 22, in a motor-vehicle accident in 2002.

Sheikh Maktoum was the oldest of the four sons of Sheikh Rashid bin Saeed and his wife Sheikha Latifa bint Hamdan Al Nahyan. Sheikh Rashid's second son, Sheikh Hamdan, was born in 1945 and has played a prominent role in Dubai and the UAE for more than 30 years. He is Dubai's deputy ruler, UAE finance and industry minister and heads Dubai Municipality, which has responsibility for urban developments everywhere in the emirate. He too is passionate about horses and has stables in Dubai, England, Ireland and the US. His wife, Rodha bint Ahmed bin Jumaa, has given him six children. Sheikh Hamdan's eldest son, Sheikh Rashid bin Hamdan, is beginning to play a role in public affairs. The fourth son, Sheikh Ahmed bin Rashid, is deputy chairman of Dubai police and public security.

Sheikh Rashid's third son, Sheikh Mohammed, born in 1949, succeeded Sheikh Maktoum as Dubai ruler and prime minister and vice-president of the UAE. Sent at the age of 20 to the Mons Officer Cadet School in Aldershot, Sheikh Mohammed excelled and was promoted to senior under officer at the school's Kohema College. He was awarded the sword of honour for achieving the highest mark of any foreign and Commonwealth officer cadet in his intake.

On November 1, 1968, Sheikh Mohammed was appointed head of the Dubai police and public security office. Following the creation of the UAE, he was made minister of defence and became the youngest defence minister in the world at the time. Working with Abu Dhabi's

Sheikh Khalifa, his principal initial task was setting up the Union Defence Force (UDF), later renamed the UAE Armed Forces. It made its first operational foray abroad in 1976 as part of the Arab deterrent force that was attempting to keep the peace in Lebanon. The first UDF chief of staff was Brigadier Freddie de Butts, who'd commanded the Trucial Oman Scouts from 1964–67. De Butts held the post for two years before retiring. He died aged 89 in August 2005.

Sheikh Mohammed's first major project was supervising the construction of the Dubai Drydocks. In August 1977, he was made head of a committee mandated to upgrade Dubai Airport and given responsibility for Dubai's oil industry. In 1985, Sheikh Mohammed approved the establishment of Emirates airline and took control of Jebel Ali Free Zone. He was appointed Dubai crown prince on January 4, 1995. This made him Dubai's effective chief operating officer and signalled the quickening of the development drive that has transformed Dubai.

The Dubai Executive Council was formed to streamline decision-making. It now includes his uncle, Sheikh Ahmed bin Saeed Al Maktoum, chairman of the Emirates group, who was born in 1958. Other members include Emaar Properties chairman Mohammed Ali Alabbar and Sultan bin Sulayem, chairman of the Dubai World holding group which owns DP World, Jebel Ali Free Zone and Nakheel, the real estate developer. Its secretary general is Mohammed Gergawi, who also heads the Dubai Development & Investment Authority and Dubai Holdings, a group set up at the end of 2004 to manage the Dubai government's commercial businesses. In January 2006, Gergawi was appointed to the UAE cabinet.

Sheikh Mohammed married Sheikha Hind in 1979. Their eldest son, Sheikh Rashid bin Mohammed, who is in his mid-20s, graduated from Sandhurst and shares his father's interest in endurance horse-racing and owning racehorses. His second son, Sheikh Hamdan bin Mohammed, born in 1982, was appointed chairman of the executive council in 2006 and crown prince on February 1, 2008. He is also a product of Sandhurst. Next in age are Sheikh Maktoum bin Mohammed, a former student at the American University in Dubai and chairman of the TECOM free zone, who was named deputy ruler on February 1, 2008; Sheikh Ahmed bin Mohammed, a world champion endurance horse-rider; and Sheikh Mayed bin Mohammed, a star graduate from Sandhurst in August 2006.

Like most of his family, Sheikh Mohammed loves horses. The Al Maktoums own Godolphin, a race-horse stable which, since it was created in 1992, has produced a string of champions that have won top races at Ascot, Epsom, Newmarket, the Curragh, Longchamps and Rome. Some of the world's finest racing horses are nurtured during the winter at the Al Maktoum's Al Quoz stables in Dubai and put through their paces in the emirate's racing season which culminates in March in the mile-and-a-quarter Dubai World Cup, the richest horse race on earth. They are then unleashed to run in Europe in the spring and summer. No stable has a longer roll of honour of classic winners in the past decade than Godolphin. In Dubai Millennium, the 2000 Dubai World Cup champion who died prematurely the following year, the family had one of the most brilliant thoroughbreds in racing history.

When the World Cup was launched in 1996, the vision was to create a race that would attract the best horses from North America, where most racing is done on dirt, and Europe, where turf predominates. It is now one of the great events in the horse-racing calendar but it has yet to overcome all the objections to flying horses more than 12 hours from the US to compete in Dubai.

Sheikh Mohammed has also made long-distance, endurance horse racing an international sport. He was 2003 European champion and the UAE national team, including his son Sheikh Hamdan bin Mohammed, were winners in the 2005 event. The biennial world championship was held in Dubai at the end of January 2005 with the UAE providing 12 competitors.

Horse racing overshadows camel racing in the UAE but there are now about a dozen camel race tracks in the federation. The image of the sport suffered as a result of charges that camel jockeys, usually boys aged as young as eight, were effectively slaves. In July 2005, Sheikh Khalifa ratified a law banning children aged under 18 from participating in the races. The UAE and Qatar are now using robot jockeys operated by computer.

A shared love of horses was a factor in Sheikh Mohammed's marriage in April 2004 to Princess Haya, daughter of Jordan's late King Hussein and half-sister of King Abdullah. Princess Haya is a graduate in philosophy, politics and economics from St Hilda's College, Oxford, and an equestrian who represented Jordan in the 2000 Sydney Olympics. Daughter of her father's third wife, Alia, Princess Haya achieved her ambition of bringing a world-class show-jumping event to Dubai with the Al Maktoum Memorial Challenge that was held at the Emirates Riding Centre in January 2006. It offered a total prize fund of US$1.25 million, the biggest in showjumping. The winner took home $250,000.

Sheikh Mohammed enjoys reading, reciting and writing poetry. Lines he has penned are being shaped into the structure of The Palm Jebel Ali, one of the four artificial island complexes being built off Dubai's coast, so you'll soon be able to read them from 10,000 m. He sponsors an annual Koran recitation competition that's highly regarded in the Islamic World. Sheikh Mohammed is a formidable character who is now ploughing his energies into his dual role as Dubai's ruler and UAE vice-president and prime minister. Some argue he is the most influential Arab since Abdelaziz Al Saud who created Saudi Arabia in the first three decades of the 20th century.

## Dubai: vanguard of the New Gulf

In February 2006, Dubai was propelled to the top of the US political agenda when Senator Hillary Clinton launched a campaign to block DP World's acquisition of the management contract for six US ports held by P&O which the company was about to buy. President Bush twice went on the record publicly to assert the deal was sound and that American security would not be endangered. Its critics, reminding the world that two of the 19 attackers on 9/11 were from the UAE, responded with wounding suggestions about the federation's role in the war against terror. This was probably the first time most Americans had heard about Dubai and the UAE. DP World responded by deciding to put the US ports up for sale.

Dubai, the vanguard of the New Gulf, is now a city of about 1.4 million people, a figure forecast to rise to more than four million by 2020. But its origins are humble and it is barely mentioned in the region's sparse early records.

Some people believe the town's name is derived either from the word *dhub*, the Arabic term for the spiny tailed agama (lizard), or from another Arabic word that means 'land devastated by locusts'. However, Sheikh Mohammed's website provides several other theories as to how Dubai was named.

One theory is that the word is a combination of the Farsi words for 'two' and 'brothers', referring to Deira and Bur Dubai. Others believe Dubai was named by people who considered its souk a smaller version of a thriving market in Dibba on the East Coast, which was a major regional centre before the coming of Islam. Yet another possibility is that the name came from a word meaning 'money' – people from Dubai were commonly believed to have money because it was a prosperous trading centre. What is also of interest is that there's another town named Dubai in Saudi Arabia.

At the start of the 19th century, Dubai occupied what is now Shindagha with a subsidiary settlement across the creek in Deira. It then had a population that could be numbered in the hundreds. At that time, Dubai Creek was a largely uninvolved spectator in rivalries between the Al Nahyan of Abu Dhabi, the sultan of Muscat, tribes owing allegiance to the Al Saud of central Arabia and the Al Qassimi. The British concluded a preliminary agreement at the end of 1819 with its emir, Sheikh Mohammed bin Hazza, who was recognized as ruler of both sides of the creek. Dubai subsequently was a signatory to the January 1820 General Treaty of Peace.

Sheikh Mohammed bin Hazza remained the headman of Dubai until 1833 when about 800 people of the Al Bu Falasah, led by Ubaid bin Said and Maktoum bin Buti, settled on the south coast of Dubai Creek. Outnumbering the original residents, the newcomers became the dominant force. Maktoum outlived his partner and became Dubai's paramount sheikh. He was to rule until his death in 1852, becoming the founding father of the Al Maktoum dynasty. A fort, built around 1800, and a mosque formed the centre of the Al Maktoum settlement. The Al Maktoum domain extended into the hinterland and encompassed Khawaneej, Awir and the Hatta enclave adjacent to the land of the sultan of Muscat. The original Maritime Truce of 1835 was renewed several times and then converted into a 10-year treaty in June 1843. The Al Maktoum were recognized by the British for the first time as sovereign rulers in the Treaty of Perpetual Maritime Peace of 1853.

Dubai benefited from the smooth transfer of power from Sheikh Maktoum to his brother Sheikh Saeed and to his son Sheikh Hasher in 1859. Sheikh Hasher's death in 1886 created a void that was filled for the first and last time in Dubai history after an internecine power struggle. His elder son Sheikh Maktoum and his brother, Sheikh Rashid, fell out and divided the Dubai community. In the end, Sheikh Rashid emerged as emir, though supporters of Sheikh Maktoum were to dispute his right to rule.

Sheikh Rashid's legacy was principally diplomatic. He supported Sheikh Zayed of Abu Dhabi in a tribal war in the interior in 1891. In March 1892, he signed the exclusive agreement with Britain. Sheikh Rashid died in 1894 and was succeeded by Sheikh Maktoum bin Hasher who was endorsed by the Dubai *majlis*, an informal grouping of leading local figures that had played a key role in the development of the emirate. There were mutterings of discontent from two sons of the late ruler Sheikh Rashid: Sheikh Butti and Sheikh Saeed. They were arrested and exiled to Sharjah for planning to replace the new ruler.

### Dubai becomes a free port

Sheikh Maktoum's rule was to witness a radical new development. On the Persian side of the Gulf, Lingah had been, for more than a century, the principal Al Qassimi port in the lower Gulf. Arab families had dominated the area at least since the 1720s. The Persian government in the second half of the 19th century sought to extinguish its independence. In 1887, Tehran took control by force and replaced Arabs in positions of responsibility with Persian officials. New taxes were imposed on Lingah's traders, eliminating the port's competitive advantage and it started to decline.

In 1902, the Persian government delegated Lingah's administration to Belgian officials who announced new regulations. A five per cent tax was imposed on all goods passing through the port. Sheikh Maktoum had the previous year declared Dubai a free port, abolished all tariffs and started to lure Lingah's traders. People crossed the Gulf to settle in Ra's al-Khaimah, Sharjah and elsewhere in the Gulf. But Dubai was the principal beneficiary. Some date the start of Dubai's rise to the arrival of the Persian-speaking Sunni Muslims, known throughout Arabia as Huwala Arabs.

In 1902, a steam-powered ship from India bypassed Lingah and sailed directly to Dubai. Within two decades of the free-trade initiative, the population of Dubai had doubled to 20,000 people. The twin ports of Dubai and Deira were by then the liveliest trading and pearling centres on the coast of what is now the UAE. The migrants included merchants from the Bastak district of the Fars province. The part of Dubai where they settled was as a consequence named Bastakiya. Their lasting contribution is houses with high windtowers designed to capture breezes and reduce humidity within – an early, natural form of air conditioning.

Sheikh Maktoum was also witness to the first flourish of 20th century British ambition in Arabia. Travelling by horseback to Sharjah on the morning of November 21, 1903, he boarded a Royal Navy sloop carrying Lord Curzon, viceroy of India and the most senior British government representative to have entered the Gulf at that point. Dubai's ruler heard Curzon deliver a promise that Britain would continue to protect the area provided local rulers governed with justice and respected the rights of foreign traders. Since most Dubai merchants were subjects of British India, this was as much a statement of self-interest as of principle.

Sheikh Maktoum died in 1908 and was succeeded by his cousin, Sheikh Butti bin Suhail. During his rule, the key events were a storm which wrecked pearling vessels and a raid on Shindagha by British forces trying to prevent weapon smuggling in which 37 Dubaians and four British sailors died.

### The rule of Sheikh Saeed

Sheikh Butti bin Suhail died in 1912. His successor was Sheikh Saeed, son of Sheikh Maktoum. Sheikh Saeed's long rule, which lasted until 1958, bridged the gap from the Arabian past of poverty, smuggling and tribal rivalries to the rise of the modern Gulf economy.

Born in 1878, he was a simple man, uncomfortable with high office, who loved hunting and other pastoral activities. Deeply religious, Sheikh Saeed had to cope with a world changing at an unprecedented pace. Relations with Sharjah deteriorated, partly caused by commercial rivalry. Dubai was sucked into the internecine conflict that swept Abu Dhabi in the 1920s. There were concerns about the ambitions of the Al Saud.

In 1927, the Persian government opened a customs post on Henjam

Island that had long been settled by the Bani Yas. The island's ruler, Sheikh Ahmed, who was also Sheikh Saeed's father-in-law, was expelled from the island in May 1928. The following month, Persian troops landed on the Greater Tunb Island, also settled for generations by Arabs and ruled by the Al Qassimi family, and established a customs post.

A boat sailing from Dubai was intercepted and its passengers taken to Lingah where they were imprisoned and robbed. The passengers were eventually freed and compensated for their losses, but the affair created an impression of weakness and challenged the credibility of the British, Dubai's Gulf guardian. A further challenge was the collapse of pearling. The distress was compounded by world depression.

Despite a well-established business community, Dubai by the end of the 1930s still had no mains water and practically no healthcare services. The depression hit the Persian side of the Gulf even harder and thousands moved from Bushire to Dubai in 1934 alone. The population influx, together with the unsettled economic and political conditions in the 1930s, accelerated social change. New ideas and discontent with the status quo produced a reform movement that pressed for political modernization including the granting of power to Sheikh Saeed's *majlis*.

Confrontation was triggered by the activities of Sheikh Butti and Sheikh Saeed, who had been expelled to Sharjah in 1894 but had moved to Deira during the rule of Sheikh Butti bin Suhail. The discontent they fostered found an echo in the aspirations of a reform movement that had already latched on to the failure of the British government to act against Iran following its seizure of the Greater Tunb Island.

Sheikh Rashid, Sheikh Saeed's son through Sheikha Hessa bint Al Murr, was born in 1912. He started to act on behalf of his father when he was barely out of his teens and played an increasingly significant role in the dramas that developed in the 1930s.

Discontent among sections of the Dubai population raised fears of rebellion. In October 1934 Sheikh Saeed, with British support, reasserted his control by demanding oaths of loyalty from all the town's leading figures. A new crisis developed in 1938. In July, news reached Dubai that Kuwait's ruler had recognized a legislative council. Sheikh Saeed's critics demanded an equivalent concession. An agreement was brokered by Britain and signed on October 20, 1938. It established an elected *majlis* with Sheikh Saeed as its president. The *majlis* was ineffective and charged with corruption and incompetence. Attempts to take more control over government were resented.

On March 29, 1939, the day Sheikh Rashid married Sheikha Latifa bint Hamdan Al Nahyan, Sheikh Saeed dissolved the *majlis*. Bedouins attending the wedding seized *majlis* members. There was little resistance but at least one death. *Majlis* members that did not accept the new arrangements were expelled to Sharjah where some continued to plot against Sheikh Saeed.

The *majlis* rebels' final flourish came in January 1940 when they attacked Sheikh Rashid and his retainers near Deira. The following week, there was a stand-off between the two sides near Khan on the Sharjah side of the border. There were occasional exchanges of shots and cannonballs were fired from ancient cannons only to be gathered up and fired back. The fighting continued until an agreement was reached with the rebels in March 1940 under the mediation of the rulers of Umm al-Qaiwain, Ajman and Ra's al-Khaimah. The leaders of the *majlis* movement were paid off and returned to exile.

Despite depression and political divisions, Dubai continued to enter the modern age. The first car was imported into Dubai in 1930. Sheikh Saeed bought his first vehicle in 1932 and Sheikh Rashid, the effective governor of Dubai, took to driving the second official car around Dubai from 1934. Dubai gave Britain permission in 1937 to build an airfield to serve as a stopover for Imperial Airways that had in 1932 launched the first long-distance, scheduled airline service to connect the UK with India. The UK opted instead to build an airstrip in Sharjah where an RAF base was created in 1939. Dubai continued to woo Imperial. In 1940, the airline reached an agreement for its flying boats to land in the creek.

Saeed was the first ruler of the Trucial Coast to sign an oil-concession agreement, striking a deal with Petroleum Concessions Limited (PCL), the subsidiary of the London-based consortium IPC, in 1935. This was ratified in 1937. Exploration started soon after but with no success until 1964. The Second World War hit the Gulf economy. Dubai emerged as the region's most active trading centre. It was the site of the region's first post office, which opened during the early stages of the war.

BBME opened its first Arabian branch in Deira in October 1946. It moved to a site on the Bur Dubai side of the creek in 1953. The Trucial States Council held its first meeting in Dubai in 1952. In 1954, London upgraded its political presence in what is now the UAE to political-agency status, equivalent to an embassy, and this was sited in Dubai. In 1956, the first five-year development plan in the Trucial States was launched and managed through the agency. Dubai was selected in 1965 to be the site of the headquarters of the Trucial States Development Office.

One of the elements driving the Dubai economy in the 1950s was gold trade with India. This was often referred to as smuggling since Dubai's gold merchants avoided paying customs duty to the Indian authorities. "Although many referred to Dubai as the centre for gold-smuggling, this was incorrect, for the trade did not contravene Dubai laws," BBME chief executive in the UAE, Derrick Patterson, wrote in

*MEED* in 1986. "It was in fact genuine re-export business." BBME played a role in the adoption in the late 1950s of the Gulf rupee, a version of the Indian currency that was not legal tender in India itself but circulated widely in the Gulf.

## The rule of Sheikh Rashid

After a period of ill-health, Sheikh Saeed died on September 10, 1958. His son, Sheikh Rashid, immediately became ruler. At the time, Dubai's population was no more than 30,000 people, including foreigners. Shrewd and accessible, Sheikh Rashid pushed for the commercial development of Dubai when other Gulf rulers were trying to keep out the modern world.

Sir James Craig, British political agent in Dubai in the 1960s, describes Sheikh Rashid as the most intelligent man he's ever met. His boldest early initiative was dredging Dubai Creek to reverse the build-up of silt that threatened to kill off the shipping business. Gray Mackenzie & Company, the British imperial trading firm, had erected a cargo crane in Dubai port in 1951 and trans-shipment to other parts of the Gulf was flourishing. Paying for the project entailed borrowing £500,000. The long-term results were to be spectacularly positive. Completed between the end of 1958 and the summer of 1959, the dredging established Dubai as the best port in the region.

Sheikh Rashid over time effectively introduced many of the changes demanded by the *majlis* movement, even appointing some of its vocal supporters to posts of responsibility. Among his first steps was to set up a municipal council and establish a police force to replace the ruler's guards. Mahdi Al Tajir, a government official seconded from Bahrain who was later appointed UAE ambassador to the UK, was made head of customs. Ahmed bin Sulayem was made his deputy.

The centre of Dubai's decision-making was Sheikh Rashid's *majlis*, an informal grouping of nationals, Indians and Europeans who met almost nightly to brainstorm. But the ruler made the big decisions. Establishing Dubai as a regional aviation centre was an early preoccupation. Gold-bullion flights arrived in Dubai weekly and would land on a compacted sand-and-salt road in Deira. But Sheikh Rashid wanted more. In 1959, he appointed International Aeradio to build a landing strip and an air-traffic control system. British assent to a permanent airfield was eventually granted. Studies suggested it should be built near Jebel Ali, but it was decided to locate the airport in Qusais. The airfield was opened on September 30, 1960, initially only being served by Bahrain-based Gulf Air. BOAC started weekly return flights connecting London and Dubai in 1964.

The first bridge across the creek was built with financial assistance from the ruler of Qatar, Sheikh Ali Al Thani, whose son Sheikh Ahmed married Sheikha Mariam, Sheikh Rashid's eldest daughter, in 1958. The Dubai Electricity Company was floated to finance a power-generation programme. A comprehensive town plan was completed in 1965. The Dubai police, established in 1956, was strengthened. By 1975, it had a complement of 1,500 officers and men. The BBME's Dubai monopoly was broken in 1963 with the opening of the National Bank of Dubai, a joint venture with the National Bank of Kuwait. A second foreign bank, the First National City Bank of New York, opened its doors in January 1964.

The land for a Roman Catholic mission to serve the growing number of Catholics living and working in Dubai was donated in 1966. Sheikh Rashid himself laid the foundation stone for what was to become St Mary's Church. Sheikh Rashid commissioned the construction of a new port outside the creek with 16 berths, far larger than many believed to be necessary. Port Rashid was opened on October 5, 1971. The 1960s construction boom created some of the best-known names in Dubai business, including the Al Naboodah, Dutco, Lootah and Khansaheb construction companies.

**Oil in Dubai**

Frustrated by the failure of the IPC consortium to find oil, Dubai in 1954 granted CFP, later TOTAL, and the Spanish Petroleum Company (Hispanoil) an offshore concession which they worked through the Dubai Marine Areas (Duma) consortium. Continental Oil Company (Conoco) of the US bought the PCL onshore concession in 1963 and formed the Dubai Petroleum Company (DPC) that acquired 50 per cent of Duma. Oil was discovered in the offshore Fateh Field in 1966 and production started at the end of 1969. In 1970, the South-West Fateh Field was discovered. Subsequently, two further offshore finds, named the Falah and Rashid fields, were made. Much of the engineering work on onshore and offshore facilities was done by Chicago Bridge & Iron Company of the US on a strip of beach south of Jumeirah that was as a result called Chicago Beach. Today, the engineering yard has gone and has been replaced by the Burj Al Arab and the Jumeirah Beach hotels.

Dubai was the first Arab Gulf state to nationalize oil and gas operations. A deal signed in July 1975 called for a payment of US$110 million in compensation to Conoco, CFP and Hispanoil. A 60 per cent share in the restructured DPC was acquired by the Dubai government and full nationalization was completed in 2006. The only onshore deposit is the Margham Field, originally discovered by Arco, which lies in the desert south of the Dubai–Hatta highway. It is now owned by the Dubai Government.

Dubai's oil production has been in decline since hitting a peak of

400,000 b/d in 1990 and now could be less than 200,000 b/d. Some say it could be as low as 100,000 b/d. This is a rate that will exhaust proven reserves in about 20 years. Also in 1990, Dubai created the Dubai Natural Gas Company (Dugas) which worked in partnership with Scimitar Oil to process gas from its offshore oil fields. Today, Dugas gas is piped to Dubai Aluminium (Dubal) and is used to fuel adjacent electric power and desalination plants. A gas terminal at Jebel Ali Port was opened in 1980. Rising demand made it inevitable that other sources would have to be found and, in May 2005, Dubai signed up for Dolphin Energy gas supplied from Qatar.

### Dubai joins the federation and flourishes

When news came in early 1968 that Britain was going to withdraw from the Gulf by 1971, logic suggested Dubai should throw in its lot with its richer and more conservative southern neighbour. The journey to federation would be a long and demanding one that eventually reached its conclusion with the establishment of the UAE.

The economic atmosphere in the Gulf was transformed two years later by OPEC's actions that raised the price of crude oil by more than 300 per cent between the summer of 1973 and the spring of 1974. The influx of funds led to a boom in Dubai and other Arabian oil-exporting states. Sheikh Rashid dreamed bigger dreams than anyone else. The story is told that he held a meeting at dawn in 1972 at the top of Jebel Ali, a hill about 60 m high that lies more than 30 km from the centre of Dubai. Pointing to the coast below the *jebel*, Sheikh Rashid said: "Down there . . . I want to build a port." He envisaged Jebel Ali would be big enough to accommodate aircraft carriers. Work began in the summer of 1976. The budget was fixed at more than US$750 million, equivalent to at least US$4 billion in 2007 values. The first phase comprising 65 berths was finished in 1983.

Only weeks after announcing Jebel Ali Port, Sheikh Rashid announced plans to build Dubai Drydocks near Port Rashid. Plans to grant the US Navy limited basing rights in Dubai ports were stymied by the federal government in 1978. Sheikh Rashid cast around for some productive use for Jebel Ali and had another brainwave. He created a free zone around the harbour in which the rules that applied to businesses operating in the UAE would not operate. Provided a business was selling goods outside the UAE, foreigners were free of the federal requirement that their operations should have majority local-ownership.

The zone was incorporated as the Jebel Ali Free Zone Authority in January 1985. The first success story was in textiles. Indian manufacturers were bumping up against their US export quotas under the multifibre agreement, an import-control system established in the 1970s. They spotted an opportunity to invest in textile plants in Jebel Ali and export to the US from the UAE, which had no quota under the agreement. By the late 1980s, Jebel Ali was one of the region's biggest textile manufacturing centres.

Dubai Cable Company (Ducab) was founded in 1977 on a site south of Jebel Ali and it opened a plant in Abu Dhabi earlier this decade. Dubal, which occupies a site adjacent to Jebel Ali, started operating in 1979. The World Trade Centre was opened in 1980 and was for years Arabia's tallest building.

Iraq's invasion of Iran in September 1980 provided a massive boost to the Dubai economy. With the major ports of the north Gulf either knocked out or seen as serious insurance risks, shipping lines used Dubai as a trans-shipment centre. Large vessels would dock, transfer their cargoes to smaller local ships and leave the Gulf quickly to save insurance premiums. The Kuwait Crisis of 1990–91 created a fresh opportunity. All the states of the GCC joined the anti-Saddam coalition. They opened up the southern Gulf to unrestricted operations by the navies of the coalition. Jebel Ali came into its own. The big money spinners were the aircraft carriers. When they docked in Jebel Ali for repairs, provisions and rest and recreation for their crews, millions of dollars were pumped into the local economy.

Sheikh Rashid was struck down with a stroke in May 1981 and never fully recovered. The death of his wife Latifa in May 1983 was a further crushing blow. Increasingly, government duties were transferred to his sons. Sheikh Rashid died aged 78 on October 7, 1990. He was succeeded by Sheikh Maktoum bin Rashid, his eldest son who ruled until his death on January 4, 2006.

**Building new Dubai**
Dubai is the centre of one of the world's great construction booms. At the latest count, there were about US$200 billion worth of projects under way or planned across the emirate. There are several motivations for the remarkable building programme. The first is the need to develop an alternative to the dwindling oil output. The answer is to promote Dubai as a world service centre, attracting income by providing a base for businesses operating in the region and beyond.

Its twin ports are the cornerstones of the economy. In 2006, they handled more than seven million containers, more than any other Middle East port. DP World, which manages Port Rashid and Jebel Ali, has built up an international portfolio of port-management contracts and bought P&O in 2006.

Aviation is the second pillar of Dubai's modern economy. By the start of the 1980s, Dubai was the most profitable destination for Gulf Air, the Manama-based airline then owned by Abu Dhabi, Bahrain, Oman and Qatar. But its open-skies policy was challenged by the airline that persistently called for protection for itself and restrictions on other carriers. Late in 1984, Gulf Air published its schedules for the following year. They called for a reduction in the number of flights into Dubai. On March 25, 1985, the new schedules went into effect. The number of Gulf Air flights to Dubai was cut by 84 a week to 39.

A fortnight later, Sheikh Mohammed bin Rashid approved the creation of a new airline and pledged the US$10 million needed to set it up. In May, UAE president Sheikh Zayed approved Dubai's plans. Emirates was founded with Maurice Flanagan, previously head of Dubai National Air Travel Agency (DNATA) and a former BA executive, as chief executive and Sheikh Ahmed bin Saeed Al Maktoum as chairman. The first two Emirates aircraft were an Airbus A300 B4 and a Boeing 737, both on wet lease; the first flight left Dubai bound for Karachi in October 1985. Direct flights to the UK and Germany began in 1987, the year Emirates received its first new aircraft. It is now one of the world's fastest-growing international airlines and Flanagan forecasts it could be carrying more than 150 million passengers by 2025. Dubai's Department of Civil Aviation forecasts that the number passing through the airport will rise to almost 70 million people in 2012 and will increase to as much as 190 million passengers a year when combined with Al Maktoum International Airport. Tourism is rising. Some seven million people are estimated to have visited Dubai in 2006. The target is to have 15 million tourists within a decade.

A second factor behind the project boom is the fact that Dubai has only 65 km of coast, a small ratio to its landmass. To compensate, the emirate is converting sea into land at a rate that would impress the Dutch. In 2001, plans were unveiled for the construction of an offshore island in the shape of a palm tree that would offer luxury and beachfront accommodation in more than 5,000 homes and thousands of first-class hotel rooms. The Palm Jumeirah's government-owned developer Nakheel ('palm' in Arabic) also offered one of the first opportunities for non-UAE nationals to buy a Dubai home. Prices were pitched low to attract buyers in the nervous months after 9/11 and before the 2003 Iraq War.

The response was unexpectedly enormous. Those who put down the deposit for a house or an apartment to be built on Palm Jumeirah had by 2007 recorded a capital gain up to 300 per cent.

The first Palm residents moved into their new homes in November 2006. Construction of the first big Palm hotel project got under way in 2005 with the start of piling on the Atlantis project, a 2,000-bed hotel and water park complex owned by Kerzner, the international hotel group part-owned by Dubai. In October 2005, New York property developer Donald Trump announced plans to brand a building on The Palm's trunk the Trump Tower. A monorail that will carry up to 5,000 people an hour each way to the Atlantis is to be completed in 2008.

The Palm Jebel Ali, the second Palm island, will have 17 fronds and luxury water homes. In October 2004, Sheikh Mohammed announced a third and much larger Palm island off the Deira coast, near Dubai's border with Sharjah. This will have a 16 km trunk and 41 fronds each up to 4 km long. Its crescent will stretch 20 km. The Palm Deira will have total land area of more than 130 km², roughly the area of Manhattan. The project will not be completed before 2015 at the earliest.

The fourth giant Nakheel offshore project is The World. This involves creating up to 300 islands arranged to represent the map of the world in the sea five kilometres off the Dubai coast. The project will create more than five million square metres of land, including 90,000 m² of beach. It's scheduled to open in 2008, but work might take longer. The islands are being sold to private developers who'll be free to develop their own concepts for housing and other facilities, subject to final approval by Nakheel. In January 2008, Nakheel announced it was planning a new offshore development named The Universe. It will comprise artificial islands in the shape of the sun, the moon and the planets that will be created between The World and the Dubai coast.

Building at speed on land reclaimed from the sea presented unprecedented engineering challenges. Unforeseen construction issues and the soaring price of building materials raised costs. To deal with the increased flow of traffic on the road linking Palm Jumeirah with the coast, the trunk has been widened and the road expanded to five lanes each way. The Palm Jumeirah's peak permanent population is forecast at more than 70,000 people.

Nakheel's largest project is Dubai Waterfront, a 25-year programme for developing the southern part of Dubai that could involve investment of up to US$40 billion. It will create a city for 1.5 million people. Plans call for a canal more than 75 km long that will run from the Waterfront into the desert, head north around the new Al Maktoum International Airport at Jebel Ali and cut back to the coast. Another development with a target population of 1.5 million is planned along the canal's route. The first sales of development plots for Dubai Waterfront's Madinat Al Arab section began at the end of 2005.

To complete a portfolio that probably involves the world's most ambitious construction programme, Nakheel is working on eight onshore schemes. In 2005, it completed the Ibn Battuta Mall, the biggest single-floor shopping centre on earth. It has already sold more than US$15 billion worth of real estate.

The Nakheel schemes complement earlier achievements. In the late 1990s, work was completed on the Burj Al Arab (The Arab Tower), now an iconic symbol of Dubai, which stands on an artificial island off Dubai's Jumeirah Beach. Jumeirah Emirates Towers was opened in

2000 and at the time boasted the tallest building in the Middle East and Europe. This was followed with the opening in 2003 of the Dubai Marina, a gigantic complex built by Emaar Properties, a joint stock company listed on the Dubai Financial Market (DFM). By the end of 2010, up to 200 residential towers will be completed within the marina area. Alongside, 36 tower blocks have been completed in the Jumeirah Beach Residences project, a development by Dubai Properties, another government agency.

Emaar's biggest scheme is the US$20 billion Downtown Dubai project, just south of Jumeirah Emirates Towers. At its heart is Burj Dubai, planned to be the world's tallest building at about 800 m, and Dubai Mall, which for a while will be the world's largest shopping centre. Dubai Properties unveiled in December 2004 plans to build Business Bay, a multi-billion-dollar commercial and residential free-zone district. The development, which will comprise office and residential towers, hotels, gardens and related infrastructure works, will cover an area of six million square metres. It's scheduled for completion in 2012 and involves extending Dubai Creek to Sheikh Zayed Road and from there through Jumeirah to the Gulf.

Dubailand is planned to be the largest integrated leisure project on earth. Larger than Washington DC, it will comprise dozens of schemes including the City of Arabia, the Snowdome indoor skiing complex and Dubai Sports City, a residential district housing 70,000 people that will have four sports stadiums and a golf course at its heart. Sports City will host the International Cricket Council (ICC) and a Manchester United Soccer School. It also aims to attract major sporting events such as Tri Nations rugby matches and the hockey world cup. Dubailand aims to eventually attract up to 100 million visitors a year. Plans were unveiled in May 2006 for the Bawadi project in Dubailand. It will have more than 30 themed hotels.

Dozens of other major projects are planned. To deal with the massive population increase they all entail, Dubai is pressing ahead with one of the world's largest urban-transport development schemes. Work is under way on the elevated Dubai Metro, comprising two initial lines. One will extend from the airport to a point near the Gulf coast, and then pass under the creek before heading south alongside Sheikh Zayed Road to Jebel Ali. Plans to extend the line to Abu Dhabi are under consideration. The trains will be remotely controlled, all the stations will be enclosed and air-conditioned, and there will be a train every 90 seconds. The project will be completed in 2010. Privately-financed monorail lines will connect with the line to serve Dubai International Financial Centre (DIFC), Palm Jumeirah, City of Arabia, Downtown Dubai and Dubai Festival City which overlooks Dubai Creek. There are plans for a high-speed light-rail link that will run from Dubai

International Airport to Palm Jebel Ali and at least one more line.

To cope with an annual 15 per cent increase in cars, more than 100 km of major highways and flyovers were being built in different parts of the emirate in the summer of 2007. Plans call for several new bridges over Dubai Creek, including a replacement for Garhoud Bridge, to complement the recently completed Business Bay Bridge.

Dubai's aviation plans are equally amazing. In January 2005, the Department of Civil Aviation announced it would build an airport complex called Al Maktoum International Airport at Jebel Ali. Up to three runways will be built at first, but there will be room for six. The goal is to have an airport handling up to 120 million passengers and 10 million tonnes of freight every year. A new town called Logistics City with up to 850 towers is planned for the complex. Emirates has been crucial to Dubai's rapid growth. The airline now has almost four times as many daily flights from Dubai to the UK as BA. It was offering 42 direct flights a week to Perth, Melbourne and Sydney at the end of 2006 and had applied for 42 more. Its objective is to offer potential passengers the ability to go anywhere on earth with just one stop.

Anticipating further big growth, Emirates has ordered more than 200 wide-bodied jets, including 66 A380 aircraft. In December 2005, an A380 in Emirates' livery flew over Dubai to launch the city's biennial air show. Reflecting its rising international reputation, Dermot Mannion, the airline's operations manager, was appointed chief executive of Aer Lingus in April 2005. He replaced Willie Walsh, who is now chief executive of BA.

Emirates' hand is behind the success of the annual Dubai Rugby Sevens. In 2006, the three-day competition involved hundreds of games and players. The South African team beat New Zealand in a competitive final in unusual monsoon-type conditions. The Kiwis returned at the end of 2007 to defeat Fiji in a thrilling final. The Sevens and the Dubai World Cup horse race are among a growing number of events that attract tourists from beyond the Gulf region. The Dubai Desert Classic, played at the Emirates Golf Club and won for the second time in 2008 by Tiger Woods, is on the European PGA tour. The Dubai Tennis Championship was won in 2007 by reigning Wimbledon champion Roger Federer, the champion's fourth Dubai title in five years.

Emirates is one of the biggest spenders on sponsorships of sports events. It was the exclusive airline sponsor of the 2006 FIFA World Cup Finals in Germany. It's reported that it cost the airline US$30 million. The scale of Dubai's ambitions was unmistakably declared on October 5, 2004 when Emirates announced it was to invest £100 million in sponsorship to secure the rights over the shirts of the Arsenal football team and to name the new Arsenal ground in north London for a total of 15 years effective 2006. The deal marked the end of the airline's four-year relationship with Chelsea Football Club, now in the hands of Russian billionaire Roman Abramovich. In the biggest Emirates deal so far, the airline announced in April 2006 that it had a US$195 million deal to sponsor FIFA until 2014. In a rare setback for the emirate, a bid by Dubai International Capital (DIC) for Liverpool football club was rejected early in 2007. In December, DIC confirmed it had reopened talks with the club about a possible buy-out.

### The Jumeirah Beach effect

Jumeirah Beach is Arabia's glamour holiday resort, a name to bandy with Bondi, Malibu and Copacabana. It stretches more than 16 km from near Dubai Creek to Jebel Ali. Little more than 20 years ago, Jumeirah was a quiet retreat where people lived in walled fishermen's cottages a few paces from the beach. Today, it is the site of some of the world's most glamorous hotels. The Burj Al Arab, which has an atrium big enough to accommodate the Eiffel Tower, sits on its own island connected by bridge to the shore. It is for the moment Dubai's definitive landmark. Famously, a helipad near its summit was converted into a tennis court where Andre Agassi and Roger Federer played a couple of games in early 2005 to promote the Dubai Tennis Championship.

Onshore is the Jumeirah Beach Hotel. Next door is the Wild Wadi water park. On an adjacent site is Madinat Jumeirah, a themed complex comprising two hotels, a shopping centre designed in traditional souk style, a conference centre and some 40 restaurants. A canal used by *abras*, traditional Dubai water taxis, threads through the development and connects with Al Qasr hotel and the Masayaf villa network.

Continuing further south, you come to the homes of leading sheikhs. Then comes the Royal Mirage complex run by Kerzner International, the Mina Seyahi, the Dubai Marina, the Dubai International Marine Club, the Metropolitan, the Habtoor Grand, the Royal Meridien, the Ritz Carlton, the Oasis, the Hilton and the Sheraton. The Grosvenor House, which is owned by Emirates chairman Sheikh Ahmed bin Saeed Al Maktoum, will soon have a matching twin. Most of the gaps between hotels are being closed off as in-fill developments extend the brick and concrete sea front to Jebel Ali.

The hotel boom in Dubai has given birth to a new international hotel-management company in the form of Jumeirah. It manages Jumeirah Emirates Towers, Burj Al Arab, the Jumeirah Beach Hotel, Jumeirah Beach Club Resort & Spa, Madinat Jumeirah and the Bab Al Shams Desert Resort & Spa opened in 2004. The company's fast growing international portfolio includes the Jumeirah Carlton Towers and the Jumeirah Lowndes Hotel in London and New York's Jumeirah Essex House, bought by the Dubai Investment Group in 2005.

Dubai is now well and truly on the rock circuit. Visiting acts range from golden oldies such as Pink Floyd and Cliff Richard to contemporary superstars of the calibre of Robbie Williams, Shakira and Aerosmith . . . with just about every act in between. Of course, all the top Arab stars appear regularly in Dubai, while classical music, opera, ballet and musicals are also performed. In fact, all of The Three Tenors have sung in Dubai but only as individuals. Andrea Bocelli, the blind Italian tenor, thrilled the DIFC's first anniversary party.

Jim Davidson, the British comedian, is now living permanently in Dubai. British comics Frank Carson and Ronnie Corbett performed at the city's first comedy week in November 2005. British radio personality Chris Tarrant of *Who Wants to be a Millionaire?* and Tim Rice, lyricist for Andrew Lloyd-Webber musicals, came to play in a charity cricket match for the Lord's Taverner's team. Michael Jackson visited for a week. Benazir Bhutto lived in exile in the city prior to her murder in Pakistan in December 2007 and was joined by her husband in early 2005 after his release from a Pakistani prison.

Soccer legends Pele, Bobby Charlton, and Franz Beckenbauer have attended the annual Soccerex exhibition. In November 2005, Manchester United manager Alex Ferguson arrived for the opening of Dubai's Manchester United Soccer School. European teams are increasingly using Dubai as a mid-season training and recreation centre while English football stars, including David Beckham, are said to have bought villas on The Palm Jumeirah. And, in January 2006, England football coach Sven-Goran Ericsson was shamed when *The News of the World*, the British Sunday tabloid, published an embarrassing report about what he said in Dubai to one of its reporters posing as a rich Arab businessman.

The growing cast of celebrity visitors and residents find much to enjoy, including Dubai's growing reputation for top-class dining inspired by star chefs such as Gordon Ramsay and Michel Roux.

Rising affluence inevitably brings with it temptation. The city was shocked in April 2007 when an armed gang raided a shop in the up-market Wafi City shopping mall and escaped with US$ 2 million worth of jewellery. There have also been other, less dramatic, incidents. Like other major cities, Dubai has prostitutes, although a government clamp-down is reducing their numbers. And people die in Dubai road accidents at an unacceptably high rate. Nevertheless, residents almost entirely live free from fear of crime. A survey by the Dubai police in the summer of 2004 of more than 2,000 people living in Dubai found almost 85 per cent of them felt safe.

### The Al Maktoum family tree

| | |
|---|---|
| Maktoum bin Buti ... ... ... ... ... ... ... ... ... ... ... ... | 1833–1852 |
| Saeed bin Buti ... ... ... ... ... ... ... ... ... ... ... ... ... | 1852–1859 |

| | |
|---|---|
| Hasher bin Maktoum ... ... ... ... ... ... ... ... ... ... ... | 1859–1886 |
| Rashid bin Maktoum ... ... ... ... ... ... ... ... ... ... ... | 1886–1894 |
| Maktoum bin Hasher ... ... ... ... ... ... ... ... ... ... ... | 1894–1906 |
| Butti bin Suhail .. ... ... ... ... ... ... ... ... ... ... ... | 1906–1912 |
| Saeed bin Maktoum . ... ... ... ... ... ... ... ... ... ... ... | 1912–1958 |
| Rashid bin Saeed ... ... ... ... ... ... ... ... ... ... ... | 1958–1990 |
| Maktoum bin Rashid ... ... ... ... ... ... ... ... ... ... ... | 1990–2006 |
| Mohammed bin Rashid . ... ... ... ... ... ... ... ... ... ... | 2006– |

Source: *Father of Dubai: Sheikh Rashid bin Saeed Al Maktoum*, Media Prima, London, 1999.

### The Al Qassimi dynasty (Al Qawasim)

There's a pleasing break in the built-up area that extends south from Dubai to the northern limits of Umm al-Qaiwain. Beyond, there's a glimpse of the mangroves and sandflats that once stretched along the length of the UAE's Gulf coast. This is a journey in time as well as space, through a landscape that was settled more than 7,000 years ago.

Ra's al-Khaimah is the most northerly part of the UAE. It encompasses little more than half the area of greater London and had a population, including foreigners, at the end of 2007 of about 200,000. The people of Ra's al-Khaimah are admired for their open-mindedness and appetite for work. But the emirate, with its splendid mountain hinterland, is one of the poorest of the seven that make up the UAE. This is quickly changing.

Sheikh Saud bin Saqr Al Qassimi, crown prince and deputy ruler of the emirate, replaced his elder brother Khaled as heir to his father, Sheikh Saqr, in April 2003. Disrupting the pattern in any Gulf state is a highly sensitive issue. Sheikh Saud prefers to look forward, but there are clues about why it happened in his diagnosis of the problems Ra's al-Khaimah faces. "I had felt that Ra's al-Khaimah had been left behind," he said in an interview with *MEED* in 2004. "We were not in our opinion harnessing our potential."

Sheikh Saud, born in 1954 and the ruler's fourth son, speaks English fluently and went to university in the US. On his return in 1979, he was appointed chief of the ruler's court and was made chairman of Ra's al-Khaimah municipal council in 1986. His aim is to turn Ra's al-Khaimah into a growth economy.

"We would like our men and women working in Dubai to return to Ra's al-Khaimah." Sheikh Saud said. "This emirate has a wonderful history and a proud people. I want that kind of history reflected in the future so it can be a vibrant member of the federation and one that co-operates in the economic miracle that's taking place in the UAE."

Sheikh Saud is a member of the rising generation of leaders that's

building the New Gulf, but for whom the past still matters. The growing collaboration among emirates is conditioned by a history of rivalry.
The partnership between the Al Maktoum and the Al Nahyan is the
cornerstone of the modern UAE. But, in many respects, the authors of
the idea of a strong independent state in south-eastern Arabia were the
Al Qassimi of Ra's al-Khaimah and Sharjah.

### The origins of Ra's al-Khaimah

For 1,000 years after the coming of Islam, Julfar on the northern Gulf
coast of what is now the UAE was the region's busiest port. A Muslim
fleet sailed from the town to attack the Persian Empire in 637. It was
the starting point for invasions in 696 and 750 to suppress the Ibadhi
movement, a segment of the Kharijites who settled in the Hajar Mountains. The Persians landed in 972 and stayed for some time. But
Julfar's reputation was as a trading centre that served as a link in the
chain of commerce connecting the Mediterranean, Mesopotamia and
China. In the 15th century, it fell under the control of the kingdom of
Hormuz. When the Portuguese forced Hormuz into submission at the
start of the 16th century, Julfar's wealth was a source of the power the
newcomers enjoyed. Expelled from Persia in 1622, the Portuguese
temporarily moved their base to the town and built a fort. They were
displaced by the returning Persians, who built a port nearby. Julfar
then disappears from the records.

Archaeologists believe the town was sited north of Ra's al-Khaimah
creek. The area has produced finds dating back to before the rise of
Islam. Julfar's disappearance may be connected with the rise of Ra's al-
Khaimah which first gets a mention at the end of the 15th century.

The Al Qassimi started to emerge as a force in the lower Gulf at the
start of the 18th century. They are a group rather than a tribe whose
origins are unclear but it appears they started as a small clan that
managed to impose itself over other tribes on both sides of the waterway. Their sway originally extended eastwards, across the Hajar Mountains, to the UAE's east coast, where the Al Sharqiyin (people of the
east) are the dominant tribe in the emirate of Fujairah. It was the last
of the seven emirates to be formally recognised by the British, in 1952.

Another tribe that was formerly under Al Qassimi suzerainty is the
Al Ali, whose dominant Al Mulla section provides Umm al-Qaiwain's
ruling family.

Ra's al-Khaimah's creek was the principal Arabian base for the Al
Qassimi family. In 1747, they helped the governor of Hormuz in his
campaign against the Persians. In the ensuing war, the Al Qassimi
captured Lingah, Luft and Qeshm Island on the Persian side of the
Gulf. This marks the start of a 70-year period in which the Al Qassimi
challenged Muscat as the principal local power in south-east Arabia.

They also came into conflict with the British East India Company that was developing a trade route between India and the Gulf. The British view was that the Al Qassimi were pirates and smugglers. The Al Qassimi asserted they were merchants being squeezed out by foreigners and their local clients and that, in any case, as the local rulers they had a right to protect their own interests in adjacent waters.

The first recorded clash with the East India Company was in 1727 when the Al Qassimi established a trading post on Qeshm Island on the Persian side of the Gulf. Competition between the Al Qassimi and the partnership between the East India Company and Muscat intensified as the 18th century closed. In 1797 a British ship anchored in Bushire was attacked by Al Qassimi dhows. The Al Qassimi ruler, Sheikh Saqr bin Rashid, blamed renegades and offered compensation.

British concerns increased with the rise of the Al Saud who formed an alliance with the Al Qassimi. Sheikh Saqr died in 1803 and was succeeded by his son Sheikh Sultan. In another incident that outraged the British, two of their ships were captured by Al Qassimi sailors. One was immediately released. The second was held for a year. The Al Qassimi and the British settled their differences in an agreement that was breached in 1808 when yet another British ship, the *Minerva*, was taken and the wife of one of the vessel's officers ransomed.

While this drama was developing, Sheikh Sultan was deposed by the Al Saud and imprisoned. The Al Qassimi were leaderless at a critical moment. In 1809, a British expeditionary force of 1,400 soldiers, supported by Muscat, which had signed a friendship treaty with Britain nine years earlier, sailed to Ra's al-Khaimah. The *Minerva* was recaptured, the town seized and about 50 ships destroyed. The force then sailed across the Gulf to destroy Al Qassimi ships in Lingah and Qeshm.

The Al Qassimi quickly recovered and rebuilt their dhows. In 1814, Muscat's Sayyid Said occupied Ra's al-Khaimah on the pretext of restoring Sheikh Sultan. He was rebuffed and Ra's al-Khaimah was recovered by Sultan's nephew, Sheikh Hassan bin Rahmah, who resumed the Al Qassimi challenge.

After an attempt at diplomacy, Britain decided to break Al Qassimi seapower for good. In 1818, an Egyptian army captured Diriyah, in Central Arabia, and imprisoned the Al Saud leaders, stripping the Al Qassimi of their key ally. On July 10, 1819, the Indian presidency council, which managed British interests in India, approved a final attack. A naval expedition, again supported by Muscat, was dispatched under Major General Sir William Grant Keir. Ra's al-Khaimah was bombarded from 3–9 December. Keir then led his troops into the town and took the surrender of Sheikh Hassan bin Rahmah.

The British shelled the neighbouring town of Rams as well as a fort at Dhayah and destroyed vessels at anchor along the coast. Keir returned to Ra's al-Khaimah and destroyed about 200 Al Qassimi dhows. The town was held until the summer of 1820 and then wrecked.

Having broken the Al Qassimi fleet, Britain acted to define the peace. Keir appointed Captain Perronnet Thomson, who could speak Arabic, as a liaison officer. Thomson drafted the 1820 General Treaty of Peace imposed on all sheikhs of the area now comprising the UAE. But British rights under the treaty only encompassed the sea. Capitalizing on the power vacuum on land, Sheikh Sultan recovered control of Ra's al-Khaimah and was recognized as the ruler of all Al Qassimi territories by the British in 1823. He was to rule for 43 years.

Sheikh Sultan recovered Dibba, Khor Fakkan and Kalba from Muscat in 1832. A compromise with Sayyid Said of Muscat in 1850 made the Al Qassimi masters of all territory north of a line running from Sharjah to Kalba on the Gulf of Oman, with the exception of Shaam, on the Gulf coast of the Musandam Peninsula, and Dibba. The Al Qassimi ruler had no fixed base but moved regularly between his lands in Ra's al-Khaimah, Sharjah and Qeshm Island in what is now Iran.

One consequence of having an itinerant ruler was Ra's al-Khaimah's growing separation from Sharjah. After decades of divisions within the Al Qassimi, their domains were finally split into two. Sheikh Sultan bin Salim of Ra's al-Khaimah was recognized by the British as an independent ruler in 1921. The borders of his emirate were defined to encompass a single slab of land that extended east from the Gulf coast to the Hajar Mountains watershed plus several Gulf islands, including the Greater and Lesser Tunbs. In Sharjah, Sheikh Sultan bin Saqr seized power in 1924 and was recognized by Britain as chief of the emirate. He was to rule Sharjah until his death in 1951.

### Oil and the economy

After the First World War, thoughts turned to oil. In 1922, Ra's al-Khaimah's ruler, Sheikh Sultan bin Salim, accepted together with all the rulers of Trucial Oman a British request that oil concessions should be awarded only to British firms. One was granted in 1938 to Petroleum Development (Trucial Coast), a division of the Petroleum Concessions Limited subsidiary of IPC. Delayed by the Second World War, exploration produced disappointing results.

Some traces were found offshore in 1966 and hopes of a major find soared in 1971 when Union Oil of California reported promising developments in an offshore area. But a major strike eluded them. Gulf Oil of the US discovered the offshore Saleh Field in the early 1980s and production, managed by Gulf Offshore Ra's al-Khaimah Petroleum, started in 1984.

Ra's al-Khaimah produces some condensate, a gas that turns liquid when it comes to the surface, and gas associated with oil output. Since

1994, condensate and gas from Oman's Gulf Bukha Field have been delivered to the emirate. Oman now delivers more than one million cubic metres a day of gas. In September 1997, Ra's al-Khaimah awarded Norway's Atlantis Technology Services and Petroleum Geo Services a permit to explore the offshore Baih Field. Rakgas, set up in 1996, has exclusive hydrocarbon rights to the rest of the emirate. No major finds have been made. In January 2006, an exploratory well drilled by Indago Petroleum was declared unsuccessful. In 2007 RAK Petroleum, a company backed by the Ra's al-Khaimah government and created in 2005, took over Indago's onshore concessions in Ra's al-Khaimah and also bought a 50 per cent share in its onshore concessions in Oman.

Ra's al-Khaimah's principal export is building materials. Limestone has been quarried in the mountains behind Khor Khuwair since 1968. The state-owned Ra's al-Khaimah Rock Company now produces up to 15 million tonnes a year of crushed rock for local cement plants and export and has made the emirate the Gulf's leading cement centre. Most of Ra's al-Khaimah's rock is shipped from Mina Saqr, Ra's al-Khaimah's port. Quarrying feeds downstream building material industries. Ra's al-Khaimah Ceramics Company is the world's largest tile manufacturer. The other large Ra's al-Khaimah manufacturing company is Julphar Gulf Pharmaceuticals which boasts six factories, three of them outside the UAE. A new drive to attract manufacturing companies is now under way. A wave of manufacturing investment is coming and a new industrial zone is being built at Al Ghayl.

Ra's al-Khaimah's new frontier is tourism. The emirate's international airport opened near Digdaga in 1975. About 70,000 passengers arrive each year. RAK Airways was founded in 2006 and its first flights began in November 2007. Hotels have been built and a golf course opened in 2004. Ra's al-Khaimah's geographical isolation from the rest of the UAE was reduced with the completion in 2005 of the final phase of the Emirates Road, making high-speed travel from Dubai possible.

Tourism projects going ahead include the Mina Al Arab resort being developed by RAK Properties. The resort will extend for 15 km along the Gulf coast south of Ra's al-Khaimah town. Others are the Saraya Islands project and the Jebel Jais scheme being developed in partnership with Iranian investors. It includes a 35 km mountain road that will zig-zag up Jebel Jais to 1,500 m where a ski resort is to be opened and the mountain peak covered artificially with snow in winter. RAK Properties' US$800 million Mangrove Island development will occupy a site in Ra's al-Khaimah creek. Rakeen, a real estate firm founded in 2006, and Dubai's Khoie Properties are promoting a range of further large projects. Plans call for the number of first-class hotel rooms to be increased to more than 20,000 in 2012 from 7,000 at the start of 2007. The aim is to double the number of tourists to 2.5 million by then.

Capitalizing on the Gulf tourism boom, investors plan to build a hospitality training institute designed to accommodate up to 15,000 students at any one time in Ras al-Khaimah. In February 2006, investors announced plans to launch suborbital space flights from the emirate.

While these ideas were being unveiled, an extraordinary tale of financial shenanigans was being reported by *7Days*, the Dubai daily tabloid. In an interview with the newspaper on June 21, 2005, Sheikh Mohammed bin Saqr, son of the ruler and the emirate's former justice minister, claimed he and other investors in the emirate had been effectively swindled out of US$20 million.

In 1993, Sheikh Mohammed set up Al Wafa, a finance house aiming to invest in foreign exchange, and raised capital from Ra's al-Khaimah. Al Wafa traded through a Swiss company named Creative Finance, which was based in the canton of Zug. A decade ago, the Zug state prosecutor charged Creative Finance with being part of a criminal organization. Its assets were frozen. According to Sheikh Mohammed, none of the charges have been proven, but the company's assets are still inaccessible. Lawyers representing Al Wafa are suing for US$800 million for lost earnings and damages. Sheikh Mohammed resolutely affirms that he and the other Al Wafa investors are the case's real victims.

## The rise of Sharjah

Sharjah is the largest part of the dismembered Al Qassimi domain. It comprises four territories separated by the land of other emirates. The largest part stretches from Sharjah city to the foothills of the Hajar Mountains. There are three enclaves on the UAE East Coast, Dibba al-Hosn, which is surrounded by Fujairah and Omani territory in the bay of Dibba; Khor Fakkan and its suburbs, north of Fujairah city; and Kalba and Khor Kalba, which lie between Fujairah city and the border with Oman.

Dhaid, a settlement that lies half-way between Sharjah city and Khor Fakkan on the Arabian Sea, is Sharjah's second largest town and an important agricultural area.

The earliest settlements in the emirate could be as many as 250,000 years old, from the Lower Palaeolithic period, on the edge of the mountains, and archaeological finds from the Late Stone Age, Bronze Age, Iron Age and later periods have been made throughout the emirate. Notable sites include those of Mleiha, Jebel al-Buhais, Muwailah and Tell Abraq.

The division of the Al Qassimi lands formalized in 1921 made Sharjah independently significant. In June 1932, Sheikh Sultan bin Saqr, who'd seized power and been recognized by Britain eight years earlier, signed an agreement with Imperial Airways. This led to the construction of the first civilian airport on the coast. An airbase was used by the RAF during the Second World War. Sharjah's significance rose in 1948, the year after Indian and Pakistani independence, when the UK appointed a permanently resident political officer in the emirate to deal with the Trucial Coast. In 1949, Britain and Sharjah reached an agreement allowing the RAF to use the civilian airport and other facilities.

As was the case with the other Trucial States, Sharjah hoped oil would lift it from the poverty caused by the collapse of pearling and the 1930s recession. Petroleum Concessions Limited (PCL), the subsidiary of IPC, signed an exploration agreement in September 1939. Years of exploration produced no results. In 1969, Sheikh Saqr bin Sultan, who'd succeeded his father in 1951, granted a 40-year concession to Crescent Oil Company. Four years later, oil was discovered in the Mubarak Field near Abu Musa Island. The field was made subject to a production-sharing arrangement reached with Iran just before the UAE's creation. Production began in 1974, peaked at 35,000 b/d and now averages about 30,000 b/d. Sharjah has production and drilling rights but shares the Mubarak Field's production and revenue with Iran, which gets 50 per cent, Umm al-Qaiwain with 20 per cent, and Ajman, with 10 per cent. In 1984, Iran ceased transferring its half-share of oil revenues to Sharjah. In 1988, during the undeclared sea war in the Gulf between Iran and the US, Iranian vessels attacked Mubarak facilities, causing their closure for two months.

In November 1980, Amoco (now part of BP), which had won an onshore concession two years earlier, discovered condensate in the Sajaa and Moveyeid fields. Production rose to 35,000 b/d, all of which was exported, and Sharjah's total output hit 62,000 b/d. After Dubai and Sharjah agreed their joint border in 1981, a pipeline was built to supply Sajaa gas to power and desalination plants at Jebel Ali. Sharjah borrowed to finance economic development following the Sajaa find. But its hopes were dashed by the 1986 oil-price slump. The government suspended debt service payments and the borrowings were only regularized in the mid-1990s.

The rise in oil and gas prices in the past five years has encouraged a fresh round of exploration. Crescent Petroleum, which operates the Mubarak Field, began an offshore drilling operation in 1999. Crescent has also announced the start of seismic work in Sharjah's desert interior. The first phase of a project to supply natural gas to residences and commercial and industrial premises began in March 1999. Sharjah will be the first Gulf state with piped domestic gas supplies.

### The rule of Sheikh Sultan
Sheikh Saqr bin Sultan, who broke IPC's monopoly over Sharjah oil, succeeded his father at the age of 25 and was a consistent thorn in Bri-

tain's flesh. His relations with the ruler of neighbouring Dubai, Sheikh Rashid, were also poor.

In 1965, he proposed opening an Arab League office, a suggestion that was treated as unfriendly by Britain in view of its worries about Egyptian dominance of the body.

This provoked an offer from King Faisal of Saudi Arabia, an opponent of Egyptian influence in Arabia, to donate £1 million for the development of the Trucial States. The UK eventually announced it would donate the same amount and that Saudi aid was not needed. The issue climaxed when Britain told deputy Arab League secretary general, Sayeed Nofal, that he could not fly to Sharjah to meet Sheikh Saqr and the airspace of Abu Dhabi, Dubai and Sharjah was closed to prevent him from doing so.

Sheikh Saqr's attitude displeased London so much that the British government threatened to withdraw its protection. There are various accounts of what happened next. But the version believed by most is that Sheikh Saqr was called to a meeting with Britain's political agent in Sharjah and shown a document calling for his deposition that had been supposedly signed by the Al Qassimi family council.

Sheikh Saqr was put on a plane and sent into exile. The succession passed to Sheikh Khaled bin Mohammed Al Qassimi who'd previously run a paint shop in Dubai and was a great friend of Dubai's ruler, Sheikh Rashid bin Saeed. The legacy was bitter. On July 17, 1970, explosives placed under the chair habitually used by Sheikh Khaled in a room where he greeted Sharjah personalities were detonated in an apparent assassination attempt. It had a deadly echo 18 months later.

In early 1972, a few weeks after the formal establishment of the UAE federation, Sheikh Saqr, the former ruler, secretly returned to Sharjah from exile in Cairo. On the evening of January 25, leading a band of 17 followers, he fought his way into the ruler's palace and declared himself restored. Sheikh Saqr's claim to rule was dismissed by other Al Qassimi family members. He and his followers surrendered the next morning.

The body of Sheikh Khaled, then aged 45, was found among the dead and wounded. Sheikh Saqr was exiled for the second and last time. At the end of an eventful year, Dr Sheikh Sultan bin Mohammed, brother of Sheikh Khaled and the first education minister of the UAE, was made Sharjah's ruler and has held power ever since. In 1974, Sheikh Saqr and his accomplices were convicted by a federal court to prison sentences for their role in Khaled's death. Sheikh Saqr, despite the conviction, was released in January 1975 but went again into exile, returning many years later to live under effective house arrest in Abu Dhabi until his death.

Sheikh Sultan is the only Gulf ruler with a doctorate, which he earned from the University of Exeter for a thesis that challenged the British allegation that the Al Qassimi were pirates. Born in 1939 and educated in Cairo, he participated as a young man in demonstrations against British rule and Israeli aggression against the Arab nation. Sharjah broke the mould with the launch soon after independence of the Voice of the United Arab Emirates Radio, a station emulating Egypt's nationalist Voice of the Arabs (Sawt al-Arab). The Sharjah-based *Al Khaleej*, the UAE's first independent daily paper, was started in October 1970 and continues to report with enviable freedom.

Sheikh Sultan has concentrated on developing Sharjah as a Sharia-compliant alternative to Dubai. Alcohol was banned in 1985, a decision that hit government earnings just as the oil price was about to tumble. The economic shock that followed helped to produce the gravest political crisis of Sheikh Sultan's rule. On June 17, 1987, the official federal government news agency WAM reported he'd abdicated and had been replaced by his elder brother, Sheikh Abdelaziz bin Mohammed, then aged 50. Dubai refused to accept the change and issued a statement disputing the version of events published by WAM. It claimed Sheikh Sultan had actually been deposed by force, denounced this as unacceptable and called for his reinstatement. This was eventually achieved and Sheikh Abdelaziz went into internal exile.

The oil price recovery has put Sharjah's finances on a firmer footing. The emirate is now looking to the future with confidence. Cheaper and more intimate than Dubai, Sharjah is the quiet person's favoured resting place. There's much to admire in its corniche, striking souks, fine public buildings, international airport and university. Sharjah's dedication to preserving its heritage and architecture – and to promoting the arts – was recognized in 1998 when it was awarded the title 'Cultural Capital of the Arab World' by UNESCO.

Sharjah is used as a dormitory town by tens of thousands of people who work in Dubai but choose to live in Sharjah because the rents are lower. People travelling between Dubai and Sharjah, however, quickly discover that the rivalry between the two close neighbours complicates life – especially when the few roads linking the cities become bottlenecks during rush hour.

## Family tree of the Al Qassimi of Ra's al-Khaimah and Sharjah

| | |
|---|---|
| Sultan bin Saqr ... ... ... ... ... ... ... ... ... ... ... ... ... | 1803–1866 |
| Khaled bin Sultan ... ... ... ... ... ... ... ... ... ... ... ... | 1866–1868 |
| Salim bin Sultan . ... ... ... ... ... ... ... ... ... ... ... ... | 1868–1883 |
| Sultan bin Saqr ... ... ... ... ... ... ... ... ... ... ... ... ... | 1883–1914 |
| Khaled bin Ahmed ... ... ... ... ... ... ... ... ... ... ... ... | 1914–1924 |
| Sultan bin Saqr (independent ruler of Sharjah).. ... ... ... | 1924–1951 |
| Sultan bin Salim (independent ruler of Ra's al-Khaimah) | 1921–1948 |

## Sharjah

Saqr bin Sultan ... ... ... ... ... ... ... ... ... ... ... ... ... 1951–1965
Khaled bin Mohammed   ... ... ... ... ... ... ... ... ... ... 1965–1972
Dr Sultan bin Mohammed . ... ... ... ... ... ... ... ... ... 1972–

## Ra's al-Khaimah

Saqr bin Mohammed   ... ... ... ... ... ... ... ... ... ... ... 1948–

## Ajman, Umm al-Qaiwain and Fujairah

The emirate of Ajman, with a land area of about 260 km², is the small-est of the UAE seven. Most of its estimated population of 120,000 live in the built-up area on a sand-spit that runs parallel to the coast north of Sharjah and in a shallow hinterland. The rest are found in two en-claves in the UAE interior: Masfut, which lies near the Dubai enclave of Hatta, and Manama.

Ajman was defined by the claims of the Al Bukhuraban section of the Al Nuaimi family. This is a division of the Al Naim tribal confedera-tion that has branches across the northern and eastern parts of the UAE and northern Oman. The Al Naim historically associated them-selves with the Ghafiri tribal section, which put them at loggerheads with the rulers of Abu Dhabi.

Like the Al Qassimi, the Al Naim adopted Wahhabism in the early 19th century. It was the second last of the Trucial States to grant a concession to PCL, eventually signing up in 1951. Nothing so far has been found though there were hopes in the early 1980s that the con-cession-holder, Unigulf Oil, would make a significant strike. To survive economically, Ajman was quick to offer itself as an expatriate retreat.

The Ajman Kempinski Hotel is affectionately regarded as being one of the first places in the UAE where foreigners could holiday as if they were in the Mediterranean. A free zone has been established.

The ruler, Sheikh Humaid bin Rashid Al Nuaimi, who was born in 1930, succeeded his father Sheikh Rashid in September 1981. His son, Sheikh Ammar bin Humaid Al Nuaimi, is crown prince.

## Family tree of the Al Naim of Ajman

Rashid . ... ... ... ... ... ... ... ... ... ... ... ... ... ... ... until 1838
Humaid bin Rashid .. ... ... ... ... ... ... 1838–1841 and 1848–1873
Abdelaziz bin Rashid   ... ... ... ... ... ... ... ... ... ... ... 1841–1848
Rashid bin Humaid .. ... ... ... ... ... ... ... ... ... ... ... 1873–1891
Maktoum bin Rashid   ... ... ... ... ... ... ... ... ... ... ... 1891–1900
Abdelaziz bin Humaid .. ... ... ... ... ... ... ... ... ... ... 1900–1910
Humaid bin Abdelaziz .. ... ... ... ... ... ... ... ... ... ... 1910–1928
Rashid bin Humaid .. ... ... ... ... ... ... ... ... ... ... ... 1928–1981
Humaid bin Rashid .. ... ... ... ... ... ... ... ... ... ... ... 1981–

Source: *The UAE: A MEED Practical Guide*, 2004

Umm al-Qaiwain has a land area of little more than 1,550 km$^2$ and a population in 2006 of about 50,000 people. It forms a wedge between Sharjah and Ra's al-Khaimah. The emirate's territory is defined by the claims of the Al Ali tribe that make up almost all its population. They are related to people living in the Shibkuh district of southern Iran. The ruling Al Mualla family was recognized by the British in the 1820 General Treaty of Peace. The present ruler, Sheikh Rashid, succeeded his father who died in 1981.

History has left its mark on the emirate. In about 2000 BC, Umm al-Qaiwain was the site of one of the Gulf's most important city states. Believed to cover more than 2.5 km$^2$ in extent, the settlement was located at Al Door on the main road to Ra's al-Khaimah. Finds show that Al Door minted its own coins. This suggests the town was the capital of a petty kingdom. The name of the town has not yet been discovered but some speculate it might have been Omana, reported to be the largest town in the region in the Roman era.

Today, Umm al-Qaiwain's principal attractions are its unspoilt beaches, enclosed lagoon, flying and horse-riding. Its secondary centre is Falaj al-Mualla in the emirate's farming area. Sinaiyah Island, which lies about a kilometre from the coast, has been made into a nature reserve.

**Family tree of the Al Ali of Umm al-Qaiwain**

| | |
|---|---|
| Abdullah bin Rashid | until 1853 |
| Salim bin Abdullah | 1853 until about 1873 |
| Ahmed bin Abdullah | 1873–1904 |
| Rashid bin Ahmed | 1904–1922 |
| Abdullah bin Rashid | 1922–1923 |
| Hamad bin Ibrahim | 1923–1929 |
| Ahmed bin Rashid | 1929–1981 |
| Rashid bin Ahmed | 1981– |

Source: *The UAE: A MEED Practical Guide*, 2004

Fujairah is the only one of the seven emirates without access to the Gulf. But its control of most of the UAE's 64 km of Arabian Sea coast, on the Gulf of Oman, more than makes up for the disadvantage.

The town of Fujairah is built on a site that's been settled for more than 3,500 years and contains some of the UAE's most interesting archaeological finds. The local department of archaeology is renovating the Palace at Wadi Hail which is situated in the wadi of the same name, some 11 km outside Fujairah town. It was once occupied by a cadet branch of the Sharqiyin, the emirate's ruling family. The site comprises a walled enclosure not much more than 50 m across at its widest and contains a two-storey fort in south Arabian style, in addition to petroglyphs (rock engravings) nearby.

Lacking oil, Fujairah depends upon support from the federal government and Abu Dhabi, with which it is historically connected. It has an international airport with one of the longest runways in the region and a container terminal serves shipping lines that operate around Arabia's southern coast. A bunker terminal opened in the early 1990s is the emirate's largest industry. Fujairah is now the second largest bunkering port in the world.

Abu Dhabi financed a power-and-water complex to be supplied with Qatari gas through the Dolphin Pipeline. Future hopes include exploiting the emirate's coastline and historical legacy. The Le Meridien Al Aqah Beach Resort was opened in 2003 and has been joined by other resorts serving UAE residents and the millions forecast to visit the UAE.

A total of US$800 million worth of projects are planned. They include a refinery to be supplied with crude oil from Abu Dhabi and a major development at the airport, as well as a number of property developments. Fujairah's ruler from 1952 was Sheikh Mohammed bin Hamad Al Sharqi who that year secured Britain's recognition as an independent ruler. He died in September 1974 and was succeeded by his son, Sheikh Hamad bin Mohammed Al Sharqi, the present ruler.

## Family tree of the Sharqiyin of Fujairah

Abdullah bin Saif
Hamad bin Abdullah
Saif bin Hamad
Mohammed bin Hamad    ... ... ... ... ... ... ... ... ... ...    1952–1974
Hamad bin Mohammed    ... ... ... ... ... ... ... ... ... ...    1974–

Source: *The UAE: A MEED Practical Guide*, 2004

## The making of the UAE

The seven emirates that now form the UAE were brought together in a process that started in 1952 when Britain established the Trucial States Council to promote development. One of its first steps was to create a security force. The Trucial Oman Levies, later to be called the Trucial Oman Scouts, were formed in 1953.

In January 1961, UK cabinet minister Edward Heath toured the Gulf ahead of the promulgation of full Kuwaiti independence later that year. It was inevitable that the other Gulf states subject to British protection would eventually follow the Kuwaiti lead and Heath came to test the views of the rulers. In Dubai, he met Sheikh Rashid. This meeting led to Dubai's ruler making a visit to London later that year in which the idea of a union among the Trucial States was officially discussed for the first time. Heath's role in Gulf history was largely overlooked in the obituaries following his death in the summer of 2005.

The idea of federation was also championed by the independent states of the region. In 1964, the Arab League proposed the Trucial States Council should be financially supported by Iran, Kuwait and Saudi Arabia. This was opposed by London, which pressed for an association solely among the Trucial rulers that would be sympathetic to the UK.

The issue came to a head following the election of a Labour government in the UK in October 1964. Initially, UK ministers promoted initiatives to stimulate growth in neglected imperial domains. The Trucial States Development Office (TSDO) was founded in 1965 to co-ordinate economic initiatives. Easa Al Gurg, now the UAE ambassador to the UK, was appointed TSDO executive director in 1971. But pressure for more radical steps grew as Britain's financial difficulties intensified. This, coupled with longstanding Labour opposition to imperial possessions and high defence spending, led to the biggest change in British foreign policy for 20 years.

In February 1967, British defence secretary, Dennis Healey, published a White Paper which called for the liquidation of almost all British bases east of the Suez Canal. It proposed withdrawing troops from south Arabia by the end of 1968 when Aden and the British protectorates surrounding the port, brought together into the Federation of South Arabia that had been founded in 1959, were to be made independent. The timetable was accelerated and, by May 1967, a plan to withdraw from the whole Gulf was on the agenda.

By this time, the Federation of South Arabia was in turmoil and swiftly fell to the National Liberation Front (NLF). British troops were withdrawn from Aden in November 1967. British credibility was shredded further the same month by the devaluation of sterling by 13 per cent against the US dollar with no prior warning to Gulf rulers who held their savings in the British currency. Britain, nevertheless, repeated its commitment to its Gulf treaty obligations. But all illusions were finally shattered when the UK prime minister, Harold Wilson, told the House of Commons, on January 16, 1968, that British forces would leave by the end of 1971.

The announcement threw the Gulf into a mood of despondency. Iran declared in 1957 that Bahrain was its 14th province and harboured a desire to take over Abu Musa and the Greater and Lesser Tunbs. The land borders with neighbouring states were still uncertain. Radicals were in power in South Yemen and civil war was raging in North Yemen. On top of this was the threat of communist subversion.

The decision was criticized by Britain's Conservative Party, led after 1965 by Heath. It argued that withdrawal was a betrayal of rulers who depended on British protection and would tempt the Soviet Union into the Gulf. Critics of British withdrawal pointed out the cost of maintaining British Gulf bases was less than the value of British investment in the region. In 1966, almost half the UK's oil imports came from the Gulf.

The Conservative victory in the British general election of June 1970 raised Gulf hopes of a new approach. These were quickly dashed. On March 1, 1971, UK foreign secretary, Sir Alec Douglas-Home, told the House of Commons the withdrawal would proceed according to Labour's timetable. London offered the Gulf rulers a treaty of friendship to replace the defence agreements scheduled to expire on December 31 that year.

Bahrain's ruler, Sheikh Isa Al Khalifa, was the first to call for a federation for the lower Gulf, soon after Wilson's 1968 announcement. This initiative was followed by a meeting between Sheikh Zayed and Sheikh Rashid on February 18, 1968. They agreed to a union between Abu Dhabi and Dubai that would be responsible for foreign affairs, defence, security and social services. Sheikh Mohammed bin Rashid, now vice-president and prime minister of the UAE and Dubai's ruler, recalled the climax of the meeting that he attended. "So, Rashid, what do you think? Shall we create a union?" asked Sheikh Zayed.

Without hesitation, the Dubai ruler replied: "Give me your hand, Sheikh Zayed. Let us shake upon an agreement. You will be president." They called for others to join the proposed union. On February 25, 1968, the seven Trucial rulers plus those of Bahrain and Qatar met in Dubai for a constitutional conference. Qatar was included partly because Sheikh Rashid's daughter Mariam was married to Qatar's then ruler Sheikh Ahmed. Abu Dhabi's link with Bahrain was already well-established. The two emirates had been allies for a century and the Bahraini dinar was Abu Dhabi's currency from 1966 until May 1973.

At the meeting, Qatar presented a draft federal agreement proposing Sharjah, Ajman, Umm al-Qaiwain, Ra's al-Khaimah and Fujairah should first form a union to be called the United Arab Coastal Emirates (UACE). It would subsequently become part of a larger five-state union comprising the UACE, Abu Dhabi, Dubai, Bahrain and Qatar. The proposal was vetoed. After three days of bargaining, an adjusted version of the Qatari proposal was signed by all nine rulers. The agreement was to go into effect on March 30. The date came and went with no action.

A second meeting, this time between advisers rather than rulers, was held in Abu Dhabi from 18–19 May 1968. The Qatari team pressed for swift action, Abu Dhabi urged caution while Bahrain fell somewhere between these two views. A communiqué based on the meeting of the advisers was approved by the nine rulers a week later. It reaffirmed their desire to achieve union but nothing more.

A third union meeting in July 1968, again in Abu Dhabi, invited Abdul Razaq Sanhuri, who'd written the 1962 Kuwaiti constitution, to draft one for the federation. A temporary union council was established. It had its first meeting in Doha from 8–9 September under the chairmanship of Sheikh Khalifa Al Thani, Qatar's deputy ruler, who was to seize power in 1972. The rulers' fourth meeting was held in Doha from 20–22 October 1968. It agreed unified armed forces should replace British garrisons when they left in 1971.

There was a burst of diplomatic activity between the fourth and fifth meetings. The 1968 frontier agreement between Abu Dhabi and Dubai was slightly amended in Dubai's favour. Sheikh Zayed visited Kuwait and then went to Doha to sign an agreement about the continental shelf between Abu Dhabi and Qatar. He proposed joint exploitation of the Bunduq oilfield between the two emirates. Sheikh Zayed then went to see Bahrain's Sheikh Isa, who'd declared his government might opt for independence if the federation did not develop acceptably. Bahrain, Qatar and Iran set about settling unresolved border issues.

The fifth federal meeting from 10–14 May 1969 made little progress. A major issue was Bahrain's insistence that members of the proposed federal assembly should be selected on the basis of proportional representation. The other emirates objected since this would have meant that Bahrain, then the most populous of the nine, would have almost half the federal assembly seats. The sixth and last union meeting of the nine rulers was held in Abu Dhabi on October 21, 1969. A communiqué was drafted that said Sheikh Zayed should be elected president of the federation and Sheikh Rashid vice-president. Sheikh Khalifa, Qatar's deputy ruler, was to be prime minister heading a 13-member cabinet to which each of the emirates could nominate up to three members. Abu Dhabi would be the temporary federal capital until a final decision to build a new one on the border with Dubai was made.

The communiqué was never issued. The day after the Abu Dhabi meeting, Iran went public with its own concerns about the plan for federation and declared union would be unacceptable until the status of Bahrain had been clarified. Dissatisfied with the reaction to its proposals for the federal assembly and conscious of Iran's position, Bahrain's Sheikh Isa formed a new government in January 1970 in anticipation of the union of the nine not going ahead. The UN's special envoy reported in May that the overwhelming majority wanted Bahrain to be an independent, sovereign state. Iran accepted its findings.

This precipitated similar actions in Qatar. On March 2, 1970, Doha published a provisional constitution. In May, Qatar's first cabinet was announced. And yet, neither Qatar nor Bahrain was prepared to give up hope for a federation. A meeting of deputy rulers of the nine in Abu Dhabi in June 1970 made further proposals. Negotiations were interrupted by the Conservative election victory of June 1970. The new government sent Sir William Luce, a retired British diplomat with extensive experience of the Gulf, on a tour of Iran and Arab Gulf states in August. A fresh dimension emerged on July 23, when Sultan Said of Oman was deposed and replaced by his son Qaboos. The possibility of incorporating the sultanate into the federation appealed to some, but Oman's prime minister, Tariq bin Taimour, declared in October that his country would not join at that point, but might consider an association with some of the other emirates in the future.

Four days later, a deputy ruler's meeting in Abu Dhabi studied a final proposed federal agreement. Bahrain argued against the recommendation that the Union Council or assembly should have equal representation for each member state. It again pressed for representation based on population and for a census. The meeting closed with no agreement. Final efforts were made for six months to break the deadlock. Kuwaiti and Saudi help was enlisted to mediate the differences. Luce was sent on two further Gulf visits. These activities were overshadowed by Britain's final withdrawal statement of March 1971. The rulers were disappointed but accepted the inevitability of an end to British protection. Luce went on a fourth Gulf tour amid frantic efforts to get arrangements in place by the end of the year.

On July 10, the rulers of the emirates that were to become the UAE met in Dubai as members of the Trucial Council. On July 18, a communiqué announced the formation of the UAE comprising six of the seven states. Ra's al-Khaimah held back because of its desire for larger representation on the proposed Union Council. A provisional constitution was approved. The communiqué said the rulers hoped the federation would form the nucleus of 'a complete federation that will include the remaining members of the brotherly family of emirates'.

On August 14, 1971, Sheikh Isa bin Salman announced Bahrain's declaration of independence that went into effect the next day. On September 1, Qatar followed suit. The plan for a seven-member union raced ahead. On November 23, 1971, the six rulers elected Sheikh Zayed as president and Sheikh Rashid as vice-president. Sheikh Maktoum bin Rashid was made prime minister. Just a week later, an 18-member cabinet was appointed.

On December 1, the protection treaties between Britain and the seven emirates were terminated. The following day, a treaty of friendship between the UK and the UAE was signed in Dubai. On December 6, the UAE joined the Arab League. Three days later it was admitted as a member of the UN. Operational command of the Trucial Oman Scouts passed to the UAE on December 22. The first UAE government was formed. Sheikh Maktoum bin Rashid was prime minister. Sheikh Hamdan bin Rashid of Dubai was deputy premier. Sheikh Mohammed bin Rashid took the post of defence minister. Sheikh Mubarak bin Mohammed Al Nahyan was interior minister and prominent figures from each of the emirates were given portfolios.

Ra's al-Khaimah's participation still hung in the balance. The emirate was irritated by the fact it had been consulted less frequently than the larger emirates. Hopes of a major offshore oil discovery raised the possibility that it might join the federation as an oil-rich member.

The most immediate issue was the handling of Iran's claim to Abu Musa and the Greater and Lesser Tunbs. Tehran argued all three islands had belonged to Persia until the start of the 19th century when the British government of India assigned them to the Al Qassimi. Ra's al-Khaimah and Sharjah, supported by the UK, said the Iranian claim was false and argued that the Arabs who lived on Abu Musa were then subjects of a branch of the Al Qassimi family which was then based on the Persian side of the Gulf.

The shah's 1971 claim relied on maps given to the Persian government in 1903 when Lord Curzon toured the region. These showed the three islands in the same colour as mainland Persia and were interpreted in Tehran as an admission by Britain that the islands were Persian. There were about 100 people on Greater Tunb. Lesser Tunb was uninhabited. Both lie closer to the coast of Iran than to the UAE.

Sharjah and Umm al-Qaiwain had their own more minor dispute about Abu Musa. Umm al-Qaiwain did not claim the island but argued for rights to explore the seabed around it. The rulers had granted oil concessions to different American oil companies and the concession areas overlapped. Britain banned drilling until ownership of the field could be clarified. Separately, Sharjah said the inhabitants on Abu Musa were its subjects.

Britain, under pressure from the US, bent to Tehran's wishes. Sharjah settled Iran's claim by signing an agreement, which was made public on November 29, in which neither Iran nor Sharjah recognized that either had sovereignty over Abu Musa. It conceded part of Abu Musa to an Iranian garrison and equal sharing of any oil and gas found on or around the island. The agreement also called for Sharjah to pass 20 per cent of any revenue from Abu Musa to Umm al-Qaiwain and 10 per cent to Ajman. Ra's al-Khaimah, in contrast, refused to make concessions.

On November 30, the Abu Musa deal went into effect and Iranian troops landed on the island. Meanwhile, the Iranians seized the Tunbs after a brief firefight in which Iranian soldiers and members of the Ra's al-Khaimah police force were killed.

Britain, still technically obliged to defend the rights of the Trucial States, did not intervene. Feelings against Iran and Britain ran high in the Arab World. Iraq broke diplomatic relations with both countries. Libya nationalized BP's oil interests. The Kuwait national assembly demanded its government should break relations with Britain and Iran. Ra's al-Khaimah appealed to Arab heads of state and sent a delegation to the Arab League meeting on December 6, 1971. It reopened talks about membership of the UAE. One of its conditions was that the UAE "should adopt the question of Iranian occupation of the islands". This was agreed.

Ra's al-Khaimah joined the federation on February 10, 1972 and was allotted six seats in the newly-formed, 40-member Federal National Council (FNC), the same number as Sharjah. Ajman, Fujairah and Umm al-Qaiwain had four each, while Abu Dhabi and Dubai had eight each. The UAE interim constitution established the federal supreme council of the seven rulers where issues are debated collectively. The council of ministers was described in the constitution as the executive authority of the UAE but real power was retained largely by the seven emirates.

A new country had been made, but there were conflicting visions about its future. Frustrated by the slow moves towards establishing strong federal institutions, Sheikh Zayed threatened, in an interview published on August 1, 1976, to refuse a second five-year term of office as UAE president when the first one expired at the end of that year. The trigger for that crisis appeared to have been a border dispute between Dubai and Sharjah in the spring of 1976. The issue was resolved in an agreement between the two emirates five years later.

Sheikh Zayed was elected for a second and further five-year presidential terms until his death in November 2004. A new UAE cabinet was appointed in January 1977 with a smaller number of members. Sheikh Hamdan bin Mohammed Al Nahyan became deputy prime minister. But differences between Dubai and Abu Dhabi continued to simmer. In April 1977, Sheikh Zayed was reported as threatening to resign as president over Dubai's decision to breach a two-year moratorium on issuing new bank licences. Abu Dhabi complained about other emirates making no contribution to the federal budget.

A further issue was a rumbling dispute about the federal army. After the formation of the UAE, the Union Defence Force was established but most emirates maintained their own security contingents. In May 1975, the federal supreme council ruled that only the federal army was authorized to use air, ground and naval armaments. In November that year, Sharjah dismantled the Sharjah National Guard and put its forces at the disposal of the federation.

A fresh agreement about unifying UAE military forces was reached ahead of Sheikh Zayed's re-election as president in November 1976, but the larger emirates continued to exercise a measure of control over their own forces. When Sheikh Zayed appointed his son, Sheikh Sultan, as commander in chief of the UAE armed forces, divisions grew, though Sheikh Rashid subsequently stated he had no objection to the appointment and liked and respected Sheikh Zayed's second son.

Sheikh Rashid voiced his unhappiness about the way the federation was developing in an interview published in an Abu Dhabi newspaper in June 1978. Among his aspirations was a plan to establish a federal capital, to be called Karama and built on the Abu Dhabi-Dubai border. There was even talk of Dubai leaving the federation and forming a union with Ra's al-Khaimah and Umm al-Qaiwain.

The issue was finally resolved when a new cabinet was formed at the end of June 1979 with Shaikh Rashid as prime minister and Shaikh Maktoum and Shaikh Hamdan bin Mohammed as deputy premiers. The most serious crisis in the federation's history had been resolved and the process of institution building quickened, but the UAE's interim constitution was only permanently adopted in 1996.

The 1970s were a period of growing regional tension. In 1977, a hijacked Lufthansa jet landed at Dubai International Airport and left for Somalia before security forces could storm the aircraft. Sheikh Mohammed bin Rashid, the federal defence minister, declared no more hijacked planes would be allowed to land. In October the same year, gunmen in Abu Dhabi shot and killed the UAE's minister of state for foreign affairs, Saif bin Ghobash, who was escorting Syrian foreign minister, Abdel-Halim Khaddam. The assassin was attempting to kill the Syrian but instead managed to end the life of one of the first UAE nationals with a university education.

Investment in internal and external security was increased and economic convergence prioritized. Until the late 1950s, the currency most frequently used in the Trucial States was the Indian rupee, the result in large part of the trade in gold between Dubai and India. The Indian government discovered, however, that this was eroding the value of its paper currency because Gulf holders of rupees were selling them at a discount for sterling. In 1959, the gold Gulf rupee was introduced to try to remedy the problem. It was not legal tender in India but circulated in the Gulf and was convertible into sterling in areas under British control. The measure significantly reduced but did not eliminate the Indian gold trade based in Dubai. In 1966, India stopped converting gold rupees into sterling and devalued the Indian currency against the pound by 35 per cent. This forced a revolution in Gulf currencies.

Abu Dhabi adopted the Bahrain dinar as the national currency and Dubai opted for a joint currency with Qatar. In September 1966, the Qatar-Dubai currency board was created to regulate financial affairs in the two emirates and manage the Qatar-Dubai riyal. The dual currency system was abolished following independence. The UAE currency board was formed in 1973 and the UAE dirham was introduced the same year. The Central Bank of the UAE was created to replace the board in 1980.

One of its first measures was to restrict the number of branches allowed to foreign banks to eight. This policy hit the BBME, now part of HSBC, which at the time had 29 branches. Most were closed in the following two years. More than a quarter of a century after it was created, the Central Bank of the UAE still struggles to exert its influence in an economy where each of the seven emirates are technically sovereign. But important milestones have been passed. Money laundering is now largely under control and the central bank's authority is growing.

The Dubai International Financial Centre (DIFC), approved in September 2004 under the terms of a federal free zone law, is proceeding with the bank's official blessing. The talking point for the federation's finance industry at the end of 2005 was the stock exchange boom.

In September, the Dubai International Financial Exchange (DIFX) was launched and became the UAE's third stock market after the Abu Dhabi Securities Market and the Dubai Financial Market. Based in the DIFC, the new exchange is governed by international regulatory standards, not by the dictates of federal institutions.

The aim is to attract listings by international and regional companies seeking a higher standard of supervision than is yet available in the rest of the region. The case for a properly regulated and modern stock exchange was underlined in the first half of 2006 when both the Abu Dhabi and Dubai bourses went into freefall and lost half their value in less than three months. Dubai's response has been to go on the offensive. Borse Dubai, a holding company set up in August 2007 that owns the DIFX and the Dubai Financial Market, has since bought stakes in the London Stock Exchange, Nasdaq of the US and the Swedish bourse OMX. DP World listed on the DIFX at the end of 2007.

But the impetus created by the UAE's economic growth is unstoppable. In June 2006, it was announced that a new investment fund would be created to manage the financial surpluses being generated by the federal government for the first time in UAE history. UAE prime minister Sheikh Mohammed bin Rashid's strategy speech of April 2007 is evidence that economic convergence among the emirates will accelerate.

**Building a new world in the New Gulf**
On a warm May evening, an excited group of more than 400 people gathered on the breakwater that extends into the Gulf beyond Dubai's Jumeirah Beach Hotel. With the sun beginning to set, the Burj Al Arab could be seen from its most flattering perspective. The crowd mainly comprised hotel executives who'd spent three days learning how the world's biggest hotel construction programme was unfolding in the Gulf. They were enthusiastic, and now wanted some fun. To bring the

event to a suitable climax, they had been promised a trip by boat to 'Greenland', the first island in The World archipelago being built by Nakheel, the Dubai government real-estate corporation.

The World archipelago will eventually comprise 300 artificial islands in the shape of the map of the world. Each is for sale for millions of US dollars to private investors who can then build palaces, hotels or just a beach hut if they want. A large catamaran and smaller boats had been laid on for the occasion. Escorted by a policeman on a jet ski, the boats with their passengers set sail as the sun sank into the Gulf. A stiff on-shore breeze kept the travellers cool.

After 15 minutes, with The Palm Jumeirah receding on the left, they could see what appeared to be low ridges. But these were in the sea; new islands, the result of six months of dredging on a monumental scale. After 25 minutes, the boats were amongst them, nothing more than sandbanks that will in the end be part of one of the world's great leisure projects. Through a channel, a low building could be seen, and, as the boats got closer, the silhouette of palm trees. Greenland seemed to rise from the sea already grassed and landscaped. A jetty had been built and, on land, Bedouin songs were chanted by a chorus of young men amid the fragrance of burning sandalwood.

Sheikh Mohammed bin Rashid had been there the day before, bringing guests who'd attended the wedding of his daughter Sheikha Manal to Sheikh Mansour bin Zayed, son of the late President Zayed and a UAE cabinet minister. It had been the biggest dynastic marriage between the Al Maktoum and the Al Nahyan since Sheikh Rashid, father of the present Dubai ruler, married Sheikha Latifa in 1939.

On Greenland, the visitors examined the world's newest inhabited island. It is about 250 m in diameter with beach all round. The model home was big enough to accommodate a family of 10. They said that British pop singer Rod Stewart had bought Britain, the Kuwaitis have Australasia and Saudi Arabians were negotiating for Indonesia. As night closed in, Nakheel chairman Sultan bin Sulayem thanked his guests for coming and declared The World open. Fireworks noisily exploded overhead in celebration. It had taken almost a year to build Greenland. Nobody had seen anything like it before. But it is just one part of the New World emerging in old Arabia as the dream of the New Gulf goes on.

# CHRONOLOGY OF ARABIA

c4500 million BC The earth is created.

c1400 million BC The Asir and Hejaz arcs are formed.

c1400 million–1000 million BC The Asir and Hejaz arcs collide to form the Arabian shield.

c600–200 million BC Arabia is part of Gondwanaland and Pangea.

c550 million BC The sea covers most of Arabia. It withdraws and rises more than a dozen times.

c1 million BC–1000 AD Volcanic eruptions take place in the Hejaz Mountains.

c1 million BC *Homo erectus* emerges in Arabia. The Arabian drought begins.

c100000 BC *Homo erectus* is replaced by Neanderthal Man.

c50000 BC Arabia becomes arid.

c35000 BC The Neanderthals are replaced by *Homo sapiens* in Arabia.

c18000–16000 BC The peak of the Ice Age. The Gulf is largely dry land.

c12000–10000 BC Rainfall returns to Arabia.

c5000 BC The Ubaid people enter Arabia from southern Mesopotamia. Settlements develop along the coast of what becomes the UAE.

c4000 BC The new Arabian drought begins. Gold smelting begins in the Hejaz and copper smelting in Magan in south-east Arabia.

c3500 BC Rise of the Sumerian Civilization in Mesopotamia. More villages develop on the Gulf coast. Rise of the Civilization of Dilmun, centred on Bahrain.

c3000 BC The Arabian camel is domesticated. The frankincense trade from south Arabia begins. Settlements start developing on Arabian land routes.

c2500–2000 BC Umm al-Nar settlements emerge in what is now the UAE.

c2100 BC Magan starts supplying copper to Mesopotamia. Failaka Island starts to emerge as a Gulf way station.

c2000 BC The fall of the Sumerians. Al Door emerges in what is now Umm al-Qaiwain in the UAE.

c1500 BC The rise of the Hittites, Mittani and Kassites in Mesopotamia.

c1200 BC The kingdom of Saba emerges in Yemen.

c900 BC The Queen of Saba visits King Solomon in Jerusalem. The first reports of camel-riding Arabian warriors.

c700 BC The Marib Dam is built in Saba.

612 BC The Assyrian state is destroyed and replaced by the New Babylonians.

539 BC Cyrus the Great defeats the Assyrians, captures Babylon, founds the Achamaenian Empire and subsequently frees the Jews from captivity.

334–324 BC Alexander the Great destroys the Achamaenian Empire and seizes Egypt, the Levant, Mesopotamia and Persia.

324 BC General Nearchus returns to Babylon, through the Gulf from the Indus.

324–323 BC Alexander dispatches three naval expeditions to the Gulf.

322 BC Alexander's death leads to

the division of his empire. The Gulf falls under General Seleucus and his descendants. Egypt and the Red Sea are controlled by General Ptolemy and his descendants.

**230 BC** A Greek settlement is established on Failaka Island in Kuwait Bay.

**c200 BC** The Nabataean system emerges in north-west Arabia.

**30 BC** Rome defeats and seizes Egypt. The Parthians destroy the Seleucid Empire.

**25 BC** The Roman vice-consul Aellus Gallus invades Arabia.

**0** Jesus of Nazareth is born in Bethlehem.

**25** The kingdom of Saba is conquered by the Himyarites.

**106** Nabataea is absorbed into the Roman Empire.

**225** The Sasanians defeat the Parthians and establish a new Persian Empire encompassing the Gulf.

**300–600** The Ghassanid and Lakhmid states emerge as buffers between Arabia and Roman and Sasanian territories.

**300–400** Nestorian Christian bishoprics established in Abu Dhabi, Bahrain and Oman.

**325** The Sasanian King Shapur launches his campaign in Arabia.

**335** Saba is captured by the Abyssinians.

**c500** Kinda state dominates central Arabia.

**c550** Arab sailors reach China.

**570** The Marib Dam collapses for the third and last time. The great Sabaen exodus across Arabia begins.

**570** The Prophet Mohammed (PBUH) is born in Mecca.

**595** The Prophet Mohammed (PBUH) marries Khadija bin Khuwaylid.

**610** The Prophet Mohammed (PBUH) receives His first revelation on Mount Hira.

**613** The Rise and Warn revelation. The Prophet Mohammed (PBUH) goes public with the message of Islam.

**620** Lailat al-Miraj. During Ramadan, the Prophet Mohammed (PBUH) rides on Buraq to Jerusalem, ascends to heaven, meets the prophets and speaks to God.

**622** The Prophet Mohammed (PBUH) and the Muslims leave Mecca for Yathrib (Medina) on July 10, which becomes the first day of the Hijri calendar.

**624** The Muslims defeat the Meccans at Badr in March.

**625** The Battle of Uhud takes place.

**627** The Battle of the Trench won by the Muslims.

**627–29** Al Hasa and Bahrain convert to Islam.

**630** The Prophet Mohammed (PBUH) re-enters Mecca. The Azd people of south-east Arabia and the whole of south-west Arabia convert. The Muslims begin their campaign in north-west Arabia.

**632** The Prophet Mohammed (PBUH) dies in Medina. Abu Bakr becomes first caliph. The Muslims are defeated by the Byzantines at Mutah. The invasion of Persia, Mesopotamia and Levant begins.

**633** Rebels defeated by the Muslims at Dibba in south-east Arabia.

**634** Caliph Abu Bakr dies and is succeeded by Caliph Omar. The Byzantines are defeated at Ajnadayn.

**635** Damascus falls.

**636** The Sasanians are defeated at Qadisiya and the Byzantines at Yarmouk. Jerusalem falls.

**643** Egypt is conquered.

**644** Caliph Omar dies and is succeeded by Caliph Uthman.

**649–50** The Sasanian dynasty is extinguished. The definitive version of the Koran is compiled.

**656** Caliph Uthman is assassinated. Ali becomes caliph.

**657** The Battle of Siffin takes place. The Kharijites split from the forces of Caliph Ali.

**658** Caliph Ali and the rebels under Muawiya meet at Dumat al-Jandal in the 'Arbitration' to end the first Muslim civil war.

**661** Caliph Ali is assassinated in Kufa. Muawiya is recognized by the Muslim majority as caliph.

**669** Hassan, the second Shiite imam, dies and is succeeded by his brother Hussein.

**673** The first failed Muslim attempt to capture Constantinople.

**680** Caliph Muawiya dies and the civil war between Umayyads and Shiites resumes. The Shiite Imam Hussein and his followers are defeated and killed at Karbala.

**684** Work starts on the Qutbat al-Sakhrah (Dome of the Rock) on Temple Mount in Jerusalem.

**717** The second failed Muslim attempt to capture Constantinople takes place.

**750** The Abbasids take power and move the caliphate to Baghdad. The first Ibadhi imam is appointed.

**756** The Umayyad dynasty is founded in Spain.

**780** The Zaydi imamate is established in Yemen.

**886** The Qarmatians take control of southern Iraq and East Arabia.

**909** The Fatimid caliphate is founded in Tunis.

**930** The Qarmatians attack Mecca and take the black stone to Al Hasa.

**954** The black stone is returned to Mecca.

**969** The Fatimids take control of North Africa and found Cairo.

**972** The Persians occupy south-east Arabia.

**973** The Fatimids establish Cairo as their capital.

**1037** The Seljuk Turks enter Persian territories.

**1055** The Seljuks capture Baghdad.

**1071** The Seljuks defeat the Byzantine army at Manzikert.

**1078** The Qarmatian state is extinguished in the Gulf.

**1092** The Seljuk empire begins to disintegrate.

**1099** Jerusalem falls to the Crusaders.

**1171** The final Fatimid ruler dies. The Fatimids are defeated by Salah Al Din Al Ayyubi. Reynauld de Chatillon loots Medina.

**1187** The Crusaders are defeated by Salah Al Din at the Horns of Hatta.

**1250** The Mamluks depose the Ayyubids and take control of Egypt.

**1258** The Mongols capture Baghdad. The caliphate is assumed by the Mamluks.

**1260** The Mamluks defeat the Mongols at Ayn Jalut.

**1280** Osman, founder of the Ottoman dynasty, is born.

**1325** Ibn Battuta starts his journeys.

**1370** Timur forms a new Mongol confederation that conquers Iran, northern India, Anatolia and northern Syria.

**1405** Timur dies and his empire divides.

**1453** The Ottomans capture Constantinople and end the Byzantine Empire.

**1498** Vasco da Gama lands in Kerala.

**1501** Shah Ismail founds the Safavid dynasty in Persia.

**1502** Italian adventurer Ludovico di Varthema leaves Europe for Arabia.

**1506** The Portuguese admiral Albuquerque attacks Sohar, Khor

Fakkan and Muscat.

**1507** The Portuguese seize Socotra Island and defeat the Kingdom of Hormuz.

**1508** The Safavids capture Baghdad.

**1517** The Ottomans capture Cairo. The Portuguese land on Qatar.

**1521** The Portuguese-Hormuz occupy Bahrain. It is lost and recovered and used in a campaign against Al Hasa in 1545.

**1530** Portugal is absorbed by Spain.

**1534** The Ottomans capture Baghdad from the Safavids.

**1538** The Ottomans take control of Yemen.

**1546** The Ottomans capture Basra.

**1551** The Ottomans take control of Al Hasa.

**1581** The Portuguese/Spanish take Bahrain.

**1599** The East India Company is formed.

**1602** The Dutch East India Company is formed.

**1603** Bahrain falls to the Safavids.

**1616** The East India Company sets up its first Gulf warehouse in Ra's Jashk in Persia.

**1622** The Portuguese/Spanish are expelled from Hormuz.

**1623** The East India Company opens a warehouse in Bandar Abbas.

**1624** Nasr Al Yaarubi is elected Ibadhi imam in Rustaq.

**1625** The Portuguese/Spanish are expelled from south Persia.

**1628** The Ottomans lose control of Yemen.

**1631** The Portuguese/Spanish build a fort at Julfar near Ra's al-Khaimah

**1646** Imam Nasr Al Yaarubi grants trading rights in Sohar to the East India Company.

**1649** Ibadhi Imam Nasr Al Yaarubi dies.

**1650** Ibadhi Imam Sultan bin Saif Al Yaarubi declares holy war against the Portuguese and

captures Muscat.

**1652** Imam Sultan bin Saif seizes Qatar.

**1664** The French East India Company is formed.

**1670** The Bani Khalid expel the Ottomans from Al Hasa.

**1679** Imam Sultan bin Saif dies.

**1696** Imam Saif Al Yaarubi completes the recovery of Muscat's East African possessions from Portugal by taking control of Zanzibar.

**c1700** Falah emerges as the leader of the Bani Yas.

**1701** The Al Utub Bedouin migrate from central Arabia to Kuwait Bay.

**1709** The first written mention of Kuwait.

**1717–1718** The Ibadhi Imam Sultan bin Saif captures Bahrain and dies soon afterwards The appointment of his 12-year-old son as imam leads to civil war in south-east Arabia between Ghafiri and Hinawi tribal factions.

**c1720** The Al Qassimi open a trade centre on Qeshm Island.

**1722** The Safavid dynasty is extinguished. Around this time, Sunni Muslim Arabs move to Lingah and south Persia.

**1727** The East India Company forcibly closes the Al Qassimi trading centre on Qeshm Island.

**1736** Nader Shah seizes power in Persia and recovers Bahrain.

**1737** The Persians invade south-east Arabia.

**1739** The Persians capture Delhi.

**1744** Mohammed bin Saud and Mohammed bin Abdul Wahab swear to campaign for a state run on Islamic principles. The Omani national movement led by Imam Ahmed bin Said expels the Persians from south-east Arabia.

**1747** Nader Shah is assassinated. Al Qassimi forces capture Lingah,

Luft and Qeshm Island from Persia.

**1756** Sheikh Sabah Al Jaber emerges as first Al Sabah ruler of Kuwait.

**1761** A Danish mission including Carsten Niebuhr arrives in Jeddah. A Bani Yas hunting party discovers sweet water on Abu Dhabi. The Bani Yas leader Sheikh Diab founds a settlement on the island.

**1763** France loses the Seven Years' War and Britain becomes the dominant sea power in the Indian Ocean.

**1764** Kuwait's ruler Sheikh Sabah Al Jaber dies.

**1765** Mohammed bin Saud dies.

**1766** The Al Khalifa section of the Utub leave Kuwait for the Qatar Peninsula and establish Zubara.

**1775–79** The Persians besiege and occupy Basra.

**1777** The first East India Company ship, unable to enter Basra because of the Persian siege, anchors off Kuwait.

**1780** Al Hasa falls to the Al Saud.

**1781** The Persian Qajar dynasty is founded.

**1783** The Al Khalifa capture Bahrain.

**1792** Sayyid Sultan bin Ahmed becomes the ruler of Oman.

**1795** Sheikh Shakhbut bin Diab becomes the leader of the Bani Yas. The Al Saud defeat the Bani Khalid and take control of eastern Saudi Arabia.

**1797** Bahrain and Qatar accept the authority of the Al Saud.

**1798** Napoleon lands in Egypt. Britain signs a friendship treaty with Sayyid Sultan of Muscat.

**1800** Sayyid Sultan signs a second friendship treaty with Britain.

**1801** The Al Saud attack Karbala. The Al Khalifa are temporarily expelled from Bahrain by forces dispatched by Muscat, Persia and the Al Qassimi.

**1803** Abdelaziz bin Mohammed Al Saud dies. The Al Saud capture Mecca.

**1804** Muscat's Sayyid Sultan bin Ahmed dies and a two-year power struggle breaks out.

**1806** Muscat's Sayyid Said bin Sultan takes control of Oman.

**1807** The British Houses of Parliament vote to ban the slave trade.

**1809** The British fleet, supported by Muscat, attacks Ra's al-Khaimah. Ulrich Jasper Seetzen arrives in Jeddah.

**1811** The Egyptian army under Tusun is defeated by the Al Saud at Wadi Safra in the Hejaz. Forces dispatched by Muscat destroy the Murair fortress in Zubara.

**1812** Johann Burckhardt starts his expedition to Arabia. Petra is seen for the first time by a Westerner.

**1814** The Al Saud are expelled from Bahrain, Buraimi and part of the Tihama. Saud bin Abdelaziz Al Saud dies. Death of the second Kuwait leader, Sheikh Abdullah Al Sabah. Muscat captures Ra's al-Khaimah.

**1815** The Battle of Waterloo ends the Napoleonic wars and frees Britain to become a global power.

**1816** Abu Dhabi's Sheikh Shakhbut dies.

**1818** Diriyah falls to the Egyptian army. Sheikh Tahnoun replaces Sheikh Mohammed as the Abu Dhabi leader.

**1819** Captain George Sadlier sets out from Muscat on the first recorded European crossing of Arabia from coast to coast. The Al Qassimi are defeated.

**1820** The General Treaty of Peace is signed by nine lower Gulf rulers. Sayyid Said bin Sultan expels the Al Saud from Oman.

**1824** Turki bin Abdullah Al Saud returns to Arabia and makes Riyadh his capital.

**1830** The Al Saud recover Bahrain.

**1833** Abu Dhabi leader Sheikh Tahnoun is assassinated. The Al Bu Falasah secede and move to Dubai where Sheikh Maktoum bin Butti founds the Al Maktoum dynasty. The British Houses of Parliament vote to ban slavery in the British Empire.

**1835** The first maritime truce is signed by the rulers of Abu Dhabi, Dubai, Sharjah and Ajman.

**1836** Death of the third Al Sabah emir, Sheikh Jaber.

**1837** The Egyptian army captures Riyadh.

**1839** The British capture Aden.

**1840** The Egyptian army withdraws from Arabia.

**1841** Kuwait signs the maritime truce for one year and the East India Company opens its first warehouse in the emirate. Sayyid Said bin Sultan sends a ship to New York and establishes diplomatic relations with the US.

**1843** Britain signs a 10-year Maritime Truce with the Trucial states. Faisal bin Turki Al Saud returns to Arabia.

**1845** The Abu Dhabi leader Sheikh Khalifa is deposed.

**1847** The Ottomans and Persians sign the Treaty of Erzurum which places their common border along the Shatt al-Arab. The Al Thani move from Zubara to Doha.

**1849** The Ottomans regain control of Yemen.

**1850** The Al Qassimi and Muscat establish a border between their territories from Sharjah to Kalba.

**1851** Faisal bin Turki Al Saud reaches an agreement with Sheikh Mohammed bin Thani of Doha.

**1852** Sheikh Maktoum bin Butti of Dubai dies.

**1853** The Perpetual Treaty of Maritime Peace is signed by Abu Dhabi, Dubai, Sharjah and Ra's al-Khaimah, Umm al-Qaiwain and Ajman. Richard Burton travels incognito to Mecca. Sayyid Said bin Sultan transfers his court to Zanzibar.

**1854** Muscat cedes the Al Hallaniyat Islands (Kuria Muria) to Britain.

**1855** Samuel Kier builds an oil refinery in Pittsburgh. Abu Dhabi leader Sheikh Said is killed. Sheikh Zayed bin Khalifa succeeds.

**1856** Sayyid Said bin Sultan dies in the Seychelles.

**1857** The Indian rebellion against British rule begins.

**1859** The first Pennsylvania oil strike takes place. Death of the third Al Sabah emir, Sheikh Jaber.

**1861** Britain confirms the division of the Omani domains into two sultanates. Sultan Thuwainy becomes ruler of Oman. Bahrain signs the Treaty of Perpetual Maritime Peace.

**1862** William Palgrave begins his Arabian journey. The first steamship service to Kuwait begins.

**1865** The first Gulf political resident, Lewis Pelly, travels to Riyadh.

**1866** The death of the fourth Al Sabah emir, Sheikh Sabah.

**1867** Bahrain launches an attack on Doha and Wakra to suppress a rebellion by the Al Thani.

**1868** Sheikh Mohammed bin Thani is recognized by Britain as the chief of Qatar and establishes the Al Thani dynasty. Oman's Sultan Thuwainy dies.

**1869** The Suez Canal opens. Sheikh Isa Al Khalifa is recognized as joint ruler of Bahrain.

**1870** John D Rockefeller founds Standard Oil.

**1871** Sultan Azzan bin Qais dies. The Ottomans take Al Hasa and Qatar.

**1873** The Nobel Brothers Petroleum

Producing Company is founded in Baku.

**1875** The UK government becomes a shareholder in the Suez Canal.

**1876** Sultan Abdul Hamid proclaims a constitution for the Ottoman Empire and establishes a parliament. Charles Doughty begins his Arabian journey.

**1878** Sultan Abdul Hamid dissolves the Ottoman parliament. Wilfred and Lady Anne Blunt begin their Arabian journey.

**1879** The Zaydis rebel against Ottoman rule. Qatar's Sheikh Mohammed bin Thani dies.

**1880** Bahrain signs an initial exclusive agreement with Britain.

**1881** Abdelaziz bin Abdulrahman Al Saud is born.

**1885** Oil struck in Sumatra in the Dutch East Indies.

**1886** Dubai's Sheikh Hasher bin Maktoum dies.

**1888** Sheikh Isa Al Khalifa becomes the sole ruler of Bahrain. Oman's Sultan Turki bin Said dies.

**1890** The Royal Dutch Company floated.

**1891** Marcus Samuel, founder of Shell, wins a long-term contract to ship Russian oil. The Al Saud are defeated at Mulayda.

**1892** Britain signs an exclusive agreement with Abu Dhabi, Dubai, Sharjah/Ra's al-Khaimah and Umm al-Qaiwain/Ajman. The first Californian oil discovery is made. The Suez Canal opens to Samuel's oil tankers. Death of fifth Al Sabah emir of Kuwait, Sheikh Abdullah. The Dutch Reformed Church of America opens hospitals in Bahrain and Basra.

**1893** Abdulrahman bin Faisal Al Saud moves to Kuwait. The Ottomans invade Qatar.

**1894** Dubai's Sheikh Rashid bin Hasher dies.

**1895** Tribal and imamate forces occupy most of Muscat before being forced to withdraw.

**1896** Sheikh Mohammed Al Sabah, the sixth Al Sabah emir of Kuwait, dies and is succeeded by Sheikh Mubarak.

**1897** The Shell Transport & Trading Company is founded.

**1899** Britain signs an exclusive agreement with Kuwait.

**1901** The Texas oil boom starts. Sheikh Maktoum bin Hasher declares Dubai a duty free port.

**1902** Sheikh Abdelaziz Al Saud recaptures Riyadh. Ruhollah Mussawi Khomeini is born. Steam ships start direct services from India to Dubai.

**1903** The Indian viceroy, Viscount Curzon, begins his Gulf tour.

**1904** Ida Tarbell's *The History of Standard Oil* is published.

**1906** Abdelaziz Al Saud defeats the Al Rashid at Rawdat Muhanna. The shah is pressured into approving a Persian constitution and parliament.

**1908** Oil is discovered at Masjid-e-Solaiman in Persia. Sultan Abdul Hamid restores the 1876 Ottoman constitution and parliament following the Young Turk mutiny. Sharif Hussein is appointed emir of Mecca. Dubai's Sheikh Maktoum bin Hasher dies.

**1909** The US Federal Court orders the dissolution of Standard Oil, a measure that leads to the creation of Exxon, Mobil, Socal, Amoco, Sohio and Atlantic. Abu Dhabi's Sheikh Zayed bin Khalifa dies.

**1910** The British political agent to Kuwait, Captain William Shakespear, makes his first visit to Riyadh to meet Abdelaziz.

**1911** Imam Yahya of Yemen is recognized by the Ottomans.

**1912** The Turkish Petroleum Com-

pany (TPC) is formed. The first
Ikhwan settlements are founded
in central Arabia. Dubai's Sheikh
Butti bin Suhail dies. Sheikh
Rashid Bin Saeed is born.

**1913** APOC completes the Abadan
refinery. Abu Dhabi's Sheikh
Tahnoun dies. Abdelaziz Al Saud
captures Hofuf. Britain and the
Ottomans agree on, but do not
ratify, a treaty dividing Arabia into
zones of influence. Qatar's Sheikh
Qassim bin Mohammed Al Thani
dies. Britain is granted first rights
to oil exploration by Kuwait.
Oman's Sultan Faisal Bin Turki
dies.

**1914** Gertrude Bell travels across
central Arabia. TPC is promised
the Mesopotamian oil concession.
The UK's House of Commons
votes to take a 51 per cent stake
in APOC. The First World War
breaks out in Europe. Britain
declares war on the Ottoman
Empire. British and Imperial
troops land on the Fao Peninsula.
British troops capture Basra.
Egypt becomes a British
protectorate.

**1915** Omani rebels almost capture
Muscat. Sheikh Mubarak of
Kuwait dies. British and imperial troops land on the Gallipoli
Peninsula. The British high
commissioner to Cairo, Sir Henry
McMahon, begins correspondence
with Sharif Hussein of Mecca
about a possible war of rebellion against the Ottomans. The
Ottomans withdraw from Doha.
Britain recognizes Abdelaziz as
ruler of the Nejd and its dependencies which come under British
protection.

**1916** British and Imperial troops
withdraw from Gallipoli. The
secret Sykes-Picot agreement
divides the Arab World between Britain and France. Sharif
Hussein launches the Arab revolt.
Kichimatsu Mikimoto perfects the
technique of cultivating pearls.
Qatar signs an exclusive agreement with Britain.

**1917** Sheikh Jaber Al Sabah of
Kuwait dies. The Bolsheviks seize
power in Russia. The Balfour
Declaration is announced.

**1918** The Yemeni imamate is
recognized internationally. The
Ottomans sign an armistice
with the Allies and withdraw
to Anatolia. Germany signs an
armistice and ends the First World
War. The birth of Sheikh Zayed
Al Nahyan, future Abu Dhabi
ruler and president of the UAE.

**1919** The Versailles peace conference opens. Faisal bin Hussein
addresses the conference and calls
for an independent Arab state.
Abdullah bin Hussein is defeated
at Khurma in the Hejaz by the
Al Saud. The King Commission
report is completed.

**1920** The Syrian congress declares
the establishment of independent
Syria and Faisal bin Hussein as
king. The Iraqi congress declares
Abdullah bin Hussein as king.
The Kuwaitis are defeated by
the Ikhwan at Manifa. The San
Remo Treaty confirms British and
French control of the Levant and
Mesopotamia and restructures
the TPC. The Iraqi revolt against
the British mandate begins. The
French defeat the Syrians at
Maisalun and Faisal bin Hussein
leaves Syria. Abdullah bin Hussein
settles in Maan. The Ikhwan are
repulsed at Jahra in Kuwait.

**1921** Sheikh Jaber Al Sabah of
Kuwait dies. Reza Khan seizes
power in Persia. A conference
chaired by Winston Churchill in
Cairo decides to create Iraq.

Britain creates Transjordan under the rule of Hussein bin Abdullah. Abdelaziz completes the defeat of the Al Rashid. Faisal I is crowned King of Iraq. Oman's Sultan Taimour bin Faisal signs the Seeb Treaty which effectively divides Oman into two states. The Eastern Bank opens in Bahrain. Sheikh Sultan bin Salim of Ra's al-Khaimah is recognized by Britain as an independent ruler.

**1922** Abu Dhabi's Sheikh Hamdan is assassinated. Abdelaziz takes Abha. The Muhammara conference fixes the borders between Kuwait and Iraq. The Palestine mandate goes into effect. The Uqair conference redefines the borders between Iraq, Kuwait and the Nejd.

**1923** E&GS wins the Al Hasa exploration concession option. The final peace treaty between the allies and Turkey in Lausanne ends hopes of independent Kurdish and Armenian states.

**1924** E&GS wins the exploration concession for the Neutral Zone between Kuwait and the lands of Abdelaziz. Oman's Sultan Taimour bin Faisal awards an oil concession to D'Arcy Exploration. The Ottoman Sultan Mehmed is deposed by Mustafa Kemal, the caliphate abolished and the Turkish republic declared. King Hussein of the Hejaz is declared caliph. King Hussein of the Hejaz is pressured to abdicate and is replaced by his son King Ali. Abdelaziz Al Saud enters Mecca.

**1925** Iraq confirms the TPC concession. Persia's Qajar dynasty is deposed. E&GS wins the Bahrain oil concession. King Ali of the Hejaz abdicates.

**1926** Abdelaziz is declared King of the Hejaz. King Abdelaziz estab-

lishes a protectorate over the Idrisi sultanate of Asir. Reza Khan is crowned Reza Shah of Persia.

**1927** Abdelaziz is officially declared King of the Hejaz and the Najd and its dependencies. Britain recognizes the kingdom as a fully sovereign state. IPC strikes oil in Iraq. Gulf Oil buys the E&GS Bahrain and Kuwait concession. Abu Dhabi's Sheikh Sultan is killed.

**1928** Sheikh Shakhbut bin Sultan takes over as the Abu Dhabi ruler. Persian forces seize the Greater Tunb Island. US oil companies acquire 23.75 per cent of TPC. Abdelaziz begins a campaign against Ikhwan rebels. Socal buys Gulf Oil's Bahrain concession.

**1929** TPC renamed as the Iraq Petroleum Company (IPC). Abdelaziz defeats Ikhwan rebels at Zilfi.

**1930** Bertram Thomas crosses the Rub al-Khali from Salalah to Doha. Bapco is founded. King Abdelaziz annexes the Asir.

**1931** Oil drilling starts on Jebel Dukhan in Bahrain.

**1932** St John Philby begins his first Rub al-Khali journey. Imperial Airways starts a scheduled air service from London to Karachi via Basra, Bahrain and Sharjah. Oil is struck in Bahrain. Iraq joins the League of Nations and lays claim to Kuwaiti territory. The Kingdom of Saudi Arabia is declared. Sheikh Isa Al Khalifa dies after ruling for 63 years. Sultan Taimour bin Faisal abdicates in favour of his son. Mohammed bin Laden sets up a construction company.

**1933** King Abdelaziz defeats Imam Yahya in a war for the Asir. Socal signs a 60-year concession agreement with Saudi Arabia. King Faisal of Iraq dies and is succeeded by his son Ghazi. The Kuwait Oil Company (KOC) is formed by APOC and Gulf Oil.

**1934** IPC completes the Kirkuk–Tripoli pipeline. Imam Yahya of Yemen signs the Taif Treaty. Exports of Bahrain oil begin. KOC wins the Kuwait concession.

**1935** IPC wins the Dubai and Qatar concessions. Persia is renamed Iran and the APOC is renamed the Anglo-Iranian Oil Company. The KOC is awarded a 75-year oil concession in Kuwait.

**1936** St John Philby completes his expedition across south-west Arabia. Caltex is formed by Socal and Texaco. The first Saudi oil well is begun.

**1937** Aden becomes a British crown colony. IPC wins the Oman and Dhofar concession. The Iran-Iraq border is fixed along part of the Shatt al-Arab. Bahrain's Bapco refinery starts operating. The government of Qatar expels the population of Zubara and takes control of the town.

**1938** IPC is awarded the south Iraq concession. The Red Line Agreement is signed. KOC strikes oil in Kuwait. Socal strikes oil in Saudi Arabia. Kuwait sets up a legislative assembly but closes it soon after. An elected *majlis* is established in Dubai.

**1939** Kuwait sets up an appointed council. Dubai's Sheikh Saeed closes the elected *majlis*. King Ghazi of Iraq dies in a car crash and is succeeded by his son King Faisal II, who is a minor. The first Saudi oil exports begin. IPC signs oil-exploration concessions with all other Trucial State rulers. The RAF builds an airbase in Sharjah. The Second World War breaks out. IPC strikes oil in the Dukhan field in Qatar.

**1940** Italian bombers flying from the Horn of Africa bomb Dhahran and Bahrain. Sultan Qaboos is born.

**1941** IPC takes over the Mosul Petroleum Company. Reza Shah is deposed and replaced by his son Mohammed Reza Shah.

**1942** Sheikh Hamad bin Isa Al Salman dies.

**1943** The lend-lease programme is extended to Saudi Arabia.

**1944** California Arabian Standard Oil Company (Casoc) is renamed the Arabian American Oil Company (Aramco).

**1945** King Abdelaziz meets President Roosevelt at the Great Bitter Lakes in the Suez Canal and the UK prime minister, Winston Churchill, at the Fayyoum Oasis. The Arab League is formed in Cairo. Saudi Arabia declares war against the Axis. The Arabia–Bahrain pipeline opens. Tapline is formed to build a pipeline from Saudi Arabia to Sidon. The Truman Doctrine is announced. The Kurdish People's Republic of Mahabad is declared in north-west Iran.

**1946** Sheikh Zayed is appointed as Abu Dhabi ruler's representative in Al Ain. Wilfred Thesiger begins his first journey across the Empty Quarter. Kuwaiti oil exports begin. The first bank is opened in Dubai.

**1947** The Gulf political resident moves to Bahrain. The UN general assembly votes for the partition of Palestine into Arab and Jewish states. Britain unilaterally delimits the border between Bahrain and Qatar.

**1948** Imam Yahya of Yemen is assassinated. The Jewish national council proclaims the state of Israel. Arab armies simultaneously enter Arab Palestine. Kuwait awards the Neutral Zone concession to

Aminoil. The Red Line Agreement is abolished.

**1949** The first Arab-Israel War ends. Getty Oil wins the Saudi Arabian Neutral Zone concession. Saudi Arabia officially notifies the British government of claims against territory in Abu Dhabi, Oman and Qatar, including the Buraimi Oasis and a corridor to the coast between Abu Dhabi and the Qatar Peninsula. Britain rejects the Saudi territorial claim. Qatar oil exports begin.

**1950** Sheikh Ahmed of Kuwait dies. Gulf Aviation is founded in Bahrain. The first oil well in the Trucial States is spudded at Ras al-Sadr. Tapline is completed. Aramco agrees to a 50:50 profit share with Saudi Arabia.

**1951** Bahrain secures a 50:50 profit share with Bapco. A decision is made at a London conference to establish diplomatic relations between the Yemeni imamate and the UK and to fix the border between the imamate and Aden. AIOC agrees to a 50:50 profit share. The National Iranian Oil Company (NIOC) is formed. Mohammed Mossadegh becomes the Iranian prime minister. AIOC is nationalized. Winston Churchill returns as UK prime minister. Libya becomes independent. BOAC takes a 51 per cent stake in Gulf Air.

**1952** The Trucial States Council is established. Kuwait and KOC agree to a 50:50 profit split. The Saudi Arabian Monetary Agency (SAMA) is founded. The Egyptian monarchy is deposed. A Saudi military contingent moves into the Buraimi Oasis. The Buraimi standstill agreement is signed. Eisenhower is elected US president. Fujairah is recognized by the British as an independent emirate.

**1953** The Trucial Oman Scouts is formed. Abu Dhabi awards an offshore concession to the ADMA joint venture between BP and Total. Faisal II formally becomes king of Iraq. Qatar introduces 50:50 profit sharing. Mossadegh is deposed. King Abdelaziz dies and Crown Prince Saud succeeds.

**1954** Gamal Abdel Nasser becomes Egypt's prime minister. Ghalib bin Ali Hinai is elected Ibadhi imam. Iran Oil Participants Oil Consortium agreement is signed. Dubai awards its offshore concession to the Duma Consortium. Bahrain's higher executive committee is formed to press for political reforms. Nasser assumes the functions of Egyptian president. The imamate rebellion begins against Oman's Sultan Said bin Taimour.

**1955** The Kuwait Airways Corporation (KAC) is founded. Nasser announces Czech weapons purchases. Iraq and Turkey sign an anti-communist treaty that becomes known as the Baghdad Pact. A rising against Yemen's Imam Ahmed is suppressed. The Buraimi Oasis arbitration opens in Geneva. Saudi Arabia and Egypt sign a treaty of defence and friendship. The Buraimi Crisis ends with the expulsion of Saudi forces. King Saud orders the first expansion of the Great Mosque of Mecca in more than 1,000 years. Omani forces seize Nizwa and Rustaq and Imam Ghalib bin Ali Hinai flees to Saudi Arabia.

**1956** Demonstrations are held against the visit of UK foreign secretary Selwyn Lloyd to Bahrain. British troops leave the Suez Canal Zone. Nasser formally becomes Egyptian president. Oil is discovered in Algeria. President Nasser announces the nationalization of the Suez Canal. Israel invades Sinai at the start of the Second Arab-Israel War. Britain and France launch an airborne assault on the canal zone. Anti-British demonstrations take place in Bahrain. Bahraini higher executive committee members are arrested, tried and sentenced to imprisonment on St Helena. Oil exploration begins at Fahud in Oman.

**1957** UK prime minister, Anthony Eden, resigns. Osama bin Laden is born in Riyadh. King Saud visits the US and adopts the Eisenhower Doctrine. The Suez Canal re-opens. Qatar's Sheikh Abdullah bin Qassim Al Thani dies. Imamate rebels seize Bahla and Nizwa. Saudi Arabia awards the offshore Neutral Zone concession to the Japan Petroleum Trading Company (JPTC). Riyadh University is opened. The Iranian parliament claims Bahrain as Iran's 14th province.

**1958** A union between Egypt and Syria is declared. The JPTC concession is transferred to the Arabian Oil Company (AOC). King Saud hands executive authority over to Crown Prince Faisal. Oil is discovered in Abu Dhabi's offshore Umm Shaif field. The Iraqi Hashemite monarchy is deposed. AOC is awarded the Kuwait offshore Neutral Zone concession. The maritime border between Bahrain and Saudi Arabia is established and Bahrain is promised half the production of the Abu Safah field. Dubai's Sheikh Saeed dies. Oman's Sultan Said bin Taimour sells Gwadur to Pakistan.

**1959** British and Omani forces end the imamate rebellion in the Jebel Akhdar. Britain sponsors the creation of the South Arabian Federation in what will become most of South Yemen. Oil is discovered in Libya. The dredging of Dubai Creek is completed.

**1960** AOC strikes oil. OPEC is founded. IPC strikes oil in the Murban Field in Abu Dhabi. Dubai International Airport opens. Qatar's Sheikh Abdullah bin Hamad Al Thani is deposed. Crown Prince Faisal steps down from government and King Saud appoints a new cabinet. Bahrain introduces the dinar. The first bank opens in Abu Dhabi.

**1961** Kuwait becomes independent. British troops are deployed on the Iraq-Kuwait border. The Arab League agrees to protect Kuwaiti territory. King Saud's health collapses and Crown Prince Faisal returns to government. Bahrain's Sheikh Salman bin Hamad Al Khalifa dies.

**1962** The Popular Socialist Party (PSP) is formed in Aden. Abu Dhabi oil exports begin. Yemen's Imam Ahmed dies and is succeeded by his son Mohammed Al Badr. Eight days later, the army takes power in a coup. Oil is struck in Oman. Crown Prince Faisal, appointed Saudi prime minister in October, announces the abolition of slavery and other reforms. Ayatollah Khomeini criticizes the shah's reforms and calls for an Islamic constitution in Iran.

**1963** Aden joins the South Arabian Federation. Elections are held for the Kuwait national assembly. The National Front for the Liberation of South Yemen is formed in Sanaa. The Dhofar Rebellion begins. Rebellion breaks out in the Aden protectorates.

**1964** BOAC starts weekly return flights to Dubai. The Dhofar

Liberation Front is formed. Ayatollah Khomeini is deported to Turkey. King Saud abdicates in favour of Crown Prince Faisal.

**1965** Ayatollah Khomeini moves to Najaf. The Trucial States Development Office is opened in Dubai. Sharjah's Sheikh Saqr bin Sultan is deposed. Sheikh Abdullah Al Salem of Kuwait dies.

**1966** Anti-British groups merge into the Front for the Liberation of South Yemen (FLOSY). The UK government announces its intention to withdraw from south Arabia by early 1968. Oil is discovered in Dubai. Oman's Sultan Said bin Taimour escapes an assassination attempt in Salalah. Sheikh Shakhbut is replaced as ruler of Abu Dhabi by Sheikh Zayed.

**1967** Second elections to the Kuwait national assembly take place. Egypt orders the UN out of Sinai. Israel attacks Egypt, Jordan and Syria in the third Arab-Israel War. Britain withdraws from the Aden protectorates. Oman starts exporting oil. British forces evacuate Aden and the National Front for the Liberation of South Yemen forms a government. Britain returns the Hallaniyat Islands (Kuria Muria) to Oman.

**1968** The UK announces its withdrawal from east of Suez. The People's Front for the Liberation of the Arab Gulf (PFLOAG) is formed. Abu Dhabi ruler Sheikh Zayed and Dubai ruler Sheikh Rashid meet at Al Semaih and agree to form a union. The Iraqi Baath Socialist Party seizes power.

**1969** Yasser Arafat becomes chairman of the Palestine Liberation Organisation (PLO). PFLOAG fighters take control of western Dhofar. Libya's King Idris is deposed in a coup by republican army officers led by Muammar Qaddafi. Abu Dhabi's Mina Zayed and international airport open. The Neutral Zone is partitioned.

**1970** Sultan Qaboos assumes power in Oman. Bahrain increases its Bapco profit share to 55 per cent. President Nasser dies. The People's Democratic Republic of Yemen (PDRY) is declared in Aden.

**1971** The third Kuwait national assembly elections take place. The Tehran agreement between OPEC and oil companies is reached. The UK confirms its withdrawal from the Gulf will take place by the end of the year. The Tripoli agreement between OPEC and oil companies is reached. Bahrain becomes independent. Qatar declares independence. Dubai's Port Rashid opens. Iran seizes the Greater and Lesser Tunbs. The UAE is declared. Saudi Arabia recognizes the Sultanate of Oman.

**1972** Sharjah's Sheikh Khalid bin Mohammed Al Qassimi is killed in an attack on his palace led by Sheikh Saqr bin Sultan. Ra's al-Khaimah joins the UAE. Qatar's Sheikh Ahmed bin Ahmed Al Thani is deposed. The IPC concession in Iraq is nationalized. Iraq signs a friendship agreement with the Soviet Union. The PFLOAG is defeated at Mirbat by British and Omani forces. Aluminium Bahrain starts operating. BCCI is founded. Former ruler of Oman, Said bin Taimour, dies in the UK. Elections to Bahrain's constituent assembly take place.

**1973** Bahrain takes a 25 per cent stake in the Bahrain oil field and all Bapco assets. The Bahrain Monetary Agency (BMA) is formed. The UAE Currency

Board is formed and the UAE dirham is launched. OPEC approves increasing government ownership of oil in Gulf countries. The Bahrain constituent assembly approves a constitution and the creation of a national assembly. Egypt and Syria attack Israel in the Fourth Arab-Israel War. OPEC announces a 70 per cent oil price rise. Saudi Arabia announces a US oil embargo. OPEC announces further oil market price increases to US$11.65 a barrel. Iraq occupies Al Samtah and other Kuwaiti territory. Crescent Petroleum discovers oil in its Sharjah concession off Abu Musa. Elections to Bahrain's national assembly take place. Bahrain, Oman, Qatar and Abu Dhabi buy BOAC's shares in Gulf Air.

**1974** Kuwait announces plans to take a 60 per cent stake in KOC. Qatar announces a 60 per cent participation. Saudi Arabia announces plans for a 60 per cent stake in Aramco. Abu Dhabi announces a 60 per cent participation. Bahrain raises its Bapco profit share to 85 per cent. The military take power in North Yemen. The Treaty of Jeddah defines the border between Abu Dhabi and Saudi Arabia. Shell discovers the offshore North Field non-associated gas reservoir.

**1975** Bahrain increases its ownership of oil assets to 60 per cent. The fourth Kuwait national assembly elections take place. Iran and Iraq sign the Algiers Accord that defines the boundary between the two countries at the thalweg of the Shatt al-Arab. King Faisal of Saudi Arabia is assassinated and King Khaled succeeds. The Lebanese civil war begins. Dubai takes a 60 per cent stake in its oil industry. The Bahrain national

assembly is dissolved. Kuwait takes 100 per cent of the KOC concession. An end to the Dhofar Rebellion is declared.

**1976** Concorde flights to Bahrain start. Sultan Qaboos marries Kamila bint Tariq bin Taimour. Aramco and Saudi Arabia agree on the terms of full nationalization. The Kuwait national assembly is dissolved. Qatar completes the full nationalization of the oil industry. OPEC splits over prices.

**1977** OPEC unifies oil prices. Ayatollah Khomeini's son Mustafa is murdered. President Sadat travels to Tel Aviv. Iraq withdraws from Al Samtah and other Kuwaiti territory. Sheikh Sabah Al Sabah of Kuwait dies.

**1978** Anti-shah riots take place in Qom. US President Carter approves F-15 fighter sales to Saudi Arabia. Ali Abdullah Saleh becomes president of North Yemen. Ayatollah Khomeini is expelled from Iraq. Strikes cripple Iranian oil production.

**1979** The shah leaves Iran. Ayatollah Khomeini returns to Iran and establishes an Islamic republic. The Egypt-Israel peace treaty is signed. OPEC raises the benchmark oil price to US$14.65 a barrel. Militants seize the Holy Haram in Mecca.

**1980** President Saddam Hussein tears up the Algiers agreement and orders the invasion of Iran. The OPEC majority raises the oil marker (benchmark) price to US$36 a barrel. The full nationalization of Bahrain's oil industry is completed.

**1981** Kuwait national assembly elections take place. Oil prices hit US$40 a barrel on the spot market. The Gulf Co-operation Council (GCC) is founded. Iran repulses Iraqi attack on Abadan. Egypt's President Sadat is assassinated. US congress approves AWACS aircraft sales to Saudi Arabia. OPEC unites around a US$32 a barrel market price. Sultan Qaboos of Oman forms the state consultative council. An attempted coup in Bahrain is reported.

**1982** OPEC sets production limits for the first time. Israel invades Lebanon. King Khaled dies and is succeeded by King Fahd. The Fahd plan calling implicitly for the recognition of Israel is adopted by the Fez Arab League summit. Kuwait's Souq al-Manakh share crash takes place. Osama bin Laden moves to Peshawar.

**1983** OPEC reduces its combined quota to 17.5 million b/d and the marker price to US$29 a barrel. Prince Bandar bin Sultan is appointed Saudi Arabian ambassador to the US. Jebel Ali port is completed.

**1984** Iraq begins the tanker war in the Gulf. Getty Oil is taken over by Texaco. OPEC reduces quotas to 16 million b/d.

**1985** Kuwait national asssembly elections are held. The Jebel Ali Free Zone is created. An attempt to assassinate Kuwait's Sheikh Jaber Al Sabah takes place. Saudi oil production is reduced to 2.2 million b/d. Emirates Airline starts operating. OPEC abandons its price defence policy in December.

**1986** Civil war breaks out in South Yemen. Iran captures the Fao Peninsula. Qatar destroys buildings erected by Bahrain on Fasht al-Dabal. The second permanent dissolution of the Kuwait national assembly is declared. The oil price falls below US$10 a barrel. Saudi oil minister Ahmed Zaki Yamani

is dismissed. The King Fahd Causeway between Bahrain and Saudi Arabia opens. OPEC sets a US$18 a barrel marker price target and a combined quota of 17.3 million b/d in December.

**1987** The US Tower Commission report says White House staff, including Lieutenant-Colonel Oliver North, illegally supplied weapons to Iran for the release of US hostages in Lebanon. The US agrees to reflag Kuwaiti oil tankers. Sheikh Abdelaziz bin Mohammed Al Qassimi temporarily deposes Sharjah's Sheikh Sultan bin Mohammed. The UN Security Council unanimously passes Resolution 598 that fixes terms for an end to the Iran-Iraq War.

**1988** Iraq recovers the Fao Peninsula. The USS *Vincennes* shoots down an Iranian airliner over the Gulf. The Iran-Iraq War ends in August. The Kuwait Investment Office (KIO) is ordered to halve its holding of BP shares. Saudi Aramco is created.

**1989** Soviet troops leave Afghanistan. Imam Khomeini issues a fatwa calling on Muslims to kill Salman Rushdie for insulting Islam in his novel *The Satanic Verses*. Egypt, Iraq, Jordan and North Yemen set up the Arab Co-operation Council (ACC). Imam Khomeini dies in June. Osama bin Laden returns to Saudi Arabia.

**1990** Abu Dhabi takes majority control of BCCI. North Yemen and South Yemen unify. A semi-elected Kuwait assembly is formed. Saddam Hussein accuses Gulf states of harming Iraq by pushing down oil prices. Iraqi and Kuwaiti representatives meet in Jeddah. Iraq invades Kuwait. Dubai's Sheikh Rashid bin Saeed dies. Sultan Qaboos replaces the appointed state consultative council with an indirectly elected Majlis al-Shoura.

**1991** Coalition forces begin an air war in January and the land war starts in February. US President Bush announces a ceasefire. Osama bin Laden flees Saudi Arabia. Qatar refers the Bahrain border issue to the International Court of Justice (ICJ). Oman Air is founded. BCCI is closed by banking authorities. Bahrain signs a defence co-operation agreement with the US and becomes the headquarters of the US Navy's Fifth Fleet. The Kuwaiti oil fires are extinguished at the end of the year. Bin Laden arrives in Sudan.

**1992** Saudi Arabia publishes the basic law of government, a form of constitution. Al Qaeda issues its first fatwa calling for holy war against the West. Bombs are detonated at two Aden hotels used by US troops.

**1993** Unified Yemen holds its first parliamentary elections. Somali militants kill 18 US troops in Mogadishu. Saudi Arabia's Majlis al-Shoura is inaugurated.

**1994** Qatar Airways is founded. A civil war erupts in Yemen. South Yemen secedes. The South Yemeni secession is repressed. The Middle East Broadcasting Centre (MBC) is launched.

**1995** Sheikh Mohammed bin Rashid is named Dubai's crown prince. The Bahrain intifada begins. Qatar's Sheikh Khalifa Al Thani is deposed by his son, Crown Prince Hamad. Oman's finance minister Qais Al Zawawi is killed in a car crash. A car bomb at a Saudi Arabian National Guard base in Riyadh kills five Americans and two Indians. The former Qatar ruler Sheikh Khalifa sets up his

headquarters in Abu Dhabi.

**1996** A failed countercoup attempt takes place in Qatar. The UN Iraq oil-for-food resolution is passed. A truck bomb kills 19 US servicemen in Al Khobar. Osama bin Laden arrives in Jalabad. Kabul falls to the Taliban.

**1997** Sultan Qaboos issues the basic law of the state that calls for an elected *majlis*. Mohammed Khatami is elected Iranian president. OPEC raises its target production to 27.5 million b/d and starts a new oil price crash.

**1998** Osama bin Laden issues a fatwa declaring war against the US. Car bombs in Nairobi and Dar E-Salaam kill more than 200 people.

**1999** The oil price falls below US$10 a barrel. OPEC subsequently agrees to a cut in combined production. Bahrain's Sheikh Isa Al Salman dies. The US declares Afghanistan to be a state sponsor of terrorism.

**2000** Omani LNG exports start. Saudi Arabia and Yemen reach a final border agreement. Ian Henderson, Bahrain's former director of public security, retires completely. Al Qaeda carries out an attack on the USS *Cole* in Aden. The second Omani *majlis* elections take place.

**2001** A referendum approves Bahrain's national action charter. The ICJ rules on the Bahrain and Qatar border. Qatar and Saudi Arabia sign a final border agreement. On September 11, Al Qaeda hijackers fly passenger jets into New York's Twin Towers, the Pentagon and Pennsylvania. The US designates Bahrain as a major non-Nato ally.

**2002** The Bahrain constitution is unveiled. The Arab League adopts the King Abdullah plan for Middle East peace. Municipal elections are held in Bahrain. President Bush addresses the UN and charges Iraq with working on weapons of mass destruction. US marines are fired on during war games on Failaka Island. Elections to Bahrain's council of deputies take place. UN Security Council resolution 1441 is passed in November. Iraq fails to comply with UNSCR 1441. Bahrain's council of deputies opens. OPEC lifts its production target to 24.5 million b/d.

**2003** Coalition forces invade Iraq in March. Abu Dhabi launches Etihad Airways. The third Oman *majlis* elections take place. Shell revises its estimates of Omani reserves downwards.

**2004** OPEC raises its production target to 27 million b/d. Chechen leader Zelimkhan Yandarbiyev is killed by a car bomb in Doha. Car bombs detonated in Riyadh kill 32 people. The Bahrain interior minister, Sheikh Mohammed bin Khalifa, is dismissed following violence during demonstrations. Six Bahrainis are arrested on suspicion of planning attacks on US targets and then released. A second car bomb in a Riyadh compound kills 17. Foreigners are killed in attacks in Yanbu, Riyadh and Al Khobar. The Dubai International Financial Centre (DIFC) is opened. The death is announced in November of Sheikh Zayed, ruler of Abu Dhabi and president of the UAE.

**2005** A gun battle with Islamic militants in Kuwait takes place. Oman arrests several hundred people. Saudi Arabia holds municipal elections. The Kuwait national assembly approves votes for women. King Fahd dies in August and is succeeded by King Abdullah. BCCI creditors drop their case against the Bank of England. UAE president Sheikh Khalifa unveils plans for indirect elections to the UAE federal national council.

**2006** Dubai ruler and UAE prime minister and vice-president, Sheikh Maktoum bin Rashid Al Maktoum, dies in Australia in January and his brother Sheikh Mohammed succeeds. Sheikh Jaber Al Sabah of Kuwait dies 11 days later. US congress ratifies the Bahrain-US free-trade agreement. Sheikh Saad is deposed by the Kuwait national assembly on grounds of incapacity and Sheikh Sabah becomes Kuwait's ruler. Women vote for the first time in the Kuwait national assembly elections in June. Elections to Bahrain's council of deputies take place. Elections to the UAE's federal national council are held. The Asian Games are held in Qatar in December. Saddam Hussein is hanged in Baghdad.

**2007** Russian President Putin visits Saudi Arabia. Iran's President Ahmadinejad visits Saudi Arabia and the UAE. A woman wins a seat in Qatar's municipal council elections. Cyclone Gumu lashes Oman and the UAE. Elections are held for Oman's Majlis al-Shura. The GCC declares the GCC common market will start in 2008.

# INDEX

**A**

Abadan 63, 94, 102–103, 192
Abalkhail, Mohammed 141–148
Abbasids 65–67, 124–125
Abdallah bin Jiluwi 129
Abdallah Malik ibn Anas 57
Abdelaziz bin Baz 148
Abdullah bin Sabah, Sheikh 173–174,
Abdullah bin Saud 127, 160
Abdullah bin Thunayyan 161
Abraham 21, 42–44, 54–55, 124
Abu Bakr, Caliph 23, 45, 48–50, 158,
   228
Abu Dhabi Company for Onshore Oil
   Operations (ADCO) 277
Abu Dhabi Defence Force 260
Abu Dhabi Executive Council
   261–264
Abu Dhabi International Airport 265
Abu Dhabi Investment Authority
   (ADIA) 8, 261
Abu Dhabi Islands Archaeological
   Survey (ADIAS) 34
Abu Dhabi Marine Areas (ADMA)
   277
Abu Dhabi National Oil Company
   (ADNOC) 85–86, 264, 277
Abu Dhabi Petroleum Company
   (ADPC) 277
Abu Dhabi Securities Market 316
Abu Dhabi Water & Electricity
   Authority (ADWEA) 263
Abu Musa Island 26, 303, 309, 313
Abu Safah Field 194
Adnan, Nizar bin Majid bin 21
Adnani tribal group (Nizari) 21, 230,
   258, 267
Afar tribal group 21, 268
Agail tribal group 22
Ahmadinejad, President Mahmoud
   12–13, 69, 71–72
Ahmed Shah 70
Aitken, Jonathan 116
Ajlan bin Mohammed 129
Ajman tribal group 21
Al Ahmar family 22, 62
Al Ali tribal group 298, 307
Al Amiri tribal group 21
Al As, Amr ibn 47, 49
Al Asad, President Bashar 17, 255
Al Asad, President Hafez 17
Al Assaf, Ibrahim 148
Al Attiyah, Abdullah 208–209, 222
Al Ayyubi, Salah Al Din (Saladin) 59
Al Bashir, Field Marshal Omar 19

Al Bu Falah tribal group 267–268,
   270, 273
Al Bu Falasah family 268, 270, 283
Al Bu Said, Ahmed bin Said bin
   Mohammed 231
Al Bu Said, Buthaina bint Taimour 235
Al Bu Said, Sheikh Tariq bin Taimour
   241, 245, 312
Al Bu Said, Sultan Qaboos bin Said
   17, 217, 224, 231, 235, 239,
   241–245, 249, 312
Al Bu Said, Sultan Said bin Taimour
   217, 235–241, 312
Al Bu Said, Sultan Taimour 233–235,
   249
Al Dakhil, Abdulrahman ibn Muawiya
   65
Al Dawasir tribal group 21–23
Al Dhaheri tribal group 21, 268
Al Door 41, 257, 307
Alexander the Great 39, 172–173,
   189, 211
Alexandria 66, 95, 141
Al Fahim, Mohammed 272
Al Faisal, Prince Mohammed 119
Al Faleh, Matruk 159
Al Farabi, Abu Nasr 66
Al Ghafiri, Sheikh Braik bin Hamood
   bin Hamid 240–242
Al Ghafran tribal group 220
Al Ghamdi tribal group 21
Algiers Agreement 102
Algosaibi, Ghazi 141
Al Gurg, Easa 23, 273, 309
Al Hallaniyat (Kuria Muria) Islands
   22, 26, 227
Al Hamad, Abdel-Latif 182
Al Hamili, Mohammed 209
Al Hanafi, Najdah ibn Amr 58
Al Hashemi, Sheikh Sayed Ali 17, 19
Al Hussein, Imam Yahya 61–62, 77,
   131–132
Al Hussein, King Abdullah II 17, 281
Al Hussein, Princess Haya bint 281
Al Hussein, Queen Alia 281
Ali Alabbar, Mohammed 280
Ali bin Hussein, King 130, 157
Al Idrisi, Mohammed bin Ali 77,
   130–131
Alireza, Abdullah 23
Alireza, Mohammed Abdullah 135
Ali Salman, Sheikh 199, 201
Al Jaber, Sheikh Sabah 173
Al Jazeera 209, 220, 254–255
Al Kathir tribal group (Al Kathiris)
   22, 227

Al Khalifa, King Hamad bin Isa 19, 200–205
Al Khalifa, Sheikh Abdullah bin Ahmed 191, 204
Al Khalifa, Sheikh Ahmed 204
Al Khalifa, Sheikh Ali bin Khalifa 205
Al Khalifa, Sheikh Isa bin Ali 191–192, 205
Al Khalifa, Sheikh Isa bin Salman 9, 194–196, 198, 200, 205
Al Khalifa, Sheikh Khalifa bin Salman 186, 195, 198, 203–204
Al Khalifa, Sheikh Mohammed bin Abdullah 205
Al Khalifa, Sheikh Mohammed bin Khalifa 199, 202, 204
Al Khalifa, Sheikh Rashid bin Abdullah 202
Al Khalifa, Sheikh Salman bin Ahmed 204
Al Khalifa, Sheikh Salman bin Hamad 193–194, 205
Al Khalili, Imam 235–236
Al Khwarazmi, Mohammed ibn Musa 66
Al Mahdi, Imam Mohammed 56, 58
Al Mahra tribal group 22, 227
Al Maktoum, Sheikha Hind bint Maktoum bin Juma 280
Al Maktoum, Sheikh Ahmed bin Mohammed 280
Al Maktoum, Sheikh Ahmed bin Saeed 280, 291
Al Maktoum, Sheikha Manal bint Mohammed 317
Al Maktoum, Sheikha Mariam bint Rashid 216
Al Maktoum, Sheikh Hamdan bin Mohammed 280
Al Maktoum, Sheikh Hamdan bin Rashid 279, 313
Al Maktoum, Sheikh Hasher bin Maktoum 283
Al Maktoum, Sheikh Mayed bin Mohammed 280
Al Maktoum, Sheikh Maktoum bin Mohammed 280
Al Maktoum, Sheikh Maktoum bin Rashid 8, 17, 263, 279–280
Al Maktoum, Sheikh Mohammed bin Rashid 17, 216, 250, 252–254, 272, 279–281
Al Maktoum, Sheikh Rashid bin Hamdan 279
Al Maktoum, Sheikh Rashid bin Maktoum 279
Al Maktoum, Sheikh Rashid bin Saeed 259–260, 279, 285–290, 304, 309–315
Al Maktoum, Sheikh Saeed bin Maktoum 279
Al Maktoum, Sheikh Saeed bin Rashid 283–285

Al Manasir tribal group 21, 268
Al Mashaani, Mizoon bint Ahmed 235
Al Masari, Mohammed 158–159
Al Misned, Sheikha Mozah bint Nasser 8, 206, 209, 221–222
Al Mualla, Sheikh Abdullah bin Rashid 307
Al Mualla, Sheikh Ahmed bin Abdullah 307
Al Mualla, Sheikh Ahmed bin Rashid 307
Al Mualla, Sheikh Hamad bin Ibrahim 305
Al Mualla, Sheikh Rashid bin Ahmed 307
Al Mualla, Sheikh Salim bin Abdullah 307
Al Mubarak, Dr Massouma 8, 164
Al Muhairi family 268
Al Muhallab ibn Abi Safra 48
Al Mutair tribal group 21
Al Muttalib, Abd 45
Al Muttalib, Abdullah bin Abd 45
Al Naboodah construction company 288
Al Nahyan, President Khalifa bin Zayed 9, 19, 250, 252–253, 260–261
Al Nahyan, Sheikh Mohammed bin Zayed 17, 19, 262,
Al Nahyan, Sheikh Zayed bin Khalifa (Zayed the Great) 271–273
Al Nahyan, Sheikh Zayed bin Sultan 9, 17, 19, 53, 99, 218, 252, 258–260, 308–316
Al Nahyan family 262–264
Al Naim tribal group 214, 306
Al Nuaimi family 306–307
Al Qassimi, Dr Sheikh Sultan bin Mohammed 304–305
Al Qassimi family (Ra's al-Khaimah) 298–300
Al Qassimi family (Sharjah) 302–305
Al Qathani, Mohammed bin Abdullah 144
Al Rahim & Al Trahom 156
Al Rashid, Abdelaziz bin Mohammed 128–129
Al Rashid, Harun 124
Al Rashid, Mohammed 128
Al Rostamani, Dr Amina 15, 254
Al Roumi, Dr Mariam 8
Al Sabah, Sheikh Abdullah Al Salem 177–180, 185
Al Sabah, Sheikh Abdullah bin Sabah 173–174, 185
Al Sabah, Sheikh Ahmed Al Jaber 176–178, 185
Al Sabah, Sheikh Jaber Al Ahmed Al Jaber 19, 162, 166–167, 170, 180–183, 185
Al Sabah, Sheikh Jaber bin Abdullah 185

Al Sabah, Sheikh Jaber bin Mubarak
175, 185
Al Sabah, Sheikh Mohammed bin
Sabah 174, 185
Al Sabah, Sheikh Mubarak bin Sabah
75, 174–175, 178, 185
Al Sabah, Sheikh Nasser Al
Mohammed 165
Al Sabah, Sheikh Saad Al Abdullah Al
Salim 166–167, 170, 181
Al Sabah, Sheikh Sabah Al Ahmed Al
Jaber 19, 165–166, 185, 313
Al Sabah, Sheikh Sabah Al Salem
180–181, 185
Al Sabah, Sheikh Sabah bin Jaber 185
Al Sabah, Sheikh Salem bin Mubarak
175–176, 185
Al Sabah, Sheikh Saud Nasser 183
Al Saud, Abdelrahman bin Faisal
129, 174
Al Saud, Faisal 128, 174, 212
Al Saud, King Abdelaziz bin
Abdulrahman bin Faisal 62,
76–77, 82–84, 90–93, 110, 116,
118, 122, 128–136, 140–141, 148,
152, 157, 161, 174, 176, 213, 220
Al Saud, King Abdullah bin Abdelaziz
19, 65, 111, 113, 115, 117–118,
121, 131, 146, 151, 159–161, 220,
277
Al Saud, King Fahd bin Abdelaziz
9, 65, 103–104, 107, 110, 112,
115–117, 134, 140–143, 145–147,
149, 161, 199, 218
Al Saud, King Faisal bin Abdelaziz
64, 108, 116, 118–119, 135–140,
161, 196, 239,
Al Saud, King Khaled bin Abdelaziz
133, 135, 137, 140–143, 146, 161
Al Saud, King Saud bin Abdelaziz
135–137, 161
Al Saud, Mohammed bin
Abdulrahman bin Faisal 129
Al Saud, Prince Abdelaziz bin
Abdullah 117
Al Saud, Prince Abdelaziz bin Fahd
bin Abdelaziz 116
Al Saud, Prince Abdul Mohsen bin
Abdelaziz 137
Al Saud, Prince Abdulrahman bin
Abdelaziz 118
Al Saud, Prince Ahmed bin Abdelaziz
118, 141
Al Saud, Prince Alwaleed bin Talal bin
Abdelaziz 108, 119
Al Saud, Prince Badr bin Abdelaziz
137
Al Saud, Prince Bandar bin Sultan bin
Abdelaziz 111, 118–119, 145, 151
Al Saud, Prince Faisal bin Fahd bin
Abdelaziz 116
Al Saud, Prince Faisal bin Salman bin
Abdelaziz 119

Al Saud, Prince Fawwaz bin Abdelaziz
137
Al Saud, Prince Hamud bin Abdelaziz
118
Al Saud, Prince Khaled bin Faisal bin
Abdelaziz 119
Al Saud, Prince Khaled bin Sultan bin
Abdelaziz 119
Al Saud, Prince Miteb bin Abdullah
117
Al Saud, Prince Mohammed bin Fahd
bin Abdelaziz 116
Al Saud, Prince Mohammed bin Naif
bin Abdelaziz 119
Al Saud, Prince Naif bin Abdelaziz
118–119, 141
Al Saud, Prince Nawwaf bin Abdelaziz
137
Al Saud, Prince Salman bin Abdelaziz
116, 118–119, 141, 158
Al Saud, Prince Saud bin Faisal bin
Abdelaziz 119, 141
Al Saud, Prince Saud bin Naif bin
Abdelaziz 119
Al Saud, Prince Sultan bin Abdelaziz
118–119, 134, 141, 146
Al Saud, Prince Sultan bin Fahd bin
Abdelaziz 116
Al Saud, Prince Sultan bin Salman bin
Abdelaziz 119, 158
Al Saud, Prince Talal bin Abdelaziz
119, 134, 136–137
Al Saud, Prince Turki bin Abdelaziz
118
Al Saud, Prince Turki bin Faisal bin
Abdelaziz 115, 119, 152, 159
Al Saud, Saad bin Abdulrahman bin
Faisal 129
Al Saud family 20, 22, 24, 74, 81–82,
91, 108, 115, 117–118, 125–131,
136, 152–157, 173–176, 190–191,
211–213, 231–232
Al Sharqi, Sheikh Abdullah bin Saif
308
Al Sharqi, Sheikh Hamad bin
Abdullah 308
Al Sharqi, Sheikh Hamad bin
Mohammed 308
Al Sharqi, Sheikh Mohammed bin
Hamad 308
Al Sharqi family (Sharqiyin) 21, 308
Al Shirawi, Yousuf 195–196
Al Sistani, Grand Ayatollah Ali 202
Al Soulh, Princess Mona 119
Al Soulh, Riad 119
Al Sudairi, Hassa bint Ahmed 116
Al Sudairi, Sarah bint Ahmed 128
Al Sulaiman, Abdullah 133–134
Al Tamimi, Abdallah ibn Ibadh 60
Al Thani, Sheikh Abdelaziz bin Ahmed
217
Al Thani, Sheikh Abdullah bin Jassem
213–215, 223

Al Thani, Sheikh Ahmed bin Ali
216–217, 223, 287
Al Thani, Sheikh Ali bin Hamad
215–216, 223, 287
Al Thani, Sheikh Hamad bin Abdullah
213, 215
Al Thani, Sheikh Hamad bin Jassem
208–209, 219, 221
Al Thani, Sheikh Hamad bin Khalifa
8–9, 206, 208–210, 216, 219–223
Al Thani, Sheikh Jassem bin Hamad
206
Al Thani, Sheikh Jassem bin
Mohammed 212–213, 223
Al Thani, Sheikh Khalifa bin Hamad
208, 216–219, 223
Al Thani, Sheikh Mohammed bin
Hamad 222
Al Thani, Sheikh Tameem bin Hamad
17, 206, 208
Al Thani family 191–192, 211–213,
216, 219
Al Thunayyan, Iffat 119, 138
Al Waleed, Khalid bin 23, 47–48
Al Walid, Rashid bin 228
Al Wifaq National Islamic Society
201, 203–204
Al Yaarubi, Imam Sultan bin Saif 229
Al Yaarubi, Nasr bin Murshid bin
Sultan 229
Al Yamamah contract 145
Al Yousef, Mohammed bin Musa 245
Al Zawahiri, Ayman 153, 155
Al Zawawi, Qais 245
American Oil Company (Aminoil)
93–95
Amoco 88, 105, 217
Anaizah tribal confederation 20, 125,
173, 190
Anglo-Iranian Oil Company (AIOC)
94–95
Anglo-Persian Oil Company (APOC)
70, 88–94, 133, 176–177, 192,
213–214, 236
An Numan ibn Thabit (Abu Hanifa)
57
Arab Banking Corporation (ABC)
197
Arab Cooperation Council (ACC) 64
Arabian American Oil Company
(Aramco) 92–96, 100, 112, 135,
139, 141, 144, 147–149
Arabian Oil Company (AOC) 96–97
Arabian Shield 29
Arab Nationalist Movement (ANM)
239
Arab Revolt 77
Arafat, Yasser 97, 150–151, 180
Aramco Gulf Operations Company
(AGOC) 96
Aref, Dr Mohammed Reza 19
Arif, President Abdelrahman 179
Arif, President Abdel Salam 179

Ashland Oil 93
ASRY 197
Ataturk, President Kemal 56, 79
Atlantic (oil company) 88
Augustus Caesar, Emperor 40
Awair tribal group 21
Awazim tribal group 21
Ayyubids 59, 125
Azienda Generali Italiana Petroli
(Agip) 96, 139
Aziz, Tariq 71, 102, 104, 169
Azzan bin Qais, Sultan 233, 249

**B**

Bahamdan family 24
Bahrain Financial Harbour 186, 204
Bahrain International Airport 203–204
Bahrain Petroleum Company (Bapco)
91–92, 192–194
Baih Field 301
Bakil tribal group 22
Balfour-Paul, Glen 259
Balfour Declaration 13, 78
Bandar Abbas 73–75
Banians 226
Bani Fatima 262
Bani Ghafir tribal group 21, 230
Bani Hajir tribal group 21
Bani Harb tribal group 22
Bani Hina tribal group (Hinawi) 21,
226, 230–231, 235–236
Bani Khalid tribal group 21–22, 173
Bani Qitab tribal group 269
Bani Saad tribal group 22
Bani Salem tribal group 22
Bani Tameem tribal group 126
Bani Thaqit tribal group 22
Bani Yas tribal group 20–21
Bank of Credit & Commerce Inter-
national (BCCI) 265–267
Baroom family 23
Barzoft, Farzad 168
Basrah Petroleum Company 90
Battle of Ajnadayn 49
Battle of Ayn Jalut 59
Battle of Badr 46
Battle of Jarrab 130
Battle of Khurma 79
Battle of Mogadishu 154
Battle of Mulayda 128
Battle of Qadisiya 69
Battle of Rawdat Muhanna 129
Battle of Safra 127
Battle of Siffin 50, 189
Battle of the Bridge 49
Battle of the Three Kings 73
Battle of Uhud 47
Battle of Yarmuk 49
Bayt al-Hikmah 66
Beasant, John 240
Belgrave, Charles 192, 194, 213
Bell, Gertrude 82

Beverly Turk  68
Bhutto, Benazir  296
Billi tribal group  22
Bin Laden family  24, 151
Bin Mahfouz family  24, 266
Binzagr family  24
Bird, Richard  236
Blair, Tony  8, 115, 159, 209, 221
Blunt, Lady Anne  82, 124
Bonaparte, Napoleon  231
Borouge  264
Bosworth, Frederick  196
Boubiyan Island  26, 85, 171–172,
    175, 179
Boustead, Hugh  277
Bouteflika, President Abdelaziz  17
British Airways (BA)  84, 115, 196, 197
British Bank of the Middle East
    (BBME)  193, 273, 277
British Indian Steam Navigation
    Company  174
British Midland Airways (BMI)  115
British Overseas Airways Corporation
    (BOAC)  196, 287
British Petroleum (BP)  88, 98,
    100–101, 105, 183, 208
Bugshan family  24
Bul Hanine Field  215
Bull, Gerald  168
Bunduq Field  311
Bunker Hunt  98
Buraidah  22, 37, 82, 174
Buraimi Crisis  236–237, 274–277
Burckhardt, Johann  81
Burgan Field  92, 177
Burhaan Field  246
Burke, Jason  155
Bush, President George H  103,
    110–111, 149, 157, 169, 178–179
Bush, President George W  19, 105,
    106, 111–113, 150–151, 156, 209

C

California Arab Standard Oil
    Company (Casoc)  91–92
California Texas Oil Company
    (Caltex)  91
Callaghan, James  142
Camp David  143, 146, 150
Canning Award  233
Carter, President James Earl 'Jimmy'
    142–143
Casey, William  144
Cementation  243
Central Bank of Oman  226
Central Bank of the UAE  316
Central Mining & Investment
    Corporation  215
Charles, the Prince of Wales  115, 119
Cheney, Dick  13, 110–111
Chevron  88, 105, 139, 147
Chicago Bridge & Iron Company  288

Chirac, President Jacques  8, 221
Churchill, Winston  77, 79, 94,
    133–134
Cities Services Corporation  240
Citigroup  2
Clark, Alan  168
Clinton, Hillary  282
Clinton, President William Jefferson
    'Bill'  105, 119, 149–150, 154–
    155, 157, 169
Cochrane, Ronald  216
Committee for the Propagation of
    Virtue and the Prohibition of Vice
    148
Compagnie Française des Pétroles
    (CFP)  89, 92, 95, 236–238
Continental Oil Company (Conoco)
    88, 105, 288
Council of Oman  244
Cousteau, Jacques  26
Cowper-Coles, Sir Sherard  114–115
Cox, Sir Percy  131, 176, 233
Craig, Sir James  287
Crane, Charles R  132
Crescent Petroleum  303
Ctesiphon  40–41, 49
Curzon, Lord  76, 88, 234, 284, 313
Cyrus the Great  35–36, 189

D

D'Albuquerque, Alfonso  72, 229
D'Arcy Exploration Company  235
Dabbagh, Amr  160
Da Gama, Vasco  72, 229
Dahna Desert  32, 125
Dalma Island  33, 255
Dardanelles  77
Darley Arabian  68
Darwish, Abdullah  196
Das Island  26, 255, 277
Day of Dibba  48
De Butts, Brigadier Freddie  280
De Chatillon, Reynauld  66
De Covilhao, Joao Peres  72
De Gaury, Gerald  177
DeGoyler, Everette Lee  92
De Lesseps  95
Dhaid  41, 257, 302
Dhiyab bin Isa, Sheikh  278
Dhofar Defence Force  238–239
Dhofar Liberation Front (DLF)
    238–239
Dhofar Mountains  238
Diaz, Bartholomew  72
Dibba  21, 48, 73, 256, 300
Diriyah  74, 82, 125–127, 211
Di Varthema, Ludovico  81
Divided Zone  31, 94, 176
Doha International Airport  84, 209
Dohat Salwa  217, 220
Dolphin Pipeline  206, 208–209, 220,
    308

Dome of the Rock  49, 150
Doughty, Charles  82, 124
Douglas-Home, Sir Alec  310
Dubai Aluminium (Dubal)  289–290
Dubai Cable Company (Ducab)  290
Dubai Desert Classic  294
Dubai Development & Investment
    Authority  280
Dubai Drydocks  280, 289
Dubai Electricity Company  288
Dubai Executive Council  280
Dubai Holdings  280
Dubai International Airport (DIA)
    84, 280
Dubai International Capital (DIC)
    295
Dubai International Convention
    Centre  14
Dubai International Financial Centre
    (DIFC)  293, 316
Dubai International Financial
    Exchange (DIFX)  316
Dubai Investment Group  295
Dubai Islamic Bank  10
Dubailand  5, 253, 293
Dubai Marina  293
Dubai Marine Areas (Duma)  124,
    288
Dubai Media City  15, 253–254
Dubai Metro  293
Dubai Natural Gas Co (Dugas)  289
Dubai Petroleum Co (DPC)  288
Dubai Properties  293–294
Dubai Radio Network  254
Dubai Waterfront  292
Dubai World  84, 280–281
Dubai World Central  84, 292–294
Dubai World Cup  281
Dukhan Field  92
Duma  124
Dumat al-Jandal (Tayma)  37, 124
Duqm  236
Dutch East India Company  73

E

Eastern & General Syndicate (E&GS)
    90–91, 192
Eastern Bank  193
East India Company  73–74, 173–174,
    229–232, 269, 271
Eden, Sir Anthony  96, 275
Elf Aquitaine  105, 217
Emaar Properties  160, 280, 293
Emirates airline  6, 84, 197, 280, 291
Empty Quarter, The  3, 21, 27, 31–32,
    83, 128, 132, 139, 210, 235
Enron Corporation  220
Ente Nazionale Idrocarburi (ENI)  96
Etihad Airways  6, 84, 197, 265
Eurofighter jet  115, 159
Exxon  88, 92–93, 95, 98, 105, 139,
    236, 263

F

Fahd Plan  146
Fahud  237
Failaka Island  26, 39, 172–173, 184
Faisal bin Ghazi, King (Faisal II)  178
Faisal bin Hussein, King (Faisal I)
    77–79, 131
Faisal bin Musaid, Prince  140
Faisal bin Turki, Sultan  76, 233–234,
    249
Fakhro, Ali  195
Falah Field  288
Falaj al-Mualla  307
Farasan Banks  26
Farouk, King  95
Farsi, Mohammed  157
Fasht al-Dibal  214–215
Fateh Field  288
Fatima bint Mubarak, Sheikha  263
Fatimids  59–61, 65–66, 125
Fayoum Oasis  134
Federal National Council (FNC)  314
Fiennes, Sir Ranulph  241
Firqa  224, 241
First American  266
Fiver Imam Shiites  61, 226
Flanagan, Maurice  291
Ford, Henry  88
Fox Broadcasting Company  119, 209
Front for the Liberation of South
    Yemen (FLOSY)  63
Fuwairat  211–212

G

Gabriel, Archangel  44, 45
Galloway, George  200
Gardner, Frank  113
General People's Congress (GPC)
    64–65
General Treaty of Peace (1820)  74,
    191, 212
Geneva Conference  143
Georgetown University  119
Gergawi, Mohammed  280
Gerrha  37, 39
Ghanoum, Hamida Alia  152
Ghawar Field  31
Ghazi, King  178
Glaspie, April  169
globalization  7
Godolphin  68, 280
Godolphin Arabian  68
Goerner, Hugh  149
Gorbachev, Mikhail Sergeyevich  153
Gray Mackenzie & Company  193
Greater and Lesser Tunb Islands  26,
    75, 285, 300, 309–313
Gulbenkian, Calouste  89–90, 92–93
Gulf Air  84, 186, 196–197, 287, 291
Gulf Bukha Field  301
Gulf International Bank (GIB)  197

Gulf Offshore Ra's al-Khaimah
    Petroleum 300
Gulf Oil Corporation 88, 90–93, 97,
    100, 176–177
Gwadur 226, 230, 238

**H**

Hadd Janan 215
Hadhramaut 22–24, 31, 38, 63, 83,
    135, 151
Haffadh, Nada 8
Hail 33, 37, 77, 82, 128–129, 131, 174
Hajji Abdullah Alireza Company 23
Halabjeh 14
Halul Island 215, 274
Hamdan bin Qarmat 59
Hamerton Treaty 232
Hamilton, Lloyd N 133
Hammer, Armand 98
Hamriyah 272
Hanafi school of Islam 57
Hanbali school of Islam 57, 126
Haradh Oasis 128
Hariri, Rafik 145–146
Hariri, Saad 146
Hashemites 67, 83, 96, 136, 175, 178
Hatta 283
Hauf 239, 242
Hawar Islands 26, 192, 213–215,
    219–220
Healey, Dennis 309
Heath, Edward 308–309
Henderson, Ian 200
Hezbollah 154
Hili 256–257
Himyarites 38, 39, 41
Hinawi tribal group (Qahtanis) 21,
    226, 230–231, 235–236
Hira 41, 45
Hogan, James 197
Holmes, Frank 90, 176–177, 192
Holy Mosque (Mecca) 146, 155
Horns of Hattin 66
House of Ali 61
House of Wisdom 66
Hurrian people 35
Hussein (son of Caliph Ali) 57–59
Hussein, King (Sharif) 77–78,
    129–131, 157
Hussein, President Saddam 14, 19,
    71, 97, 102, 104, 111–112, 144,
    153, 156, 167, 169, 170, 180, 183,
    209
Hussein bin Talal, King 17, 67, 178, 241
Huwala 23, 190, 203

**I**

Ibadhis 10, 60–61, 65, 228
Ibn Battuta, Shams Al Din Abu
    Abdallah Mohammed 80–81
Ibri 236–237, 247–248

Idd al-Shargi Field 215
Idris I, King 98
Ikhwan 129–131, 144, 176
Illah, Abdul 178
Imam (Sayyid) Hamad 231
Imam, Mohammed bin Nasser 230
Imam Ahmed 62
Imam Ahmed bin Said 231
Imam Ali 58–59
Imam Bil'Arab 230, 248
Imam Ghalib bin Ali Hinai 236–239
Imam Khomeini 69, 71–72, 198
Imam Mohammed bin Abdallah Al
    Khalili 234–236
Imam Said 231
Imam Saif 230–231, 248
Imam Saif II 230–231
Imam Salim bin Rashid Al Kharusi
    234
Imam Sultan bin Saif 229–230, 248
Imam Sultan II 230
Imam Yahya (Yemen) 61–62, 77,
    131–132
Imperial Airways 84, 193
International Atomic Energy Agency
    (IAEA) 69–70, 107
International Court of Justice (ICJ)
    214–215, 220
International Energy Agency 4
International Petroleum Investment
    Company (IPIC) 264
Iran-Contra weapons deal 140
Iran-Iraq War 9, 14
Iranian Oil Participants Limited 95
Iranian Revolution 9, 14, 96,
    101–102, 182, 242
Iraqi National Oil Company (INOC)
    96
Iraq Invasion/War (2003) 12, 14
Iraq Petroleum Company (IPC) 90,
    91–93, 96, 98, 100, 192, 213–214,
    236, 237
Iricon Agency 95
Isa bin Nahyan, Sheikh 277
Isa bin Saleh, Sheikh 234
Isfahan 69, 73
Islamic Action Society 201, 203
Islamic Front for the Liberation of
    Bahrain 199
Islamic University, Medina 144
Ismaili Muslims 10, 59, 189
Izki military camp 240

**J**

Jabali 22, 226–227, 235
Jaber bin Zaid 60
Jafari Shiite 226
Jafurah Desert 32
Jamarat 55
Janan Island 215
Japan Petroleum Trading Company 96
Jawf 124

Jazirat al-Ghanem 227, 243
Jazirat al-Hamra 74
Jebel Akhdar 30, 227, 229, 237,
    247–248
Jebel Ali Free Zone Authority 280
Jebel Ali Port 289
Jebel Dhahran 91, 133
Jebel Dhanna 277–278
Jebel Dhofar 22, 226
Jebel Dukhan (Bahrain) 91, 133, 186
Jebel Hafit 257
Jebel Jais 301
Jebel Rahmah 54
Jebel Shams 247–248
Jerba 60
Jibrin 248
Jizan 26, 137
Jubail 33, 37, 133, 141
Juffali family 23
Juhaina tribal group 22
Julfar 73, 229, 231, 298
Julphar Gulf Pharmaceuticals 301
Jumblatt, Walid 60

**K**

Ka'bah 43–44, 47, 54–55, 189
Kaaki family 24
Kalba 73, 255–257, 300, 302
Kamal, Yousef bin Hussein 208, 222
Kanoo, Ahmed 196
Kanoo, Hajji Yusuf 193
Kanoo, Khalid 192
Karzai, President Hamid 17
Kassites 35, 188
Kathiri 24
Kazimi, Abdul Mutaleb 140
Kerzner International 291
Khadija bint Khuwaylid 45
Khalaf bin Mubarak 230
Khaled bin Ahmed, Sheikh 305
Khaled bin Musaid, Prince 140
Khamis Mushait 132
Khan, Reza 70
Khansaheb construction company
    288
Kharg Island 73
Kharijite 50, 58, 60, 65, 189
Kharj 31, 37
Khasab 227, 243
Khashoggi family 23, 140
Khatami, President Mohammed 72
Khawaneej 283
Khoja Ismailis 60, 226
Khor al-Udaid 212, 217–218, 271
Khor Fakkan 72–73, 85, 231, 256,
    302
Khorramshahr 71, 102, 176
Khorsabad 188
King-Crane Commission 132
King Abdelaziz University 152, 157
King Abdullah Economic City 7, 160
King Abdullah Financial District 160

Kingdom Centre 108
Kingdom Holding 119
King Fahd Causeway 112, 199
King Faisal Centre 119
King Faisal Foundation 119
King Khaled University 135
*Kitab al-Jabr Wal Muqabalah* 66
Kitchener, Herbert 77
Kooheji family 23
Kufa 50, 57
Kuwait Airways Corporation (KAC)
    84
Kuwait Fund for Arab Economic
    Development (KFAED) 180
Kuwait Gulf Oil Co (KGOC) 97
Kuwait Investment Authority (KIA) 8
Kuwait Investment Office (KIO) 181,
    183
Kuwait Oil Company (KOC) 91,
    177, 181, 184
Kuwait Petroleum Corporation (KPC)
    97
Kuwait University 164, 181

**L**

Lahak 81
Lakhmids 41
Lawatiyya 226
Lawrence, TE (Lawrence of Arabia)
    77–78, 83
Layla 37
League of Nations 13, 89, 178
Lebanon Invasion (1982) 14
Leigh-Pemberton, Robin 265
Lingah (Lingeh) 23, 74, 283
Linjawi family 23
Liwa 256
Liwa Energy 264
Liwa Petroleum 247
Lloyd, Selwyn 194
Longrigg, Stephen 133
Loomis, Francis 133
Lootah construction company 288
Lord Canning 233
Lord Rothschild 78
Luce, Sir William 312
Lusail 209

**M**

*Ma'ul Hayat* 172
Maan 79
Macmillan, Harold 96
Madain Saleh 40, 82, 114
Magan 34, 188, 228
Mahd al-Dhahab 34
Majid bin Said 233
Majlis al-Dawla 244
Majlis al-Nawwab 200
Majlis al-Shoura (Saudi Arabia) 120,
    148
Major, John 169

Makki family 226
Maliki school of Islam 57, 60
Mamluks 59, 67, 125
Manahil tribal group 268
Manasir tribal group 268
Manifa 176
Mannai family 23
Manzikert 66
Maqam Monument 173
Marawah Island 26, 34
Margham Field 288
Marib 38–39
Maritime Truce (1835) 75
Marwah 54
Masfut 248, 306
Masirah Island 26, 227, 237, 243
Masmak Fort 129
Merv 49
Mesaieed 215
Middle East Broadcasting Centre (MBC) 253
Mikimoto, Kichimatsu 68
Mina Saqr 301
Mina Sultan Qaboos 242
Mina Zayed 278
Mirbat 229, 241
Mirfa 275
Mishaghin family 268
Mishari bin Saud 160
Mitla 171
Mleiha 41, 257
Mocha 67
Mohamed bin Thani, Sheikh 191, 212
Mohammed, President Ali Nasir 64
Moore, Henry 157
Moresby Treaty 232
Mosaddegh, Mohammed 71, 94–97
Mosul Petroleum Company 90
Mount Soodah 132
Muawiya bin Abu Sufyan 50, 56–57, 65, 124
Mubadala Development 247
Mubarak, President Mohammed Hosni Said 146, 154
Muharraq Island 191, 193–194, 241
Mukhaizna Field 246
Mundhir ibn Sawa 47
Murair 191
Murawiec, Laurent 111
Murban 276
Murrah tribal group 21, 128, 220
Musallim Field 246
Muscat Bay 229
Muscat Securities Market (MSM) 244
Mussalim bin Nufl 238
Mustali, Imam 60
Mutah 48
Muttar tribal group 22
Muttrah 226, 240, 242
Muzdallifah 54
Mzab Valley 60

N

Nabataea 40, 114, 124
Nader Shah 70, 231
Nafud Desert 32–33, 37, 82–83
Naimi, Ali 148–149
Najaf 50, 58, 72, 101, 124, 268
Najran 22, 37–38, 61, 132, 137
Nakheel 291, 317
Nasser, President Gamal Abdel 25, 95, 135–136, 138, 178
National Bloc 179
National Democratic Action Society 201
National Democratic Front for the Liberation of the Occupied Arab Gulf 240
National Front for the Liberation of South Yemen 63
National Iranian Oil Company (NIOC) 94–95, 96, 98
National Islamic Front 153
National Liberation Front (NLF) 239
National Media Council 15, 253
Nawwal bint Tariq, Sayyida 245
Nazer, Hisham 141, 147–148
NCB 157, 266
Near East Development Corporation 90–91, 236
Negev Desert 40
Neguib, General 95
Neutral Zone 96, 176
Niebuhr, Carsten 81, 172
Night Ascent, The 46
Night of Power 53
Night of the Revelation 53
Nihavand 49
Nineveh 35
Nixon, President Richard M 99, 102, 139
Nizam of Hyderabad 24
Nizwa 136, 229, 234, 236–237, 247–248
Nobel Brothers Petroleum Producing Company 87
North Field 217

O

Obaidullah 59
Obhur Creek 157
Occidental Petroleum 98, 246–247
October War 99–100, 146
Oger International 145
Ohyama, Kiyoko 235
Olaya 108
Olayan family 22
Omana 41, 257
Oman Air 84, 197
Omar, Caliph 48–50, 65, 228
Omar, Mullah 154–155
Onassis, Aristotle 135
Osama bin Laden 111, 151–156, 184

Oud Cemetery 117
Ousman, Cyril 135

**P**

Pahlavi, Shah of Iran, Mohammed
    Reza 69–71, 94–95, 98, 101–102,
    138, 143, 152, 241
Palestine Liberation Organization
    (PLO) 97, 143, 150, 180
Palgrave, William Gifford 82
Partex 236–238
Pelly, Colonel Lewis 82, 212
Pemba 230, 232
People's Front for the Liberation
    of the Occupied Arab Gulf
    (PFLOAG) 239–241
Petra 40–41, 81, 257
Petroleum Development (Oman &
    Dhofar) Ltd 236
Petroleum Development (Qatar)
    (PDQ) 213–214
Petroleum Development (Trucial
    Coast) 273
Petroleum Development Oman
    (PDO) 237–238, 246
Petromin 139
Pharaon, Ghaith 140
Pharaon, Rashad 135, 140
Philby, Harry St John 83, 132–133,
    235
Phillips 93, 105, 139
Picot, George 77–78, 89
Port Rashid 84, 288
Powell, Colin 111, 209
Powell, Major Spike 240
Progressive Democratic Forum
    Society 201
Project Babylon 168
Prophet's Mosque 146
Putin, President 106

**Q**

Qadaffi, Muammar 98, 159
Qadisiya 49, 69
Qajar tribal group 70
Qalat al-Bahrain 188–189
Qalhat 246–247
Qarmatians 59–60, 65, 189
Qaryat al-Faw 37
Qassim 22, 36–37, 120
Qatar Airways 6, 84, 197
Qatar Financial Centre (QFC) 222
Qatargas 105
Qatar Petroleum (QP) 208, 215
Qathani tribal group 22, 230
Qeshm Island 74, 298
Qitat Jaradah 214–215
Qom 58, 100–101
Qubbat al-Sakhrah 49
Quraysh 45, 47
Quss bin Saida 132

**R**

Ra's al-Hadd 255
Ra's al-Khafji 96
Ra's al-Khaimah Ceramics Co 301
Ra's al-Khaimah Oil and Gas Co 301
Ra's al-Khaimah Rock Co 301
Ra's al-Sadr 277
Ra's Jashk 73
Ra's Laffan 206, 208–209, 217
Ra's Tanura 91–92, 133
Rabigh 22, 85, 160
Rafsanjani, President Ali Akbar
    Hashemi 69
Rakhyut 239
Rams 74
Reagan, President Ronald 144–145
Redec 140
Red Line Agreement 90–93
Reem Island 26, 264
Rezayat Group 23
Rice, Condoleezza 151, 160
*Rihla* 80
Riyadh University 135
Rockefeller, John D 87–88
Rodway, Christopher 114
Roosevelt, President Franklin Delano
    84, 92, 110, 133–134
Royal Commission for Jubail and
    Yanbu 141
Royal Dutch/Shell Group 87, 89, 93,
    95, 215, 236–237, 263, 273
Royal Saudi Air Force (RSAF) 115
Rub al-Khali 3, 247
Rumaila Field 104, 168–169, 171
Rustaq 48, 229, 231, 237
Ruwais (Qatar) 211, 256
Ruwais (UAE) 256
Ruwallah tribal group 22

**S**

Saadiyat Island 26
Saar tribal group 21
Sabic 2, 141
Sadat, President Anwar 138–139,
    143, 146, 181
Safwan 171, 175
Sahoo, Mohammed 264
Said, Sayyid 74, 232–233, 249
Saipem 139
Sakakah 33
Salalah 32, 83, 227, 235–243, 247
Saleh, President Ali Abdullah
    17, 22, 63–65
Salman, Sheikh Ali 199, 201
Samuel, Herbert 78
Samuel, Marcus 87
Samuel, Samuel 87
San Jacinto Petroleum Corporation 95
San Remo Agreement 89
Sasanian Empire 40–41, 47–49, 189
Saud bin Mohammed bin Saud 127

Saudia 84, 117, 134, 157
Saudi Arabian Monetary Agency
 (SAMA) 8, 134
Saudi Aramco 96, 100, 112, 135,
 147–149
Saudi Oger 145–146
Saudi Railways Organization 160
Saudi Research & Marketing Co 119
Sayhut 37
Sayyid Mohammed bin Ali 130
Sayyid Sultan bin Ahmed 231–232
Sayyid Turki bin Said 233
Scimitar Oil 289
Seeb 234, 236–237, 242–243, 247
Seetzen, Ulrich Jasper 81, 124
Seleucid Empire 39, 189
Shafi 57, 61–62, 227
Shagra 211
Shakespear, Captain William Henry
 Irvine 83, 130
Shammar tribal confederation 20, 22
Shams Abu Dhabi 265
Sharif (King) Hussein 77–78,
 129–131, 157
Sharqiyin family 21, 308
Shaybah Field 276
Sheffield Engineering 168
Sheffield Forgemasters 168
Shell Group 23, 87, 89, 215
Shell Oil 147
Shibkuh 307
Shiga, Shigetaka 235
Shihu tribal group 21, 227
Shuwaikh 76, 175
Shuwayhitiyah 33
Signal Oil & Gas 95
Sinaiyah Island 307
Sinclair Oil 93
Sir Bani Yas Island 26, 258
Sirri Island 23
Sitra 203
Socal 88, 91–92, 95, 132–133, 192
Socotra Archipelago 26
Sohio 88, 95, 217
Solaib tribal group 22
Souk al-Manakh 182, 183
South-West Fateh Field 288
South Arabian Federation 24, 63
Standard Chartered Bank 193
Standard Oil Co (SO) 87–88
Standard Oil of Indiana 88
Standard Oil of New Jersey 88, 92
Standard Oil of New York 88, 92
Standard Oil of Ohio (Sohio) 88, 217
Star Enterprise 147
Stark, Freya 83
Strait of Hormuz 25–26, 31, 34,
 73–74, 186, 227
Subiya 171, 184
Sudairi Seven 116, 118, 141
Suez Crisis 96–97, 137, 194, 238
Sufiism 57, 70
Sultan, Maqbool Ali 226

Sultan bin Sulayem 280
Sultan of Lahej 63
Sumerians 34, 86, 188, 228
Summan Escarpment 31
Sun Oil Company 88
Supreme Commission for Tourism 119
Supreme Petroleum Council of Abu
 Dhabi 261
Sur 246
Sur al-Lawatiyya 226
Sykes-Picot Agreement 77–78

T

Tabuk 37, 48
Taif Treaty 62, 65, 132
Taliban 19, 71, 111, 154–156
Talib bin Ali Hinai 236–237
Tameem tribal group 211
Tanuf 234
Tapline 93, 135
Taqah 229, 235
Tarawih 53
Tarbell, Ida 88
Tariki, Abdullah 97, 99, 137
Tarut Island 26, 34, 38, 125
Taweelah 85
Tayma 37
Telegraph Island 75
Tell Abraq 34, 257, 302
Texaco 88, 91–92, 94–95, 105, 139
Thaj 39
Thamarit 243
Thatcher, Margaret 243
Thatcher, Mark 243
The 9/11 Commission Report to US
 Congress 153–154, 156
The Arbitration 124
Thesiger, Sir Wilfred 83–84, 268
The Victory of Victories 49
The Wall Street Journal (italics) 158
Thomas, Bertram 83, 234–235
Thomson, Captain Perronnet 300
Thuwainy, Sultan 233, 249
Thuwainy bin Said 233, 249
Tidewater Oil 95
Tihama 61, 127
Tikrit 167
Tilmun 189
Tornado jet 115, 145
Total 105, 141, 209, 236, 247
Treaty of Erzurum 102
Treaty of Jeddah 276
Treaty of Perpetual Maritime Peace
 (1853) 75, 191, 271, 283
Treaty of Sevres 79
Trucial Oman Levies 80, 306
Trucial States Development Office
 (TDSO) 309
Truman, President Harry S 93
Tunill, Lt Col Edward 240
Turaba 130
Turki bin Abdullah 127–128

Turki bin Said, Sultan 233, 245, 249
Turkish Petroleum Co (TPC) 89–90
Tuwaiq Escarpment 108
Twelver Shiism 58, 60, 70
Twitchell, Karl S 132–133
Tylos 39, 189, 211

**U**

Uhud 46–47
Umayyads 50, 65
Umm al-Nar Island 26, 34, 257
Umm al-Nar period 257
Umm al-Qura 44
Umm Qasr 171–172, 175, 179
Unaizah 22, 37, 82
Union Defence Force (UDF) 280
Union Oil 88
United Arab Coastal Emirates 310
Unocal 88
Uqair 90, 93, 131, 176
US Army Corps of Engineers 139
US Department of Energy 3–4
US Navy 22, 155, 182, 199
Utaibi, Juhaiman bin Mohammed 144
Uyaynah 126

**V**

Van Buren, President Martin 232
Van de Vijer, Walter 246
Vatican 221
Von Bismarck, Chancellor Otto 2

**W**

Wadi al-Batin 31
Wadi al-Dawasir 31, 37
Wadi al-Ibrahim 44
Wadi al-Rimah 31
Wadi Fatima 37

Wadi Hadhramaut 22–23, 31, 38
Wadi Hanifa 31, 108
Wadi Sirhan 124
Wahhab, Mohammed bin Abdul 126–127, 137
Wakra 191, 212
Warba Island 26, 171
Wejh 83
White Revolution 101
Wilhelm, Kaiser 89
William IV, King 232
Wilson, Harold 309
Wilson, President Woodrow 89, 132
WJ Towell Group 226
Wolfowitz, Paul 111
World Islamic Front 155

**Y**

Yaariba family 73, 229
Yahya, Imam 61–62, 77, 131–132
Yamani, Ahmed Zaki 99, 137
Yamani, Hashem 148
Yanbu 22, 82–83, 112, 127, 141
Yas Island 265
Yathrib 37, 40, 46
Yemeni Socialist Party (YSP) 63–65
Yibal 237
Yousef Omair bin Yousef 264

**Z**

Zadjalis 226
Zamzam 42, 44–45, 54
Zapata Offshore 178
Zawawi, Qais 181
Zayd bin Ali 61
Zayed ibn Harithan 48
Zirku Island 255
Zora Island 271
Zubara 190–192, 211–212, 214–215
Zubayda bint Jafar 124